For my old racegoing companions Bruce and Brian

CONTENTS

INTRODUCTION
UNDER STARTER'S ORDERS

The collective catch of breath that went up when Kauto Star tipped over the fourth-last fence in the 2010 Cheltenham Gold Cup held echoes of what it must have been like when the Queen Mother's Devon Loch belly-flopped within sight of the winning post in a Grand National more than half a century before. The stunned silence betrayed a mixture of conflicting emotions: shock, momentary fear for horse and jockey, dashed dreams, the downing of a hero, the apparent collapse of the natural order, a coronation abandoned, and, on more personal notes, the loss of a dead-cert bet. Almost instantly, though, eyes swivelled back to the action that had moved a hundred yards up the course, the eerie silence replaced by renewed cheers. There is always another winner to applaud and crown champion in the Sport of Kings. Life goes on.

The disbelief felt by the tens of thousands who had descended on Cheltenham for jump racing's Blue Riband was particularly deep because the race had been hyped into an epic showdown between two horses, Kauto Star and Denman, alternate winners of the previous three Gold Cups. It was to be the decider to sort out not only which of the two stable-mates was the best, but who was quite possibly the greatest steeplechaser of all time. The marketing men had got to work in the overblown build-up: supporters of both horses wore football-style scarves like oversized betting slips around their necks. Racing was about to be taken to a new level, we were led to believe, and a new name was going to be announced in the Pantheon of the sport.

Except the gods don't always appreciate the presumption of mere mortals and, instead, let loose Fate to decide the outcome. Kauto Star had been sent off at the slightly flattering odds of 8–11 considering his propensity to plough through fences, sometimes terminally, and he duly smashed into fence

No. 8 to an audible groan. He never really recovered, and 11 fences later came the fall that was to prove calamitous. In the split-second of stunned silence that followed you could almost imagine, if not actually hear, the tut-tutting of Cheltenham's immortals as they stood waiting restlessly around the parade ring and winner's enclosure.

Racing honours its heroes, nowhere more than at Cheltenham where there are life-size bronze statues of some of the stellar-stars of jump racing: five-times winner Golden Miller, three-times winners Arkle and Best Mate, plus Dawn Run, the only horse to have won both Gold Cup and Champion Hurdle. Coming from different ages, quite what they would have made of a modern-day would-be interloper breaking into their magic circle is open to conjecture. Memories of their feats and personalities, and the hope of finding their successor, are what keep the turnstiles at Prestbury Park ticking over.

Back on the racetrack, Fate had read her formbook carefully and noted that the largely unconsidered Imperial Commander had only finished a nose behind Kauto Star at Haydock Park earlier in the season, and decided that was enough to destroy the hype without being too outrageous. The party-pooping Imperial Commander finished seven lengths ahead of the doughty Denman.

Fifty-four years earlier, Fate had shown she was no respecter of Royalty, either. The Royal Family had not won the Grand National since Ambush II did so in the colours of the Prince of Wales, later Edward VII, in 1900. When Devon Loch cleared the final fence with barely another horse in sight, it looked as if that record was about to be put right. The shock at what happened next was almost outrage that it should happen to the Queen Mother. One moment Devon Loch was about to win the Grand National, the next he was spread-eagled on the deck like a Thelwell sketch of a pony trying to clear a water jump with an overweight young rider on its back; it was a sporting disaster which has never been explained satisfactorily to this day.

But lighten up. This is the very essence of sport, the very essence of horse racing. The unpredictability is what keeps it fresh and interesting, and entices us back again and again. The objective of this myriad collection of equine tales, told through the eyes of the Telegraph's expert writers, is to celebrate this most enduring of relationships between man and beast. There is nothing like the sight of a horse at full tilt, ears pricked, nostrils flaring as it storms towards the finish line. You probably need to be on the rails, or standing at one of the fences, say Becher's Brook or The Chair at Aintree, to take in the full scale of its strength and power. But even from the comfort of a private hospitality box high up in the stands at Ascot you can still appreciate the beauty and grace of our four-legged athletes.

A day at the races is like no other, whether dressed up in your finery at a Royal meeting, or in jeans and a T-shirt at, say, Uttoxeter. Racing is a sport that unites in its democracy. It brings together a varied cast of characters, both equine and human, from the lowliest to the mega-rich, servant to king, the humble selling plater one step away from the knacker's yard to the blueblood thoroughbred destined for a life of luxury at stud. If Norton's Coin, a 100–1 outsider, can beat the demigod Desert Orchid, as he did at Cheltenham in 1990, then anything is possible.

So, this is not necessarily the moment to dump your Kauto Star scarf in the bin: there is still time for a comeback. Look at Workforce on the Flat where horses rarely have the time or opportunity to come back. Winner of the Derby at Epsom in 2010, trounced seven weeks later by stable-mate Harbinger in the King George VI and Queen Elizabeth Stakes, and yet able to come back in the autumn and finish the season by beating Europe's best in the Prix de l'Arc de Triomphe.

Apropos of nothing, you do wonder about the names horses are sometimes given: Workforce is almost weighed down by connotations of being work-manlike rather than fleet of foot, and the noun Harbinger tends to be followed by 'Of Doom', though he could equally be a messenger of good news, if not at Ascot for the concrete-booted Workforce. No, the beasts who stir the blood tend to have majestic names that match their magnificence: they are called Nijinsky, Shergar, Arkle, Red Rum, Sir Ivor, Pinza, Golden Miller, Galileo, Desert Orchid, Mill Reef, Mandarin, Aldaniti and Brigadier Gerard. Prepare to meet them again here.

The rags-to-riches, riches-to-riches stories within these covers represent a personal selection culled from the *Telegraph*'s archives, which stretch back to encompass more than 150 years of racing history. The choice of chapter head-ings is similarly down to the editor. The reports are contemporaneous and, apart from the occasional slight trim for space purposes, are as they appeared in the newspaper. Any glaring omissions are mine, and are probably deliberate.

The *Daily Telegraph* is rightly highly regarded for the standard of its horse-race tipping service. Why, only a year or two back the anonymous Marlborough went through the card at Catterick Bridge like a latter-day Frankie Dettori. Tony Stafford and Marcus Armytage have both won the prestigious naps table in the *Racing Post,* young Armytage as recently as the 2009–2010 jump racing season. And the author of this book was a member of a racing-desk team who shared £1,000 and a tin pot for coming top of a similar season-long table in the *Sporting Chronicle.* The words *Sporting* and *Chronicle* will give you a clue to how long ago that was: the Chron, the old rival to the *Sporting Life,* ceased publication in the last century. However, despite that impressive pedigree, you won't find any hot tips within these pages with which to wage war with the bookies; it isn't that sort of book. Rather, it is a celebration of the sport, and the characters who have made it what it is.

My first bet was enough to turn anyone's head. It was not always wise to oppose Lester Piggott in the Derby at Epsom, where he became so revered after nine victories in the great race that the entrance gates have been named in his honour. The favourite, the wonderfully-named Ela-Mana-Mou, was also ignored in preference to the sublimely monikered Troy. There were no workhouse Workforces in the 1979 Derby field. Indeed the way Willie Carson sent Troy tearing down the outside in the final furlong to win by miles and miles made you wonder whether he was, indeed, a Trojan Horse.

It was a great way to open the account that generally equates to handing over fistfuls of dollars to the bookmakers for an adrenalin rush that fails to last more than a few hundred yards. There have been Grand National winners like Hallo Dandy and West Tip, a decent-priced straight forecast – 'it's kosher: it's straight from the stable' – involving a horse called Spinning Saint, winners from Newmarket to Ludlow, Chester to Newbury. There would have been another National winner when Esha Ness, plucked out in the office sweep-stake, passed the post first in the 'void' race of 1993 – but despite protests, threats of legal action and appeals to the stewards, the stake money went to charity that year.

Like all punters, and every angler, there are always tales of the ones who got away. Mine was Ma Biche, Criquette Head's runner in the 1,000 Guineas of 1983. I had seen firsthand the filly's sudden burst of acceleration in front of the Newmarket grandstand in the previous autumn's Cheveley Park Stakes, and made a mental note of the name. Her declaration for the first spring Classic coincided with a scheduled day off work, so a trip to racing's head-quarters, with a bundle of fivers to be lodged temporarily with a bookie offering favourable odds, was duly planned.

'Ma Biche,' said the racing editor out of the side of his mouth not encumbered by the trademark cigar, ash piling up on the desk in front of him, as he researched his nap for the selections article in the following day's paper. 'That means "My deer" in French.' We sighed. It was irrelevant information. Or so it seemed. Later, driving home in the small hours, about to belly-flop over a humpback bridge, the brakes were slammed on as the headlights caught something large standing in the middle of the road. The car stalled as out of the shadows loomed a doe and her fawn looking dolefully straight at me. A deer, my dear, Ma Biche! It was too much of a coincidence to ignore:

the cash-point at Newmarket would have to be raided for more blue betting vouchers to stake on Mademoiselle Head's little beauty.

So, next afternoon, the would-be multi-millionaire, a life of luxury riding on the back of a sure-fire winner, set off through the back lanes of Essex, Suffolk and Cambridgeshire towards his destiny. Except halfway there: disaster! The previous night's jolt had seriously upset the internal combustion engine of the snow-white Ford and it lurched to a sudden standstill. No amount of cajoling would encourage it to re-start. As Ma Biche flew out of the stalls a dozen or so miles up the road, the disgraced motor was being towed back to the garage. To make matters worse, these were the days before mobile phones and credit accounts; equally, the rural countryside on the way back had no thatched cottages masquerading as emporia owned by Messrs Hill or Ladbroke. Ma Biche, lighter without my monkey on her back, stormed home at 5–2, a worthy favourite. Ma Biche, my dear, oh drat!

So instead of heading straight to nearby Stansted Airport to jet off to the sun courtesy of Ma Biche's largesse, it was back to a career in journalism on the *Daily Telegraph* sports desk, ostensibly to pay the car repair bill.

There was no horse-racing coverage in the first edition of the *Daily Telegraph* on 29 June, 1855. Not that it was an emerging sport: racing horses had been taking place since man could sling a leg over an animal's back and chase after a similarly adept opponent. There had been organised meetings for centuries and racecourses had sprung up all around the country; besides, the Derby had been going for more than fifty years. Anyway, the oversight was rectified within a week or two, and racing, like the weather, the City prices and the masthead, has been a mainstay of the *Telegraph* throughout the last century and a half.

In those days there were no designated sports pages, let alone separate supplements; nor were there many sports jostling for space: just cricket and rifle shooting. The 'Sporting Intelligence' column, with its tips and gossip from the racing world, would have to elbow itself some room amid the news stories and other essential reading matter of the day.

Sometimes, as now, racing became the story of the day. Reports of the Derby and Grand National, itself 17 runnings' old, consumed large slabs of type, often amounting to three- or four-thousand words, setting the scene, previewing the horses in the paddock, pointing out luminaries in the crowd, before embarking on a blow-by-blow commentary of the race, and finishing by reviewing the winner's parentage, ownership and inside leg measurement. And if there should be a Royal runner, let alone winner, the fawning and celebrations/commiserations would go through the roof. When Minoru won the Derby in 1909 for King George VII, there was almost 21st-century-style coverage with a whole broadsheet page devoted to the momentous occasion – still the only time a reigning monarch has won the race – complete with those rarely-seen, new-fangled photograph thingies.

Those who wrote the words hid behind monikers like Hotspur, Marlborough, Watchman or, in the early days, Roughscratcher, probably to escape the wrath of irate punters. Hotspur and Marlborough have endured to this day, but it wasn't until the early 1960s that their true identities were revealed. Today, Hotspur is the *nom de plume* of the racing correspondent, now J.A. McGrath; Marlborough is the resident tipster, though it was the long-time pseudonym of John Oaksey. Past Hotspurs have been B.W.R. Curling, the first to be unmasked, and Peter Scott.

Some of the *Telegraph*'s racing staff came to their roles with mud still on their breeches. Indeed, Oaksey and Marcus Armytage sometimes still had mud on their racing silks when they sat down to write their copy for the next day's editions. Oaksey rode in 11 Grand Nationals and after the majority of them had to file a colour report for the Sunday paper, often for the front page, and usually up against deadline. As examples in this book show, they were the work of a master wordsmith. He came closest to winning the race in 1963, on board Carrickbeg, who led over the last, only to lose the decision at the line by three quarters of a length. 'It still seemed possible,' he wrote of those final strides, 'and then Ayala's head appeared like Nemesis at my knee'.

Like a married woman, 'My Noble Lord', as he was called by John McCririck, was known, in his maiden days, as plain John Lawrence, and as such began writing for the *Telegraph* in 1957. When he succeeded his late father as the 2nd Baron Oaksey in 1971 he became John Oaksey, and Lord Oaksey when off duty. Since he was also known as Marlborough, it all became a bit confusing. Under all of those names he stepped up the standards for writing about the sport, not only in race reports, but in authoritative columns, full of insight and opinion, as his many entries in this book underline. He was an unashamed fan of Arkle, whom he described as 'the perfect, complete chaser'. To read his unsigned piece on Mandarin's victory in the Grand Steeplechase de Paris, filed from the British Embassy in the French capital, after the horse's bit broke and left Fred Winter effectively rudderless, is to be transported to Auteuil that June day in 1962. Not surprisingly he was Racing Journalist of the Year in 1968, three years *before* he was champion amateur jockey for the second time, and he only stopped writing daily pieces for the newspaper in 1988; he continued to contribute columns and features for years afterwards.

Unlike the 'Noble Lord', Marcus Armytage did win the Grand National, the last amateur to do so, and has been dining out ever since on Mr Frisk's success in 1990 – and periodically reminding the *Telegraph*'s readership about it. Like Oaksey, he went straight from weighing room to press box to write the report of his greatest triumph for the *Racing Post*, his then employers, while it was still fresh in the memory. The son of a racehorse trainer, Roddy Armytage, and international showjumper mother, Sue, and brother of leading female jockey Gee, racing was always in his blood. He rode 100 winners before retiring in 2000 to stand, watch and scribble from the sidelines. His article on how the jockeys left abandoned in a big, unfamiliar city after the IRA bomb warning, and subsequent evacuation of Aintree, in 1997, is one of the best humour-out-of-adversity pieces you will read.

Brough Scott, who juggled being founder and editorial director of the *Racing Post* with weekly essays for the *Sunday Telegraph*, was also a one-time jockey with more than 100 winners to his name. If Oaksey blazed the trail for excellence in racing journalism, Scott followed closely in the second wave. Three times he won Sports Feature Writer of the Year, and was equally at home writing about other sports, attending Olympic Games, Wimbledons and Tours de France, as he was at the race track.

Peter Scott, who was Hotspur from 1965 to 1991, the Telegraph's longest-serving racing correspondent of the 20th century, was a meticulous, knowledgeable journalist who would be Racing Writer of the Year in 1975. He was unusual for a tipster, despite his prowess, of being a non-gambler. He, too, had racing coursing through his veins: an aunt bred Park Top, a winner of the Coronation Cup and King George VI and Queen Elizabeth Stakes, and instilled in him his lifelong love of the sport. Jim McGrath, meanwhile, is a bookmaker's son from Melbourne, Australia, via Hong Kong, who rose to be Sir Peter O'Sullevan's successor as BBC television's senior race commentator, and was another *Telegraph* recipient of the Racing Journalist of the Year award, in 1992. Tony Stafford, still deeply immersed in the world of racing, spent thirty years at the *Telegraph*, including spells as racing editor and racing correspondent.

The growth in the newspaper's pagination and staff during the late 1980s and 90s, had a profound effect on racing coverage. Day-by-day it would continue to pump out the familiar stream of race cards, tips, reports and returns. However, when there was a big race, a big meeting, a big story, it went into overdrive. No longer would Oaksey, McGrath, Stafford or Armytage be left holding the reins. Suddenly they had support from feature writers like Paul Hayward, who cut his teeth at the *Racing Post*, Michael Calvin, Sue Mott, Andrew Baker and Jim White, as racing moved off its text-heavy pages at the back of the newspaper towards the front and on to feature-based spreads. The advent of the weekend sports supplements, followed by their midweek counterparts, pioneered by the then sports editor David Welch, himself a noted racing enthusiast, helped it compete against mainstream sports like football and cricket.

To spice up the coverage, jockeys like Peter Scudamore, Frankie Dettori, Johnny Murtagh and Tony McCoy were handed regular columns, imparting their knowledge and making helpful suggestions about the day's action ahead. Lester Piggott even wrote a first-person piece about his Frank Sinatra-like return to the saddle. Trainers and owners would be roped in to make contributions ahead of Royal Ascot or Cheltenham or Epsom. Henrietta Knight, for instance, kept readers appraised of Best Mate's progress towards his defences of the Gold Cup, and penned a moving tribute to the horse when he collapsed and died at Exeter. All tastes were catered for: from the hard-bitten gambler, kept up to date with form and movement in the market, to those who follow racing for the sheer excitement and enjoyment of the sport.

Anyway, you've seen the newspaper, now read the book.

This book would not have been possible without the help and expertise of a number of people. Consequently, my thanks must go, initially, to Sam Harrison for commissioning this collection on behalf of Aurum Press; to Caroline Buckland, Head of Books and Entertainment at Telegraph Media Group, for helping to push the project through; to Aurum – particularly my hard-working editor, Barbara Phelan – for publishing it; to the always-helpful Gavin Fuller, Lorraine Goodspeed and the rest of the staff in the Telegraph library for facilitating the research; to my trusted former colleagues Andrew Baker and Kevin Perry for keeping me on the right track; to the writers, whose love and feel for the 'sport of kings' shines through these pages; and, not least, to the boys on the racing desk, Adrian, Kevin, Danny, Brian, Miker, Stevdn, and their predecessors, who performed the original editing, and wrote the headlines. They have my admiration and appreciation.

Martin Smith
December 2010

CHAPTER I

THE CLASSIC SHOWDOWNS

In the build-up to the 2010 Cheltenham Festival, all the talk was of the showdown in the Gold Cup between Denman and Kauto Star. Paul Nicholls's stable companions had finished first and second in the previous two years, winning one apiece, and this was going to decide which of the best mates was the greatest steeplechaser, probably of all time. Amid the over-the-top hype, racing folk scratched their heads to recall on-track rivalries of similar intensity: the half-dozen magical moments that follow were on most experts' lists.

Incredibly, John Oaksey (né Lawrence) witnessed all six first-hand on Telegraph *duty – one, when Red Rum chased down Crisp in the 1973 Grand National, with a rapidly diminishing view of the protagonists from the back of his own mount. There was to be no seventh entry, though: Denman and Kauto Star failed to read the script and were soundly trounced by Imperial Commander.*

---

8 MARCH 1964

ARKLE SETTLES A THOUSAND ARGUMENTS, AND DOES IT IN RECORD TIME

John Lawrence at Cheltenham

Our wildest dreams came true yesterday afternoon as, with the Cheltenham Gold Cup between them, Mill House and Arkle rose together at the second last. Then, as Arkle swept irresistibly away, a thousand arguments were settled – and we who watched stood hats in hand, lifted clean out of ourselves by the finest racing spectacle I saw or hoped to see.

A few breathtaking seconds earlier as Mill House turned downhill towards the last three fences, anything seemed possible. For Arkle had moved up easily a length behind the favourite and, hearing him come, Willie Robinson must have known the chips were well and truly down. Three fences out with Arkle at his quarters, Mill House threw one final, almost despairing leap, but it gained him not one yard, and in a dozen strides the challenger was level.

Long before this, cheering broke out all over the stands. Now, as the Irish saw the prize within their grasp, it rose to an awesome yell of triumph. And suddenly, going to the last, as Robinson drew his whip, it was all over. With the burst of speed about which we all had talked and wondered for so long, Arkle rocketed clear, swept up and over, silky-smooth – and on to victory in record time.

Mill House never faltered, never gave up. Forced by circumstances to lead from the start, he was simply beaten by a faster horse, but both winner and victim covered themselves with glory. Both are great chasers – perhaps, no, almost certainly, the greatest of all time.

Six minutes before the last snow shower had cleared and, in hard, bright sunlight, with each fence looming black against the green, the stage was set more perfectly than any human impresario could have contrived. Trotting serenely down towards the start, Mill House looked invincible – ears cocked and shooting out his toes, a ballet dancer with the power of a tank. Beside him Arkle looked almost small – but hard as nails and superbly fit.

From the start Willie Robinson sailed straightaway into the front and at what looked an easy pace – but must have been a fast one. Arkle, pulling hard, disputed second place with Pas Seul ahead of King's Nephew – and jumped the first few fences, like all the rest, with an ideal blend of accuracy and boldness. Mill House, by contrast, 'fiddled' more than once and after the first full circuit drew an agonised gasp from the crowd by getting right under the open ditch in front of the stands. But then, as if to reassure us, he stormed off down the hill, opening a six-length gap from his pursuers.

For just a moment it seemed the race might be decided there and then. Could any horse alive, we wondered, find the speed to match those giant strides? But, turning past the farm, Pat Taaffe and Arkle gave their answer. It echoed loud and clear across the course and already a mile from home the crowd's murmur became a roar as the Duchess of Westminster's yellow jacket drew closer stride by stride.

'I was never worried at any stage,' said Pat Taaffe later. 'This is by far the best horse I rode.' Well, a great horse deserves a great jockey, and Arkle got one yesterday. He was ridden throughout with supreme confidence and perfect timing – the tactical plan of using one decisive burst carried out to the letter.

Poor Willie Robinson, bitterly disappointed, felt that Mill House had not jumped as well as he can. Possibly this was caused by lack of company and, with a pacemaker, Willie feels that there would still be hope. 'He beat me fair and square today,' he said sadly. 'But I can't believe it's right.'

I have never seen at Cheltenham, or anywhere else, enthusiasm to equal the welcome Arkle got yesterday. Mobbed, patted and pushed on every side, he walked calmly through the milling cheering crowd – and found the winner's enclosure almost too full to allow him to enter.

2 MAY 1971

BRIGADIER IN COMMAND

John Oaksey

Flat racing often seems a cold and heartless business in which pounds and pence mean more than flesh and blood. But yesterday that image was dealt a memorable blow as Mrs Jean Hislop's Brigadier Gerard stormed irresistibly home to win the 2,000 Guineas with Mill Reef and My Swallow struggling three lengths behind him. For this was not just the victory of a handsome well-bred colt, superbly trained and admirably ridden. Many 2,000 Guineas winners have been. This was something else besides.

What Brigadier Gerard carried on his back was the belief that racing can still be a sport and his name will always henceforth stay as a reminder that the joy of owning a really good horse, for some people, has a value which cannot be expressed in money terms. In this, surely the supreme moment of his long and eventful racing career, John Hislop, who bred Brigadier Gerard and owns him in partnership with his wife, Jean, remained as calm as he used to when the chips were down in an amateur Flat race or steeple-chase. Asked in the winner's enclosure how he felt now about refusing the bid of £250,000 made for his colt last year, he answered quietly: 'We didn't really refuse it. The horse was never for sale.' In fact, at the time, the Hislops' sporting gamble was roughly the equivalent of betting £200,000 at even money that Brigadier Gerard would win the 2,000 Guineas – and he started yesterday at 11-2. Needless to say, the racing world wagged its collective head and said: 'How can they do it?' But they did, and they won, and Brigadier is now, at a very conservative estimate, worth all of a million pounds.

For yesterday there was no trace of doubt or fluke about his superiority. Three furlongs from home Geoff Lewis on Mill Reef had just begun to feel really confident. 'I knew I had My Swallow beat,' he said later. 'But the moment Joe appeared it was all over.' And so it was, for while the long-awaited battle between the two favourites was being fought and won, Joe Mercer had calmly bided his time on Brigadier Gerard.

Racing wide in the middle of the course, My Swallow had led to halfway, but Mill Reef was never more than a length behind him, and when they came together with three furlongs left to go it was the little American colt who had more to spare than his gigantic rival. But behind them the Brigadier – named after Conan Doyle's second most favourite character, the brave but braggart French cavalryman – was poised to deliver a charge of which the Hussars would have been proud. He took a moment to find his full stride and Mercer tapped him once. But the response was more than he or anyone can have expected. For in 100 yards, racing down the hill into the dip, Brigadier Gerard brushed aside the two colts who last year dominated European two-year-old racing. They finished together far ahead of the others, but he was three lengths clear and going away, as decisive a winner of the 2,000 Guineas as has been seen since Tudor Minstrel.

Nijinsky's brother, Minsky, was done with after six furlongs and, finishing a fairly distant fourth, will not now run in the Epsom Derby. Mill Reef duly took his revenge on My Swallow and ran, it must be presumed, right up to his best form.

---

27 JULY 1975

IT'S GRUNDY IN RECORD TIME

John Oaksey at Ascot

In a battle worth more than all the diamonds in the world, Grundy and Bustino combined to do British racing a signal honour at Ascot yesterday. Their record-breaking King George VI and Queen Elizabeth Diamond Stakes will never be forgotten by anyone fortunate enough to have seen it. But, though the credit for this superlative race was shared between the home-bred pair, it was Grundy, our Grundy, who got home half-a-length in front. And if he retired to stud tomorrow no one can say anymore that he has not been tested to the utmost.

Because, as in last year's St Leger, Bustino's owner Lady Beaverbrook was wonderfully served by her pacemakers. First Highest, then Kinglet, led the way according to plan and when they tired, exactly half a mile from home, Joe Mercer asked Bustino to go and claim his place in the history books. The big bay four-year-old quickened like a hero, but Patrick Eddery was very much on guard. He had Grundy in second place like a flash, but even so Bustino galloped into the short straight with a clear three lengths' advantage.

He fought for every inch of it, too, and for a moment, with less than a quarter of a mile to go, all Grundy's admirers and connections (a phrase which includes every tax-payer in the British Isles) felt our confidence draining away. If there had been even a shadow of weakness in the dual Derby winner's stamina or courage, the next hundred yards would infallibly have revealed it. But instead, down went his nose and with that blond tail flying like a comet he strained every nerve to answer Eddery's call.

If Bustino had been the one-paced stayer some of us thought him last season, the race would have been over there and then. But he, too, managed somehow to find some extra speed and for a few heartbeats they raced together head to head. Bustino never gave up, even when Grundy had taken the half length by which in the end he won. That, in fact, was how they covered the last half furlong with a proud and delighted English crowd cheering them every yard of the way.

Having snatched his advantage, Grundy held it to the bitter end and, to do so, don't forget, he had made at least three lengths in the short Ascot straight at the end of a race run in two minutes 26.98 seconds — more than two seconds faster than anything seen over a mile and a half on the royal heath.

Five lengths behind the two leaders, Dahlia, winner of the last two King Georges, did everything she could to make it three and ran quite well enough in the process to suggest that she may be very nearly as good as ever. The French five-year-old On My Way was fourth, and another even older Frenchman, Card King, fifth. Still another Frenchman Ashmore, who had been only a length behind Bustino at Epsom, proved the English colt's magnificent improvement since by finishing sixth.

Small wonder in the circumstances that two of the many happy faces in the unsaddling enclosure were those of The Queen and the Levy Board chairman, Sir Desmond Plummer. For the latter, of course, recently bought three-quarters of Grundy for the National Stud and when Bustino's syndication as a stallion is announced shortly it is probable that he will stand at The Queen's stud near Sandringham. Both horses were bred in England by English stallions and out of English mares. Both have won English Classic races as this became not only one of the best, most exciting Flat races I have seen, but also one of the most encouraging and satisfactory for the whole world of British bloodstock breeding.

Grundy's trainer, Peter Walwyn, was understandably next door to speechless with excitement and delight — too moved to make any statements about his wonderful horse's future. But the National Stud's agreement with Dr Vittadini allows Grundy to have only two more races, both of them in the British Isles. Presumably the Benson and Hedges Gold Cup at York might be one possibility and the Champion Stakes another. But, with the York race in mind, many yesterday remembered only too well how the great Brigadier Gerard tasted defeat there after victory at Ascot. But anyway, as Walwyn said, who cares about the future?

I am delighted to withdraw my criticism of the decision not to race Grundy as a four-year-old. It would have been lovely to go on watching him for years, but if he can transmit the sort of courage, intelligence and acceleration we saw yesterday, well then, perhaps the sooner he goes to stud the better. Heaven knows we need a few more like him.

And though Grundy will not race outside this country, Bustino's long-range objective is definitely the Prix de l'Arc de Triomphe. Leading bookmakers made him joint favourite for that race with Allez France yesterday and, if by chance, the great French filly has lost some of her sparkle, it requires no stretch of the imagination to see Bustino and his gallant team of helpers carrying the war across the Channel.

Well though Kinglet and Highest did their job yesterday I suppose it is arguable that if Riboson could have been in the field as he was at Doncaster last year, Bustino might have got a lead for another furlong or so. But in truth this is not the time for ifs, buts or hard-luck stories. Yesterday's real story was one of triumph, both for British racing and for a sport which, at this level, can move grown men and women as much as any drama of the stage or screen.

***

I APRIL 1973

RED RUM WINS, BUT CRISP IS IMMORTAL

HEARTBREAK IN THE NATIONAL

John Oaksey, who was seventh on Proud Tarquin

The last cruel yards of Aintree's quarter-mile run-in claimed yet another victim yesterday. And as Mr Noel Le Mare's Red Rum caught Crisp close home to win the 1973 Grand National, one of the saddest, as well as finest, chapters had been written in all the great race's eventful history. For Sir Chester Manifold's Crisp had come from the other side of the world to teach us Pommies a lesson we will never forget.

From the first fence to the last he blazed a glorious lonely trail. In the end, though beaten by a weight no horse has carried to victory since 1936, he earned a sort of immortality wherever men admire brave horses. But if, which God forbid and I don't for a moment believe, this was the last Grand National, it more than lived up to its reputation, with not one, but two, supremely romantic stories.

For the race's other heroes, Brian Fletcher and Red Rum, were fulfilling the dream of a lifetime for the eight-year-old's octogenarian owner. Mr Le Mare had three dreams, in fact: to marry a beautiful woman, become a millionaire and win the National. The first two came true long ago, and last year, buying Red Rum for 6,000 guineas at Doncaster, he laid the foundations for the achievement of the third.

But when you have just ridden around the greatest steeplechase course in the world it is inevitably horses you feel for more than people. And so, with apologies to Mr Le Mare, to Brian Fletcher and Red Rum, I come back to Crisp and his rider, Richard Pitman. To me, peering ahead from Proud Tarquin's back through a kaleidoscope of hooves and tails and colours and flying brush that is the National, Richard was, almost from the start, just a speck on the horizon.

And, dismounting, tired but happy in seventh place, I still could not believe that, for the second time in a month he had known the nearest thing to heartbreak a British jumping jockey can be asked to face. Robbed of certain victory in the Gold Cup halfway up the Cheltenham hill, Richard had already paid one dreadful price for all his marvellous rides on Fred Winter's horses. And yesterday, landing over the last still 20 lengths in front, he found history repeating itself with agonising precision.

For Crisp, like Pendil, though with a far better excuse, seemed for a few disastrous strides to lose his bearings. Willing if necessary to go round again, he swerved to the left and had to be wrenched back on course with the run-in empty and stark before him. At the second-last, as he said afterwards, Richard Pitman had asked for and got yet another tremendous leap. But then he felt Crisp's stamina begin to drain away and from that fatal swerve to the finish, what had been a dream became a nightmare.

Alone from the first fence on – 'I never saw another horse till Red Rum came,' says Richard – Crisp had fearlessly cut the great fences down to size. They bear no resemblances to anything he had seen before, but he made them feel like hurdles – all of them, including Becher's, Valentine's and The Chair.

You probably know more about his triumphal progress than I, for though Proud Tarquin proved the perfect mobile grandstand, he was never, on this fast ground, able to come within miles of the leader's furious pace. Nor could anything else, though, and for all but 100 yards this Grand National was really two races – one Crisp's and the other for the rest of us. The time taken of nine minutes 1.9 seconds is a record, beating Golden Miller's time when winning in 1934 by almost 19 seconds.

Richelieu was the first casualty in my vision – crumpling over the very first fence. Not long thereafter Jeff King's hopes came to a violent end on

Ashville. Proud Tarquin, who never made a serious mistake, was already at full speed by Becher's, but he went round the Canal Turn as if he'd been doing it all his life, and as we galloped back on to the racecourse there weren't more than ten runners between us and Crisp. Of these, the colours which stay in my memory are those of Spanish Steps, Black Secret, Grey Sombrero, Rouge Autumn, Hurricane Rock, Endless Folly, Red Rum and, of course, Crisp.

For Bill Shoemark and Grey Sombrero the end, a tragic one I'm sorry to say, came at The Chair: for the big grey broke his shoulder as he fell and had to be destroyed. Charley Winking fell there, too, and as Pat Buckley landed over the huge ditch on Canharis they found his fallen body in their path.

Crisp's relentless gallop was stretching us out by now and at Becher's for the second time two or three more falls had thinned the ranks in front of Proud Tarquin until a place became at least a possibility. But he landed heavily over Valentine's, made one of his few misjudgments at the last ditch and, though still running on thereafter, made no further ground until the run-in.

Brian Fletcher had set out determined to ride a waiting race on Red Rum, but landing over Valentine's with Crisp nearly a fence in front, he knew he could afford to wait no longer. From then on, Red Rum, revelling in the fast ground, left the rest of us for dead and stormed off in what looked a vain pursuit. To the crowd, apparently, it was painfully clear quite early on that Crisp was certain to be caught. But though desperately tired and giving his rival two stone all but five pounds, he held him until the last 20 yards. And even in the end the verdict was only threequarters of a length.

Galloping under Anchor's Bridge, the well-remembered colours of Mr Raymond Guest came past me as the dual Cup winner L'Escargot began to make his claim. He had jumped so slowly early on that Tommy Carberry was never able to keep the pace he wanted. But now class told and over the last two fences L'Escargot ran past horse after horse to take third place. Not far behind him the third of three top weights, Spanish Steps, lived gallantly up to his family reputation. Like his dam Tiberetta, he finished fourth in the end. And who knows, if shown a little mercy by the handicapper, he may improve as she did on that placing another year.

Ruefully tying the strings of his cap in the weighing room, Joe Guest had wished aloud 'that this was a novice chase at Plumpton'. But Endless Folly gave him no reason to feel that way in the race, and as we straightened out for home his were the next colours in our path. Joe, had he wanted, could easily have cut Proud Tarquin off along the rails, but instead he cheerfully waved us by and so my gallant companion was able to take an honourable seventh place.

Of the many sad stories told afterwards, none was more bitter than Beltran Albuquerque's. Going to Becher's the first time his left-hand stirrup leather parted on Nereo and so a sporting quest that started in Madrid had to end prematurely at the Canal Turn. Of the other fancied horses, Princess Camilla was, according to Ron Barry, 'always just behind you, John, and always struggling'. She was one of several, in fact, baulked and stopped at the last open ditch five fences out. Astbury, Sunny Lad and Rampsman were others involved in the pile-up here – but I didn't see it. That means that none of them can have had much chance at the time, though Sunny Lad battled through to the post.

None of us had any chance, in fact. And if there was any justice in the National, which there never has been, Crisp would surely have got the reward he so richly deserved. Red Rum and Brian Fletcher deserved it, too, of course. For they alone had the strength and speed and determination to attempt what looked so hopeless a task. But this will be remembered as Australia's Grand National and the wonderful lop-eared ten-year-old who made it so will, as I say, never be forgotten.

---

15 MARCH 1979

MONKSFIELD AGAIN A TRUE CHAMPION

Marlborough (John Oaksey)

For the second year running Monksfield and Sea Pigeon fought an epic duel for the Waterford Crystal Champion Hurdle at Cheltenham yesterday. The result was the same, but this time there was a real magic in the damp grey air. I expect never to see a finer hurdle race.

Forced to make almost all his own running and headed by Sea Pigeon before the last flight, Monksfield landed on the flat with his title apparently slipping away. But no horse ever refused more stubbornly to recognise defeat and his fightback up the hill brought tears to many an eye, English as well as Irish.

It was sad that there had to be a loser and on ground far softer than he likes Sea Pigeon has probably never run a better race. The rapier of his speed, blunted a little by the mud, was simply turned aside on the steel core which Monksfield uses for a heart.

The one unsatisfactory feature of this unforgettable race was Kybo's luckless slip on landing over the second last flight. He was alongside Monksfield at the time and going so well that no one could possibly blame Bob Champion for believing that they must have come desperately close to victory.

No one can say for certain, and what might have been pays no bills, but it must be remembered that Sea Pigeon, two lengths behind in third place when Kybo fell, was going even better. Between the last two flights, in fact, he seemed to be pulling over Monksfield – but in that respect, as we ought to know by now, appearances are deceptive.

Dessie Hughes, who had already won the Arkle Challenge Trophy on Chinrullah, took Monksfield straight to the front and steered him boldly wide in search of the best ground. Both Sea Pigeon and Kybo followed his lead and those who unwisely took the conventional shorter route were all beaten a long way from home.

Monksfield, who was headed briefly at halfway by Birds Nest and Major Thompson, gave a flawless exhibition of quick, clean hurdling. Again and again he saved ground and energy in the air.

So Dessie McDonogh has proved to the hilt the point he has been quietly making all this season – namely that Monksfield is at least as good as he was last year and probably better. As for those who dared suggest that the little stallion might be losing his enthusiasm, we can only hang our heads in respectful shame.

19 MARCH 1987

PEARLYMAN IS WORTHY CHAMPION

Marlborough (John Oaksey)

The Queen Mother Champion Chase lived up to both halves of its name at Cheltenham yesterday, with Pearlyman, Very Promising and Desert Orchid fighting out a three-sided battle of champions fit for a Queen. In front for 11 fences out of 12, Desert Orchid made a most gallant attempt to rise above the left-handed spell which Cheltenham seems to cast on him. But, steered intentionally wide from the start by Colin Brown, he always seemed to be leaning slightly outwards. Round the final bend, both his pursuers were able to squeeze through on the inside rail. Pearlyman had hit the second last quite hard and again at the last Very Promising gained ground on him in the air.

'I never remember having a better ride, not even last year's Grand National', was Richard Dunwoody's tribute afterwards – but all Very Promising's boldness was to be in vain. For on the flat Pearlyman was always just getting the better of a duel which set the stands ablaze. In the end he had a neck to spare, with Desert Orchid three honourable lengths away.

The winner, who will run at Aintree on Grand National day, had given his trainer an anxious time before this race. 'For some reason he was in an awful mood,' John Edwards told us. 'I tried four different saddling boxes before we could get him in one.' The only time Pearlyman behaved like that was at Ayr last year before one of his rare defeats. But this time all was well. He is the undisputed two-mile champion – but I wish Desert Orchid's 'manager' could persuade him to defend the title at Kempton or Sandown.

CHAPTER 2

THE JOY OF RACING

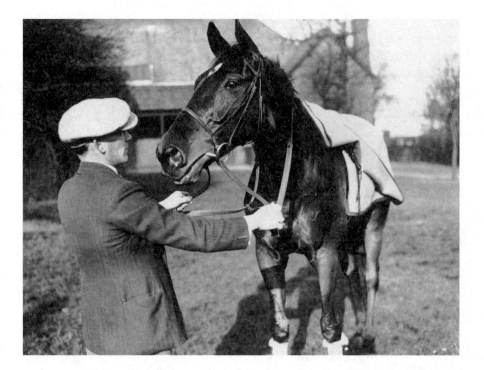

Flemington 2005, and the trainer of the three-time winner of the Melbourne Cup gushed: 'Find the youngest child in our midst and you can say he or she will probably be the only one with a chance of seeing such a feat again. We won't.' It was hyperbole in the heat of a great moment, but it summed up what attracts us to the sport.

This chapter reminds us why we go racing: in the hope of seeing a performance we will still be talking about years afterwards; a performance that lifts the spirit, gladdens the heart, quickens the pulses. There are a number of contenders here, from an outstanding against-the-odds victory for Mandarin, coaxed home in Paris by Fred Winter; the serial winners of National Hunt, from Golden Miller to Best Mate; the sleek thoroughbreds of the Flat, earning millions for their connections; to rags-to-riches stories you couldn't make up.

---

18 JUNE 1962

HEROIC MANDARIN GAINS HIS GREATEST TRIUMPH

BIT BREAKS AND WINTER RIDES THREE MILES WITHOUT BRIDLE

Marlborough

Without a bridle – with only his own great heart and Fred Winter's matchless strength to keep him going – Madame K. Hennessy's Mandarin yesterday afternoon became the first English-trained horse to win the Grand Steeplechase de Paris at Auteuil since Silvo in 1925. The bit broke in Mandarin's mouth after only three fences and for three twisting, hazardous miles Fred Winter had neither brakes nor steering. So when in the end, unbelievably, Mandarin thrust his head across the line in front we who were here knew beyond doubt we had seen a feat of courage, skill and horsemanship never excelled on this or any other racecourse.

For a few dreadful moments, however – staggering dazed and hoarse from the stands – we did *not* know if this was victory or just a bitter heroic defeat. A photo had been called for. Then the right number was in the frame and as Winter and Mandarin pushed their way back through the wondering crowd a cheer went up – from French throats as well as English – that would have made the Irish yell at Cheltenham sound like a feeble whimper.

Forty minutes later the incredible Winter was back in the same enclosure, having won the Grande Course de Haies for four-year-olds on Beaver II. For a French jockey I imagine this would be a formidable double. For an Englishman in these circumstances it simply proved what we already knew – that Fred Winter has no equal in the world.

But once more this was Mandarin's day and as he bounded past the stands, a gay, determined bundle of fire and muscle, already up in front and pulling Winter's arms out, there was no hint of the disaster to come. The little horse was wearing his usual bridle, the one with a rubber-covered bit in which he won both the Hennessy and Cheltenham Gold Cups last season. But going to the fourth (a privet fence nearly six feet high) some hidden fault appeared, the bit parted and Winter found the reins loose and useless in his hands.

'What could I do?' he said afterwards to Bryan Marshall. 'I couldn't steer him, I couldn't stop – and I was much too frightened to jump off!' In fact, of course, the thought of giving up occurred neither to horse nor jockey. On they went, pitching dangerously over the big water, and it was not till the second circuit that we in the stands realised the desperate situation they were in. Desperate indeed it was! Quite apart from the near impossibility of steering without reins round this tortuous figure-of-eight, Mandarin, a horse who always leans hard on his bridle, must have felt horribly ill at ease and out of balance. As for Winter, his task defies description.

'I could give him no help at all,' was how the jockey put it, and no doubt by his own high standards that was true. But if I saw a horse given all possible assistance it was Mandarin yesterday and I do not believe any other man could have got him there. Round most of the bends Winter managed to keep a horse or two outside him, and the French champion Daumas, upside on Taillefer when the bit broke, did his best to help.

Close-up fourth down the far side for the last time Mandarin flicked cleanly over the post and rails that undid him three years ago – and then, at the junction of the courses, the worst all-but happened. For three strides coming to the turn it seemed Mandarin was going to run out the wrong side of a marker flag. His own good sense and some magic of Winter's kept him on the course, but the hesitation had cost precious lengths and round the last bend he was only fifth, six lengths behind the leader.

'Just wait till Fred gets him straightened out.' Dave Dick's voice behind me was much more hopeful than confident. But a moment later, going to the Bullfinch two from home, the impossible began to come true. With all the stops pulled fully out, Mandarin's head appeared like a bullet through the dark-brown barrier – and by the last, answering, as he has always done, Winter's every demand, the little hero was actually in front. He made no mistake and landed perhaps a length clear, but up the long run-in, hard and brilliantly though Winter rode, like a man sculling without oars, Mandarin was tiring. Inch by inch Lumino crept up and at the line not one of us could really be sure.

But all *was* well and as Mandarin walked away, dog-tired but sound, his faithful attendants quite speechless with delight, the dreams of his owner, Madame Hennessy, had been realised. At an age when many jumpers are past their best, and after many hardships, her wonderful horse had come back to triumph in the land of his birth – to a triumph even finer than any in his long career. For Fulke Walwyn, too, it was a moment never to be forgotten. After the Gold Cup, at Cheltenham last March, there seemed to be no more fields left to conquer. Understandably, Mandarin's devoted trainer had grave doubts about subjecting him to another gruelling race in Paris – but he could sleep sound last night (if he slept at all) in the knowledge that the risk so boldly taken has brilliantly come off.

I never expect to be more moved by a man and a horse than I was by Winter and Mandarin yesterday afternoon. Separately, they have always been superb. Together, yesterday, taking disaster by the throat and turning it to victory, they have surely earned a place of honour that will be secure as long as men talk, or read, or think of horses.

---

7 NOVEMBER 1965

ARKLE SHATTERS NORMAL RULES AND THEORIES

John Lawrence

Blue skies, clear light – and the greatest horse in the world. Sandown Park had all these yesterday and as Arkle came home alone in the Gallaher Gold Cup it had much more besides. For all the normal rules and theories about racing were being shattered. The impossible was happening before our eyes. We were watching a miracle in the shape of a horse. It was in the end an effortless victory, one of the easiest, Pat Taaffe says, in Arkle's whole career.

But that hadn't always been how it looked. For one heart-stopping moment down the railway straight Mill House had his hour – and never let it be forgotten. Superbly ridden by David Nicholson, the big horse stormed away from Arkle over the three close fences. It was like the good old days of his supremacy and, glancing back at least four lengths to Arkle, even the most convinced began to doubt. But we couldn't see inside Pat Taaffe's head – or inside Arkle's heart. There all was calm and confident. 'I hoped he'd take a rest,' said Pat. 'But he really never stopped pulling.'

What Arkle felt no one can say – but perhaps, since he is a kind-hearted horse, it was pity for his rival. And round the final turn England's hopes, so high a moment earlier, were dashed for good. In a dozen easy strides Arkle swept up beside Mill House. Before the Pond he was in front and as he landed over it the stands were shaken by a mighty cheer. It wasn't by any means the first.

Both horses were clapped in the parade ring, Arkle was applauded walking down to canter to the start and – something I've never heard before on an English racecourse – a roar greeted the field as they passed the stands *first time round!* By that stage Arkle was in front and had shown once again that extraordinary intelligence is among his many qualities. For down the back side, as Mill House sailed along ahead of him jumping the others silly, the favourite settled calmly well behind at ease in Pat Taaffe's hands.

But Arkle has been to Sandown before. He *knows* where the finish is and galloping round towards the Pond not bothering to count he decided it was time to go. For 100 yards Taaffe was a passenger and yet again poor Mill House saw beside him the form he must by now hate worse than death itself. It did not, to his eternal credit, stop him trying. But second time round the same thing happened and that was just too much.

David Nicholson, humane, as well as skilful, did not persevere and Rondetto, running a marvellous race for a horse probably not yet fully fit, passed Mill House, landing over the last to finish second. As he did so Arkle was nearly home. Scarcely ever off the bit, he won by 20 lengths in record time (the first horse to break six minutes over three miles round Sandown) and had made no shadow of a mistake.

'Weight will stop a train,' said Tom Dreaper afterwards – but 16 pounds had made not an ounce of difference and I do not really see how Arkle can be handicapped again. To describe his greatness fully no words or comparisons are adequate. He is not just the best I saw, he is like something from another world. When they made him I suspect they threw away the mould – so long may he live and flourish – a delight to watch – a thing to marvel at – a miracle.

---

18 MARCH 1966

ARKLE STROLLS HOME IN THIRD GOLD CUP

30 LENGTHS TO SPARE DESPITE BLUNDER

Hotspur (Peter Scott)

Arkle, a spray of shamrock in his browband for luck on St Patrick's Day, survived an 11th-fence blunder with complete nonchalance and won his third Cheltenham Gold Cup yesterday afternoon by a strolling 30 lengths. The widest winning margin in Gold Cup history could have been trebled at least had jockey Pat Taaffe wished. Never was Arkle remotely at full stretch.

The champion hacked along for the first mile, allowing Dormant and Snaigow to lead. At the eighth fence he jumped his way to the front. Arkle's error at the end of the first full circuit was probably a lapse in concentration. He hit the fence hard, but imperturbable Taaffe hardly shifted in the saddle. As if to atone, Arkle stood well back at the following jump – a ditch – and cleared it with plenty to spare. Dormant and Snaigow were allowed to keep within reasonable touch until racing down towards the third fence from home. Arkle, still on a light rein, accelerated clear and from that point defeat was no longer a possibility.

Dormant outstayed Snaigow to take second place ten lengths in front of Lord Cadogan's horse. Sartorius was another eight lengths behind Snaigow, earning fourth money of £516, but Hanch, the other runner, broke the pastern of his near hind when falling three fences from home and was later destroyed in the racecourse stables.

Winner now of £72,092 in stakes, Arkle returns to England for the Whitbread Gold Cup at Sandown Park in April. This race last year provided the richest of the 25 National Hunt victories Anne, Duchess of Westminster's champion has so far achieved. 'Only if the ground really firmed up might we have second thoughts about Arkle and the Whitbread,' said his trainer's wife, Mrs Tom Dreaper.

While Arkle was almost unbackable at 1–10 for yesterday's race his ever-growing fame brought a slightly bigger Gold Cup crowd to see him than came last year when Mill House was also in the field. Excluding club members, 22,250 paid for admission. Everyone had his money's worth. Arkle was in the parade ring a full five minutes before his opponents and filing past the stands he played to his public. Prancing, aloof, head high, Arkle was clearly satisfied with the homage received.

It was at Cheltenham, in the Massey-Ferguson Gold Cup of December 1964 that Arkle was last beaten. Flying Wild won that race in receipt of 32 pounds and, as if in tribute to her great compatriot, she chose yesterday afternoon to recover form after a spell at stud. With Irish Imp clearly amiss and a beaten horse at halfway, Flying Wild's task in the Cathcart Challenge Cup was simple. She could not have achieved it with greater fluency.

14 MARCH 2003

BEST MATE EVOKES SPIRIT OF ARKLE

Marcus Armytage

The ghost of Arkle haunts the parish of Prestbury, hanging around as the mist and dark descend on racing's most famous backdrop, Cleeve Hill, on a Gold Cup evening. It drifts on the breeze among the losing betting slips, a monkey riding on the back of every horse to win the race. Universally acclaimed the greatest steeplechaser, almost beyond comparison, winner of three Cheltenham Gold Cups in the Sixties, and so good they had to change the handicapping system to give his rivals a chance, 'Himself', as he was affectionately known, has had no peer. To mention another horse in the same breath as Arkle was blasphemy, even jump racing's more recent household names, Red Rum and Desert Orchid. We may not have found his better but yesterday, perhaps, in Best Mate we found his equal. This may just have been racing's answer to the Second Coming.

The eight-year-old destroyed the best chasers either side of the Irish Sea and English Channel to become only the sixth horse to win a second Gold Cup. Ironically, in beating a field of 14 others, he beat more horses in one Gold Cup than Arkle, who raced against three or four runners each year, did in three from 1964 to 1966. Never was such a demolition job completed with such immaculate athletic accuracy or authority. Never can favourite backers have had such a comfortable ride. He and jockey Jim Culloty, riding in the claret and blue colours of Aston Villa fan Jim Lewis, looked the winners fully a mile from home. He left his rivals toiling in his wake from the third last to take his place in history alongside Easter Hero, Golden Miller, Cottage Rake, Arkle and the last to do it, the inappropriately named L'Escargot in 1970 and 1971. Underrated by history, L'Escargot also went on to beat Red Rum in a Grand National. Best Mate will probably never get the opportunity to tackle Aintree.

The bookmakers, who have taken such a financial bashing at this year's Festival as a succession of favourites waltzed in, are taking no chances on Best Mate equalling the post-War record shared by Arkle and Cottage Rake by winning a third next year. He is already 2–1. His victory at 13–8 yesterday delivered not so much the *coup de grâce* to the old enemy but the bankruptcy notices, and there's no reason why, at his age, he cannot go on and win several more. This time he improved on last year's win to beat Truckers Tavern, a 33–1 shot, long on stamina, by ten lengths with the rest strung out like washing behind him. The novice Beef Or Salmon, the big Irish hope only a year younger than Best Mate, but in terms of experience a boy among men, turned over at the third.

Two minutes earlier, his trainer, Michael Hourigan, a small round man with an outdoor face, stood full of expectation on the stands, a camera focused on his every move. 'He's the new Bono,' said the Irish cameraman. That's as maybe, but not this year. While Best Mate galloped imperiously on, floating, Hourigan's horse, never previously vanquished over fences, stood disorientated, surprised and shaken but otherwise none the worse, following the first fall of his career. The Gold Cup remains a tall order for novices. For Best Mate's trainer, Henrietta Knight, the former biology teacher at a girls' public school, it's getting harder not easier. She won't watch a race live and often won't watch it at all.

'This morning was the worst,' she said, relieved that it was all over. 'The horse's temperament is brilliant, but mine isn't. I nearly cracked this time. I said I'd only train on this scale for five more years, but at that stage I was wishing I'd said five minutes. I usually take myself off shopping, but everywhere I went it was "Good luck" or "How's Best Mate?" I couldn't get away from it. There was even more pressure on this time and I've had all these statistics thrown at me, like horses don't win the King George and Gold Cup in the same season [only Arkle and Desert Orchid had done it]. They'll have to change that now.' Terry Biddlecombe, her husband and former jump jockey, rode against Arkle and reckons that comparison can now be drawn. 'Arkle was brilliant and this fellow is as good, or at least we'll find out next year,' he said.

When Best Mate first started winning, Knight said she believed that the horse thought he was Arkle. At that stage, if that was the case, the horse was the only one to believe it. Yesterday he put up a convincing argument and a lot more people will be converted to the idea. An exorcist, it seems, has been at work in the Cheltenham area.

---

8 MARCH 1933

NOTABLE DOUBLE EVENT FOR MISS D. PAGET

GOLDEN MILLER AND INSURANCE AGAIN TRIUMPH AT CHELTENHAM

Hotspur

A woman has the good fortune to own not only the best steeplechaser in the country, but the champion hurdle racer. The Honourable Miss Dorothy Paget takes this unique position through her ownership of Golden Miller and

Insurance, the one the winner at the National Hunt meeting at Cheltenham yesterday of the Gold Cup and the other successful for the Champion Hurdle Challenge Cup. As if it were not enough for all men owners to have been thus overwhelmed, for the first time in racing history we had it demonstrated that both the horses mentioned were capable of winning these championship trophies for the second year in succession.

In the case of the chaser Golden Miller, especially, it was a 100 per cent victory, not only placing the horse above all others, but giving him a great chance when the time comes the week after next of winning the Grand National. The first contributor to the double 'double event' was Insurance. For the moment I prefer to discuss what Golden Miller did if only because his was by far the more spectacular performance, and everyone loves a chaser rather more than a hurdler, though everyone should love a good horse. I have frequently written that he is an exceptionally good-looking, and, indeed, impressive horse. He is commanding and of high class, as we judge steeple-chasers in the top standard.

In the field of seven it will be understood that he easily carried off the honours in the paddock before even going out to race. Kellsboro Jack is an excellent type, but he was sweating and anxious. I do not like to see these symptoms in a chaser just before going out to race. Thomond II is unorthodox in physique, because he is so light as to be even frail looking, but he is full of grit, and would have won now had Golden Miller made any fatal mistake. Holmes is slightly undersized, but must be made of tough stuff.

Miss Paget's horse was always racing well up, and never further away than second or third. If there was any surprise in the race it was that Delaneige should have made such a fine show, though when the favourite was called on he rapidly drew away. Thomond II went with him, but the effort spent itself very quickly, leaving Golden Miller to jump and race on his own. And how rapidly he did jump and get away from the fences! Two or three of them he treated as if they were trifling hurdles.

Miss Paget proudly led in each of her heroes, and in reflecting on their triumphs one must add a congratulatory word to the big part played by the trainer, Basil Briscoe. He bought both horses on her behalf, both also from the same man, the late Mr Phillip Carr, who being a good seller as well as a good judge, did not exactly give them away. Miss Paget is the first owner since the pre-War days of the late Sir Charles Assheton-Smith to be in a position to pay for the best. As in his case, money has demonstrated the importance of its power. We may be certain now that Golden Miller will run for the Grand National, and, all going well, I can at least prophecy that he will start favourite.

Now as to Insurance, the champion hurdler: he retained his honours by winning for the second year in succession the Champion Hurdle Challenge Cup. One was left in no sort of doubt that he was the best of the quintet, because he won what was a slow-run race for more than half the distance (which was against one with his exceptional stamina), and then held off in succession each of his opponents.

---

13 MARCH 1936

GOLDEN MILLER IS FAVOURITE AT 7–1 FOR 'NATIONAL' AFTER CHELTENHAM TRIUMPH

FIFTH SUCCESSIVE GOLD CUP WIN — WITH NEW JOCKEY RIDING

Hotspur

Golden Miller vindicated himself yesterday afternoon by a glorious victory in the Cheltenham Gold Cup, and for the fifth year in succession brought the trophy to Miss Paget – a record that may never be beaten, unless he beats it himself by winning again next season. I expected to see him win easily. Actually, he finished a dozen lengths in front of Royal Mail. Everything was in his favour except, perhaps, the ground, which had been a good deal cut into, and the opposition was as weak, or weaker, as he has faced in the event.

He did nothing better than he has done before. He had, for instance, an easy race by comparison with his struggle with Thomond II last year, and he should actually be the better for it. His jumping, if not orthodox, and such as would almost inevitably bring him to grief at Liverpool – was a delight to watch, for he flicked over each fence, gaining ground every time and giving his new jockey, Evan Williams, something to do to keep him under restraint. He certainly chanced a few of the obstacles, notably the fence after the water, but then he has always done this on courses other than Liverpool, and was doing it each time he ran during the season in which he won the Grand National. There was never a suggestion, at any point in the race, that he was in two minds whether to cut it or not. He went straight into each fence, was over and gone.

At the last, where he had drawn out ten lengths clear, Williams steadied him and he did not clear it as quickly as he had jumped the others. It is needless to say that when he came away up the hill alone there was a hurricane of cheering, for he is still the most popular steeplechaser in training, and it is also needless to say that Miss Paget was delighted.

There was strong hostility displayed in the betting towards his chance, for he opened at evens and at the close was 21 to 20 against — a remarkably good price, considering that there was only one serious lapse, on the part of the horse himself, to be forgiven. Royal Mail and Brienz were joint second favourites. Southern Hero, as last year, made the running, but he stayed on nothing like as long, for Royal Mail had taken the lead from him when they had gone less than half a mile. The field was soon reduced to five. The outclassed Fouquet, who was bringing up the rear, fell at the fence after the water first time round. Royal Mail continued to lead from Southern Hero and Golden Miller, with Brienz tracking them, and Kellsboro Jack tailing along behind. It was after they had passed the water the second time round that Golden Miller moved up and became second as they came to the bottom. He drew up to Royal Mail and then headed him.

The further he went, the further he draw away from them, always racing effortlessly on the bit, and, to all appearances, thoroughly enjoying his task. There was then no shadow of doubt about his winning. Under pressure, the others tried to keep with the leaders, but none of them had a chance. Kellsboro Jack made up a good deal of ground coming up the hill, and managed to beat Brienz, who was tiring, by two lengths for third place.

There was nothing in the performance of Golden Miller to go into ecstasies about. It was only what one would have expected the real Golden Miller to do, but the mercurial members of the Ring, who had been pounding him unmercifully before the race, as if he were a deteriorated horse, immediately made him favourite for the Grand National again at 7 to 1 — and Reynoldstown was knocked out to 15 to 2. Viewed in the cold light of reason, Golden Miller's prospects in the Grand National seem to be exactly as they were before he went to Newbury and refused. The general view of the horse is always to forgive him one lapse, but, if he does wrong two or three times, to cast him off. Although he has won the Grand National once, Golden Miller is not a true Liverpool jumper. Maturity has not mellowed him or steadied him in this respect.

---

10 MARCH 1950

COTTAGE RAKE LANDS GOLD CUP HAT-TRICK

BEATS FINNURE BY TEN LENGTHS

Hotspur

Cottage Rake yesterday joined Golden Miller as the second horse to win the Cheltenham Gold Cup three years in succession. Thanks partly to the brilliant opportunism of his jockey, Aubrey Brabazon, Cottage Rake won very easily by ten lengths from Finnure. Brabazon sapped his field after turning for home, and instead of the close finish expected the race became a procession. It was the easiest Gold Cup victory since the days of Golden Miller. It is a pity Cottage Rake has not yet been allowed to take his chance in the Grand National. He stays so well I think he would acquit himself with credit. Over Park courses he is certainly a smasher. A National triumph would entitle him to be considered on the same plane as 'The Miller'.

Brabazon showed once again that he is a great man for the big occasion. It was a very poor gallop for the first mile and a half with Nagara and Clarendon alternately making the running. Contrary to expectations, Brabazon took Cottage Rake to the front approaching the stands for the first time with the other five bunched close up. Going away from the stands again, Cottage Rake was asked to quicken. He went into a six lengths' lead and from that moment was never headed. The tubed Rideo made a bad mistake at the water and thereafter was not a factor. Clarendon was beaten at the same time.

When the fence at the bottom end of the course was reached, Cottage Rake was nearly six lengths in front of Finnure and Garde Toi, who were almost level. Making the final turn for home Cottage Rake was about four lengths clear of Finnure, but Brabazon had evidently decided to slip his field directly he rounded the bend. This he most successfully did and came to the next fence at least a dozen lengths in front of Finnure – with his race apparently won. Finnure toiled throughout the last half-mile to get at Cottage Rake, but in vain. It was rather a sad anti-climax.

Nevertheless, all honours to Cottage Rake for a smashing performance; to his jockey, winner of the last two Champion Hurdles and Gold Cups; and to his trainer, Vincent O'Brien. I thought Cottage Rake would not be quite as good this year as he was last. I was wrong.

---

3 APRIL 1977

RED RUM IS FIRST TO WIN NATIONAL TREBLE

John Oaksey

The sun came out at Aintree yesterday to illuminate perhaps the happiest scene witnessed on a British racecourse. Red Rum had come to claim his kingdom and as he galloped home alone, the first horse to win a third Grand National, the roar which welcomed him was echoed round the world. Now it can surely be said without fear of contradiction that in the British Isles at least there has never been a racehorse more famous or more universally admired. As Tommy Stack and Red Rum pulled up they were at once surrounded by a delighted, jostling mob. The two police horses who traditionally escort Grand National winners home needed all their strength and weight to force a path back to the winner's enclosure.

After Friday's gales which had seemed at the time to be washing Red Rum's chances down the drain, a glorious sunny day was only one of several well-deserved favours which fortune offered the hero. As he sailed over his beloved fences, cool, economical, sure-footed as a cat, no less than four other horses fell when still in front of him, all potential dangers. By the fence after Becher's second time round there were only loose ones left. Even they played their part by standing aside before the end like a guard of honour.

But falls and disasters are part of the Grand National and let no one suppose that luck was the basic reason for this golden piece of sporting history. Red Rum's genius is the sort which creates its own good fortune. From start to finish, foot perfect as always, his progress was as relentless as the script of a well-rehearsed romance with an ending so happy that it brought tears to your eyes.

Five horses fell at the very first fence, bringing down two others in the chaos. They were the well-fancied Pengrail, Duffle Coat, Spittin Image, the only grey in the field Willy What, and Huperade, the oldest horse in the field. His 40-year-old amateur rider, Mr John Carden, was kicked in the chest, the only jockey hurt badly enough to need a trip to hospital. The two brought down were War Bonnet and High Ken, whose trainer-rider John Edwards had wasted long and hard to take the mount.

For him all the pain and effort ended in bitter disappointment, but though these disasters occurred in the middle of the field, not far from Red Rum's path, this was not one of Tommy Stack's only two really anxious moments. The first of these came at Becher's second time when Andy Pandy, who had been jumping superbly, toppled over in the lead. Red Rum needed all his famous agility to avoid being tripped up. Though that left him in front with only riderless horses for company, it was they who then became Tommy Stack's second nightmare. Round the Canal Turn one of them could so easily have gone straight on and carried Red Rum wide off course. But they all turned according to the book over Valentine's, Tommy Stack pulled calmly back to give them a chance to get out of his way. That way, in fact, only became completely clear two fences from home where the remaining loose horses ran out safely to the right. From then on, with Churchtown Boy tiring visibly in second place, it was a triumphal progress all the way.

Andy Pandy had been the fourth leader to disappear. Boom Docker was 15 lengths in front as the survivors galloped past the stand after one circuit and though he cleared the Chair, Sage Merlin fell heavily in second place. Red Rum was sixth by now and at the first fence second time round the band in front of him was cut again. Boom Docker had seemed till then to be enjoying every moment of the race. But he clearly considers that four and a half miles is twice as far as a race should be and, running down the fence he had jumped so well first time, he declined to take any further part.

That left Andy Pandy alone in front going so strongly and jumping so well that his trainer Fred Rimmell must have had dreams of a fifth Grand National winner to go with the four he has already trained. But the famous drop which claimed Captain Becher in 1839 was just too much for Andy Pandy and last year's winning rider John Burke. The horse leapt the fence dead right, but jumped it just too well, failed to get his undercarriage down in time and, as I've said, very nearly proved a fatal obstacle to Red Rum coming up behind him.

Winter Rain fell at that same fence. But as Red Rum and his riderless attendants swerved round the Canal, another threat materialised behind them. Churchtown Boy had won the Topham Trophy over nearly three miles of the Grand National course on Thursday and now, jumping as well as he had then, he made a most gallant attempt for his own place in the history books. No horse has won both races in the same year, but, though Churchtown Boy had to be content with second place in the end, even that achievement outdid Irish Lizard, who won the Topham and finished third to Early Mist in 1953. Taffy Salaman, the tough Welsh jockey who trains Churchtown Boy, had received an anonymous telegram yesterday morning telling him that the horse would only run 'at your own peril'. Taffy, needless to say, took no notice and on the long run down from Valentine's there seemed to us in the stands an awful possibility that the 22 pounds Red Rum was giving Churchtown Boy might turn the scale.

But the gallant pursuer does not really stay beyond three miles and it was now, with a mile to go, that Red Rum's matchless stamina came into its own. He flicked over fence after fence and, crossing the Melling Road, Tommy Stack looked round to see what for him must have been the happiest possible sight. For Martin Blackshaw had begun to kick and push on Churchtown Boy. The gap was growing, not shrinking and as the three loose horses in front ran out before the second last that left only two fences between Red Rum and what so many had thought an impossible achievement.

30 SEPTEMBER 1996

MY SEVEN-TIMER WAS LIKE WINNING THE LOTTERY JACKPOT

Frankie Dettori

In some ways it was a relief when Sunbeam Dance was beaten in the first race yesterday and we stopped at seven in a row. The pressure was off and I had a few moments to think about Saturday, and just how astonishing it all was. Of course, it was a shame that the people who came to Ascot hoping to see me do it again were disappointed from the start, but if we are to attract people to the great sport of racing, it is important they know the difference between fantasy and fact. Like the Lottery, if it's your day you can win, but for most people you buy the ticket and wait for next week. Nobody rode all seven winners in a seven-race card in England. Not just in my time here, in my lifetime, or even in old Lester's time. Nobody. Ever.

It was only after I came back in with Sunbeam Dance yesterday that the importance of what I'd done truly began to sink in. On Saturday night, when I went home in the car, I thought I'd got it in perspective, but even then there was the hope of carrying it on to eight, nine, or, less probably, ten winners in a row. Yesterday told me the real merit of Saturday's effort: the skill of all the trainers and their teams in getting the horses there at their peak. Especially Godolphin. Their four wins in a single day was in danger of being thought of as being secondary to my seven-timer. But for a stable of not much more than 40 horses to prepare four of them to win a Group Three, Group Two, England's top all-aged mile Group One, and then a 19-runner handicap against the strongest opposition, is mind-blowing.

I have to thank Sheikh Mohammed for letting me into his team, first as John Gosden's jockey, and then as the main rider for Godolphin. I feel I have an affinity with both men, a feeling that goes beyond the normal trainer-jockey or owner-jockey relationship. I was thrilled to win on Decorated Hero for John Gosden on Saturday and even though I could only watch from Medaaly's back in the Royal Lodge yesterday, it was great to see John get another big win in a Group Two race with Benny The Dip so soon after we won the St Leger together. Maybe we will be able to team up on him in the Derby next year. I suppose yesterday ended up as a bit of an anti-climax, but it was great to finish on a winning note again for John with Altamura.

But to come back to Saturday and that magical moment when Fujiyama Crest showed he'd read the script, too, and stuck that brave head out to beat

Pat Eddery on Northern Fleet. He was so tired, as if he too felt the occasion, but, of course, he'd carried nine stones ten pounds for two miles around Ascot. Ray Cochrane later asked if I'd heard the crowd as we turned into the straight. I told him, the noise as we went past the post was better than Wembley when England played in the European Championship. I felt like Nick Faldo coming up the 72nd hole in The Open with a five-stroke lead; like Pete Sampras serving for the title at Wimbledon. I was so grateful that so many people stayed on even after the presentations on Saturday. As I said then, racing is known as the Sport of Kings; I think we should try to make it the Sport of Everyone. When I think about the seven wins in one day, I cannot believe it. On the way to Ascot on Saturday morning, I had a bad feeling about Mark of Esteem's big race. I was worried that the race would be messy, but luckily I was always in the right position, and when he quickened the response was electric.

On Saturday night I went home, collected Catherine, my fiancée, and went for a drink with Simon Crisford, Godolphin's manager. We had a quiet meal, then I went home and was in bed, exhausted after all the excitement, by 11. When I got up yesterday I read all the papers, and it was a change that the nice part of winning was not spoiled by stories of whip bans or trainers complaining about me jumping off in the winner's enclosure. Two leaps off two winners on one day is another record for British racing! There were so many messages from all around the world on my answerphone, and it took me two hours to play them all back. But the most important call was the one from my dad. He once rode six winners on a seven-race card back home in Italy, but never all seven. His congratulations meant everything to me. He didn't see the races, but watched the results come up one by one on the BBC World Service Teletext. He thought it had broken.

---

22 DECEMBER 2001

IT'S HIGH FIVE FOR BRILLIANT McCOY

Brough Scott

It was cold at Ascot, so cold that racing only went ahead after four freezing foot-stamping stewards' inspections. But Tony McCoy was hot, five winners hot. What hungover Boxing Day punter will resist the name of his King George ride on Boxing Day – Best Mate. There was nothing dull in this repetition of excellence. Tarxien, Wahiba Sands, Shooting Light and – after (for him) the humiliation of only being eighth behind winner Marble Arch in The Ladbroke on Westender – Seebald and Alvino. Different horses, different distances, different rides, but through all of them shone the most astounding mixture of mental and physical commitment to be seen anywhere in sport today.

Shooting Light, in the Tote Silver Cup, was the star turn, positively sprinting clear of Siberian Gale and his seven other rivals up the final Ascot hill. With fancied horses like Ad Hoc, Dusk Duel and, to a lesser extent Arctic Camper, running disappointingly, Shooting Light might have been a shade flattered by the ease of this success. But there is no doubt that he is a remarkably improved chaser since he moved to Martin Pipe this season. With Pipe responsible for the first four of McCoy's winners, and the loser Westender, this was cue once again for some other trainers to start dark mutterings that such success – these winners took his total to 149 – was somehow 'not natural'. While it is true that Shooting Light's improvement can be officially assessed at two stone this season, he was always a talented if sometimes inconsistent horse with previous handler Pat Murphy, and the change to the noticeably more intensive training regime perfected by Pipe is much more likely to be the answer than some easily alleged 'magic mushroom' nonsense.

So intensive is the regime that some horses have trouble standing up to the pressure season after season. But while they are right, they buckle down to their tasks with all the workaholic grit of their trainer. Both Tarxien, in the novice hurdle, and Seebald, in the novice chase, were winning for the sixth consecutive time this season, while Wahiba Sands (two races) and Shooting Light (three) remain unbeaten. As a tribute to collective good health and athleticism this is hard to better.

McCoy completed his five-timer with a comparatively easy victory on the Henrietta Knight-trained Alvino in the National Hunt Flat race. But even here, all the ingredients of the champion's zenith shone out through the frosty gloom. In his early days – he was first champion jockey six seasons ago – there was an element of impetuosity in the way McCoy threw himself at every challenge. Now, as on Alvino, and indeed on each of the other four winners, he is as happy to settle his horse easily into the middle of the pack as to set off in one of those macho, all-the-way trailblazers of his early days.

But when McCoy clamps down into the athlete beneath, the compulsion he engenders into and after a fence is more complete than any jump jockey I have seen. For Shooting Light's race I stood down at the last fence. McCoy and his blinkered partner were well clear, but there was never any question of any easing up of the rhythm. Fifty yards from the fence, McCoy pulled the whip across into his right hand, cracking Shooting Light down the shoulder to instil one final sense of urgency. The champion's long, honed face was creased into teeth-flashing effort as they came into the obstacle. Six full strides from it he thrust his body and legs down into the horse, the last three strides extending into the leap. It was bolder, braver and more committed than any jump so far. But faint heart leads to faltering. With this champion, commitment is the only way. Afterwards, McCoy mockingly cursed Frankie Dettori. 'If he hadn't done his seven-timer I might have been famous,' he said. Not famous enough to make even the final three in BBC Sports Personality of the Year, though.

8 JUNE 1953

GORDON RICHARDS ENDS DERBY HOODOO ON PINZA

GAME AUREOLE NOT QUITE GOOD ENOUGH

Hotspur

If The Queen's colt Aureole could not win the Derby on Saturday, as would certainly have been a fitting climax to Coronation Week, then a victory for Pinza, ridden by Gordon Richards, owned by Sir Victor Sassoon, bred by Mr Fred Darling, and trained by Darling's former head lad, N. Bertie, was the second best result. It was Gordon Richards's first victory in the race at his 28th attempt, and now, having fulfilled a life-long ambition, it may be that Pinza will prove his last Derby mount.

Sir Victor Sassoon was also gaining his first Derby triumph. This staunch supporter of racing, who won the 1,000 Guineas and the Oaks with Exhibitionist, in 1937, has thoroughly deserved his success. For Mr Darling – trainer of a succession of Derby winners, and owner and trainer of Pont l'Eveque, who won a substitute Derby at Newmarket in 1940 – Pinza's victory completes the chapter.

At the December Sales of 1949, Mr J.A. Dewar bought on behalf of Mr Darling for 2,000 guineas the ten-year-old mare Pasqua, carrying a foal destined to be Pinza. Mr Darling knew the value of the blood, for he had trained Pasqua's half-brother Pasch to win the 2,000 Guineas of 1938 for the late Mr 'Manna' Morriss, and to finish third in the Derby to Bois Roussel and Scottish Union. Yet once again the Derby illustrated the glorious uncertainty of racing, for Pinza was bought by Sir Victor Sassoon against the advice of Mr Darling, who sent up three yearlings to the Newmarket July Sales in 1951 and told Sir Victor which one he thought most promising. It was not Pinza, who was sold for 1,500 guineas – a small sum compared with some of the prices his owner has paid for yearlings in the last 20 years. Pinza, however, has already won more than £24,000 in stake money for Sir Victor, and no doubt by the time he has finished his worth will run well into six figures. But so much for the story of the winner. Let us turn to the race.

Aureole was inclined to play up in the parade, but by the time he had got to the starting post he was quiet again and did not take much out of himself. The start was a good one, and among those soon conspicuous were City Scandal, Mountain King and Shikarnpur with Victory Roll, Star of the Forest, Nearula, Pinza and Aureole reasonably well placed. After half a mile Shikarnpur had gone into the lead, and coming to the top of the hill he was followed by Victory Roll, Mountain King, Pinza (on the rails), Nearula, Aureole, Pharel and Premonition among others.

From that point the pace increased noticeably, and before they had come to Tattenham Corner, Shikarnpur and Pinza – on whom Gordon Richards was lucky to get a clear run – were out clear of the remainder, with Shikarnpur some four lengths ahead. The positions were the same going into the straight, with Pinza, in turn, four or five lengths ahead of a group which included Mountain King, Good Brandy, Star of the Forest, Pharel, Aureole and Nearula. Mountain King, Good Brandy and Star of the Forest were in trouble a furlong later, while Gordon Richards was almost on the tail of Shikarnpur, waiting for the moment to challenge. The champion jockey asked Pinza to win his race about a quarter of a mile from home. The colt drew up to Shikarnpur without ado, and with more than a furlong to go held a clear lead from Shikarnpur with his race apparently won.

The only danger now was Aureole, whom Carr brought to challenge wide of Pinza. Aureole ran on well, but was not quite good enough and could not get to Pinza, who won decisively by four lengths. Pink Horse finished fast to take third place from a tiring Shikarnpur with Chatsworth (who never promised to win) fifth, Pharel sixth, the rank outsider Timberland, seventh.

---

3 JUNE 2007

DETTORI'S SUFFERING ENDS WITH RUTHLESS DERBY WIN

Brough Scott

Frankie Dettori, in tune with the times, in tune with the horse and now, at last, in tune with the Derby. In the end it was gloriously, ruthlessly simple, but the vast, nationwide explosion of joy as Authorized powered

Dettori past the winning post only happened because of the tightening knot of worry beginning to bite into the psyche of horse and rider alike. Dettori had been through panic enough when he damaged a knee in a fall last week, and when he had to rush his son to hospital a couple of days ago. But when Authorized got into the paddock, it was clear the tension was getting to him, too.

With temperatures in the high 70s, Authorized was becoming a very hot favourite indeed. Every now and then he was dancing on the spot and chucking his white splashed forehead up and down in annoyance. He might not have known he was risking punters a fortune, but he knew something was up. Dettori's impassive, far-away focus in the parade showed he was feeling it, too. But in the race you would not have known it. With the Epsom outsider Kid Mambo setting a good gallop from the start, Dettori, from his wide draw, ensured himself of as good a position as possible for the first right-hand dogleg on the upward climb and then settled in towards the back of the field as Kid Mambo and the Ballydoyle outsider Anton Chekhov kept up the tempo at the lead. Dettori was towards the back and on the outside, but this was a no-risk strategy. He should be on the best horse. He had the others covered. 'I counted ten horses in front of me,' he said afterwards, 'but I thought as long as they did not slow up and bunch us, I could have a clear run at them. I expected a dogfight, but it was so smooth it was like an oil painting. It was beautiful, so smooth and great.'

Close up, there was one of those gorgeous feelings of historic inevitability. A little green-silked figure pumping behind the mane of the big bay colt who, with his tongue flopping out of the side of the mouth, was making his big stride force him clear of his rivals as the whole 100,000 crowd roared in salute. Three swift times Dettori's whip smacked his back to keep up the pressure, but as he came to the line, those familiar Italian teeth were flashing in delight and there was the first of an endless series of war-whoops. The victory by five lengths, two-and-a-half lengths and a head from Eagle Mountain, Aqaleem and Lucarno, was so decisive that everyone now could abandon themselves in delight. What luck it has been for British racing that Dettori's instinct is to share his delight as wide as possible. He was scheduled to parade sedately in front of the massed photographers and then return to the unsaddling circle. But he could see and hear the clamouring fans in the grandstand and on the infield on either side of the now empty racetrack up ahead. He signalled the photographers apart and rode up the course for his lap of glory.

At last he had a partner to give him the one racing honour that has eluded him. That he had was thanks to the talents of 44-year-old Peter

Chapple-Hyam, a portly figure sweating under the black top hat and now cautioning in his Tommy Cooper voice: 'It's all about the horse.' Chapple-Hyam won the 1992 Derby with Dr Devious, and his three seasons back from an unhappy spell in Hong Kong have confirmed that he has the crucial trainer's gift of being both able to spot talent and to deliver it. Yesterday he also had the services of one of the greatest sets of gifts rolled into a jockey's frame. Sometimes it is easy to miss the skills beneath the showmanship. But if anyone questioned Dettori's ability to rise to the highest challenge on the greatest stage they needed to watch this race.

And if anyone doubted that his knee injury would eliminate the trademark 'flying dismount', they should have been beside him as he turned to press through the throng to the unsaddling enclosure. 'No,' he said to someone advising caution. 'Clear the area. I am going to do a flyer and if the knee cracks, hey, I've still won the Derby.'

Long after the racing was over he finally came out of the changing room, a tired, dapper, limping little figure in a smart suit and a pink shirt carrying a glass of Champagne in one hand and a trophy bag in the other. His mobile phone already showed 65 text messages. 'I am really drained,' he said, 'but this is the most satisfying moment of my career. When my five children grow up I want to be able to tell them that I won the big honours in my sport. I don't want to retire, but this has been the day that was wanted.' For Dettori, of course, but after Henry Cecil's hugely welcomed comeback win in the Oaks with Light Shift on Friday, this was the day that racing itself needed more than any other. Her Majesty was there, too. After yesterday, is it really too soon for 'Arise Sir Frankie'?

---

11 APRIL 2010

BEING PULLED OVER BY POLICE FAILED TO RUIN MY DAY

A.P. McCoy, Grand National-winning jockey

Quite apart from the fact that I was beginning to think it might never happen, I never, for a moment, thought winning the Grand National would be quite so emotional. Maybe it is because I had been trying for so long and had so often walked out of Aintree on a Saturday night disappointed and deflated, but, until you win it, you have no idea of the effect it will have on you. Not many things have reduced me to tears, but I found it incredibly emotional that wave after wave of well-wishers were so genuinely pleased and happy for me. Two of the first people to congratulate me were Ted Walsh, Ruby's father, and Martin Pipe, my old boss, two of the biggest names in the sport. I could see how happy they were for me and, for some reason, it just opened the floodgates.

I know well enough no one has a divine right to win this race, it can happen to anyone. But now when I do retire I will retire a happy man. It would have always irked me if I hadn't won it. I had always tried to comfort myself with the thought that better jockeys than myself, like John Francome, Peter Scudamore didn't win it and that Jonjo O'Neill, Don't Push It's trainer, couldn't even get round. Each year you come back hoping for, though never expecting, better luck. But by the time I had jumped five fences on Saturday my mentality changed and my mood was much more optimistic because I felt the horse was loving it. Don't Push It is a very special animal and you have no idea how well he is going to be looked after when J.P. McManus retires him. There's no way he will let me have him – he will live a life of luxury at J.P.'s stud in Ireland, and if I come back in another life I wouldn't mind coming back as Don't Push It.

After the racing and all the interviews were done I drove into Liverpool and I hadn't gone more than a few hundred yards when the police pulled me over for talking on my mobile phone. I couldn't believe it when they did me for three points – you would have thought that on Saturday of all days they might have let me off, especially as I was on the phone to my mum at home in Ireland. My driver, Barney Jones, who had the week off, is really pleased, though, because it means he can keep his job a bit longer! Hundreds of racegoers were walking back into Liverpool; they were cheering as they went past and telling the police not to do me. One, who lived in Melling Road, said if it was an on-the-spot fine he would even pay it for me. They would have had to lock me up to spoil my day, though.

I have had hundreds of texts from people, from close friends, people I haven't seen for years and people I've never met. I even got one from Liam Brady, who was my childhood hero, and from Sir Alex Ferguson. Back in Liverpool I dropped in to see Ruby Walsh who missed the ride on Big Fella Thanks after falling in the Aintree Hurdle earlier in the afternoon. We went out to the official winners' party, where there were quite a lot of my weighing-room colleagues in very good form. Even those who'd had heavy falls were on a high from the thrill they'd had – it's that sort of race. When that finished we continued back at the hotel and I eventually climbed back into bed at 5 a.m.

On Sunday I drove to Jackdaw's Castle to see Don't Push It. Jonjo wasn't in great shape – he's not the sort of man to hold back on the celebrations. I flew to Southwell to ride in the afternoon and last night flew out to Ireland to stay the night with J.P. It might be a day or two before everything returns to normal.

---

9 FEBRUARY 2009

TONY McCOY ACHIEVES 3,000TH WIN – FINALLY

Andrew Baker

The Tyser and Co. Beginners' Steeple Chase (Class 4) is a very long way from being the most charismatic race on the National Hunt calendar. Plumpton, for all its charms, is hardly Cheltenham or Aintree. But this humble fixture at this bucolic venue provided Tony McCoy with the chance to finally claim his 3,000th winner over jumps. Restless d'Artaix was the name of the horse, and, while he may go on to great things, his place in racing history is already secured.

In gathering darkness and driving rain, the 13-times champion sprayed Champagne around the already sodden parade ring. Teetotal, he won't have touched a drop himself, but he was happy to drink in the enthusiastic acclaim of the fans gathered around him.

It might all have happened a short while earlier. McCoy was cruising home in the previous race, eight lengths clear on Miss Sarenne coming to the final hurdle: surely that 3,000th winner was in the bag . . . But Plumpton on Monday was more of a quagmire than a racecourse, and the mare's hooves skidded straight on as she landed, and McCoy went over her head and hit the floor hard. Quickly, he was on his feet, helping up the horse and then leading her back to the parade ring, with commiserating cries from the grandstand ringing in his ears.

Plumpton was hardly overrun, but in such foul conditions that was understandable. The course is regarded by local fans as 'Cheltenham in miniature', but that is more a tribute to the undulations of the left-handed track than to the atmosphere, such as it is. It is enjoyable as long as you stay indoors. The rain was relentless and the gusting wind icy. The race commentator was in trouble after the first couple of fences of each contest as jockeys' silks rapidly became a uniform mud-brown. As the afternoon wore on, assorted obstacles were dolled off or preceded by men waving warning flags, as the course became increasingly waterlogged.

Had history not been in the making, the card might well have been abandoned, as horses were splashing through increasingly vast puddles, and spectators scuttled from bar to bookie and back sheltering under improvised newspaper hats. The big screen opposite the grandstand fizzled out halfway through the afternoon, so fans who wanted a glimpse of the great champion's celebrations had to brave the torrenting rain or press their noses to the steamed-up windows of the Members' Bar.

Perhaps it would have been more appropriate for McCoy to have ridden winner No. 3,000 at one of Britain's more iconic venues, or even one of the nation's more rugged or rural courses. But it somehow suits the man and the sport that the mark should have been made at a modest track in unspeakable weather. It was the climatic conditions, of course, that had kept McCoy's many fans on tenterhooks for so many days and the jockey himself at home, waiting for the next call from his agent telling of yet another meeting snowed off, frozen off or drowned out. Plumpton represented a wet window of opportunity, a chance to register the magic number before the dreadful weather closed in again.

Throughout the often-postponed saga it has been clear that the least excited of all those involved was the great jockey himself. What counts for McCoy is the win, not the number of winners, as you could tell as he cleared the last at around 4.30, rising and landing parallel with Timmy Murphy on The Package. As they started up the final hill, McCoy went to work on Restless D'Artaix, driving the inexperienced chaser through the bottomless mud, knees working the flanks, elbows flailing, determination personified.

The sparse and soaking crowd cheered with a volume that belied their number as their hero steered his exhausted mount into the winner's enclosure. It was a well-named ride for the record: horse and rider, both restless.

---

30 MAY 1968

UNIQUE PARTNERSHIP OF HORSE AND RIDER

SIR IVOR AND PIGGOTT SUPERB

Marlborough

'I don't know how good the others are – but I know he's an awful lot better.' That was how Lester Piggott summed it up yesterday after he and Sir Ivor had given a performance which, for sheer style and flawless elegance, has surely never been bettered on Epsom Downs. They say – and it is true – that a jockey can't run without his horse. But it's also true that a great horse deserves a great jockey and it is for that, the perfect harmony of two outstanding talents, that yesterday's great race will always be remembered.

Fonteyn and Nureyev, Charlton and Best, Crosby and Hope – Piggott and Sir Ivor are members of that same exclusive club. And yesterday afternoon, matching each other, they were equally superb. Two furlongs out, as Remand tried and failed to challenge Connaught, the leader seemed to us in the stands uncatchable. Uncatchable, that is, until you glanced back and saw Piggott on the favourite – taking, you would have thought, about as much interest in the proceedings as a rank non-trier in a selling plate.

To wait so long in such a race required a unique blend of confidence and nerve, but the tactics were entirely logical. We know now that Sir Ivor stays every yard of the Derby distance – but Piggott didn't know it then. And so, to make the best use of his mount's known phenomenal speed, he sat still longer than nine men out of ten would dare. When he did pull out to pass Remand, Sir Ivor, every bit as calm and unconcerned, took a stride or so to realise the time had come. For a moment there, with Connaught three lengths clear and running as if the hounds of Hell were after him, even Piggott may have felt a twinge of doubt. But if so he has already forgotten it. 'I always knew I could pick them up whenever I wanted,' he says. And pick them up he did – like a Ferrari in the old crocks' race.

To poor Sandy Barclay, who had ridden Connaught so beautifully, the winning post was heartbreakingly near. Connaught, to his eternal credit, had never faltered after striking the front and must have been giving his rider the feeling 'nothing can stop me now'. When a good horse works at home, lesser animals are often 'jumped in' to take him along at various stages of the gallop. And that, as Barclay said afterwards, was how if felt as Sir Ivor caught and passed him a hundred yards from home. The time of the Derby was fast, but I'd dearly love to know how long the winner took to cover the last furlong. Sir Gordon Richards, asked his opinion of Sir Ivor, expressed it in one word – 'Class' – and we saw the perfect living definition of that word yesterday afternoon.

---

30 JULY 1968

RIBERO SLAMS SIR IVOR

John Lawrence at The Curragh

Two furlongs from home in the Irish Sweeps Derby here yesterday Lester Piggott glanced sideways. He was looking at Sir Ivor – in his own words the best horse he has ridden – and a couple of heartbeats later, moving his hands on Ribero's neck, he scattered those words and a million others across the sunlit Curragh. For in those seconds we saw the impossible happen. Stepping gracefully into the footsteps of his full brother Ribocco, Ribero strode irresistibly away.

That Sir Ivor should be beaten at all was hard enough to believe; that he should be beaten like this – treated almost contemptuously by a horse who last time out finished a dozen lengths behind Connaught at Ascot – was as strange and inexplicable as anything seen in a Classic race. My first reaction to it is a feeling of heartfelt sympathy for Liam Ward, who had taken Piggott's place, as was his right on his home track before an adoring Irish crowd. Ward's only consolation must be that he rode the favourite flawlessly. Sir Ivor suffered no interference, was given every conceivable chance. He was beaten fair and square and no one who saw him at Epsom can believe they were watching the same horse here.

There had been no premonition of disaster – unless it was in the press handouts supplied by the thoughtful management of this superbly organised event. They contained biographies of every runner and the favourite's was headed 'WINNER – SIR IVOR'. Perhaps the Fates took this as an intolerable affront, but as Sir Ivor, looking if anything better than ever, cantered down in the sunshine, there was no sign of their displeasure.

From a perfect start – the favourite was last but one to be installed and had only a minute or so to wait – Ward settled him two from last while Giolla Mear and Stitch shared the lead ahead of Ribero. Piggott, using very different tactics from those he adopted at Ascot, was never worse than third. But before the turn for home Sir Ivor had moved up easily on his quarters and quite early in the straight these two came on with the race between them.

And now for the first time there *was* a doubt. Two furlongs out Sir Ivor was still on a tight rein, but so was his opponent. A moment later the crowd gave a great collective groan as Ward felt for his whip. 'He just died in my hands,' the disconsolate jockey said afterwards, and that was precisely how it looked. In place of the deadly burst of speed we saw at Epsom on Derby Day, there was nothing. It was Ribero who accelerated like a champion, storming away ridden only with hands and heels to win by two very comfortable lengths. 'I was always going easily,' said Piggott, 'but when I looked round two furlongs out I thought I was looking at the winner. When he collapsed it shocked me as much as anyone.' Yesterday's race was run on good going at a true gallop throughout and if you had not been at Epsom you might say Sir Ivor failed to stay. A more feasible explanation is of course that he had, after all, caught the virus which has swept Vincent O'Brien's stable. This incredible result throws the rest of the season wide open.

4 JUNE 1970

NIJINSKY FASTEST DERBY WINNER SINCE MAHMOUD

Hotspur (Peter Scott)

Nijinsky, running Epsom's mile and a half faster than any Derby winner since Mahmoud in 1936, stretched his unbeaten record to eight races yesterday with a display of sheer brilliance. For the first time in his life, Nijinsky started at odds against. Mr Charles Engelhard's colt, the third Derby winner for his Irish trainer Vincent O'Brien, and Lester Piggott's fifth, won by a comfortably decisive two and a half lengths from Gyr, with Stintino, another French challenger, three lengths behind in third place.

Nijinsky, taught by skilled training and jockeyship to conserve his brilliant speed, settled down in the middle of the field. He was, in fact, running lazily and Piggott had to produce the whip to rouse him up. Once that happened Nijinsky's great stride took him past Gyr just over a furlong from home. Then the gap between an excellent horse and a rapidly outstanding champion rapidly widened.

Mr Charles Engelhard, Nijinsky's American owner, had never seen his colt run until yesterday. He intimated that Nijinsky will retire to stud at the end of this season. It is also odds against his running for the St Leger in an attempt to become the first Triple Crown winner since Bahram in 1935. Mr Engelhard, a lavish supporter of international racing, said: 'The Derby, to my mind, remains paramount among the great international Classics and I always hoped to live to see this day.'

Lester Piggott's five wins now puts him only one behind the Derby riding record, held jointly by Steve Donoghue and Jem Robinson, an early 19th-century champion. Nijinksy, Canadian-bred, was bought on Mr Engelhard's behalf from his Ontario breeder, Mr E.P. Taylor, as a yearling by Vincent O'Brien for $84,000 (roughly £35,000).

---

10 JUNE 2002

STAMINA WAS THE KEY

Johnny Murtagh

As I anticipated in my *Telegraph* column on Saturday, High Chaparral gave me my second Vodafone Derby. He answered my every call and as spare rides go, they don't come much better. When I won on Sinndar it was total elation; this time it was high emotion. The early part of the race didn't go quite as I'd expected. High Chaparral was the first to load in the stalls. I probably got him a bit too relaxed. He didn't jump just as fast as I'd hoped and consequently I was a bit further back than I wanted to be, following Mick Kinane on Hawk Wing – I had thought it would have been him following me – but there was a lot of pace up front so I told myself not to panic.

The key to beating Hawk Wing was always going to be stamina so about five furlongs out, I started getting closer, easing past Bandari, who was beginning to drop away. Once round Tattenham Corner, I gave him a crack to go and catch the two pacemakers, Moon Ballad and Coshocton. I hit the front before the two-furlong pole and about a furlong and a half out, I felt Mick come to me, but he never got closer than half a length. I knew High Chaparral would stay and I knew once Hawk Wing didn't get past me quickly, I'd rally and win. They say the last furlong was slow (14.32 seconds) but I really put the pressure on between the three pole (11.39 seconds and 12.25 seconds) and the furlong pole to take the sting out of Hawk Wing.

The Derby remains the race we all want to win and I'm very fortunate to have won it twice now. I'm sure Mick is disappointed to have picked the wrong one on this occasion, but he has the compensation of knowing that he'll ride High Chaparral next time. He's a big man and will take it well. He was in a similar position when he rode Commander In Chief (the 1993 Derby winner). It happens. Making the wrong choice is always disappointing – even in a maiden. Mick seemed to be in good form on the plane on the way home.

----

4 JUNE 1981

SHERGAR'S TEN-LENGTH TRIUMPH

John Oaksey

All sorts of records were put in danger at Epsom yesterday when 19-year-old Walter Swinburn rode the Aga Khan's Shergar to the easiest and most predictable Derby triumph of the century. Lester Piggott, who finished fourth on Shotgun, was three months younger than Swinburn when he first won the race on Never Say Die and historians allege that a 16-year-old apprentice called Parsons won in 1862. But certainly no younger man has ridden the Derby favourite – let alone one who started at odds as short as 10–11. As for winning margins, a few early 19th-century judges contented themselves with verdicts like 'won very easily'. But since they started counting lengths, no Derby has been won by ten.

The present Aga Khan's grandfather, who dominated British racing in the 1930s, owned five Derby winners between 1930 and 1952. But neither Mahmoud, who still holds the Derby course record, nor Bahram, who was never beaten, made anything like the impression left on the Epsom crowd by Shergar yesterday.

The favourite's countless backers (including two friends who staked £40,000 each at Ladbroke's Mill Hill betting shop) never really had a single uneasy moment. By the top of Tattenham Corner, Walter Swinburn and Shergar were poised in third place with ample elbow room, and as they turned for home the favourite cruised effortlessly up beside the leaders. Watched by his mother and father (a former champion jockey of Ireland), Walter hardly needed the 'miraculous medal' they had given him for luck. When asked about his tactics in the straight, he said simply: 'I won't look back.' But in the end he had to – because Shergar had gone so far in front that his rider could not hear the others.

In fact, Shergar was chased home by Mr Paul Mellon's Glint of Gold whose father, Mill Reef, won the Derby ten years ago. Struck into after two furlongs, Glint of Gold had been involved in one of the race's only hard-luck stories. As he was snatched up, Kalaglow galloped into him and, according to his rider, Greville Starkey, was almost down.

So, at the end of a glorious day, Shergar left Epsom for Newmarket poised securely at the summit of European racing. In the unlikely event of the Aga Khan deciding to sell or syndicate Shergar, he could scarcely be valued at less than £10 million. Troy was syndicated two years ago at £7.2 million and Spectacular Bid, the most valuable horse in training syndicated so far, was thought worth $22 million in the United States. Admittedly both had accomplished more in a sense than Shergar, but for a horse who has won his last three races by ten, 12 and ten lengths, the sky is apt to be the limit.

Tracing back Shergar's pedigree you come after seven generations in the female line to Mumtaz Mahal, the famous 'flying filly'. She was one of the very first yearlings bought by George Lambton when the then Aga Khan asked him to lay the foundations of the family's racing venture. So, quite apart from all the happiness and laughter which filled the air on Epsom Downs yesterday, there must, I imagine, have been some rejoicing in Paradise, too.

25 JULY 1971

MILL REEF HAS HIS FINEST HOUR

John Lawrence

The great Mill Reef – and there is no doubt *now* about the adjective – achieved his finest hour so far at Ascot yesterday. Without frills or fuss he won the King George VI and Queen Elizabeth Stakes by a cool six lengths, and in 21 years the great race has seen few if any more utterly convincing winners. Better than Nijinsky? Well, no one can make that more than an opinion and if, by magic, you could wipe away 12 months and super-impose last year's King George on yesterday, what an agonising choice it would present.

'Good big ones beat good little ones' would be one possible answer and another school of thought holds that Nijinsky's instant explosive acceleration would still give him an edge. But all my admittedly prejudiced money would be on Mr Paul Mellon's colt – and when he has won the Prix de l'Arc de Triomphe don't say I didn't tell you. The great French prize is now his autumn target (with or without a preparatory race), and there is no chance now of a return match with Brigadier Gerard, at least until next year. Because among the many hostile theories of which Mill Reef disposed forever yesterday was the one that his best distance is ten furlongs.

Two furlongs from home, it's true, the £31,558 first prize might just as well have been in Mellon's bank account. But throughout the final quarter mile Mill Reef drew inexorably further ahead and if (which God forbid) he happened now to be aimed at the St Leger I would not personally have much doubt about his stamina. For yesterday the gallop, set by Ortis's pacemaker Loud, was fast and furious from the beginning. And yet, having lain well back as far as Swinley Bottom, Geoff Lewis calmly let Mill Reef cruise through his field until, with three furlongs to go, just before the final turn, only Ortis and Politico were left to beat. And already, for all the chance they had, these two good four-year-olds might have been handicappers leading Mill Reef in a gallop on the Kingsclere Downs. As they straightened out for home Ortis showed briefly in front of Politico, but now Lewis could see no need to keep us waiting any longer.

From start to finish he had secured for the favourite the clearest possible run, and now poised three horses off the rail he gently moved his hands. In 50 yards the Italian Derby winner was brushed aside like an autumn leaf, and with almost two furlongs left the stands erupted with the sort of half hysterical cheer which only true greatness inspires on a racecourse. Where Lester Piggott would probably have sat still — as indeed he did on Nijinsky a year ago — Lewis rode Mill Reef with hands and heels until the final 50 yards. But that, if anything, made his triumph all the more impressive, for here there was no need for guesswork. We *know* he is *at least* six lengths better than any of this distinguished field.

---

3 OCTOBER 2010

WORKFORCE DIGS DEEP TO WIN PRIX DE L'ARC DE TRIOMPHE

Hotspur (J.A. McGrath at Longchamp)

Brave decisions are not always rewarded in racing, but owner Khalid Abdulla celebrated his fourth win in the Prix de l'Arc de Triomphe after placing the utmost faith in a trainer, who had not only never won the race, but for whom Europe's richest all-aged contest had threatened to become a jinx. Regardless of the fact that Sir Michael Stoute had won ten trainers' titles, five Epsom Derbys and just about every other major race in the calendar during his 38-year training career, he had never enjoyed much luck at Longchamp.

Pilsudski had twice been runner-up in the Arc for him, Opera House had finished third, and horses as classy as Shahrastani, Ezzoud, Golan and Conduit could finish no closer than fourth. There were also many others who finished out with the washing. So why would Workforce, who had been annihilated by stablemate Harbinger in Ascot's King George, suddenly become the one to turn it around? But that he did after Prince Khalid followed Stoute's guidance when the colt 'had ticked all the boxes' after several bits of serious work and elected to run.

In terms of performance, nothing could live with the second Abdulla Arc winner, Dancing Brave, but Workforce would certainly slot in ahead of the owner's other Longchamp stars Rainbow Quest and Rail Link. A seven-length winner of the Derby on lightning-fast ground in summer, and now a gutsy winner of the Arc against older opposition on soft ground in autumn. He is both versatile and top class. Here, Workforce was able to settle much better, back in the field, smothered up on the inside rail. He had more than half the field in front of him half a mile out, and it is to Ryan Moore's great credit that he was able to secure a direct passage through the pack before it disintegrated into interference that took the stewards nearly 30 minutes to sort out.

Nakayama Festa, who had given a glimpse of his promise when a close second to Duncan in the Prix Foy, emerged from the pack as the main serious challenger to Workforce halfway up the home straight. With victory within his grasp, Moore was never going to let his colt falter, nor was he going to let little-known Masyoshi Ebina from Japan upstage him in Europe's biggest race. Workforce prevailed by a head for the first truly British win in the Arc in 21 years – Godolphin, who have three Arc wins, are a Dubai stable for record purposes – with Nakayama Festa battling hard for his second, with two and a half lengths back to French Oaks winner Sarafina, who suffered bad interference in running before finishing third. Local favourite Behkabad took fourth.

Stoute was in a state of mild shock after Workforce had fallen apart in the King George. He recalled: 'We were totally baffled. Ryan thought he had got the tactics wrong, that he had been too aggressive with him early in the race. I thought that I had trained him too hard for the race. He had been outstanding at Epsom, yet he ran an inexplicably bad race at Ascot. But I was satisfied that he was right to run his race in the Arc. We waited until his final gallop because we wanted everything to be right.'

Stoute and the Abdulla camp had kept the media waiting until Thursday before confirming Workforce's participation, but he had insisted all along that the decision would be a late one, and that the owner would have the final call after he had reported in.

This was one of the outstanding training performances of our time, yet it seemed in danger of being overshadowed by the mild controversy over the lateness of news regarding the colt's running plans. 'The punters knew where they stood,' Stoute argued. 'It was just a few tetchy journalists who were unhappy.' Nobody would have quibbled had Abdulla ducked the Arc with Workforce, but he deserves high praise for a brave decision. It was an extraordinary comeback from an extraordinary colt.

---

5 NOVEMBER 2006

OUIJA BOARD SPELLS OUT HER TRUE CREDENTIALS

Brough Scott

She only gets better. Ouija Board, already the most travelled mare in the whole history of the Turf, became the first British-trained horse to win two Breeders' Cup races with a nailing smooth three-length victory under Frankie Dettori in the Filly and Mare Turf. This tenth victory in 21 runs took her winnings in Lord Derby's historic black silks to over £3 million.

This year she has already run in Hong Kong, Dubai, Epsom, Ascot, Goodwood and Leopardstown. Now, as last year, she aims to sign off in Japan and Hong Kong. No wonder Frankie Dettori said afterwards: 'It was awesome, the best she has been. She has some great gears; they always get you out of trouble.'

He had played his own part flawlessly enough and was to double up brilliantly with Red Rocks in the mile-and-a-half Breeders' Cup Turf. On Ouija Board he kept cool along the rail as the field stacked up before the final turn, and then spinning out wide to cut down his main rival Wait A While before the furlong pole. Ouija Board possesses a turn of foot to die for. Used like this she can claim to rank in the very highest rank of champions.

How lucky we all are that the skill of her Ed Dunlop training team, and the enthusiasm of her owner Edward Derby, has kept her in action for a fourth season. Her victory under Dettori in the Nassau Stakes was the highlight of our domestic summer. Now she has given our greatest moment overseas as well. It was back in 1780 that the 12th Earl Derby gave his name to the most famous race in sport. But with Ouija Board the 19th holder of the title has made a contribution that should live just as long. 'She's quite literally changed the lives of her connections,' the proud owner said afterwards surrounded by what on these big days appear to be a growing family. 'I can say we have travelled the world about four times over with her, and I think she has earned a happy retirement at the end of this year. We look forward to racing her daughters and children in the future.'

Back home at Knowsley, Edward Derby already has three of the largest and best-kept leather scrapbooks you will find. This afternoon must have given him material enough to fill another one and with the prospect of Japan and Hong Kong before Ouija Board's impending matrimonials to super sire Kingmambo, he must be a stationer's delight.

---

2 NOVEMBER 2005

SOMERSET LASS IS NOW A LEGEND

Hotspur (J.A. McGrath in Melbourne)

It was not the right time to raise the subject but Makybe Diva, who earned legendary status in Australian racing by winning the Melbourne Cup a record third time, is British-bred. While my fellow countrymen were rejoicing in the fact that a successor to the mighty Phar Lap had been unanimously appointed, there was really no escaping that this modern-day champion, a daughter of the tough Irish Derby winner Desert King, was foaled at the Britton House Stud, in Somerset.

This West Country 'lass', who has become an Australian sporting icon, has twice been through the famous Tattersalls Sales ring in Newmarket, first being carried (in utero) by her mother Tugela — who fetched 60,000 guineas in 1998 — and a year later, when she was led out unsold (19,000 guineas was the final offer) at the December Foal Sale. Makybe Diva's mother was once owned by Khalid Abdulla's Juddmonte Farms, but was sold at the end of her juvenile career for 21,000 guineas. Bought by Ballylinch Stud, she was put in foal to Desert King and re-offered the following year. The rest is racing history, certainly in Australia, where debate rages on whether she is better than Phar Lap, or even Carbine, who made his name 40 years earlier.

Yesterday provided one of those racing occasions you can never forget, a day you would like to be able to recall on cold winter's evenings when memories seem to take on such a warm glow. As Lee Freedman, the great mare's trainer, said: 'Find the youngest child in our midst and you can say he or she will probably be the only one with a chance of seeing such a feat again. We won't.'

Freedman, who was winning his fifth Melbourne Cup, has done a remarkable job with Makybe Diva, but praise for the trainer is surpassed on this occasion by the accolade heaped on the jockey, Glen Boss, who possesses nerves of steel. Boss adhered to the conventional demands on Australian jockeys riding at Flemington, by sticking close to the inside rail, even as the challengers jostled their way into the sweep into the home straight. He had Makybe Diva on the inside in 14th place, sitting with a double handful, and with the weight of expectation of a nation desperate to witness a historic triple coronation. Boss sat and waited, then angled the great mare a little to the right and the gaps started to come. She was in front 300 yards out and then held on to win by a length and a quarter from the strong-finishing On A Jeune. If Boss had been beaten, he would have been run out of the country. No surprise then that he burst into tears as he rode back to the winner's enclosure. Emotions could no longer be kept in check.

News that Makybe Diva had been retired after the race somehow seemed appropriate. She had gone out on a high. As the celebrations continued long into the night, a few National Hunt stalwarts listened to a race at Exeter. They returned with stunned looks on their faces. Another triple champion, Best Mate, had died with his racing plates on. Different code, different parts of the world, but the message very much the same. Enjoy them while we have them.

5 APRIL 1981

A CHAMPION DAY OUT FOR ALDANITI

John Oaksey

Very nearly all the dreams came true at Aintree yesterday when Bob Champion and Aldaniti won the Sun Grand National by four lengths from John Thorne and Spartan Missile. The only real losers were sickness, injury, old age and pessimism. If, for instance, John Thorne had to be beaten, there is not the shadow of doubt that the man he most wanted to see in front of him was Bob Champion. 'I have no excuses and the horse made no mistakes,' he said afterwards. 'I am very proud of him – and even prouder of Bob.'

The whole racing world and anyone else who knows the amazing facts will echo those words. Eighteen months ago, in the throes of a new and painful system of treatment for cancer, Champion had lost all his hair and about two stone in weight. If he had been normal, he would surely have lost all hope as well, but that was never the case. In fact, amazingly enough, as he has often said long before yesterday, one of the thoughts which kept him going was the possibility of riding Aldaniti in last year's Grand National. In the final weeks of his treatment Aldaniti was due to reappear on the racecourse at Sandown and Bob got leave from hospital to see him run. It is not easy to imagine how he must have felt when Aldaniti pulled up hobbling lame – broken down for the second time in a career which has been plagued by injury. But even then Bob refused to despair. 'We'll just have to come back together,' he told Aldaniti's owner Mrs Valda Embericos – and there and then she and her husband made up their minds to spare neither time nor expense in the search for a cure to Aldaniti's unsoundness.

'Even I thought they were crackers,' trainer Josh Gifford said yesterday – but in fact he, like the owners, kept hoping against hope that if his stable jockey did manage to ride again, Aldaniti would be there to carry him. Well, thanks to the new cure and the tireless care of doctors and nurses (two of them were at Aintree yesterday and backed him) Bob did overcome the cancer which at one time seemed so certain to kill him. He rode again for the first time in America and won, last summer, and this season with 30 winners already to his credit, has been at least as good and strong as ever.

That was one miracle, and Aldaniti himself is another quite apart from two breakdowns (major tendon strains), he broke a bone in his leg at one time and should by all the rules of science be a cripple. Instead, thanks first to the patience of Mrs Embericos, and second to the skill of Josh

Gifford, he came back this season to win at Ascot. After that race Gifford said the horse was most unlikely to run again before the National. 'There is only one race we want to win,' he said — and yesterday they won it.

People have been saying lately that Aintree and the Grand National are both moribund, but no one would have thought it yesterday afternoon as the 39 runners set off in blazing sunshine and in front of stands packed almost as they used to be in the golden pre-War days. It remains to be seen what Mr Davies will do with Aintree, but it will, I believe, take something stronger than lack of money to kill this unique occasion.

The fences are unique, too, and to Bob Champion's relief, Aldaniti hit the first of them. It taught him a priceless lesson and from then on, taking no more liberties, his jumping was both bold and without flaw. For some others the early fences were not so happy. Another Captain and Barney Maclyvie fell at the first and Mr Aidan O'Connell's long cherished dream of completing the National course disappeared with Chumson at the fourth. Kilkiwell fell there, too, and so did another large and sporting amateur Mr John Carden on Bryan Boru. Delmoss, who had led for a long way in a previous National, got only this far yesterday.

Both John Thorne and Bob Champion had lined up towards the outside and, galloping down towards Becher's for the first time, both had plenty of elbow room. Spartan Missile had overjumped at the famous Brook in the past, but this time he was foot perfect. Carrow Boy, Choral Festival and Zongalero led them round the Canal, but Carrow Boy was badly hampered and almost brought down at the tenth. Kininvie fell there, too. Drumroan, No Gypsy and Another Prospect had all gone at much the same time, and Tenecoon fell at the 11th.

By that time, Aldaniti had jumped his way up into the leading group and crossed the Melling Road for the first time with Sebastian, Royal Stuart, Royal Mail and Facify. Spartan Missile had lost a length or two at this stage, but he like all the other leaders sailed safely over The Chair. At that stage, in fact, Spartan Missile was ninth with Aldaniti, Royal Stuart and Zongalero (who hit the big fence quite hard), sharing the lead together.

---

16 MARCH 1990

GRIFFITHS' FARM HACK DESTROYS A LEGEND

Michael Calvin

Sirrell Griffiths will be telling the story of Norton's Coin for the rest of his life. When milking at Rwyth Farm, Nantgaredig, is no longer a media event, he may even come to believe it. A £450 horse, named after a motorbike and conditioned by chickens, destroys a legend in the six minutes and 30.9 seconds it took to complete this most unlikely Cheltenham Gold Cup. Suddenly, Mike Tyson has an affinity with Desert Orchid. England's cricketers can identify with Griffiths, the humble hill farmer who has helped make 1990 the year of the underdog. It is, indeed, a mad, mad, sporting world. Buster Douglas arrives home in Columbus, Ohio, the world heavyweight champion. Graham McCourt gives Ivor Davies the opportunity to bellow *Cymru Am Byth* within earshot of the Queen Mother.

Ivor shared yesterday morning's three-hour journey to Cheltenham with Griffiths and Norton's Coin in a cattle truck. When the prizes are being given out, and the status of instant celebrity beckoned, both still had mud on their scuffed brown shoes. Their weatherbeaten faces, flushed with emotion, radiated delight. Ivor, who had helped when they began milking at 3.45 a.m., said: 'I tell you, this couldn't have happened to a nicer fellow. Fair play to him.' He went off to marshal the coachload of 51 villagers who had travelled from West Wales. They planned to brave the traffic jams and spend the night laying siege to The Railway, Nantgaredig's only public house. There was much to celebrate, thanks to the permit trainer and the horse the official racecard dismissed as 'more of a candidate for last place than first'. Griffiths was one of the few who had not taken the local book-makers' offer of 200–1. 'Not a penny on him,' he confirmed with a smile. 'I can't possibly believe all this, can I? I only hope the bookmaker doesn't go broke. He's a nice man.'

For those less intimately involved with a truly local hero, it was a time to dust off the phrases about the compelling unpredictability of sport. The uncharitable were quietly enjoying the blow to the cottage industry of Desert Orchid Inc. It would be wrong to diminish the achievements of the grey, who has come to represent honesty of endeavour in an era in which human heroes tend to be flawed. His gentle decline, and inability to sustain the pace in the final stages of yesterday's race, carried echoes of the anti-climactic end to the athletics career of Sebastian Coe. Both, in their way, were almost too perfect. Coe the calm, collected golden boy of Conservative Central Office; Desert Orchid the almost human animal, plaited and playing to the crowd like a ham actor. Dessie's defeat was a triumph of hope over expectation, of genuine affection over the bleak ritual of scientific preparation pioneered by trainers like Martin Pipe.

The 12 stone Norton's Coin carried yesterday was like a featherweight compared to the 15-and-a-half stones of his trainer, whose concession to fitness, at the age of 50, is to ride him on his daily rounds on his farm. Welsh hill farming can be a punishing existence. It breeds a suspicion of the superficial. In the depths of winter, commonsense can, quite literally, be a lifesaver.

Once Griffiths recognised Norton's Coin had potential beyond his appointed station as a point-to-pointer, he prepared in the only way he knew. He stabled the horse with bantams, who pecked at his heels and tested his temperament. All big-race horses must cope with big-race crowds, big-race distractions. None are as infuriating as those he became accustomed to on the farm, as a favourite family pet. 'Nobody is going to buy him on looks,' reflected Griffiths, speaking softly. 'He never holds his head up, shows himself off. He mopes around the farm. But when he has someone on his back he's different, he's got his release.'

Griffiths was unwinding slowly, reliving the last frantic yards of 28 fateful furlongs. He had not been consumed by nerves beforehand, because he had not expected to win. 'As he went to that final fence I just said, "Please, God, don't fall",' he recalled. 'I could see then, he was second at least. That would have been wonderful.' Instead, he will carry to his grave the image of McCourt punching the air as he crossed the line first. We did not recognise the significance of it at the time, but the jockey carried his whip in his hand. He had used it to drive the horse to the line. He was operating on instinct, conscious of the bedlam breaking out in the crowd and of his responsibility to his connections. The Stewards took a stern view, and soured one of his greatest days by punishing him for his commitment. They failed to recognise that the occasion demanded a sense of perspective.

---

18 MARCH 1983

BREGAWN LEADS AS DICKINSON TAKES FIRST FIVE GOLD CUP PLACES

Hotspur (Peter Scott)

Bregawn, Captain John, Wayward Lad, Silver Buck and Ashley House were cheered as a team when they walked back in front of the packed grandstands after giving trainer Michael Dickinson the first five places in yesterday's Tote Cheltenham Gold Cup. Dickinson continues to break records and exhaust superlatives. His Gold Cup quintet accomplished a *tour de force* unprecedented in modern big-race history, and one which it is difficult to visualise being surpassed.

Dickinson had steadfastly avoided predictions about which of his five would prove best, but backers made the correct choice. Bregawn, at 100–30, became the first outright favourite to win the Gold Cup since Arkle in 1966. Sensing that a big race is no occasion for foolery, Bregawn showed none of the reluctance to line up that has characterised his recent appearances. Whiggie Gee disputed the lead with him over the first six fences. Bregawn then went ahead and was not passed again. Captain John, recovering from a mistake three fences from home, drew nearly level at the last, but Bregawn shook him off and went five lengths clear.

Wayward Lad, keeping far behind while Bregawn ensured a strong gallop, began to move up a mile from home. He looked the danger rounding the last bend, but could not quite sustain his effort. A training interruption caused by Wayward Lad's injured back may have counted at the point where peak fitness tells. He is a year younger than Bregawn and Captain John, so a Gold Cup triumph next year is well on the cards for him. Yesterday was Bregawn's day and how superbly he rose to the occasion. Graham Bradley, who had also ridden him when Bregawn finished second to Silver Buck last year, was fully justified in yesterday's bold tactics that made full use of his mount's stamina. Bregawn, whose big-race successes this season also include the Hennessy Gold Cup, was named after a mountain in Tipperary by his owner Mr Jim Kennelly.

Silver Buck's overnight odds of 5–2 lengthened to 5–1. His chance of a second Cheltenham Gold Cup victory disappeared when he began to tire two fences from home. Winner of 29 races worth a National Hunt prize-money earnings record of £150,387, Silver Buck may soon be retired. But this decision has not yet been agreed between Dickinson and Silver Buck's owner, Mrs Feather.

The trainer's immediate post-race reaction was that none of yesterday's first four would race again this season and that he would wait a week before deciding whether Ashley House will carry top weight in the Grand National. Dickinson, whose first-money earnings this season are now an amazing £345,000, began his young career as a successful amateur rider. A fall at Cartmel damaged his liver and ended his riding career. Three years ago he took over his father Tony's stable.

---

17 MARCH 2007

KAUTO STAR WINS GOLD CUP

Marcus Armytage

The question that has perpetuated the Sport Of Kings as it has splashed through the mud and guts of this very wet winter was answered in emphatic style on a spring afternoon yesterday when Ruby Walsh brought Kauto

Star home safely and in front in the totesport Cheltenham Gold Cup. Since Christmas, Kauto Star has split racing opinion like he split the birch of the last fence at Kempton on Boxing Day. His ability has never been questioned nor has the exceptional versatility that makes him the best horse at all distances since Desert Orchid, but there appeared to be only two possible outcomes to the 2007 Gold Cup. He wins or he falls. Second or third has never been an option. Walsh is either carried triumphantly on a wave of euphoria into the winner's enclosure or he gets a lift back in an ambulance. The experts, and my goodness there were 65,000 of us at Cheltenham alone, have been either for him or agin' him but, yesterday, the ayes had it.

When this week is over Walsh, 27, winner of two Grand Nationals and developing the wise mind of his loquacious father Ted, might be a whiter shade of grey than he was at the start of the meeting. But outwardly he never showed pressure and, crucially, Kauto Star never sensed it. If Kauto Star felt anything from Walsh it might have been that brief moment going to the last when he realised the race was won and where he made his solitary mistake, one which, unlike some of his previous blunders, did not wake those people who look after the Richter Scale.

'Everyone had an opinion,' said Walsh afterwards. 'Will he stand up? Will he get the trip? That's part of racing. Sure there was pressure, there was £1 million riding on it and he was favourite. Pressure's part of the job and I only play a very small part – it's Paul Nicholls and the team who had done the work and they had him spot on today.'

When Walsh sits down to show the grandchildren his scrapbook, it is unlikely any race will compare with the 2000 Grand National which he won on Papillon for 'the old man', because blood is thicker even than gold. But this race will come close. 'I've always considered it the best race and everyone wants to ride the best horse in the best race,' he explained. 'He's a very, very good horse.'

After winning his prep-race at Newbury, where he again blundered at the last, some were even beginning to question the jockey's role. But yesterday Walsh made it look easy despite having had a confidence-shattering fall in the previous race where he was fired into the ground. Almost immediately the reins were looped, not taut as they had been at Newbury, and once Kauto Star cleared the first bogey, the fence in front of the stands where he had fallen in last year's Champion Chase, Walsh looked like he was enjoying the horse again, something I am not convinced he has since the King George. 'Once he settled the only question was when to press the button,' he said, making it sound easy. 'When I moved off the inside and saw A.P. slip through I thought, "Jesus, what have I done?" so I kept him tight. I can't make a horse stay but today we found out he does stay. And if you came and saw him school you'd wonder how he ever made a mistake — but that's him.' After this performance, there are no more questions to be answered.

---

16 MARCH 2008

DENMAN WINS THIS ROUND, BUT THE DEBATE IS NOT OVER

Brough Scott

There was beauty in the brutal simplicity of it all. Denman's whole life had led to this. He would set off to attack round Cheltenham's great anvil of dreams and gallop and jump until the best horse in the world was battered into submission behind him. It was what he had been bred and trained and raced for. It would be two circuits, 22 fences and six minutes of fulfilment on the hoof.

To be exact, the big attack did not come until they started the second circuit. Until then Denman had been tracking the grey Neptune Collonges, while Kauto Star just kept track along the inside about four lengths away. Until then you could not spot a chink in the defending champion. Some of us thought he looked a touch tight, his skin dull in the paddock, but maybe that was more our nerves than his. Then, just as Sam Thomas decided to play Denman from the front, Ruby Walsh had a problem. At the 11th fence, the second-last on the final circuit, Kauto galloped in and clouted it. This happens. But you don't want it to happen too often. They came thundering towards us at the 12th, the final fence in this Gold Cup next time. When he had approached it for the first time, the second jump of the race, Kauto Star had put in such a huge spring-heeled leap that he landed almost too steeply. This time he didn't. Kauto galloped in again and clouted it.

It wasn't dangerous, like it used to be a year ago. But he had missed it. Walsh has a poker player's stillness about him, but he now knew his hand wasn't perfect.

Not that he betrayed anything down the back stretch. Denman was piling it on up ahead of Neptune Collonges, the lesser horses were already being driven. But Kauto was neat enough. It didn't matter that he was still five lengths adrift at the 17th, the last open ditch. But it did at the 18th at the top of the hill, for he galloped in and clouted hard again. Denman was launching off down the hill and Walsh had the stick up. Kauto was in trouble. There was no mistaking it. The champion had taken the equivalent of a knock-down. He was on his feet but the contender was pummelling him. Kauto got good jumps at the 19th and 20th but he couldn't even take Neptune Collonges. There was a roar from the crowd as Denman's name was called, but also a strange muted feel. For Kauto this was not going to be just defeat, but humiliation. Yet he had not become a 15-victory, six-season champion without being a battler.

The game looked up as Thomas thundered round the last turn for those final two fences with a widening gap behind him. But Walsh dug deep as he drove Kauto up the inside to that penultimate fence and the horse's long white blaze came up with a mighty leap to finally take second. As Denman came towards us, the roll of his forelegs showed the strain was biting. If he was to blunder and Kauto could get another big jump there was just a chance of the equivalent of a last-round knock-out. But Denman kept his rhythm. He landed weary but running. Kauto drove in but clouted, and as he came away from the fence he staggered slightly sideways. You should always look at the forelegs. Denman's were no longer moving easily, but at least they were rolling. Kauto's had lost their bite. It was over.

Afterwards the mind was in a muddle. Denman was the new champion. Thomas well deserved his arm-punching elation. The ownership 'odd couple' of Paul Barber and Harry Findlay had their belief fully vindicated and Paul Nicholls's achievement of training the first three home recalled the 1983 Famous Five of Michael Dickinson. Yet this had not been Arkle versus Mill House after all. That cold clear day in 1964, both sets of supporters could still believe as they swung for home, and then Arkle changed it all. Here the champion had been in trouble too early. We can't be really sure until the re-match.

With this bizarre, stable-companions, all-good-friends, no-edge rivalry, there was no chance of one of those wound-licking 'I will follow him to the end of the earth and then I will beat him' declarations which Jimmy Connors would say after another defeat by Bjorn Borg. But it seemed important to walk back to the wash-down with the loser.

Sonja Warburton has been Kauto Star's closest companion. 'The most important thing is that they are all home safely,' she said patting her horse's sweat-soaked neck. 'But I think the ground was a bit sticky for him. For me he is still a champion.' The small knot of fans broke into spontaneous, sympathetic applause as she led Kauto out into the ring after his wash-over. They did the same in more cheery mode when lofty, grey-suited young Harry Fry came up with Denman. Away in the paddock you could hear the loudspeaker calling Jess Allen to the podium as groom to the winner. The two horses circled together with the familiarity of the stable-mates they are. Kauto Star still tall and grand, Denman even bigger, but that low chestnut neck making him look slightly less than the 17 hands that he is.

Eventually Allen came up to join us. She will become a mother in the summer. 'I could feel the baby kicking on the run-in,' she said. But even that wide-eyed wonder could not stem thoughts of her four-legged hero. 'Yesterday morning,' she said, 'I put my hand on the bottom of his neck and for the first time ever it was just one slab of muscle. Paul asked me how he was. I said he had never been fitter.' The two horses were led off to share a box home to Somerset. They don't look as if they argue, but we have to hope the debate is not over. Seven lengths was the verdict. It was decisive but not necessarily final. Next March, let's hope it's not only the daffodils that are blooming.

---

19 MARCH 2010

IMPERIAL COMMANDER WINS GOLD CUP

Hotspur (J.A. McGrath)

Nigel Twiston-Davies once shunned publicity with such determination he refused to be interviewed by Des Lynam on the BBC after training the winner of the Grand National. But, following his first Cheltenham Gold Cup triumph with Imperial Commander, there was no stopping this reformed character. Imperial Commander completely upstaged a field of star chasers that included the winners of three previous Gold Cups in Kauto Star and Denman, and did so in a manner that mocked the doubters, who reckoned he wouldn't stay the three miles, two and a half furlongs.

Then, 40 minutes later, as he was discussing the Gold Cup with reporters, Twiston-Davies watched on television as his son Sam, 17, made almost all of the running to win the Christie's Foxhunter Chase on Baby Run, and delivered a colourful commentary that included plenty of encouragement and a sprinkling of expletives. Asked which had given him the most pleasure, Twiston-Davies replied: 'To be dreadfully honest, it would have to be the Foxhunters. I'm hugely proud of Sam, who rode a beautiful race. This takes the biscuit. Winning the Gold Cup and then the Foxhunters with a horse I own and train, ridden by my son – the two together made this day great.

'The first Grand National [with Earth Summit in 1998] was unbelievable, but despite this, my greatest day at Cheltenham will always be when Tipping Tim won his first Mackeson,' he added. That may be the case, but most of the 67,716 crowd are more likely to recall the supreme performance of Imperial Commander, as he fought tenaciously to overwhelm Denman, whose menacing intimidation had raised levels of tension and excitement several times during an incident-packed Gold Cup. The winning margin, seven lengths, reflected Imperial Commander's superiority. For the second successive year, Denman was runner-up, with 23 lengths back to Grand National winner Mon Mome, who finished powerfully to snatch third from the gallant Carruthers on the line.

I cannot remember as much tension and expectation in the minutes prior to a Gold Cup, the crowd divided over whether it would be the year of Kauto Star or Denman. After the field had settled into a rhythm, the first drama occurred when Kauto Star blundered badly at the eighth, a mistake that left his followers groaning as they watched the giant screens.

'I was in trouble from the moment he made that mistake,' Ruby Walsh said. 'I couldn't get a position, and I couldn't get him travelling. You can't make mistakes like that against that calibre of horse, because they just take your position, and it's very hard to get it back.'

Meanwhile, Tony McCoy had Denman stalking Carruthers up front, with the pace picking up noticeably from the point of Kauto Star's narrow escape. It was as if the trailblazers sensed the favourite had just been set his biggest task and they were going to ensure he had little chance of getting back. McCoy, of course, was also out to deliver his reply to a small critical element, who had argued that he wasn't the right jockey for Denman. No doubt they will be dining on humble pie for some time as the 14-times champion and 'The Tank' inspired each other so much that Denman soared over several fences with spectacular leaps and gave his all.

Four fences out, Kauto Star fell heavily, ending any slim chance he had of landing a third Gold Cup. The relief was tangible when the horse picked himself up and Walsh was able to climb back into the saddle and hack him back. Imperial Commander had been sitting in fourth, one off the rail, most of the way, and when Paddy Brennan went for him approaching the home bend, it became evident that Denman would be forced to produce another of his gut-busting efforts to repel him. The Twiston-Davies horse had already fought a duel with the other big name, Kauto Star, at Haydock Park in November, failing by only a nose, and here he was serving it up to the 2008 Gold Cup winner, but on his favourite course and following a relatively light campaign. He won emphatically.

Brennan said: 'We knew we had a serious horse. He actually hit a flat spot a couple of strides before the last, but has then picked up again and sprinted away after it.' McCoy was full of praise for Denman: 'He ran a great race and ran his heart out. No excuses. I can't say I would have done this or that different. It's frustrating as it's my fourth second in the race.'

28 APRIL 1958

TAXIDERMIST BEATS THE 'CHASING 'STARS'

MR J. LAWRENCE RIDES GREAT RACE TO WIN WHITBREAD GOLD CUP

Hotspur

Taxidermist, owned in partnership by Mrs Peter Hastings and Mrs Fulke Walwyn, both wives of trainers, and ridden with brilliant judgment by my colleague, Mr John Lawrence, alone prevented the three top weights, Mandarin, Kerstin and Much Obliged, from sweeping the board in the Whitbread Gold Cup at Sandown on Saturday. In a field of 31, which was considerably smaller than expected, Taxidermist won by four lengths from Mandarin. Both first and second are trained by Fulke Walwyn who thus becomes the leading trainer of the 1957–58 National Hunt season now drawing rapidly to a close.

Mr Lawrence was the only amateur rider in the race. As he persistently hides his light under a bushel I must repeat that he rode a brilliant race on the winner. Indeed his riding has been one of the features of the National Hunt season. When I saw him win his first race under National Hunt Rules at Sandown two years ago on Mr A.J. Sellar's Pyrene at the Grand Military meeting I thought he would make a good jockey if given the chance, but I do not think anyone could have foreseen that he would improve a couple of stone in the course of a season. He is now certainly the equal of most of the professionals. Perhaps also, from a sporting point of view, he will one day hold as high a place in National Hunt racing as did the late Lord Mildmay a few years ago.

Two days before Saturday's race, John Lawrence was still walking about with an arm in a sling as the result of dislocating his shoulder very badly at Towcester on Easter Monday. Taxidermist was his first ride in public since then and he rode tightly strapped up. He tells me that the strapping did not worry him in the heat of battle, but he looked none too comfortable as he got up on Taxidermist in the parade ring before the race.

I must add that it was a lovely sight as the horses cantered down to the post in the spring sunshine and I hope perhaps Sir Alfred Munnings will put it on canvas. It was a splendid race and Taxidermist was a worthy winner. He finished four lengths in front of Mandarin with Kerstin two lengths farther away in third and Much Obliged fourth. Once again the horses who ran in the National made little show.

Looking back on the race it is possible that Madden, on Mandarin, made too much use of his horse as he was carrying top weight, but he steered clear of trouble by so doing. Kerstin ran a most gallant race, as also did last year's winner, Much Obliged, who was carrying a seven-pound penalty for his success at Wetherby. It was most satisfactory to see the three top horses in the fighting line and leading the field less than a mile from home. The conditions by which the top weight cannot carry more than 12 stone does give the best chasers a reasonable chance in a handicap and has contributed to the great success of the two Whitbread Gold Cups which have so far been run.

CHAPTER 3

THE SPORT OF KINGS ...
AND QUEENS

The soon-to-be George V rushed to his father's deathbed and told him his horse, Witch of Air, had won. 'I am very glad,' said Edward VII. Somehow fitting, they were his last words, as the old king loved horses almost as much as he loved women. As Prince of Wales, he won the Derby and St Leger with Persimmon in 1896 and Diamond Jubilee in 1900, as well as the Grand National with Ambush II. He is still the only reigning monarch to have won the Derby, and to crown Minoru's feat in 1909, the Telegraph devoted a whole page.

Similarly, on the morning of her Coronation, our present Queen was all ears for news of Aureole, her horse who was due to run at Epsom three days later. Her eldest offspring, Prince Charles and Princess Anne, even donned racing silks and rode in public. The Sport of Kings, indeed.

---

31 MARCH 1900

THE GRAND NATIONAL

PRINCE OF WALES'S VICTORY
ENTHUSIASTIC RECEPTION

Our Special Correspondent

Another Grand National is over, and the foremost sportsman in the land has established a unique record. To the Blue Riband of the Turf he has added the Blue Riband of the Chase, giving a distinction to the great Liverpool event which will live in horse-racing history. Slowly but surely the Prince is making his mark upon the pages of Weatherby. A St Leger, a One Thousand, an Eclipse, an Ascot Cup, a Goodwood Cup, a Manchester Cup – these are trifles not to be despised. All the achievements of Royal owners in the past days – days over which we linger with the veneration begotten by lapse of time – are put into the shade by the good fortune, the result of judgment and patience, attending the Prince's stud. Ireland will rejoice at the victory of a horse who celebrated St Patrick's Day by a complementary triumph in a contest intrinsically insignificant. Whatever grievances the 'distressful country' may claim, she has nothing to say against the Liverpool Grand National, where her sons have, over and over again, proved the mettle they are made of. And the Liverpool multitude was demonstratively pleased also.

Ambush, Anthony and Aintree made up an alliterative combination to which no superstitious mortal could be insensible. The more prosaic of us, looking on the handsome quarter-sheet prepared for the Prince's candidate — a sheet emblazoned with the three feathers, the rose, the shamrock and the thistle — hoped that the artistic adornment would seem as attractive after the contest as it did before. For gorgeous clothing does not win races, and when horses and money go flying in the air the nervous apprehensions of the late Mr Frederick Swindells are liable to be repeated in our own breasts. Inspiriting weather made the multitude glad, and a huge attendance was a foregone conclusion. The mass of holiday-makers gathered together when the numbers were hoisted for the opening race showed us that, war or no war, people are disinclined to be deprived of their accustomed measure of enjoyment.

It is scarcely necessary to say that with the crowds at Aintree keen for the victory of the Prince of Wales, the ladies especially desired a decisive triumph for the Royal colours. Perfectly useless it was to explain to them that Grand National chances depended upon age, and the apportionment of weight, and the skill of rival jockeys, and many other elements of good or ill fortune. They would hear nothing of these things. A horse was a horse, and should have as good a chance as any other. When, however, he happened to be the property of the first gentleman in the land, what possible reason was there for supposing that he would, could or should be beaten? If the Lancashire lasses had been aware of another fact, their hopes would have derived additional fortification. For it was exactly nine and twenty years ago to a day that the Prince of Wales first exhibited his jacket on a racecourse — and in a steeplechase, too. In the Challenge Cup, at the 10th Royal Hussars' meeting, held at Egham, on 31 March, 1871, his Royal Highness's aged gelding Champion, ridden by Captain Bulkeley, ran second to Lord Valentia's Wellington. The Prince, moreover, had sought Liverpool honours in 1884, when The Scot ran unplaced to Voluptuary, an animal who has won an enormous number of Grand Nationals since then on theatre stages in a popular Drury Lane drama. In 1889 Magic failed to obtain a situation, and Hettie fell; but last year's failure by Ambush II, whom the Prince originally bought for £500, was wiped out yesterday. And it was wiped out to the general joy, after the public had experienced a strain of suspense and anxiety more than usually pronounced.

Having been the principal guest of the Earl of Derby at Knowsley on Thursday evening the Prince had assisted in the perpetuation of a custom established by a progenitor of the noble lord. The great 'racing Earl' set the practice of entertaining influential friends at Knowsley during the Aintree meeting, which in a very short time superseded the older Liverpool fixture held on the Maghull course. A cock-pit, a bowling green, a cricket ground, and conveniences for trap balls and fives, were part of the original equipment of Aintree's racing establishment, and from Lord Derby's social parties sprang the Knowsley Dinner Stakes, which remained a feature of the programme at the gathering in July. The course has undergone much transformation since then, and what with extensions of and improvements to the stands, Aintree is obviously leaving no stone unturned to maintain its popularity.

I fancy that numbers of Liverpudlians – horrible word, 'Liverpudlians' – together with the strangers within their gates must have had sore throats last night. Never was there a more 'cheering' day. The demonstrations commenced with the arrival of the Knowsley party in open carriages, the Prince of Wales being in the first with Lady Derby. Ireland came tremendously to the fore, and with English and Hibernian flags fluttering in the breeze we all felt that there would be a mighty 'slump' in popular emotion if anything went wrong with the big race. Disappointment is so often the antidote of enthusiasm that it was hard to repress the conviction that we were holloaing before we were out of the wood. Nevertheless, the crowd gave a right royal greeting to the Prince, and received a right royal acknowledgement. Then it settled down to a languid enjoyment of the three races preceding the National, and by the time that momentous event 'came on the carpet' we were all in a condition of ill-concealed agitation. It was necessary to forego the paddock inspection if one wanted a good place for watching the struggle, and the appearance of the horses on the course came as a pleasant relief to the tension. What with the people on the rails and the scattering throngs on other parts of the course – either massed around the big jumps or scurrying from point to point to see the horses pass and re-pass – there was plenty of animation during the contest. Emphatically the race was a battle to be seen and remembered. That Hidden Mystery should have fallen a victim to the chances of the game was a matter of general regret; and, while the victory of Ambush II proved far more popular than any other could possibly have been, the splendid fight of grand old Manifesto caused us a sigh of regret that success had not, for the third time, attended his gallant efforts. At the last fence the veteran was up alongside the Prince's representative, and it was only in the run-home that his welter burden made him bite the dust. No sooner did the populace perceive that Ambush II had the verdict safe than a long roar of cheering broke forth. Up went hats, away went sticks, while vociferations from thousands of throats exultantly rent the air. Cheers for horse, cheers for rider, cheers for owner were given again and again, for Ambush II was decidedly the people's horse, and the Prince, as he stepped down to meet the winner, must have felt that the triumph was not to himself alone. His Royal Highness was obviously very pleased that an anxious time had concluded so satisfactorily, and for the rest of the afternoon handshakings and congratulations were incessant. No doubt there was a 'hot time' in Liverpool city last night; and those of us who sped south, if deprived of a share in these demonstrative rejoicings, had at least the satisfaction of having witnessed a fine race, worthy of the Grand National's best traditions.

---

27 MAY 1909

THE KING'S DERBY – MINORU'S BRILLIANT VICTORY

HIS MAJESTY'S TRIUMPH
SCENES OF ENTHUSIASM
SIR MARTIN'S FALL

Never in the history of Epsom or the Derby has such a thrilling scene been witnessed on the famous Downs as that which was associated with the triumph of Minoru in the Blue Riband yesterday. The bubbling enthusiasm which permeated the huge crowd bursting with loyalty and the love of a splendid sport was a sight which will never fade from the memory of those who were fortunate enough to witness it. It was a Royal victory in every sense of the word, and it is no exaggeration to say that the excitement was even greater than when Persimmon and Diamond Jubilee respectively won the prize. For one thing, his Majesty had not then ascended the Throne, and that he should, as King of England, achieve the highest ambition of every sportsman marks a red-letter day in the annals of the Turf.

It is extremely regrettable that the Fates were not more propitious in a meteorological sense. If ever Royal weather could have been eminently desired, it was surely upon such a memorable occasion as this. The morning was perfectly miserable, rain falling in torrents, and although the sun shone forth fitfully at short intervals during the afternoon the leaden clouds imparted a sombre appearance to a spectacle which is usually marked by brilliancy and colour. Those who patronised the road must have had far from a pleasant experience, but all discomforts were compensated by The King's magnificent victory. Needless to say, everybody was delighted, and in the circumstances questions of weather mattered little. There is no doubt but that the wretched morning influenced the attendance to a lamentable extent, and it was nothing like the record crowd it promised to be.

The King and Queen were present, and were accompanied by the Prince and Princess of Wales, Princess Victoria, and Prince Christian. Few of the leading lights of the Turf were missing, and altogether it was a representative gathering. Many Americans were to be met with, and among others I noticed Mr J. Huggins, who trained Lord William Beresford's horses in the zenith of the Sloan era, when the Heath House stable carried almost all before it. Like Mr Croker, he was much impressed with the prospects of Sir Martin, who became a very strong order in the market, and eventually ousted Minoru from the position of favourite. It was generally considered that upon all public form as exemplified this season Minoru, Sir Martin and Louviers were entitled to primary consideration, and it must be confessed that, in spite of his American reputation and his smart victory in a minor affair at Newmarket, Sir Martin had scarcely such overwhelming claims as the 2,000 Guineas winner Minoru.

Many people professed to believe that superior condition alone gave Minoru the spoils in the first of the Classic races, and that he could not be made any better. The theory was completely exploded yesterday, for the son of Cyllene and Mother Siegel stripped the picture of a grandly-trained blood-like thoroughbred. He was by far the handsomest colt in the paddock. He held quite a levee in one corner, where he was surrounded by a critical crowd. I thought he looked heavier than he did on Guineas day. He carried a lot of muscle about his quarters and thighs, and his exquisite quality was well defined. Richard Marsh seemed supremely satisfied, and I may say that he was reasonably confident of victory.

In the preliminary canter nothing went better than Minoru, who is a particularly light-actioned horse, with a beautiful low sweeping stride. Both Sir Martin and Bayardo moved well, the last named apparently revelling in the altered condition as regards going. Minoru had been fortunate enough to draw the number one, or inside, position, and this seemed a happy augury. There was no inordinate delay at the post, and the start appeared to be a capital one. Brooklands, who had been started to ensure an adequate pace for Louviers, faithfully discharged his mission, and he was closely attended by his stable companion and Phaleron, with Sir Martin, Minoru, and Bayardo next, until they turned down the hill, where William the Fourth drew into third place, with Minoru and Bayardo at his heels.

About halfway down the hill, and just before reaching Tattenham Corner, there was a lot of bunching together, and in the scrimmaging Sir Martin fell. His rider, J.H. Martin, had a miraculous escape from serious injury, and was lucky to get off with a shaking and a few bruises. During the contretemps William the Fourth was much hampered, and, losing several lengths, he had to come round on the outside. When the accident happened Louviers had taken up the running from Minoru, and the pair came into the straight in front of Valens, Bayardo, and William the Fourth. Immediately the line for home was entered Minoru closed with Louviers, whom he headed a few strides later. Then ensued a struggle as desperate and thrilling as anything which has been seen on a racecourse. The excitement was intense.

Both horses ran on in the gamest possible way. In the dip Minoru appeared to falter slightly, and for a moment it seemed as though he would succumb to Mr Raphael's colt. Both Stern and Herbert Jones rode magnificently. Responding to the latter's call in the most indomitable way, Minoru put forth a fresh effort, and, amid a scene of unparalleled enthusiasm, won by a head. William the Fourth, who was running on all the way up the straight, was only half a length behind Louviers, and just managed to keep Valens out of third berth. Even before the winning number was hoisted the vast crowd gave themselves up to the spirit of the moment. The cheering was deafening, and thousands and thousands of people rushed on to the course in front of the unsaddling enclosure in order to catch a glimpse of the Royal visitors.

From the Royal box The King and Queen gracefully bowed their acknowledgements. Everybody seemed to go almost mad with delight. His Majesty, followed by the Prince of Wales, hurried down the steps into the enclosure, and passed out through the gates on to the course amid the frantically cheering crowd. The police were powerless to keep them back, and as he waited for Minoru to return many of the spectators endeavoured to shake His Majesty by the hand. He accepted the humour of the situation in the good-natured way so splendidly characteristic of the finest sportsman in the land. Probably it was one of the happiest moments of his life. The cheering increased in volume as His Majesty personally led his gallant horse back to the enclosure.

It was a great and glorious occasion, and apart from the splendid popularity of the victory, it is recognised that it must inevitably do a power of good to the Turf. Richard Marsh was not forgotten in the crowning moments of triumph. Perhaps few can really appreciate how much is due to him. No man could possibly have exercised more patience and perseverance with a horse than he has done with Minoru. Last year he was totally averse to hurrying the colt in any way, for he always entertained a high opinion of him, and now the excellence of his judgment has been thoroughly demonstrated. Herbert Jones never rode a finer race, and to win two Derbys for His Majesty is a feat of which he will always have reason to feel proud. Colonel Hall-Walker, who leased Minoru to His Majesty, was naturally immensely gratified, and perhaps future historians may have to write of yesterday's celebration of the Derby as the greatest of all time.

31 JULY 2000

EVERYONE'S FAVOURITE OWNER

John Oaksey

It was Anthony Mildmay – Lord Mildmay on his father's death in 1947 – who first suggested (in 1949) that Queen Elizabeth, as she then was, should buy a steeplechaser.

The leading amateur rider in each of the first five post-War seasons, Lord Mildmay was a well-known figure, universally loved and admired, in the world of National Hunt racing. Riding his own horse, Davy Jones, in the 1936 Grand National, he had been robbed of victory by sheer bad luck when a rein came unbuckled between the last two fences. Bad luck struck again in 1948 when painful cramp, the result of previous falls, left him riding Cromwell virtually blind from the Canal Turn. Even so, they finished a close third to Sheila's Cottage.

It was during the next year's Royal Ascot meeting that Lord Mildmay, a guest at Windsor Castle, found himself sitting at dinner between The Queen and her daughter, Princess Elizabeth. The King's Hyperion filly, Avila, had won the Coronation Stakes that day and it may have been while drinking to her victory that Lord Mildmay made his suggestion. Jumping was then very much a poor relation of the Flat but the great owner-rider, famous for his charm, would have argued with the conviction of a man who knew his subject inside-out. He also, very definitely, practised what he preached and, who knows, The Queen may have found herself wondering whether the rather less formal world of jumping might not suit her better than the starchy Flat. Anyway, the message got across. The Queen asked Mildmay to find her and her daughter a steeplechaser and send it to be trained (as all the Mildmay horses were) by his great friend Peter Cazalet at Fairlawne in Kent. Queen Elizabeth knew Fairlawne well, having first gone there when she was 12 to stay with Cazalet's sister.

It is difficult now to imagine the effect in those unprosperous and still heavily-rationed years of the appearance at, say, Fontwell Park, of a chaser trained by Cazalet for The Queen and her daughter. Was this really the 'poor relation', a sport for the needy and greedy? Queen Elizabeth certainly did not think so. She loved the jumping crowds – and they loved her. They treasured her smiling presence and the enthusiastic interest she so clearly took in the sport from top to bottom, steward to stable lad.

Cazalet's stable jockey, Tony Grantham, had enjoyed a good ride on an eight-year-old called Monaveen in the 1949 Grand National and, after prolonged inquiry and negotiation, he was Mildmay and Cazalet's choice – the first chaser owned jointly by The Queen and her daughter. Monaveen could hardly have made a more appropriate start – winning the new Queen Elizabeth Chase at Hurst Park and finishing a highly respectable fifth in Freebooter's 1950 Grand National. After that race, The Queen wrote to Cazalet describing the thrill Monaveen had given her. 'The next thing,' she said, 'is to try to win a Grand National, if not next year the year after that.' But the cruel Fates must have been listening. Poor Monaveen himself never had another chance. He was killed at the water trying to win the Hurst Park race again.

His death was not Fairlawne's only tragedy that year. The same cramp which robbed Lord Mildmay of the 1948 Grand National was almost certainly to blame for his untimely death. On 12 May, 1950, it recurred during one of his customary morning keep-fit swims. He was never seen alive again. News of the 41-year-old amateur's death plunged the racing world into mourning. The loss of her friend and chosen racing adviser must have been a bitter blow to Queen Elizabeth.

Nevertheless, determined to pursue her new hobby as she knew Mildmay would have wished, she bought his most promising youngster, the French-bred Manicou. Amazingly, for a five-year-old still entire and in only his third race over fences, he delighted Kempton Park's Boxing Day crowd by winning the King George VI Chase. Sadly Manicou was not sound enough to win again, but he redeemed himself at stud, siring good winners including two of Queen Elizabeth's great favourites The Rip and Isle of Man.

The story of Devon Loch, the next Royal star at Fairlawne, is too painful and well known to need much telling. I know that the Queen Mother herself hates watching the replay of that unexplained collapse 50 yards from the line in the 1956 Grand National.

It was, of course, poor Dick Francis who had the dream of winning a National for everyone's favourite owner turn inexplicably into a nightmare. No one, not even he, will ever know what went wrong and the only redeeming feature of the tragedy is that, by causing Dick to write his autobiography, *Sport of Queens,* it launched his career as one of the world's best-selling novelists. He rode in the Injured Jockeys' Fund landau during the Queen Mother's birthday pageant.

One other certainty about the 1956 Grand National is that no owner, robbed of a longed-for prize for no visible reason, has behaved so supremely as the Queen Mother that awful day at Aintree. Apart from consoling the Fairlawne team, her first smiling reaction was to congratulate Mrs Carver, owner of the winner, ESB. Four days later she went down to Fairlawne, still smiling, to give presents to all who had been involved. 'Mementoes,' she said, 'of a terrible, yet glorious day.'

Devon Loch, of course, was by no means the end of Cazalet's service to his favourite owner. Not long before he died of cancer in 1973, the grey Inch Arran and David Mould won the Topham Trophy – Mould's 106th winner in the Royal colours and the 250th Cazalet sent from Fairlawne. (A footnote to this triumph is that David Mould's car broke down on the way to Aintree. Engaged 'just in case' by Cazalet's distraught head lad, Jim Fairgrieve, I was standing by, dressed in the Royal colours and ready to weigh in when a frantic Mould rushed up. 'He's sure to have run away with you anyway,' was his somewhat uncharitable comment.)

As her story shows, Queen Elizabeth has seen all too many of her jockeys – and, even sadder, her horses – injured on the racecourse. In 1971 she accepted an invitation to become patron of the Injured Jockeys' Fund and, without her constant encouragement and support, the Fund would not be in anything like its present healthy state. Its trustees are, from time to time, privileged to enter-tain Her Majesty and, to one special lunch in the Goring Hotel, we invited all those still alive who have been lucky enough to ride a winner in the famous blue and buff stripes, black cap and gold tassel which Queen Elizabeth inherited from her great uncle, Lord Strathmore. To my infinite regret, I never had that honour. I remember, with shame, hitting the front at least half a mile too soon on her Sunbridge in the National Hunt Chase. He should certainly have won and another near-miss, as I have said, was Inch Arran in 1973.

After Cazalet's death, the Queen Mother moved most of her horses to a very different but even more distinguished trainer. Fulke Walwyn, the master of Saxon House, Lambourn, was one of the very few men to have both trained and ridden a Grand National winner. His record in the other great chases, notably the Whitbread and Hennessy, was second to none and, much as she missed her many friends at Fairlawne, the Queen Mother was made every bit as welcome at Saxon House. There, as with all her other trainers, her visits are a constant source of pleasure to the lads. She has a phenomenal memory for details of their lives and families and her evident devotion to the horses warms their hearts.

For most owners, a setback like Devon Loch's collapse might well destroy their keenness altogether. For the Queen Mother, it did just the opposite. From 1960 until his death, Cazalet sent out an average of eight winners a season in the Royal colours and, though the number of her horses reduced in the move to Lambourn, winners kept coming. Many of them in recent years had been bred by the owner herself at Sandringham and in several cases the Queen Mother watches their careers almost from start to finish. Her present trainer, Nicky

Henderson, recalls, with admiration and pride, discussions of young 'future prospects' unlikely to see a racecourse for the next three or four years.

Numerically, the Queen Mother's heroes have been Game Spirit (21 wins and a race named after him at Newbury), Gay Record (the awkward customer whom Jack O'Donoghue conned and cajoled into becoming her 200th winner), and her special favourite, Double Star (who shared with Laffy and The Rip that famous Lingfield treble in 1961). Double Star was himself 17 times a winner in six seasons, and The Rip, whom the Queen Mother discovered herself, won 13. The French-bred Makaldar and New Zealander The Argonaut won 15 apiece, the brothers Inch Arran and Isle of Man 14, and last, but by no means least, Special Cargo – whose Whitbread Gold Cup victory in 1984 remains the most exciting race of any kind I have seen. The happiest sight of all that famous day was the look on the Queen Mother's face when, having promised beforehand to present the Cup, she found herself receiving it from Colonel Whitbread. They don't make moments like that any more and the cheers around the Sandown Park winner's enclosure that day expressed the affection and gratitude which all supporters of British jumping felt then and will always feel for this brave, beautiful, infinitely lovable lady.

---

31 MAY 1996

THE QUEEN HAS IMPRESSIVE RACING PEDIGREE

John Oaksey

Forty-three years ago, when one of her Ladies in Waiting asked The Queen if all was well on the morning of her Coronation the reply was: 'Yes thanks. The Captain just rang to say Aureole went fine...' So though Aureole did not quite win Pinza's Derby (run three days after the Coronation) the Royal trainer, Captain Boyd-Rochfort, would certainly not have been surprised to hear that his principal owner is attending this year's Derby in preference to a football match.

Even if the Coronation story was apocryphal, The Queen's devotion to racing and racehorses has been admirably apparent for most of her 70 years. She was 16, in fact, when her father King George VI took her down to Beckhampton to watch the final pre-Classic gallops of Big Game and Sun Chariot – both leased from the National Stud and therefore trained by Fred Darling, not Boyd-Rochfort. Sun Chariot, as it happened, was on her very worst behaviour. She got down on her knees 'roaring like a bull' and, eventually, forcing her rider Gordon Richards to bale out. Sir Gordon (knighted in the Coronation Honours) told Darling that it was the only time 'I had to clean my boots between first and second lots...' Sun Chariot won three War-time Classics to go with Big Game's 2,000 Guineas but, for security reasons, Princess Elizabeth and her sister were not allowed to go racing – or appear much anywhere – in the early years of the War. Indeed, the rumour that they had been evacuated to Canada was, intentionally, never contradicted.

So the first Royal Classic victory witnessed by our present Queen was Hypericum's 1,000 Guineas in 1946. It was a pretty nerve-racking affair since Hypericum – not quite as good as Sun Chariot but almost as temperamental – ejected Doug Smith before the start and was loose for nearly a quarter of an hour. The Queen had already watched her first Derby – the 1945 substitute run at Newmarket. The King's useful but slightly one-paced Rising Light (the Princess's first great favourite among her father's stable) was fifth to Dante. Winner of four races that year Rising Light was also second to Chamossaire in the St Leger. When Princess Elizabeth married Prince Philip in 1947 her wedding present from the Aga Khan was a thoroughbred filly called Astrakhan. But though Astrakhan did win a minor Flat race she was not the first winner to carry the Princess's colours. That honour, of course, went to a jumper – the brave but ill-fated Monaveen, winner of four steeplechases including the Queen Elizabeth Chase at Hurst Park.

Bought on the advice of Lord Mildmay, whose brainwave it was to champion the winter game at a Windsor Castle dinner party during Royal Ascot, Monaveen was owned in partnership by the Princess and her mother. It was only after his death that Princess Elizabeth decided to concentrate on Flat racing – leaving the winter game to Queen Elizabeth, the Queen Mother. Both women, we all hope, will be at Epsom a week tomorrow and, though The Queen has no runner this year, there is still plenty of time for her to emulate the Epsom triumph of her great uncle, Edward VII, whose Minoru is still the only Derby winner (in 1909) to carry the colours of a reigning monarch.

---

22 MARCH 1981

CARRY ON JUMPING, CHARLES

John Oaksey

Opinions differ, of course, but unless you happen to be a disciple of W. Hamilton, MP, it is perfectly feasible to argue that the health and well-being of Prince Charles are as crucial to the future of Great Britain as those of any other single human being. So when he hit the ground twice in five days last week – and was seen to do so on the nation's television screens – it was both inevitable and understandable that loyal cries of warning and dismay should be heard on many sides.

Opposition to the Prince's race-riding exploits takes two main forms. First you get the straightforward 'safety-first-at-all costs' brigade – whose members regard steeplechasing as a nasty, dangerous pastime, the risk of which an heir to the throne should not under any circumstances be exposed to. But there are also some people who affected shock and surprise when Prince Charles did not immediately ride in triumph into the winner's enclosure, behaving like a combined reincarnation of Lester Piggott, John Francome and Fred Archer.

The quick answer to the first group is, of course, that they need an entirely different Prince – and to the second, that if he wanted instant, effortless success he should have chosen an entirely different sport. The safety-first argument seems to me particularly ridiculous. If Prince Charles's parents and/or advisors had wanted him to avoid all risk of physical injury, they would presumably have forbidden (or, anyway, done their best to discourage) parachuting, flying, windsurfing, scuba-diving, hunting, skiing – to name just a few of the violent forms of exercise to which he has become addicted.

Everyone knows that jumping jockeys get hurt, but I remember how, while once attempting to obtain a horse's eye-view of Aintree from a helicopter, I kept trying to persuade the pilot to fly lower. 'Look,' he said finally, in a tone of patient exasperation, 'if one of your bloody horses hits the fences you'd get carried away in a nice comfortable ambulance. If we touch one, they scrape us off with a trowel.'

A comparable difference exists between most steeplechasing injuries and those involved in many of Prince Charles's other occupations. If things go seriously wrong when you are parachuting or deep-sea diving, for instance, you do not expect to get away with a broken collarbone. For a fully-employed professional jockey who cannot or does not pick his rides, broken bones are an accepted occupational hazard, and even amateurs sometimes get them. But, touching all available wood, cases of serious brain damage or paraplegia are happily rare nowadays, and the total of jockeys actually killed since the last War is, thank God, still in single figures.

The other line of criticism is based, even more absurdly in my opinion, on Prince Charles's record of two falls from four steeplechase rides. In fact, that compares pretty well with the vast majority of beginners. I rode in eight point-to-points before managing to complete the course! But there are in any case several reasons why any such criticism is both totally unrealistic and unfair. For one thing, very few would-be amateurs who take up the game in their early thirties are anything like as bush as Prince Charles. Chris Collins did work his way to the amateur championship while building up a highly successful and profitable business, but he was very much more his own boss than the Prince, and no pitiless glare of publicity followed his every move.

Quite apart from his unique position and countless responsibilities, Prince Charles has suffered one unbelievably cruel stroke of bad luck this season. With so little time at their disposal, he and his trainer, Nick Gaselee, had decided to concentrate on building up a partnership between the Prince and one particular horse, Allibar. Prince Charles rode him happily and well at Ludlow, took him out hunting several times and came to regard him as a trusted friend. There is no substitute for that kind of confidence, but owing to shortage of time and opportunity, no effort was made to widen the Prince's experience and teach him the knack of adapting to different horses and different situations. No one was to blame for this, but when poor Allibar dropped dead the Prince had only two days to get used to Good Prospect, a horse of entirely different size, character, action and jumping methods.

So, at Sandown Park and Cheltenham, things went wrong – just two of those infuriating, undignified disasters to which the rest of us beginners were able to become accustomed to in the unreported seclusion of point-to-point or unimportant country meetings. Even when I pulled up a hot favourite at Cheltenham, thinking (wrongly as it turned out) that I had gone the wrong way, the newspaper coverage amounted to a couple of back-page paragraphs.

Happily, Prince Charles has long been accustomed to excessive publicity and, as his triumphantly successful courtship shows, does not allow it to blow him off course. The only effect of two well-publicised 'failures' will, I am sure, be to strengthen his determination. 'Nothing else I've done compares with this,' he said the other day, and there is not much doubt that the highly infectious bug of riding over fences at speed has bitten him good and proper. He also believes – and said for quotation the other day – that steeplechasing is 'a part of our way of life'. Who knows, he might even one day persuade the Levy Board of that when it is splitting up prize money between jumping and the Flat!

But those in any case are, I suspect, two excellent and convincing reasons why the Prince will not give up until he has mastered enough of jumping's basic skills to appreciate its charm and excitement to the full. The risks and difficulties which, as he has already learnt, lie ahead, only make it that much more certain that he will try again, and keep on trying. Because that, by the grace of God, is the kind of Prince we are lucky enough to have.

———————

27 JULY 1987

ROYAL EXCITEMENT AS PRINCESS ROMPS HOME

Tony Stafford

Among the massive crowds for Diamond Day at Ascot on Saturday, one urgent voice in the stands exhorted: 'Don't be so cool, do something.' This self-confessed plea came not from an ordinary punter, but from The Queen as she shouted home the Princess Royal in the Dresden Diamond Stakes. Many proud parents in the crowd could sympathise with The Queen, who added later: 'But everybody else said, "She doesn't need to".' That indeed was the situation as the Princess Royal and Ten No Trumps provided the perfect curtain-raiser to Reference Point's spectacular success just over an hour later.

This was not the case of a privileged rider getting on an overwhelming favourite and simply steering the horse home. The Princess Royal showed the fruits of many years' experience at the top of the horse trials world, honed into Flat-racing sharpness by her tutor David Nicholson. And just how professional Nicholson — known universally as 'The Duke', a title which he may even aspire to one day at this rate — is can be gauged by the manner in which he guided his pupil straight to the scales to weigh-in while the celebrations were at their height.

By this time The Queen, Prince Philip and Queen Elizabeth the Queen Mother had all come down to the winner's enclosure and were behaving as happily and animatedly as any parent and grandparent of a young apprentice winning his or her first race. The pleasure was clearly doubled by the fact that the Princess Royal was winning on her mother's own racecourse. But The Queen's acute sense of protocol was such that she hung back from the actual winner's enclosure, leaving that honour to connections of the winner, satisfying herself with a happy 'Well done' as the Princess carried her saddle past.

CHAPTER 4

THE MEN IN THE SADDLE

The role of jockey can be both underplayed and overplayed. Some, like Pat Taaffe, would sit immobile, like a dead-weight, and allow Arkle to find his own way home. Lester Piggott, meanwhile, would position his charges perfectly coming around Tattenham Corner in the Derby and ambush the leaders with a devastating burst of acceleration. Others will be a whirl of arms, legs and whips as they put everything into the run-in around The Elbow in the National or up the hill in the Gold Cup at Cheltenham.

Violet Johnstone's article from the Young Topics column, a Telegraph staple in the 1960s, examines the pros and cons involved in becoming a jockey. For every McCoy or Piggott passing the finishing post first, there will be a dozen more bringing up the rear and infuriating those with money riding on their every move. It's a great life, but chiefly when you're winning.

23 JULY 1966

BECOMING A JOCKEY ISN'T A JOY RIDE

YOUNG TOPICS

Violet Johnstone

Fifteen-year-old David Morgan has no doubt about what he's going to do when he leaves school this term. 'When I was ten the idea of becoming a jockey interested me,' he says, 'and at the end of this month I'm leaving Bermondsey to start my career at Newmarket.' This is the reward for several years of perseverance, for it has taken David scores of letters to jockeys and trainers – including Lester Piggott, who was very encouraging – to win a place at one of our leading stables.

David's riding experience runs to no more than a few holiday-time canters in North Wales, but he has the first essential for becoming a jockey: the right build. He is four feet ten inches tall and weighs about six and a half stone. 'I never have to diet,' says David, 'if I did, I wouldn't go in for racing.' He is going to be apprenticed for five years, at 30 shillings a week. His hours? Seven a.m. to 11 a.m., a 4 p.m. to 7 p.m. spell, every second Sunday off. At first David will be mainly concerned with feeding and exercising the horses, and cleaning the stables.

'In my spare time there'll be the Jockeys' and Trainers' Institute to go to for snooker, and as I'm taking my bike with me I shall be able to get about a bit,' he says. 'During the summer there will be race meetings to go to with the horses and, of course, the exercising goes on right through the winter.

'My friends and relations say that with me "in the business" I'll be able to pass tips on to them,' David joked. 'Actually, I think gambling is a complete waste of money.' He accepts the hazards of riding quite philosophically. 'I expect I shall break my collarbone – it's the weakest spot – quite a few times in the next few years,' he said, with impressive matter-of-factness. He is clearly convinced that the odd painful tumble is a small price to pay for a job which offers him companionship with man and beast, plenty of fresh air, and an uncommon amount of thrills. And he has, incidentally, as an added spur to his ambition, the desire to prove his headmaster emphatically wrong. The latter, remembering a previous student's failure to make the grade on the back of a horse, tactfully told David that he didn't think it would work out for him either.

What are the chances for youngsters in racing today? We asked Hotspur, *The Daily Telegraph's* Racing Correspondent, for his opinion. Girls – though they have no chance of becoming jockeys – are as welcome as boys in racing stables, he says. Nearly all are short of 'lads' (there are no stable lasses!). Luck, weight and choosing the right stable are the crucial factors in becoming a successful jockey. There are certain trainers who seldom give any of their lads a ride in public. Others, like Geoff Barling, Tom Masson, Frenchy Nicholson, Sam Armstrong or Staff Ingham, teach with great pains, taking a calculated risk in persuading some not always eager owners to 'give the boy a chance' when perhaps a fashionable jockey is available. Apprentices who have not ridden a certain number of winners can claim weight allowances on a sliding scale in most races. In a policy designed to help their chances, the Jockey Club have recently extended that scale.

As a lad your ambitions can be frustrated by increasing weight. Hands and feet give an indication of how much you are likely to grow, and a fair-minded trainer will leave you with no false illusions on that score. But if you show real talent and are heavy you can turn your attention to riding over fences and hurdles where you can afford to be at least two stones heavier. Alternatively, you can concentrate on rising to some senior position in your own stable. The life is still hard, as Harry Carr describes in his autobiography, *Queen's Jockey*. But his account should inspire those hoping to succeed in a chancy, but eventually highly-paid, and exciting, career.

3 JUNE 2001

PIGGOTT'S 50-YEAR-OLD LOVE AFFAIR

Brough Scott

If he was impressed by the anniversary he was not going to show it. Fifty years ago at the supposedly tender age of 15, Lester Piggott had his first ride in the Derby. There were 33 runners and his mount Zucchero, who eventually finished ninth, was notoriously temperamental. 'No,' said Lester in that distinctive nasal mutter as he toyed with some prawns in The Three Blackbirds pub at Wood Ditton last week, 'there wasn't much pressure. Nobody fancied him very much.'

With Lester it was ever thus. It is not that he is shy about his triumphs. His home in Newmarket is a shrine to the astonishing talent and determination which brought him a record nine Derbies and over 5,000 winners worldwide in a 48-year career which finally closed in 1995 and which for sustained cutting-edge excellence surpasses anything in the whole history of 20th-century sport. Most times he is just not the talking type.

In 1970, he gave me a lift down to Epsom the day after he had ridden the still unbeaten Nijinsky to his fifth and arguably most impressive of all Derbies. 'Be outside Harrods at 10.30,' was the five-word conversation the night before. Next morning the big Mercedes slid up the Brompton Road kerb and the lean figure in the wrap-around dark blue glasses considerately got out to help me, on crutches from a racing accident, into the car. 'Doesn't look too good,' he said. After that, the silence.

The Piggott silence is special because it dares you to start babbling away like an idiot to be finally countered by a monosyllabic grunt. On that drive in 1970, I tried desperately to hold my tongue from pressing the burning question of what it had felt like when he pulled out the mighty Nijinsky and cut down the French star Gyr in one of the most memorable of Epsom finishes. Finally, by about Ewell (a couple of miles from Epsom), he told it as it was. 'I wanted to switch him off,' he said, the voice so quiet that in any other car it would have been inaudible, 'but when I wanted to quicken he had gone to sleep on me. I had to drop him a couple to wake him up. Then he did it.' That was all and yet everything.

At that stage he was in his pomp, without question to my mind the most dominant jockey that I have seen. He was 34 years old and well on his way to the eighth of his 11 jockeys' championships. Two years earlier he had beaten the Americans on their own soil on Sir Ivor in the Washington International as part of a career-long globe trot which eventually scored winners in no less than 36 countries worldwide. He could do anything and often did. But to appreciate the force that he became, you need to understand the boy wonder he was when that unique Derby journey began.

Wednesday, 30 May, 1951: King George VI had opened the Festival of Britain on The South Bank at the beginning of the month, the spies Burgess and Maclean had bolted the previous Friday, 83 luckless miners had been killed at Easington Colliery on Tuesday and a 77-year-old Winston Churchill was not going to win the election over the Labour Government until October. On to this Epsom stage rode 15-year-old Lester Keith Piggott and he was already no stranger to it. At the April meeting he had won both the Grand Metropolitan Handicap and Blue Riband Trial, the latter with Zucchero on one of his Derby partner's going days. Lester's first winner had come at Haydock Park back in August 1948, and after passing 14 (the school leaving age) on 5 November, 1949, he was hot enough to become champion apprentice in 1950, a feat he was to duplicate in 1951 despite a leg smash in August which put him out for the season.

'Oh yes, he was The Housewives' Choice all right,' said Sir Peter O'Sullevan on Friday morning. 'They loved him for riding winners but he had already collected more suspensions than David Beckham has hair styles.' Five years ago Sir Peter, Lester's longest-standing friend and confidant, wrote the eloquent tribute adorning The Piggott Gates at Epsom racecourse which ends with the perfect phrase 'an iconoclast who became an icon'. Back in 1951, his *Daily Express* column gave an equally apt description for the time. 'A potential genius,' wrote O'Sullevan, 'with the look of a wilful cherub.'

Lester was still small, he was to ride at seven stone four at Royal Ascot, but his as yet unlined face bore the frown of a boy determined to thrive in a man's world. At this stage he could not do it by power, so it had to be by cheek, concentration and unique understanding of the mind of the thorough-bred machine. Piggott had a long line of champion jockeys on both sides of his pedigree. His father was a trainer. He was an only child and partly deaf. Lester always denies this but you don't have to play too much of the amateur psychologist to see why he could humour horses like Zucchero where others failed.

'He was a real good horse when he was in the mood,' says O'Sullevan of Zucchero in the mellifluous tones that were still calling the Grand National in his 81st year. With typical attention to detail he has a 50-year-old ante-post voucher on the coffee table of his Chelsea flat. 'Lester won twice on Zucchero in July and I had this fiver each-way on him at 200–1 when he was second to Supreme Court in the first King George at Ascot.' The O'Sullevan memories have already spawned the best-selling book *Calling The Horses*, but as he recalled Piggott's brilliance and daring and match-winning cool he also stressed the extraordinary self-discipline with which Lester kept his weight 21 pounds under its natural ten stone over a 40-year period. 'No other professional athlete,' says Sir Peter admiringly, 'can have performed to such a standard for so long under so ruthless a regime.'

By the time Lester rode his first Derby winner, Never Say Die in 1954, he had grown to five feet seven inches and was already struggling to do eight and a half stone. 'I thought I was bound to end up jumping,' he told me much later, and his thoughts of following his father and grandfather's careers had taken shape enough for him to have ridden a winner at the Cheltenham Festival that March. Incidentally, and there are a lot of 'incidentallys' in the Piggott story, it was at that Cheltenham that he first met the legendary trainer Vincent O'Brien, who would later saddle not just Nijinsky but Sir Ivor, Roberto and The Minstrel as Piggott Derby winners. At that stage O'Brien was the jumping king. 'If you want a ride in the Grand National,' he said to the genius on the grow, 'give me a ring.'

The tales of the personal battle between Lester and his own body are full of stories of cigars and black coffee, of sauna baths and of sweat-suited drives to the races with the car heater switched to tropical. But in truth he got himself into a routine where he ate well but sparingly. When I had the 'blood out of a stone' pain and privilege of ghosting his *Evening Standard* column in the 1970s we would meet for lunch on a day off, he would order Dover Sole and a gin and tonic. There would be no 'wolfing down' followed by the discreet trip to the 'loo' which some of the American bulimic 'chuckers' do. But at the end of the meal the fish would be half finished, the drink still part drunk.

One day he told of the time when the war on weight became total. 'I was down in the south of France in February,' he recalled. 'On the scales I was 11 stone. When I got back to England I worked and worked but was still pushing nine stone at the Lincoln meeting in March, was cheating to do eight stone eight at the Craven in April. I thought it would never come off. But we had some winners. It was the year of Crepello, 1957, and,' he added with one of the most cold-blooded bits of self-denying understatement you will hear, 'I never let it go up again.' He was no longer a thin man with a fat man trying to get out. If you are prepared to be that hard on yourself, professional rivals and media hasslers are unlikely to be given the kid-glove treatment. And while it is highly likely that his most famous suspension, for six months after Derby winner Never Say Die was involved in a scrimmage at Royal Ascot, was unfairly severe, there was an undeniable streak of violence in Piggott.

Poor Tony Murray went to his grave vowing that a bad fall at Windsor was caused by Lester deliberately putting him over the rails, and only on Friday a reporter came up with a tale of how years ago he had been pestering Eve Lodge for news of Lester's Derby ride only for the door to be flung open and the Piggott fist to smash in his teeth much to the delight of the waiting cameraman. This touch of utter ruthlessness was an essential part of his dominance in the saddle. The thundering capsule of the horse race as the field runs tightly packed to the turn, is no place for the faint-hearted. Half tons worth of thoroughbred are jammed in together, shoulders banging, hooves clipping. The squeamish want to pull wide or pull back. The hard men know where they want to be and make sure you know it too.

Nowhere is this more true than at Epsom. Its horseshoe-shaped helter-skelter contours would never be allowed by current course-building regulations. 'In the old days before camera patrol,' recalls O'Sullevan, 'interviewing the jockeys afterwards was like talking to them at the Grand National. They were full of tales of how rough and dangerous it had been. But not Lester. He had the nerve and the reactions and the brilliance to get a position and create space around him. He never had hard-luck stories.' The most common of these is that the horse 'could not come down the hill'. The sharp descent through Tattenham Corner and the heavy left-hand camber of the straight run home is, after all, the greatest single natural hazard on any racecourse anywhere. Many jockeys will wax eloquent about the difficulty of keeping a horse balanced as the ground drops away from you and the pace hots up. It seemed a rich vein to tap for this Piggott ghost writer when we came to the pre-Epsom piece. 'It's not a problem,' he muttered, 'they all come down the hill first time.'

Hard though this reticence might have been on a word-hungry hack you could once again understand what he was saying. The way he rode the track with his insistence on getting a good position by the top of the hill meant that his horses simply cruised down the slope. Look back at the videos and see the Piggott balance and poise and you can appreciate his simple summing up 'they just roll down the first time. It's when they come back again that they often check and want to get out of it'.

If the core principles of Piggott's brilliance remained constant, the actual mechanics of his riding began to change. The Derby victories of Never Say Die (1954), Crepello (1957) and St Paddy (1960) all reveal a jockey riding in a more traditional, longer-leathered style. But by the time Sir Ivor (1968) and Nijinsky (1970) came around, the Piggott method had become the short-stirruped, bent-hairpin style which became his trademark and which inspired the traditionalist rebuke of 'not so much a jockey as a talented acrobat'. To ride so short actually makes more demands on your balance and strength and indeed courage which was a quality with which Piggott has been quite incredibly endowed. Say what you like about Lester's behaviour (and many did!), no one doubted the quite astounding physical courage which underpinned his talent.

Appropriately enough one of the greatest examples happened at Epsom. In the 1977 Oaks, three days after he had won the Derby on The Minstrel, his saddle slipped on the way to the start and he was hung up underneath his now runaway filly Durtal, his foot trapped in the stirrup iron. 'That was bad,' he conceded. 'I only got free because she bumped into a concrete post which snapped the stirrup iron. I could have been killed y'know.' There was a slightly sad-eyed pause as he contemplated this early trip to the everlasting bonfire. Then he moved into something akin to triumph as he added: 'It knocked me about a bit. But I rode in the last race.' How did he get on? Another pause, and then the smile which has always so surprisingly melted the frozen tundra of the face. 'Yeah, I won it.'

While imitators of his new short-stirruped style found themselves losing both forward pushing power and lateral control, Piggott's own balance and strength and courage developed a unique way of rolling the horse beneath him. With his backside hoist high and the reins gathered up in hands which were still and nerveless, the gunfighter is always the best metaphor for Lester's coolness under fire. Balance and strength and courage were crucial and in his most revealing interview (with *The Observer's* Kenneth Harris which began with the four unpromising answers of 'born to it', 'no', 'yes' and 'motor racing') Lester likened the strength needed to ride short to that in standing on one leg compared to walking down the road. But all of this is as nothing if you don't have the understanding of what is beneath you and then the nerve to wait to play your hand. Play the video of Sir Ivor's final furlong cutting down of the leader Connaught a hundred times and again and again you will find yourself echoing the words of the horse's breeder standing next to trainer Vincent O'Brien. 'He cannot win from there.' But he did.

Of course this totally single-minded self-interest caused problems when it came to such contractual things as which horse he was supposed to ride. As far as Piggott was concerned the longer he could juggle his options the better and when it came close to Derby time the 'what will Lester ride?' charade became almost as comical to outsiders as it was aggravating to those involved. Never more so than one year when he was due to ride a final trial on some fading O'Brien hot-pot (I think it was Apalachee) early in the morning and I had arranged to ring him at nine o'clock to rush the news to the *Evening Standard* first edition. For reasons of efficiency I phoned from the newspaper office. For strange reasons of secrecy I had to ring Tipperary and say it was Mr Robinson. Piggott came on the line, muttered something unintelligible and put the phone down. We had both 'He does run' and 'He doesn't run' stories ready. I turned to my fellow hacks, took a deep breath and with fraudulent bravado pointed to the 'He doesn't run' option. Tails, I won.

Naturally he wasn't doing this stint just to help the fund of newspaper knowledge and the world now knows that his obsession with stuffing his wallet rather than his stomach eventually saw him serve a year behind bars for trying to bluff the taxman. Despite all the warnings, his squirrel-like miserliness just would not let him reveal where the cash was stashed even when the Inland Revenue were on the trail. Many of us thought that locking up this wildest of spirits would break him on the wheel. Which is why what happened next is almost the most remarkable twist in the whole Piggott saga. He had retired from riding for two years before he went to jail. He then had an unhappy few months trying to come to terms with what the future might hold only, on Vincent O'Brien's invitation, to leap back into the past. At 54, he took to the saddle again in October and 12 days into the comeback crossed the Atlantic to produce a vintage last-furlong swoop to take the Breeders' Cup Turf on Royal Academy, in money terms, the most valuable race of his whole career.

He won another Classic, the 2,000 Guineas on Rodrigo de Triano, and rode in four more Derbies, hardly the safest of afternoon activities for grandfathers in their closing fifties, but for Piggott it would always be the stage that would remain his own. Each June, albeit sometimes with some reluctance, he would come out to the TV cameras and tell us that 'yes, this really is the biggest day. It's what all the buzz is about'. One year he tried particularly hard except that as he began to speak the Guards band started up behind us. It was not a very equal contest.

So how does he feel about it now? Do the Piggott Gates and the perennial agitation mean much to him? After all the years of privation the lined features keep something mournful about them. As he ponders the question and sips his coke you remember the late Jack Leach's immortal description, 'a face like a well-kept grave'. Then he shrugged and began to answer. 'They invite us each year,' he muttered. 'They are very nice. It's a great day. It's good to be part of it.' In the famous interview Kenneth Harris arranged to raise his hand when he wanted more words from his victim. But in a world of airwaves crammed to bursting with verbosity there was something rather touching in the utterly laconic nature of the response. After an hour and a half's perfectly pleasant, though sometimes silent conversation, the word count on the transcribed tape came to 582.

He was looking fit, the forearms still powerful beneath the smart gold golf shirt, still a swagger in the walk before he slid into the Mercedes and the tyres bit the gravel to depart. He and his wife Susan are quite involved in son-in-law William Haggas's stable, for which Lester bought Ascot winner Superstar Leo last year. He sees a lot of his grandson and of his own son Jamie from his now ended relationship with former assistant Anna Ludlow. He goes his own way.

There is a story which, if it isn't true, ought to be. One evening Lester was seated at dinner next to Sir Michael Stoute. The champion trainer is a notoriously focused individual and was quite soon quizzing Lester on what he was doing. How often was he riding out? Was he going to the sales? What did he think of the three-year-olds? The silver-haired old legend took it for a bit then gave one of his little twists of the mouth and glanced off into the mid distance before coming back with his reply. 'Do I,' muttered Lester Piggott with his funny snuffling laugh, 'have to do anything?'

---

17 OCTOBER 1990

EXPERIENCE AND JUDGMENT KEY FACTORS FOR US OVER-50S

Lester Piggott

It shows it can be done. The most satisfying thing about my comeback so far, is that all those people who have this thing in their mind that when you have passed the age of 50, your life is just about over, have been proved wrong. You see it everywhere, in all walks of life. Once you're over the age of 50, they want to replace you with a youngster, forgetting that the older person has experience and the judgment which a raw youngster will take years to acquire.

Obviously, taking seven rides over two days was not an easy way to start. But it gets easier with every ride and as the days go on, the easier it will be. It was particularly nice for me that the first winner was on a horse of our own. I had intended to make Nicholas my first ride, but if you're a jockey and you are offered attractive rides, especially for people you have worked with before, you have to take them. That's why I started on Monday.

It was also good that the first winner was for Henryk de Kwiatkowski. He has been with us since we set up the stable, and we've had nice horses from him. Apart from Nicholas, we have Batzushka and I am looking forward to riding him at Newmarket on Friday. Henryk did say that he wanted to fly over to see the race, but he sometimes has been unlucky when he comes over. He was thrilled with the news about the win, though, and I'm delighted to have my first winner in his colours. Nicholas was my first ride for Susan and I hope that I will be able to ride many more winners for her. At least I should be able to keep the ride on this one next time he runs!

It was great, too, to win for Eric Eldin. He was a friend and weighing-room colleague for so many years and, like so many trainers, he deserves more luck than he's been having recently. His horse, Shining Jewel, showed a lot of promise at Newmarket earlier in the year when, on his first run, he was third to Lord Florey. Eric said the horse had been a bit disappointing, but yesterday was his day and he came and won very easily.

It was an unusual experience yesterday to go to Chepstow. It must be 20 years or more since I've ridden there, and I definitely haven't crossed the Severn Bridge before! The course is a bit out of the way, and yet a lot of people travelled there and it was wonderful to get such a warm reception from everyone after both the winners. The jockeys were all great, especially the older ones, and it was as though my coming back showed that they could stay around for a while as well.

As I've said before, there is no substitute for experience in most careers and, for a jockey, experience is the most crucial ingredient of all. It feels just like the old times, it's great. I don't regret not having come back earlier – I've had a good break. Now that the most difficult part is over – the first winner was always going to be the most important barrier – I hope that I'll be able to have a few good rides before the end of the season.

There's almost a month of this season to go and some important races still to come and I hope to be able to pick up some rides in those races, but it won't be easy. But at least, with these winners behind me, I'll now be able to go into them in the right frame of mind.

---

28 JANUARY 1996

FAME GALLOPING UP FOR THE REAL MCCOY

Brough Scott

Too much body, but an awful lot of head. Tony McCoy, 21, is now more than 20 winners clear in the jockeys' championship but, as people suddenly study every racecourse move of his lean and saunaed-down frame, they should remember that mind is always more important than matter. The opening barrage of facts is apt to overwhelm sensible judgment. Anthony Peter McCoy arrived from Ireland at Toby Balding's Hampshire stables in August 1994, an unsung ex-Flat race apprentice with 13 winners to his name and, as yet, not one ride in a steeplechase. By the end of last season he had ridden 74 winners, a record for a 'conditional' jockey. By Thursday evening he had ridden 108 more. It is the most sensational start in the whole history of the game, yet he is still so new to us that it is hard to give him his due.

Up until a month ago most professionals would not put McCoy near the very top bracket occupied by the likes of Dunwoody, Maguire, Williamson and Osborne. They ascribed his flood of winners to a willingness, unlike Dunwoody and Osborne, to go flat out for the title from the very start of the new 12-month jumping season, and to the luck of avoiding the injuries which have so curtailed both Williamson and Maguire this term. They said that with super-agent Dave Roberts booking the mounts, McCoy was just riding the crest of a great wave of confidence as yet unhampered by public setback. Even Dave Roberts (also agent to Maguire and Williamson) agreed with this assessment. But after the last ten days neither he nor we can be quite so sure.

The season's first hundred came up a week ago Thursday as part of a treble at Nottingham. A Kempton double on Saturday included victory on his first ride for Jenny Pitman, followed by the Bic Lanzarote Hurdle, his biggest career success to date. On to this week with a winner at Leicester on Tuesday and then another at Folkestone on a reluctant-looking partner called North Bannister, who had even the normally phlegmatic Roberts wowing in wonder. 'I looked at the way he got the horse up,' says the man who has revolutionised the booking system, 'and had to ask myself, "Could Adrian or Norman have done any better?" Tony knows he has a bit to learn, but he listens and he is learning very quick.'

Roberts was not the only 'pro' to be impressed. That same day champion trainer David Nicholson, whose stable jockey Maguire had been hurt in a pile-up at Nottingham, had rung to engage McCoy for former King George winner Barton Bank at Cheltenham. It was the sort of compliment to turn many a young head. But as we drove the 40 miles from Toby Balding's yard at Fyfield to Paul Nicholls's operation near Shepton Mallett on Thursday morning, you soon realised that it is a wise old skull on McCoy's still so youthful shoulders. It is also a very lean one. A year ago McCoy was eight pounds lighter and one-and-a-half inches shorter than the five feet ten inches and nine stone 13 he checks in of an afternoon. This unusually late development now necessitates a regime to make even the Spartans wince. Before North Bannister on Wednesday there had been one cup of tea and a wheat cracker followed by an hour and a quarter to shed three pounds in the sauna.

We had shared a meal of typical Balding generosity that evening (but on his part only Diet-Pepsi), yet the only fuel next morning before four rides, two winners and two pounds shed in the sauna at Wincanton, was a bowl of Frosties and a cup of tea. 'I do feel tired afterwards,' he says of this jockey's routine, which continues to defy all physiological sense, 'but the sauna is the only way to shift the weight and the adrenalin carries you through.' His mobile phone rings. It is Dave Roberts to agree plans. McCoy's voice drops and suddenly he is a long way from discussing unfulfilled schooldays in Randallstown, County Antrim, but a few years back.

'He came over from Jim Bolger's in Ireland apparently a lot less experienced than Adrian Maguire was when he had joined us a couple of years earlier,' Toby Balding had said, 'but he actually settled in quicker. He has a very good grasp of the racing scene.' The learning curve has been steep, no part steeper than the previously unfamiliar craft of organising half a ton of steeplechaser for take-off. That was precisely the role which Paul Nicholls was now needing for a talented, but as yet untried novice called Blue Laws in a freezing field near Castle Cary. 'At the start of the season,' Nicholls said, watching McCoy and stable 'conditional' Mark Griffiths attacking the four-fence lane of schooling obstacles, 'people said I was mad to take on someone so inexperienced. But straight away I could see there would be no problem. He is so calm and balanced. Look at that!' Blue Laws, with McCoy's long body wrapped low and deep around him, jumped like a particularly nimble springbok. Make sure he is on your list.

At Wincanton later, on an afternoon when even a Yak would have sought shelter, the second of the two McCoy winners was first-attempt novice Samlee in a three-mile chase that was always going to sort the men from the boys. Only ten of the 16 starters completed and not all Samlee's efforts, particularly a sort of banking leap at the second last, looked good for the digestion. 'What I have noticed about Tony,' said Grand National winner Brendan Powell, who had prudently pulled up in the straight, 'is his quite remarkable perseverance. He gets very low into his horse and really inspires them. It's in his head.'

Master trainer Jim Bolger, who never dishes compliments out too freely, says from his County Carlow base: 'His parents must take much of the credit. He came to me at 15 and was always a solid performer. He did not set the world on fire as an apprentice. He got a bit heavy and he broke his leg quite badly. Not a star yet on the track, but already a star in attitude. He had been very well brought up.'

The plot thickens the nearer to home you get. McCoy had gone to Bolger and to morning gallops on Classic winners like St Jovite and Jet

Ski Lady, on the recommendation of Billy Rock. It was to Rock's rather more rustic point-to-point yard at Cullybackey, near Ballymena, that the then tiny tyro used to cycle from his parents' post office and village store 12 miles to the south at Moneyglass, very close to the shores of Lough Neagh. 'Anthony [Tony is a recent English application] was first brought to me by his father Peader, who is one of my oldest friends and bred the Cheltenham winner Thumbs Up,' says Rock. 'To begin with it was just Saturdays, then once in midweek, then all week, too. At 15, you could put him in charge of everything and I paid him a full wage. The teachers would ring up just to check he was safe, but accepted it was his future. It was probably against the law.'

Young McCoy will be back in County Antrim to see his parents, four sisters and brother this weekend. He will, of course, visit Billy Rock, but the trainer will not be awe-struck by any new-found pre-eminence. 'When Anthony came, he was about five stone nothing and yet straight away you could put him on great big horses that grown lads couldn't hold one side of,' says Billy. 'I remember ringing Jim Bolger and saying, "I have a young feller here who one day will be a champion jockey". I should be reading tea leaves or something.'

---

2 APRIL 2002

TONY McCOY'S DIARY

THE CHAMPION JOCKEY GIVES A DAY-BY-DAY ACCOUNT OF LIFE IN AND OUT OF THE SADDLE IN THE COUNTDOWN TO BEATING SIR GORDON RICHARDS'S RECORD OF 269 WINNERS IN A SEASON

Sunday, 3 March: Got roped into a Cheltenham preview race night for Jim Bolger, ex-boss, in Wexford. No getting out of that one. Flew from Heathrow at lunchtime with Mick Fitzgerald – which ruled out sleep. Needed ice pack on ear afterwards. Met up with old colleagues.

Monday, 4 March: Arrived at East Midlands. Jimmy McCarthy picked me up from airport and took me on to Market Rasen, which was appreciated by Gee Armytage, my assistant, as much as it was me as it saved her having to drive. I arrived at Market Rasen very heavy, ten stones 11 pounds, which put me in a bad mood.

Tuesday, 5 March: Turned down another of many invitations, a race night in Ireland, but did four pre-recorded interviews on the mobile on the way to Exeter, three of which were incomprehensible. Driven by Steve Taylor, who is writing my book.

Wednesday, 6 March: Drove self to Bangor earlier than usual to go via Cheltenham to do a promotional photo for JCB, sponsors of the Triumph Hurdle. More sweating. Weight not great.

Thursday, 7 March: Still feeling grotty. Everyone beginning to assume I'm going to break Sir Gordon Richards's record. Lots of TV people want to do interviews and mini-documentaries. The record seems such a formality to them, and it's beginning to wreck my head. I am signed up to a DVD with Lace International, which I think will be good.

One winner. Went on to Cafe Royal in London for one of the few previews I agreed to do. Back home 2 a.m.

Friday, 8 March: Cameraman from Lace here. Set off early to London to Chris Coleman's shop called Copperfield. He's a good tailor who keeps me well dressed. I was picking up my Cheltenham suits. They had me arriving in a Rolls-Royce. It certainly isn't my style. On to Sandown, and back to London for last preview. Had agreed ages ago to do something for Richard Dunwoody – think he was a jockey once. His benefit dinner had been cancelled just after September 11 and restaged tonight.

Saturday, 9 March: Got up, watched *Morning Line* in the Hilton. Sandown – last important racing day before Cheltenham. Four rides, Polar Red most important. He won, but had a hard race.

Sunday, 10 March: Mothers' Day. Sponsored a fence at the Old Berks Hunt team chase. I'm also paying for Easter eggs for the young racegoers at Plumpton on Easter Saturday. Gee said how much Fitzy would like to help out too, so he has been dropped in it for half.

Monday, 11 March: Radio 5 Live followed me around at Stratford to get my last-minute thoughts before tomorrow. Rode a winner for Jonjo O'Neill and J.P. McManus.

Tuesday, 12 March: Cheltenham, and no winners. Woke up ten stone four. Had a sweat for an hour in bath. *Morning Line*. Walked course while on phone doing web-chat for Channel 4. Sauna. Champion Hurdle. Cantering. Valimarix had to win. Fell coming down hill. Utter dejection. Genuinely pleased for Dean Gallagher.

Wednesday, 13 March: No winners. Gave *Morning Line* a miss. Looking forward to today, but not ready for unnecessary inquests or people telling me to be cheerful. Cranked up sauna. Just a Jaffa cake and cup of tea for breakfast. Did ten stone two on Golden Alpha. Very disappointing. Only beat the groundsman home. Supreme Developer is not quite ready for the hassle of the Festival Bumper. To make matter worse Jamie Spencer, a former lodger, wins it. He will be good when he learns to keep one straight. Watched Manchester United. Very dull – unlike Arsenal.

Thursday, 14 March: Woke up. Apparently, according to the papers, haven't had a winner for two days. Triumph Hurdle. First person I met in parade ring is Alex Ferguson. Also tried to cheer me up. After Dunwoody, Sir Alex is the second worst loser in sport. Londoner, the banker, pulled up. Exit Swinger – another second. Beaten by another bloody former lodger, David Casey, his first Cheltenham winner. All I need now is for Seamus Durack with a broken leg to come and beat me. Two chances remaining. Royal Auclair. Made all, needed an aggressive ride, so he got me on the perfect day. Halfway down chute began to realise that I had a lot of supporters out there. I acknowledge their applause.

Friday, 15 March: Chepstow. One winner. Claiming Hurdle. Running Times. Banker. Reading between lines, I'm not a great loser. Must ring Dunwoody and Ferguson for advice. Bed early.

Saturday, 16 March: Thought I was doing OK with 264 winners so far, but a punter at Uttoxeter reminds me I'm having a bad run. Three rides, three losers.

Sunday, 17 March: Met Luke Harvey and Jim Culloty to celebrate his Gold Cup win.

Monday, 18 March: Heathrow. 8.45 a.m. to Glasgow. Ayr for one. Taxi to races. Met Sue Mott. Spoke about my depressing week. Sense of humour beginning to return. One ride, one banker. Beaten.

Tuesday, 19 March: Hereford. Two rides, both beaten out of sight, but the day is taken over by the serious spinal injury to Joe Tizzard.

Wednesday, 20 March: Ludlow. Three rides, no winners. Baclama very disappointing in the seller.

Thursday, 21 March: Wincanton. Back in the winner's enclosure for Venetia Williams. Folly Road was third, ran okay. Can't blame Norman Williamson for taking the week off and heading for the Alps. Maybe he's right, but he's a married man. Taking holidays when I could be riding isn't for me – at the moment.

Friday, 22 March: Newbury. Tristan Ludlow disappointed. Thought he'd run well, but was beaten a long way. Bangor tomorrow will save me, I know it will.

Saturday, 23 March: Bangor for four rides, two certainties. Gone Far, a real nice horse, just tootled round a poor fourth. I'm now beginning to wonder how on earth I've ridden 265 winners this season.

Sunday-Wednesday, 24-27 March: Got to Malaga at breakfast. Arrived Marbella with Fitzy and James Blackshaw, owner of Shadow Leader. Played golf, few quiet nights out, back home for 7.30 p.m. each day. This is on a need-to-know basis.

Thursday, 28 March: Exeter. Raring to go, but back in the groove with three beaten favourites.

Good Friday: Quiet morning with Lace International. Afternoon show jumping at the Lambourn Open Day. Fitzy wins, but on a former international showjumper. Bungee-jumped off a crane backwards.

Saturday, 30 March: Newton Abbot. Seven rides, one winner. At least the one I fancied, Polar Champ, won.

Easter Day: Meet Richard Dunwoody in the evening for a drink. He tells me he's off across the Arctic after the London Marathon. That boy's not happy unless he's punishing himself. He's crackers.

Easter Monday: Chepstow. Five rides, five favourites. One winner.

Tuesday, 2 April: Schooled all Martin Pipe's Grand National entries this morning. Looking at one winner at best. My first ride, Shampooed, runs a good race to win by a couple of lengths. Riding for the neighbour, Charlie Morlock. His Shepherds Rest is an old character who knows more about racing than I do. Charlie tells me to just sit there without moving on him and he'll win if he wants. Not allowed to push, shove, slap or beat. He wants. Winner 269 and we're equal. Valfonic for Martin next. His jumping eventually warms up, and the fast ground gets him home. That's No. 270. It's a big, big relief. The crowd appreciate it as much as I do. Back home to The Pheasant for a celebration.

---

14 JANUARY 1968

A CHAMPION – IN AND OUT OF THE SADDLE

John Lawrence

Five years ago, the day after the 1963 Grand National, I went to see Stan Mellor in a Liverpool hospital. Minus six teeth and with ten fractures in the bones of his face, he was conscious, cheerful – and totally unrecognisable. As we walked out someone broke the gloomy, sickened silence. 'Well, with that lot,' they said, 'it must be long odds on he'll never ride again.'

Last week, watching Stalbridge Colonist lifted up the Sandown hill to win the Mildmay, I thought about those words, with which, when they were spoken, none of us had the heart to argue. So I went to see Stan again to ask, among other things, how that pessimistic prophecy so signally failed to come true. It was soon quite evident that no such thought had occurred to him. 'The fall' (Eastern Harvest went at the second flight of the Schweppes Gold Trophy, leaving him a human football under the feet of 40 rivals) 'never really bothered me,' he says. 'It hurt at the time and I thought I'd broken my back as well. But then, one night, fast asleep and a bit dopey, I took off that shroud thing they make you wear in hospital and sleepwalked stark naked around the ward. The night nurse was afraid to stop me (she *says* she looked the other way) and in the morning my back was fine.'

But for the fall, in fact, Stan Mellor would have been champion jockey for the fourth successive time that season. Next year, by his standards, he didn't ride many winners. 'But I'd got married in the meanwhile, don't forget, and that,' with a smile at his tiny, startlingly pretty wife Elaine 'put the cap on it properly.' 'That' was also one of the wisest things Stan did and a good example of the quick, correct decisions which have controlled his life. The first time he took Elaine out (she was 17 and had fancied him since she was 12), he asked her to marry him. In fact, there is some doubt who did the asking, but three years later they were married and now with two daughters Elaine runs their home near Bicester so well and so hospitably that 'we often seem to have more people here than there are beds'.

Much earlier, in 1952, 15 years old and the son of a timber merchant in Manchester, Stan Mellor had made another almost equally important decision – to join George Owen's Cheshire stable. 'It was pure luck,' he says. 'I chose from three trainers. One was Mr Owen, one gave up a year later, and the other was warned off.' George Owen is, with Bob Turnell and Ryan Price, one of the three greatest living producers of National Hunt jockeys. Three champions, Dick Francis, Tim Brookshaw, and Stan himself – and the former leading amateur Stephen Davenport – all got their start on his horses. 'He never tells you much,' Stan says, 'just weighs you up and then if he thinks you're worth it gives you a *real* chance. I suppose he chooses carefully in the first place, but once he's chosen he'll stand by you whatever happens.'

Stan weighed just over seven stone, when he decided to give racing a try. 'People told me I was too small and too weak, that I'd never stand the falls. And now' – this with a broad grin and no trace of bitterness – 'they all say, "Of course, you're so lucky you don't have to worry about your weight".' What he did worry about in those early days was his strength, or lack of it, and his inability to ride a proper finish. 'I practised for hours in my bedroom squatting on an upturned chair. It was John Hislop's book *Steeplechasing* that helped me most, but when I told John that I'm not all sure he was very flattered.' For the strength he took up weight-lifting in a Manchester gym owned by a former Mr Great Britain. 'There were all these great mountains of muscle heaving huge weights about, and there was me in the corner sweating to lift a few pounds. I felt an idiot, but the old boy who ran the gym said, "Never you mind about them, it's what you do for yourself that counts" I've always remembered that – I think there's a lesson in it somewhere.'

From the age of eight Stan has ridden, showjumping on his father's ponies with great success, and it didn't take George Owen long to recognise his potential. After only three seasons he succeeded Tim Brookshaw as stable jockey, and in 1958 his name appeared in the list for the first time – tenth with 26 winners. He was still strictly a Midlands name, almost unheard of in the fashionable South, but two years later, riding for Roy Whiston as well as George Owen, all that was changed. Stan suddenly caught fire, rocketed up the list and beat Fred Winter by one for the title – riding two winners on the last day of all. 'I knew I wasn't a good champion,' he says. 'How could you think any different when Fred was still riding? He was out on his own and watching him made us all realise what a lot we'd got to learn.' But 'good' champion or no, Stan rode 117 winners in 1960–61 and 80 the season after that. And the endless grind of those two achievements has given him some very decided views about the title – views in which, needless to say, sour grapes play no part whatever.

'I honestly don't regret losing it,' he says. 'Based on your total of winners it's a real killer. The strain of chasing all over the country from August to June makes you ride worse, not better, and apart from the honour, what do you get out of it? There wasn't even Champagne [the Bollinger Trophy] in my day, just a lot of speeches and dinners and people wanting to be introduced to the champion. It's hell, I tell you, it burns you out. And for Josh [Gifford] and Terry [Biddlecombe], who have to waste like crazy, it must be 100 times worse.' Stan's ideal would be a situation like that in France with two classes of meetings, top ones at which top jockeys are paid a fee that really allows them to make (and save) some real money, and second class, cheaper ones for the up-and-coming brigade. 'They don't even have a champion as such in France,' he says. 'You're just leading jockey at Auteuil or wherever it may be. The best men only ride two or three days a week. They don't have to worry about the gaffs.

'All I really want to do now is what I've got – two or three good trainers [his chief claims are from Frank Cundell, Tom Jones and Roddy Armytage] and the time to concentrate on doing as good a job as I can for them. Of course, if the chance came again I don't say I wouldn't have a go, but I don't miss it and I'm not going to knock myself out.' Stan is 30 now – still under nine stone soaking wet in colours – and with only a few grey hairs at his temple to show the strain of 15 years in one of the toughest jobs there is. Chairman of the Professional Jockeys' Association and a tireless worker for the Injured National Hunt Jockeys' Fund, Stan has already taken Fred Winter's place as the acknowledged elder statesman of the profession. He would like to see higher riding fees – 'we've only had one small rise in the 15 years since I started, but with things as they are you can't really ask, can you?'

Something of a fanatic about physical fitness, he would also like to see official help for young jockeys trying to keep fit and learn their job – a small gymnasium with a professional instructor, for instance, on the major courses. 'As it is, we just drive to the races, change and walk out stiff and cold to do what after all is a fairly intensive physical job. What other athlete would try to do his best without a warm-up?' But elder statesman or not, Stan doesn't feel old and it makes him laugh when journalists call him a veteran. 'With a bit of luck I could have five or six years yet,' he says. 'But, of course, the competition is far hotter now than when I started. Now when you say you can't ride a horse they don't look too disappointed. There are 20 or 30 others who'll do it just as well. Ten years ago there weren't more than a dozen.'

'Just as well', is, of course, a gross exaggeration, as anyone who saw Stalbridge Colonist win at Sandown would testify. The standard of jockey-ship is probably higher than before, but Stan Mellor's place in the very top flight – as a jockey and as a man – is unquestioned. 'Unfulfilled ambitions?' I asked, and he grinned, reluctant to tempt the Fates by naming them. But I think I know one. No English National Hunt jockey has ridden 1,000 winners in this country. Only Fred Winter, with 880, and Ernie Piggott (Lester's grandfather), with 700 here and 300 more in France, come close. Stan has 725 so far. Five or six more years, touch wood, at his present rate could see him reach that pinnacle and if that day does come I hope I'm there to cheer. For, by then, no one, not even Fred Winter himself, will have done more for the good of National Hunt racing than the small, gallant, infinitely charming man whom I visited that gloomy day five years ago in Liverpool.

---

14 APRIL 1985

FRANCOME FLICKS OFF THE COMPUTER

John Oaksey on the retirement of a unique jump jockey

If the autobiography John Francome plans to finish this summer is halfway as funny as his after-dinner speaking, and half as frank as his descriptions of racing's powers-that-be, we can expect the most entertaining book by a jockey since Jack Leach's immortal *Sods I Have Cut on the Turf*. But, sadly, however well he writes, John may be unable to throw light on the most unique and individual facet of his complicated art.

Somewhere beneath that mop of curly hair lies an invisible, indescribable computer into which his eyes feed the ground line of each approaching fence, the length and speed of his horse's stride and a dozen other rapidly varying factors. The signals by which, through Francome's hands or legs or both, it passes its conclusions to the horse are likewise invisible and indescribable. John McEnroe would find it easier to analyse his service – for which Francome, an incurable tennis addict, would cheerfully give up at least 100 of his 1,138 winners! Viv Richards's on-drive or Ballesteros chipping out of impenetrable rough are comparable sporting mysteries. They are things of beauty, too, as was the sight of John Francome presenting a horse at a fence. More in-born than acquired. I doubt if we shall see it done so well and so consistently again.

John worked tirelessly, though, on the parts of his job which *could* be learnt or improved. For more than half his riding life he was, by the highest standards, not an outstandingly strong finisher. But, steadily, he made himself stronger and more effective: even if, on two equally tired horses and especially in heavy ground, I would still back Fred Winter to beat him from the second last. Incidentally, it is Francome's horsemanship as opposed to his tactical jockeyship which Fred himself singles out as unique.

But comparing great riders of different ages is even more pointless than trying the same thing with horses. These two very different men were the best I have personally seen. But what mattered much more was the partnership between them, unbroken for 15 eventful seasons. Blessed with a highly developed sense of humour, quick wit and a quicker tongue, John Francome has always taken Sinatra's advice to 'Do it my way'. What the world thinks does not worry him, either; or does not seem to. It makes John far more amusing, less predictable and better company. Woe betide pomposity or self-importance in his presence. When you least expect it that lazy Wiltshire drawl delivers a lethal puncturing one-liner. No wonder they already miss him in the changing room. But racing, whether you like it or not, does contain people who do take themselves quite seriously.

Some are stewards, whose job is to enforce the rules, including the one which requires jockeys 'to achieve the best possible placing'. Some are owners, who expect 'the best possible placing' in return for the money they spend. For reasons which seemed good to him – chiefly an understandable conviction that he knew better than anyone when the horse he was riding had had enough – John Francome has repeatedly fallen foul of both groups. And in all the resulting clashes, he would undoubtedly have come off worse without the unfailing support of a man as universally respected as Fred Winter. Throughout the trauma of the John Banks affair, Fred was the rock on which his jockey's reputation rested. The racing world *knew* that if he even suspected any *real* wrong-doing, as opposed to technical infringement of the rules, the partnership would have been severed there and then. But it remained intact and, with it, John's good name.

However big a debt of gratitude the great jockey owes his trainer, those who have backed and watched and been thrilled by his exploits for a dozen years owe him an even bigger one. From countless memories, my own favourite is of Uncle Bing winning the Topham in the colours Lord Mildmay made famous before John Francome was born. Landing dog-tired over the last, Uncle Bing was gathered and lifted and held together every yard of the run-in.

With the championship wide open next season, there will be a fresh fascination in who comes out on top: the ex-champion Jonjo O'Neill, John's co-champion Peter Scudamore, or a 'new' face like Hywel Davies, Steve Smith Eccles, Richard Dunwoody or Graham Bradley? Whoever makes it, I don't believe we shall readily compare him with the man who hung up his boots on Tuesday.

<hr>

8 APRIL 1993

ASCOT WINNER TOPS OFF AN EMOTIONAL DAY

Peter Scudamore

My last day as a jockey started early yesterday with a phone call from, of all people, Jimmy Tarbuck. We'd never met before, but he just wanted to say: 'Well done, good luck'. It was lovely to think that people you don't even know can be so kind. Soon after that John Francome called. He had not read a newspaper or heard any news, but had been contacted by a reporter for his reaction.

John told him: 'Well, he's been around for too long, he should have gone ages ago'. It was only when John mentioned 'the red flag' that the journalist realised they were talking at cross purposes and said he was asking about my retirement. After that, the phone kept on ringing, and all the time I was trying not to think too much about it.

I'm sure some people might be critical of me packing up when I did, thinking I should have carried on to the end of the season and tried to catch Richard (Dunwoody) for the championship. But I didn't really want to struggle on around the little tracks any more. OK, Cheltenham, Aintree or Ascot still excite me, but jump racing is all about battling away on a rotten day at Worcester or in a novice chase in the cold at Devon. They're hard days, but real jumping days. No, in the end I felt I owed it to Martin (Pipe) and Nigel (Twiston-Davies) to stop when I felt ready. This way, Martin has a couple of months in which to decide what he wants to do about jockeys next season, and I have a chance to work out what I want to do.

It was a strange feeling setting off for Ascot. I'm sure I'll feel like an outsider from now on, but the jockeys yesterday couldn't have been friendlier. There is a special camaraderie among jump jockeys – unlike, I'm sure, in any other sport. Nobody's up there too long; every time you go out for a ride you can only feel respect for the skill and bravery of the other riders.

Yesterday, I tried to play it down a bit and we had a laugh and a joke together about what John Francome said (he's still revered in the weighing room). Before racing, there were a couple of television interviews and then it was down to business on Grand Hawk, my first ride of the day. He isn't always brilliant at the start and it took us a while to get in front. Jimmy Frost and I probably went a bit too fast too early. Even so, Grand Hawk ran a great race, though Hebridean beat us, as he had done at Huntingdon.

I thought Dagobertin would be a certainty on my next ride, after his good runs over fences. He jumped a bit better, but I'm not really 'clicky' about him. He'll win soon, though, I'm sure. Then came my last ride and the most touching moment was having my cap tied for the last time by my valet, Andy Townend. I tried to put my emotions in perspective. As Phil Bull would have said, it was only another horse race, after all.

I wasn't getting too wound up, but when I was given a clap into the paddock, and again down to the start, it brought a tear to the eye. In the race, I just tried hard to concentrate. Nigel had said beforehand that there was no need to make all, as Sweet Duke had 12 stone and, luckily, I had a good run, following Jamie (Osborne) all the way. I went to the front on a good stride, still not thinking about winning, just plugging away – and he kept jumping and galloping. It was only afterwards that I realised how important it was to win on my last ride. And it was nice, too, that it was not an over-big racing occasion – just a nice meeting. It took nothing away from the racing, and maybe added a bit.

So, now, what to do next? Sometimes, retirement is a difficult choice, but my partnership with Nigel Twiston-Davies can't be going too badly. It had five winners in all yesterday. People in racing know we are partners, but we are more than that. We have been friends since pony club days. Then Nigel moved away to the Cotswolds and bought a farm. Four years ago, the farm wasn't going too well, so I suggested buying one of the houses and half the farm from him, but he was to hold the training licence until I packed up riding, when I would take over. Now, though, he is so well known he'll have to keep the licence and I'll be the assistant, helping out where I can. Certainly, I'll spend more time there and, hopefully, there will be more to do.

----

3 DECEMBER 1995

RETURN OF THE EASY RIDER

Brough Scott

A smile lost but now found again. It is not an uncommon phenomenon as a desperately committed champion rediscovers the joy in doing what made him great. Richard Dunwoody was smiling at Thurles on Thursday. Thurles was too. For though Richard was born on 18 January, 1964, in Belfast, and has been based on the mainland since before he rode his first winner in 1983, the people of southern Ireland greet him as one of their own. 'You're very welcome,' they said as we navigated the soft Tarmacadam which for some reason was being laid outside Thurles' slightly dilapidated old weighing room just an hour before the first race.

Dunwoody smiled at the absurdity of it, a man comfortable with himself, a three-times British champion about to ride his 30th winner of the Irish season, only seven short of his score across the sea, which this time last year was already 71. Who would have thought it? Who would have thought ten months ago that this most stone-faced and obsessional of all jockeys could have reinvented a new, relaxed, twin-track persona so late into his career? Ten months ago Dunwoody was returning from a 30-day ban with a mind so daunted by the prospect of another relentless duel for the jockeys' title with Adrian Maguire, and the daily pressure of holding down the incessant demands of the Martin Pipe stable, that he was little short of total breakdown. On the eve of his comeback this hardest of the hard men collapsed in tears in conversation with one confidant, and his behaviour was so strange that his agent Robert Parsons was under the impression he was going to ride one winner and then announce his retirement from riding altogether.

The winner duly came, the announcement didn't, the long drag to the third championship continued, but the seed of change was irrevocably set. 'He had things to work out,' says Parsons diplomatically, referring not just to Richard's ending of the Martin Pipe connection, but to the achievement of an amicable settlement with his long suffering wife, Carole. 'Yet once he had come back from suspension it was as if there was a little man inside him determined to get a better system through.' And have a bit more to eat. This season Richard is keeping his five feet nine inch frame to ten stone four or five, some six pounds heavier than in the past, and it is only now that he is off that endless sauna-bath routine and the constant 'ride everything' quest that the new 12-month season brings to a title leader, that you can measure the damage it was doing to his persona. 'He's still very hard on himself,' says Parsons, chiding Dunwoody for boiling off four pounds to ride a not exactly brilliant animal on Friday, 'but it used to be ridiculous. Ten minutes after the last race he'd be on the phone in his car going through the rides for the next few days.'

Stories of Dunwoody taking days off are now told with disbelieving delight on both sides of the Irish Sea. 'I rang his mobile on Tuesday,' said Edward O'Grady, for whom he was to ride the classy Ventana Canyon at Thurles. 'There was a lot of noise on the line. I imagined he was talking from the jockeys' room at Fontwell. No, he was having lunch at San Lorenzo. And I think it's tremendous,' added Edward, the astutest of all Ireland's jumping trainers and saddler of Dunwoody's ride Sound Man at Sandown yesterday. 'He's starting to see some of the benefits a champion should. Certainly his trips over here, [he starred on Ireland's top chaser Merry Gale at Punchestown last Saturday] have become very, very popular. Our crowds love the idea of having such a great rider around.'

On Thursday it was the knowledgeable if windchilled race fans of Tipperary who were to have the treat. As Dunwoody was legged up on the breath-takingly handsome Ventana Canyon, there was the chance to take in just how much he has achieved and how. There have been 1,302 UK winners (second only to Scudamore). He is the only current jockey to have won the Champion Hurdle, the Gold Cup and the Grand National (West Tip in 1986, Miinnehoma in '94), and the man who shared Desert Orchid's glorious sunset years with the Irish Grand National and the King George VI in 1990. And here he was on a big, talented, but worryingly cautious novice making a first shot over fences in the gathering gloom at Thurles.

It's not a precious world, jump racing, but at its heart there is an amalgam of balance and nerve and strength and judgment which make the crossing of a steeplechase obstacle the most intriguing of all the daily challenges in sport. No one does it better than Dunwoody. His body low and deep, his balance at one with his horse, his mind locked into that other one inside the bridle. As they thundered past and over the fence in front of us, Ventana Canyon in second place was still hesitant, but at least he was getting the instructions right. Away towards the crowd, the odd dog-collared priest sheltered under the old blue corrugated roofs of the stands, and then the field swept off up the undulations of the far side with Dunwoody having to put his partner up in rhythm to pull back the trailblazing leader. Ventana Canyon was safe but unspectacular at the third last and still had three lengths to make up as they spun downhill off the far turn. Dunwoody's legs clamped in to impress urgency. Ventana Canyon closed the gap, but as they reached the fence he ducked left behind the leader, who himself got too low and capsized slap in front. The horse must do the side-stepping; the jockey just keeps cool and helps him balance. In a split second, the danger was past and Dunwoody drove his debutant firm and sure towards the last of the fences. Ventana Canyon measured and committed himself.

What might yet be a top-class career was launched. The 5 a.m. alarm call, the long slog from Richard's Faringdon base to Stansted airport, the 7.10 flight to Dublin, that red Budget rentacar, the Kildare, Portlaoise, Abbeyleix road to Thurles, and the swollen River Suir, had been worth it. The craftsman had done his job. On the way home, he would talk about it. About the need to find a rhythm in the race, and in life itself. 'It's only now I realise just how close to the line I had got,' he says, huge hands on the wheel, the voice very quiet but with its searching intelligence coming through.

'You look at those pictures of Schumacher on the podium after winning the world title and he was ecstatic. Yet after I beat Adrian in '94 [197 winners to 194] I was so drained I felt nothing but relief. Last year's problems were partly the dread of going through all that again. I made the break. I did things I wanted to. Rode in America and in the big Festivals in Ireland. There are Dermot Weld and Edward O'Grady's horses over here and I have some good ones lined up in England. It's going very well.'

The reference to Schumacher reminds you that Emma, Richard's new girlfriend, has been part of the motor rather than the horse racing scene. David Coulthard, rather than David Nicholson, is the type of man he will spend leisure with, no ambitions as a horse-trainer here. It's a wider world and one as a man and as a champion he can well measure up to, even if the mould-breaking sponsorship deal he has with Saab is still a long way short of the millions the Grand Prix drivers draw.

At the airport, the man at the Budget desk recognises him, but not many others do. A genuinely great champion, still to a large part of the public unsung. 'I think there will be other things,' he says with that smile again, 'but for now I want to enjoy the riding while I can.'

---

4 MARCH 2005

PROOF THAT MAN CAN CLEAR ANY OBSTACLE

Marcus Armytage

Paul Carberry is a law unto himself. The week after next he rides Harchibald, favourite for the Champion Hurdle, and Beef Or Salmon, Ireland's best hope of toppling Best Mate in the Cheltenham Gold Cup. The temptation, with such chances in two races he has never won before, might have been to wrap himself in cotton wool. Not Carberry. 'When you wrap yourself up, that's when you get hurt,' he says. On Tuesday and today, as he has done every Tuesday and Friday of the winter, he has been whipping-in with the Ward Union Hunt looking for bigger, wider and deeper obstacles to clear in pursuit of a 'carted' stag – a red deer that comes from a park and is returned there afterwards – across the Meath countryside.

Previous injuries sustained pursuing his passion have included a butt in the stomach from a stag and a chipped vertebra, though this did not stop him winning the first race at the Cheltenham Festival a fortnight later. It was to hunt with the 'Wards' that, after a successful three-year stint in Britain as first jockey to owner Robert Ogden, Carberry returned home where, despite good prize-money, the chances of winning some of it are limited to just three or four days a week. Though champion twice, the job of jockey is verging on part-time. Not for him the commuter status of Ruby Walsh, pursuing successful careers either side of the Irish Sea. Twice a week, Carberry's focus is the lead hounds and how best to keep up with them.

The best way to explore this aspect of the jockey's life is to borrow one of his seven hunters, join him for the meet, at Kilmessan, and confirm that the man really is fearless. But in those parts Carberry is the rule rather than the exception. It's an Ireland thing, why most of our jump jockeys are Irish. With us were about 50 other lunatics, from farmers to housewives, with whom fear just does not register when they are on the back of a horse.

Several people took pride in telling me that the septuagenarian in a flat cap had a picture of himself sitting on the back of his stallion while it covered a mare. Another, Aidan O'Connell, who rode in the Grand National three times as an amateur, wore a top hat, a Champagne-coloured swallow-tail coat with green trimming, green breeches and a red carnation – like something straight out of another century.

Being invited to ride Carberry's hunter, Juicy, is like being on Amberleigh House in the Grand National – almost guaranteed not to fall – but I regretted not having checked the small print of my travel insurance when the first person I was introduced to in the pub beforehand was the local undertaker, who offered his business card. When I hunted with Carberry a year ago he hit the deck twice, and then, before we had jumped an obstacle, one follower had ridden into a tree, gashing his neck badly and just missing his jugular, though to judge by the amount of blood it looked like he had scored a direct hit. I, therefore, approached the first obstacle – an eight-foot bank and ditch with a hedge atop and a dangling loop of wire halfway up the bank – with a mixture of disappointment (that all jugulars were still intact) and trepidation: it resembled a tank trap. Disappointment was short-lived. The first two horses and riders failed to make the top with the partnerships intact. At the second, five were down but, as we warmed up, the loose horse count dropped until we came to a collapsed bridge, where bodies and empty saddles outnumbered survivors.

The amateur jockey Gordon Elliot lost his hat early on in a 'swamp'. 'It was so wet I couldn't have put it back on,' he explained before taking on, hatless, more high-tensile wire with Carberry, and there was I wondering whether I should have been wearing a body-protector. After two hours and ten minutes the stag went to bay in a back garden where, had he arrived two minutes later, the cement-mixing lorry waiting in the drive would have by then delivered. Comedy, they say, is all about timing.

Washing off the horses in a river required us, first, to get to the river. Carberry was straight in through a building site, over a couple of walls that will shortly define the boundaries of some Dublin commuter's bijou kitchen. Carberry, 31, is a man of action rather than words. He is hard to fathom. Horses, and teaching them to jump, are what make him tick. He is not materialistic, just as long as he earns enough to keep him in hunters. He is, arguably, the most natural horseman you will find at next week's Festival.

'Paul is Paul,' trainer Dermot Weld said over Christmas. He had told him not to win too far. After the last, Carberry had taken a pull and won by a short head. 'People don't tend to tell me not to win too far now,' says the jockey who loves that sort of challenge.

Stories of Carberry are legend: of the day a man on his way hunting parked his trailer outside a chemist's shop. While he was in there, Carberry unloaded his horse and rode it into the pub. Of how when one trainer was away he would get his £100,000 two-year-olds jumping large round bales of straw. Of how he swung from the rafters of the winner's enclosure at Aintree when led in after his Grand National triumph on Bobbyjo. These stories, and his reputation as a party animal and something of a head-banger, all suggest an extrovert, but he seems quite the opposite. 'A bit mad but in no way a fool,' says Tony McCoy with admiration. 'Less harum-scarum than he used to be,' says Harchibald's trainer, Noel Meade.

Carberry is not influenced by what other people think and he is not showy. His antics do not require an audience. He will take a young hunter out, on his own, and just ride it in a straight line, jumping anything in his path. Spending a day with him no more scratches the surface than a briar whipping your face atop one of those Meath banks. In a world where the successful modern sportsman is expected to lead the life of a Trappist monk, Carberry does not bow to convention.

22 FEBRUARY 2003

HOUSE GUEST WALSH TRACKS CHAMPION'S EVERY MOVE

Sue Mott

An off-duty jockey is a creature of strange and sprawling bonelessness. So Ruby Walsh was at full sag yesterday morning, awaiting the results of ground inspections at Warwick and Kempton Park. He lay across a couch at Tony McCoy's house near Lambourn. McCoy himself was predictably and deeply asleep upstairs, despite the hammering, drilling, sanding and banging of two workmen on the premises. Now, you are not talking stately home here. The table decoration in the dining room consisted of a set of shinpads and the garden looked like – and was – a ploughed field. But the living room in which Walsh has ensconced himself is an accidental shrine to its owner. Cups, trophies, more Waterford Crystal than a flower arranging class at the Women's Institute: the unmistakable swag of a champion.

Walsh wasn't the least put out. He has trophies himself, albeit a smaller collection on a smaller set of shelves in his 'humble abode' near Kilkenny. But he is not intimidated. The boy who won the Grand National at 19 on a 10–1 horse trained by his father has already experienced one of the miracles of sport. 'It wasn't realistic, was it? All I was looking for was a safe, fun ride. I never dreamed he'd win it, Papillon. Ah, it was the greatest day of my life.'

If he wasn't McCoy's friend, he might be his stalker. They talk in glowing terms of the racer in Walsh. He is not Ruby red for stop, that is for sure. Last year at the Cheltenham Festival he won as many races as McCoy – one – and the similarities do not end there. They are fiendish horsemen, Irish, determined and regularly liable to win. 'Hah! It's a fictional rivalry,' said Walsh, indulging in a little modest fiction himself. 'I don't feel it at all. There are better riders than me. There's a list of them. People pick me out and I don't know why. Obviously he's the best. We all have to raise our standards to equal McCoy.'

Walsh is the younger man by five years. When McCoy was closing in on the first of his seven champion jockey titles, Walsh was being concussed by a butt from Commanche Court as a temporary stable lad at Cheltenham. You still cannot talk in strict terms of parity. But Walsh has the look, the style and the reputation of a serious challenger.

It is most annoying that they are on such good terms. A Tysonesque feud would be much more dramatically satisfying. Instead Walsh is saying: 'It's very good of him to have me at his house', having stayed the night in the frost-bitten confusion of cancelled race meetings. Walsh is possibly exaggerating the compliment intended by the champion. He has everyone to stay. Gee Armytage, his manager, finds stray individuals in the kitchen all the time making tea, toast and free with the facilities. McCoy would probably have his horses in for the night, given the opportunity.

So he and Walsh share a laugh and a roof and the most brutal-natured sport man has yet devised. But they are not of a similar temperament. 'I don't know,' said Walsh, thinking about it. 'I've never thought about it. But, erm, I don't think we are. He's very enthusiastic about winning. But then I like to think I am, too.' He was being diplomatic. McCoy is famous for being grimly mad about winning. At last year's Cheltenham, he endured the desperate tragedy of his wonderhorse being killed after a mystery fall in the Champion Hurdle. Grief and fury fused and the champion went into an introverted silence. He was roundly criticised. But Walsh understood. 'Put it this way, if Commanche Court had broken his neck on his way down the hill to win the Gold Cup, I don't think you'd have got much talking out of me for a week. There's more to this game than winning and putting on a smile. That doesn't make a hero. It's more personal.'

So when Walsh's sole win of Cheltenham 2002 (alongside three seconds, two thirds and two fourths) was at the expense of McCoy on a cast-off stable-mate that McCoy could have chosen to ride in the Mildmay of Flete, he appreciated the irony. 'Look, there's no love lost coming down the hill. Everyone is there to win. Friendship goes out of the window. Temporarily.'

McCoy rode off without any public sign of congratulation. But he shook the victor's hand in the locker-room later. Racing is like trench warfare. There is little point in being antagonistic to those on the same side in similar, imminent danger. McCoy once kept quiet about a broken leg and continued to pull on his riding boots. Walsh broke a leg in 1999, came back far too soon, reopened the fracture and soon after won the National with an obstructive lump of scar tissue inside his right boot. They all have gruesome stories, the jockeys, which they tell with detached and marvellous relish. 'I went to Czechoslovakia to ride in their big cross-country race. I was in a prep race just to get a feel of the track. I got a feel of it, all right. I was swinging into the straight and you know the white rails you have at a racecourse – joined together like gutter – well, one of the joins was open. I came on and hit the round pipe full on with my leg. My bone broke with one snap. I came off four strides later. It was agony. But that's the joys of racing,' he said laconically.

And so is this: the lead-up to Cheltenham, less than three weeks away. Anything can happen: accidents to horse, accidents to rider, suspensions, sackings, failures of nerve, failures of fan belt on the horsebox. This is a tricky, electric time when Walsh will use his whip conspicuously less than usual and take special note of magpies. He is not in the least superstitious, he insists, but a man charged with riding at least two or three fancied horses cannot afford to take chances. The exact count is unclear. Thanks to an unusual pooling of his great talent among his father, Ted, Willie Mullins, the Irish trainer, and the West Country-based trainer, Paul Nicholls, Walsh is not entirely clear of his mounts. And why bother to worry? 'Adrian Maguire was booked to ride Florida Pearl in the Gold Cup last year and look what happened to him,' he said. Indeed, the fall suffered by Maguire leading up to last year's Cheltenham broke his neck and very nearly his heart by pitching him into early retirement. Put it this way, not many jockeys wear ostentatious plasters and Alice bands to show off their latest cuts and bruises.

But if Walsh is pushed he will show you the corner of a card held still close to his chest. 'I'm hopeless at tipping,' he said by way of preface. 'I always put the mockers on my horses. So I prefer to talk about somebody else's and put the mockers on them instead.' Still, he likes the French-bred Azertyuiop (named after the top row of a keyboard, as arranged in France). 'He has an outstanding chance in the Arkle. I've ridden his last three runs. He's won all three. He's jumped very well, he's extremely quick, he knows Cheltenham. He's athletic and intelligent.' Walsh's instructions to himself on the horse are pretty simple. 'Steer.'

His father, who won four times at Cheltenham, gave him the advice as a child that he still carries into the weighing room as a 23-year-old professional. 'Sit quiet, sit in deep, try not to interfere.' His horses seem to wear him. His long legs fold around them, a picture of synchronised will. Ted Walsh always made his son watch Richard Dunwoody. 'Very, very strong and very, very stylish.' And very, very ruthless. 'Ah, there's a difference to being ruthless on a horse and carrying it off the racecourse with you. You don't have to be ruthless to win.' His schooling, however, was hardly gentle. Ted Walsh sent him out as a teenager to jump nearly every obstacle he could find in County Kildare and County Limerick. 'Hedges, drains, banks, walls, ditches. I'd jump them high as I could find. Falling off didn't matter. I had my first fall pretty much as soon as I had my first ride.'

His first Cheltenham memory goes back to 1986, when he remembers sitting on the floor at home, aged six, watching his father win his last race at Cheltenham before promising his wife on the phone that he was retiring from racing. So then he trained. Horses are wired into the Walsh family genealogy. His grandfather, Ruby, was a trainer. His great grandfather, as far as he knows, was a horse trader from County Cork. Every fence Ruby Junior goes over at Cheltenham could be construed as a genetic leap. His first victory was as an amateur in the bumper on Alexander Banquet in 1998. A year later he was second in the Triumph Hurdle. In 2000 he was third in the Hurdle. Last year was the victory on Blowing Wind. Whether the rate of progress continues is down to skill, luck and the same indomitable will that governs his temporary landlord.

The late news came in. Warwick was off. Kempton was on. So together they piled into McCoy's mud-ridden BMW with the shy M6COY number plates and set about their latest day's work. Walsh came second in the first. McCoy had three winners and a fall. 'Ah,' you could almost hear Walsh saying, 'the joys of racing.'

---

28 MARCH 1971

MAKING OF A CHAMPION

Geoff Lewis, the man most likely to knock Lester Piggott off his throne this season, is reminiscent of Gordon Richards at his best, says John Lawrence

With Nijinsky safe in his Kentucky harem, the Flat racing season which began last week, has only one unquestioned reigning champion. He is, of course, Lester Piggott and the bookmakers, influenced perhaps by the recent fate of such fallen idols as Cassius Clay, Henry Cooper and Persian War, make him only an even-money shot to retain the title he has held for the past seven years. There is at least one place in England – a light and airy red brick house less than two miles from Tattenham Corner – where those odds are considered pretty generous. And this opinion is worth noticing, because the house belongs to Geoff Lewis who, according to the bookies and almost everyone else in racing, is the man most likely to knock Lester off his throne.

In appearance, in manner and in many of their attitudes to life the champion and his challenger could scarcely be more different. Lester Piggott's face, pale, ascetic, almost tragic, might have come straight from an El Greco canvas, but Geoff Lewis's, irrepressibly cheerful and almost chubby by contrast, would be much more at home on one by Franz Hals. It is the sort of laughing Cockney face Norman Wisdom would be glad to borrow – a face, which, except for the thicket of greying hair above it, you wouldn't be surprised to find on a page boy in a posh London hotel.

Which, in fact, is precisely where it was 17 years ago when Tim Molony, then champion jumping jockey of Great Britain, noticed a stocky figure, complete with smart blue buttons, as he passed through the front door of the Waldorf. 'You're the right shape to make a jockey,' he said – and remembering the moment now, Geoff Lewis laughs. 'I suppose I must say the same thing to about a dozen boys a year. You just say it and walk away. But perhaps it means a lot to them – or anyway it did to me.'

Geoff is one of 13 children, with nine sisters and three brothers – 'Talk about women's liberation, they had us *surrounded*' – and his father, a London builder, was none too keen on the notion of racing as a career. 'If you don't make it you'll come back here aged 20 and trained for nothing,' he warned – and the sad fact is that for every successful Flat race jockey there are an awful lot of boys who learn the hard way how right he was.

But Geoff hated his life as a page boy. The stammer which is now an attractive and barely noticeable hesitation except in moments of great excitement was then a full-scale impediment to his speech and it made the job a nightmare. 'With my size and weight,' he says, 'there seemed to be only one alternative.' And so at the age of 15, still weighing well under five stone soaking wet, he handed in his uniform at the Waldorf and set forth for Epsom to be bound apprentice to Ron Smyth, himself a former champion National Hunt jockey and then, as now, a successful trainer of both jumpers and Flat race horses.

Having at that time never so much as fallen off a seaside donkey, Geoff Lewis had a fair amount of leeway to make up on the men who are now his contemporaries, rivals and friends. By the time he rode his first winners in 1953, Lester Piggott (who is only two months older) had ridden well over 200, and Joe Mercer, though still an apprentice, won the Oaks that year on Ambiguity. At that time, what's more, Geoff's chance of even setting out on the same golden road seemed far from certain to materialise. Or rather it seemed all too possible that he had missed it. Because the year before, riding a supposed certainty at Lewes, he had been told, on pain of dire penalties, not in any circumstances to strike the front before the final furlong. 'Well, they crawled for half a mile, and there I am, yanking the poor bloody thing's back teeth out to stay behind, when suddenly, whoosh, off they go and leave me 50 yards.' He can smile now, but then, hauled before the stewards to explain his tactics and offered practically no more rides that season, it must have seemed to a nervous 17-year-old stable lad the end of the world.

Perhaps partly because of that painful memory Geoff, like most jockeys worth the name, dislikes being tied down too firmly before a race. 'The best guv'nors are the ones who give the fewest orders,' he says – and in that as in many other respects his ideal of the perfect man to ride for was the late Captain Peter Hastings-Bass. 'Give him a chance, come the shortest way, and if you get shut in, well, never mind – there'll always be another day.' To a young jockey riding good horses for the first time, as Geoff was when he went to Kingsclere in 1959, those are the perfect orders. 'They give you the confidence to sit and wait, and in this business confidence is more than half the battle.'

But it can easily be shattered – by good horses as well as bad ones – and as it happened Captain Hastings-Bass's untimely death in 1964 coincided with the appearance of the best – and most difficult – horse Geoff Lewis had up to then been asked to ride. His name was Silly Season and, though brilliant at two and three when he finished second in the 2,000 Guineas and won the Champion Stakes, he became, as a four-year-old, the original jockey's night-mare. The trouble was that, though ready and able to pass almost any rival, Silly Season then took the view that he had done enough and, quite irre-spective of anything his jockey might do, stopped as though caught in quick-sand. When such a horse starts hot favourite for an important race – as Silly Season did repeatedly in 1966 – the strain on his rider is more than doubled. Complex problems of horsemanship and split-second judgment are not widely appreciated among the average racecourse crowd, and when things go wrong – as they often did with Silly Season – the air is filled with cries of wounded punters baying blindly for the jockey's blood. 'He came just a bit too early for me,' Geoff says of Silly Season. 'I think I could handle him now, but I simply didn't have the confidence in those days.'

'Confidence' – the word recurs continually when Geoff Lewis talks about his riding life, but last week, watching him unpack five brand new saddles just arrived from Australia (he buys a new set every year and gives the old ones away) I got the strong impression that self-doubt is no longer one of his problems, if it ever was. Even now he gives himself no more than just a fair chance of becoming champion this season – and reckons both Joe Mercer and Frankie Durr much more feasible 'outsiders' than the bookmakers appear to. But an invitation to ride Noel Murless's horses is the biggest compliment an English jockey can be paid, and to Geoff Lewis, I suspect, it means a great deal more than just the chance to earn a lot of money.

For the Silly Season saga was not the only crisis of confidence in his career. Another, even worse, came in the second half of 1969, when for an agonising period nothing would go right on the horses that really mattered. It began with a disastrous Eclipse Stakes at Sandown, in which Geoff, on the red-hot favourite Park Top, was beaten by Lester Piggott on Wolver Hollow. 'I just didn't want to come back in after that one,' he says. 'If there had been a hole in the ground I'd have gone down it.' In fact, under orders again not to hit the front too soon, he had quite understandably waited a bit too long on Park Top, and while he searched in vain for an opening, Piggott stole calmly through along the rail. The critics (this one included) had a field day, and to rub salt in the wound Lester proceeded to win the King George VI and Queen

Elizabeth Stakes on Park Top, with a ride universally hailed at the time as a perfect example of his genius.

In fact, as Geoff says without a trace of bitterness, it was really a perfect example of how luck favours the man in form. Dead last on the inside rail turning into the short Ascot straight, Lester should by rights have been in a distinctly awkward position – when a French jockey, dropping one rein as he went for his whip, let his horse run wide, taking the whole field with him and leaving a gap on the rails wide enough for 20 Park Tops. 'And that Lester,' Geoff remembers, 'all he said when he came in was "the so and so dropped his rein, would you believe it, he dropped his *rein*".'

Park Top was only the first of Geoff's misfortunes that year, for after winning the Irish Derby brilliantly on Prince Regent he had a bad run on the same horse in the Arc de Triomphe, and a nightmare ride on the notoriously unmanoeuvrable Gyr. Etienne Pollet, who trained them both, 'jocked him off' as a result and what might have been a tremendous season ended in doubt and gloom.

But gloom doesn't fit Geoff Lewis very well and despite all these ups and downs his style of riding, steadily developing over the years and more reminiscent of Sir Gordon Richards at his best than any other living jockey, is now a technically perfect example of the English method. Broad-shouldered and short in the leg, he looks like a successful boxer (which as a stable lad he was) and in a tight finish is the absolute embodiment of strength and determination scientifically, and above all rhythmically, applied.

Though married to the daughter of the famous Australian jockey Jim Munro, and a great friend and admirer of Scobie Breasley and Bill Williamson, Geoff has not borrowed any of their methods. 'If I sat as still as Scobie used to and got beat,' he says, 'I'd always think I hadn't done enough – though mind you *he* got every ounce out of them. But I just like to work on a horse, that's all.' Well, this season, barring accidents, he will have plenty to work on – the 2,000 Guineas and Derby favourite Mill Reef ('the best horse I've ridden, and pretty sure, in my opinion, to stay the Derby distance') and the pick of Noel Murless's, John Sutcliffe's and Ian Balding's powerful stables. It looks a tremendously strong hand, and there are two more important factors tipping the scales for Geoff and against Lester Piggott. One is that he rides abroad much less than the champion and another is his weight – a fairly comfortable eight stone one or two.

There is a sauna bath in the garden of Lewis's house, but though he uses it a good deal his diet compared with Lester Piggott's is positively lavish. 'I'm dead lucky that way,' he says. 'I just don't know how Lester does it.' This last is typical of the perfectly genuine admiration Geoff Lewis feels for his great rival – and typical of the man himself. Gay, courageous and generous (when interviewed on television he invariably gives his fee to charity), Geoff Lewis will, if he wins the championship, adorn it. Looking at a newspaper headline last week, 'Why I can beat Lester', he said ruefully: 'I wish I felt as confident as they make me sound.' But with two winners at Doncaster he's off to a flying start and if all goes well this season all I know for certain is that it couldn't happen to a nicer man.

---

21 MARCH 1985

CAUTHEN READY TO ASSERT SUPREMACY

Tony Stafford

For the past three decades, the riding exploits of Lester Piggott have dominated the thoughts of racing enthusiasts, even to the exclusion of such exceptionally gifted rivals as Willie Carson, Pat Eddery and Joe Mercer. But there is a strong possibility that for the second half of the 1980s, and probably a considerable time after, a new supreme talent will take over, one with extra dimensions which even the 11-times champion could not equal. Fittingly, Steve Cauthen, the 1984 champion jockey, follows Piggott as stable jockey to champion trainer Henry Cecil at Newmarket.

By the end of the year, a hitherto unsuspecting public will come to appreciate the many attributes of this gifted young American. Cauthen, still only 24, has a track record of six steadily-progressing seasons with Barry Hills's stable, following two years' unprecedented success as an apprentice in the United States. Few 24-year-olds could boast such extraordinary success in two such different and demanding environments, and Cauthen has already acquired maturity beyond his years.

'It's just the effect of growing older,' he says, without extending the line of argument to the fact that he was still young enough at the beginning of the last year's championship season to have been classed as an apprentice had he not recorded the small matter of 487 victories in 1977. Such is his maturity that jockeys much more senior in years and experience turn to him to express their views publicly. 'That's one nice thing about the weighing room here,' he says. 'Lester's getting on, and anyway he keeps himself to himself. Some of the other lads find it less easy to express themselves, so gradually they've tended to look upon me as something of a spokesman when the occasion arises.'

It is easy to see why. Cauthen speaks freely, eloquently and easily and takes great pains to help keep the press informed. 'I try to be available whenever possible. Obviously, from time to time people try to manufacture stories and then I'm less happy about it, but generally I believe it's in all our interests to publicise the sport. As television coverage of racing is reduced, it falls on professionals inside the sport to keep the names of the top horses, trainers and jockeys in the minds of the public. Then it's much more likely that when they can get to a good meeting, they'll come along and help boost attendances. Without them, racing can't get very far,' he says.

The Kentucky-born Cauthen has been very much in the public eye since he went to the small country racetrack of River Downs soon after his 16th birthday and rode the first of many winners in his short, two-year stint in the United States. 'Before then, that was my whole ambition, to ride a winner at River Downs. But obviously, once the winners came along it was all very exciting and I just got swept along with it,' he says. 'Jockeys back home cannot ride in public before their 16th birthday, and even working on the track is not strictly allowed. But the people down there got to know me and turned a blind eye.

'It all started four years earlier. I decided when I was 12 years old to be a jockey and went to my father, who said if that's what I wanted to do, he'd support me. I worked at it day after day – yes, those stories about me practising on hay bales in the barn are all true – and I'm afraid things like school, where I'd been two grades above the level for my age, took second place. But after those two years, exciting as they were with 487 winners in a year and the Triple Crown on Affirmed, I was beginning to feel the effects of being on the treadmill. In the United States racing is a 365-days-a-year business. You get into the position where even if you need a weekend off, you can't take one, because someone else will be in for your best rides.'

Most people in the United States, amazed at Cauthen's decision to accept Robert Sangster's offer to ride in Britain at the beginning of the 1979 season, took the fact that he had recently gone through a losing sequence of more than 100 as the major factor. 'It wasn't that at all,' says Cauthen. 'I knew Robert Sangster owned one of the largest strings of top horses in the world and was thrilled at the chance to ride for him. Also, when I was younger I'd read about such great jockeys as Steve Donoghue and Sir Gordon Richards and was keen to see the racing scene in England.'

Within a month of his first ride over here, Cauthen had already won a Classic, the 2,000 Guineas on Tap On Wood. 'It was marvellous to win the race for Barry Hills. He's an emotional man and a great friend, and I'll never forget the look on his face when I came in to unsaddle. A sort of "I've shown them" look.' Though Cauthen is now Henry Cecil's stable jockey, he will still ride for Hills on occasions, and could well get off the mark for the new season today on the Lambourn trainer's Poquito Queen. But however soon the young champion gets going, there are few people prepared to bet against his repeating last year's championship success. And few indeed who could claim that the United States had sent out a better sporting ambassador.

------

9 NOVEMBER 2003

A FINAL PAT ON THE BACK

Brough Scott

Just before Pat Eddery loaded up into the stalls for the very last time, a rabbit ran out from underneath an advertising hoarding and sprinted towards the winning post. Eddery's mount, Gamut, was odds-on favourite, but after 37 years and 4,632 winners, one more conjuring trick was too much to ask. Eleven championships, three Derbies, four Arcs de Triomphe, 73 Royal Ascot victories, not to mention 28 seasonal centuries, count for nothing to the horse you walk towards when the mounting bell rings.

Pat's first partner, Rio Branco, had never been to the racecourse in her life before, and it showed. She was a tiny two-year-old filly with a woolly winter coat trace-clipped along her neck. As she left the paddock she jumped right, like a startled cat. Many a younger jockey would tighten the reins with a twinge of terror. Pat stayed limpet-still in the saddle, reached out his right hand for a reassuring stroke on the shoulder and set Rio Branco off towards the very first start of her career. She didn't do at all badly, running on to be seventh after being baffled when the stalls had opened.

Understanding horses has been at the heart of Pat's genius. When he first came to Frenchie Nicholson's Cheltenham stables back in 1967 – and I was around to remember – it was immediately obvious that here was a seal in water, a man, or rather a neat, smiling, child-faced 16-year-old, in his element. He did not ride a winner that first year, but by the time Alvaro started off the 4,500 flood that day at Epsom in April 1969, it was already clear that this was a talent that could get a tune out of all sorts of four-legged fiddles.

But not, yesterday, out of a big rather common-looking chestnut called Colourful Life whose career so far has included successes over both hurdles and fences but never yet on the Flat. The booking of Eddery on his bow-out day encouraged many punters and, one rather suspects, the owners to think the omission could now be rectified. Colourful Life looked like a carthorse compared to little Rio Branco, but he thundered round close to the leaders and looked a possible winner until appearing to lose his action and hanging badly in towards the rails in the straight. As he galumphed, hind legs swinging awkwardly, past the post back in ninth place, another Eddery dream was over.

There have been countless such reverses over the years and not all of them washed easily over the connections. This one did not yesterday. Colourful Life was led back to unsaddle, the jockey dismounted, pulled the elastic girths out to unbuckle and turned to explain about the problems in the straight before ducking under the rails and scuttling back to the weighing room. The large owner clamped a phone to his ear and said: 'That was the worst f****** ride I have ever seen.'

Such a hilariously downbeat cameo was almost matched when Eddery contested much of the running on the Martin Pipe favourite Chubbes in the next, only to be summoned by the stewards and formally cautioned for excessive use of the whip. Fears that this might be breached into a full-scale suspension if Gamut got into a slogging match for Eddery's final ride, were sadly alleviated three furlongs from the finish when it became clear that the odds-on favourite was never going to have the zip to reel in the front-running Scott's View. It was a bad result for conspiracy theorists. This race would surely have been fixed. Instead Pat came back to affectionate cheers while Scott's View's rider Joe Fanning had to put up with a round of good-natured booing.

So it was over, four decades of Eddery in the saddle, of the master craftsman who rode in the best sustained duel (Grundy-Bustino) and the best sling-shot waiting race (Dancing Brave's Arc) that I have seen. He could be as brilliant and happy winning a selling race at Salisbury as masterminding something as big time as El Gran Senor's epic 2,000 Guineas run at Newmarket. He may have been bumping and unorthodox in a finish, but over the years he was a pillar of sustained excellence unmatched in the Flat race field.

Easy, genial and modest in private, he was almost Piggott-style monosyllabic in public and beside some generous thanks to those who had supported him he wasn't any different at Doncaster. The jockeys gathered for an unsaddling enclosure presentation which was almost immediately reduced to chaos when Dettori and Duffield disgraced their seniority by producing foam sprays from their breeches and coating their departing idol. Back in the weighing room it apparently got worse, Eddery's socks, scarf, even underpants being cut to pieces, cream cakes put in his shoes. After five minutes Pat had somehow brushed himself down, said his goodbyes and with no ceremony slipped out the backdoor into the night and his new life running an owning operation from his stud farm in Buckinghamshire.

Meanwhile, a slightly weird-looking gentleman with lank hair, dark glasses and a cap, on which was emblazoned the statement 'Kevin – Pat Eddery's No.

1 Fan' – waited stoically for an autograph. After each race he had mistakenly rushed up only to be swatted away as Eddery ran to the weighing room. Alas, poor Kevin, let's hope he hasn't been trying this for 37 years. Treasure the memories, but put yesterday in the comedy tray.

---

10 AUGUST 2003

RIDING HIGH AS AN EDDERY IS NO CERTAINTY IN RACING

Andrew Alderson

Under a bright evening sun, Paul Eddery is returning to the racetrack where he rode his first winner – a horse called Tufu – 24 years ago. Times have changed. Wolverhampton's grass track has been replaced by an all-weather surface and the jockey has lost the knack of riding winners for the first time in his career. As Paul's older brother, Pat, prepares to retire this year after a glorious career and more than 4,600 winners, the younger Eddery is facing lean days. When he arrived at Wolverhampton for his sole ride at the meeting (and his first of the week), Paul, who like his brother was once one of the country's leading jockeys, faced the ignominy of having no winners from 133 rides this season.

At the age of 40, he also figured all too prominently in the *Racing Post's* list of 'cold' jockeys: he had gone 306 days and 158 rides since his last winner. After 75 seconds of action in the six-furlong opener, those figures had both gone up by one: Bonny Ruan, Paul's 20–1 mount, faded to finish eighth of 13 runners. Within 15 minutes of passing the winning post, Paul had changed from his racing silks into a pink short-sleeved shirt and navy trousers. As he sat on a wooden bench outside the paddock bar, he spoke of his hopes of rejuvenating his career when he is the only member of the famous racing family still riding next year.

He retains his love of racing: on Wednesday, after getting up at 6.30 a.m. to ride work, he embarked on a four-hour, 300-mile round trip from Newmarket to the Midlands for one ride that paid £75.60. Paul, who now books his own rides, has no plans to follow Pat into retirement. Yet racing is a cruel sport: when the winners dry up so do the good mounts. 'It's my longest run without a winner, but that's racing. I think I am riding as well now as ever. If I start riding winners, who knows what is around the corner?'

He was born in Dublin on 14 July, 1963, the second youngest of 12 children. Racing was in his blood. His father, Jimmy, had been champion jockey in Ireland and his maternal grandfather, Jack Moylan, had been a leading jump jockey who had ridden the runner-up in the 1928 Grand National. All six brothers — John, Michael, Pat, Robert, Paul and David — have ridden either on the Flat or over jumps, but all bar Pat and Paul have now retired. Paul first sat on a race-horse at the age of seven and, after moving to England aged 12, used to ride out when he was at school. He shone more on the gallops than in the class-room and, at 16, began an apprenticeship with Reg Hollinshead: a four-year stint from 1979 that gave him some of his fondest memories.

Because of their age difference — Pat left home at 16 when Paul was five — the brothers were never close. And, though Pat has few peers as a jockey, he has never been a great communicator. So when Paul started in racing, Pat, already a four-time champion jockey, was everything but helpful. 'When we were first in the weighing room together, he didn't speak to me. Pat had started off fending for himself and he thought it was right that I should have to do the same,' said Paul, who is divorced with a 12-year-old son, Charles, who is already showing promise as a jockey.

Paul left Hollinshead's yard to become second jockey for Henry Cecil, then the country's leading trainer. He spent his first year as understudy to Lester Piggott, his second as understudy to Steve Cauthen. 'It was a great two years and a time when Mr Cecil was winning just about everything,' said Paul. 'Lester was a legend and, although he didn't say much, you learnt from just watching him. Steve was one of the nicest jockeys I have met: an absolute gentleman.'

In 1986, Paul took up an offer as first jockey to Peter Walwyn, succeeding another racing legend, Joe Mercer. He rode a Royal Ascot winner — one of four in all — for the stable, but he was not retained for a second year. Since then the quietly spoken jockey has ridden as a freelance. He has often been the 'nearly man' in a career that has brought more than 1,000 winners worldwide. In the late Eighties he often rode for Geoff Wragg, including Most Welcome who finished second in the 1987 Derby. When opportunities dried up in the Nineties, he adopted a 'have saddle, will travel' approach to his career. He has ridden in Macau, Malaysia, Mauritius, Australia, Hong Kong, Germany, Italy, Spain, Austria and India (where he enjoyed a four-month stint this winter).

Paul, who rides at eight stone two, is full of admiration for Pat, who is retiring after being champion jockey 11 times in a career spanning 37 seasons. Pat is second in the all-time list of British winners after Sir Gordon Richards. Without a hint of jealousy, Paul, who now lives with his girlfriend, Charlotte Fitsall, outside Newmarket, said: 'Pat has had the sort of career that most jockeys only dream about. I may not have had his success, but I have ridden some big winners, seen the world and I can't complain. Racing will give me up before I give it up.' Whereas most brothers drift apart, Pat and Paul have become closer. Indeed, the younger Eddery now looks upon his older brother as his best friend in racing. 'I'll miss Pat when he's no longer riding,' said Paul. 'And I'll miss those lifts to meetings in his private plane even more!'

---

8 JUNE 2001

FEAR OF NOT WINNING DRIVES MURTAGH

Sue Mott

Just over a year ago, the jockey Johnny Murtagh thought he had lost the will to win. Thirteen of his mounts came second. It seemed like an equine conspiracy. What do you do? He went to the doctor, though a vet might have been more to the point. The doctor sent him to a sports psychologist in Dublin and the rest is extraordinary personal history.

'So after crying with him for half an hour, telling him what was going wrong and how I'd lost, he says, "You haven't lost the will to win, you've lost the will to work".'

Murtagh revamped himself. New agent, new masseur, new diet, new fitness regime. He focused his fathomless blue eyes on the winning post and promptly won the Derby on Sinndar. Followed by the Irish Derby, the Irish Oaks, the Yorkshire Oaks, the Arc, the Dubai Champion Stakes, Newmarket, the *Racing Post* Trophy, Doncaster, the Breeders' Cup and a Blue Riband race in Japan. Twelve Group One races in all. It seemed that Dame Fortune rejoiced in his character reformation and deposited all her eggs in one basket case.

For a religious man it seemed entirely apt that he could thread a horse through the eye of a needle, as he did in the Breeders' Cup Turf in Kentucky last November, when he converted ninth off the bend on the Aga Khan's Kalanisi into steel-nerved, find-the-gap, opportunistic victory. He never forgets what Willie Shoemaker once told him: 'If you lose your head, your ass goes with it.' He knows that. At 31, he has a chequered past, or at least one big, black square circa 1993–94 when alcohol, disillusion and going missing from Leopardstown conspired to send him to a clinic. It was a mental squeal of brakes on the limo ride to fame and fortune and he is utterly sick with discussion on this sore subject.

'Oh I know it makes a good story. But it's history now,' he said evenly, unblinkingly, and ever-so-quietly intimidatingly. 'Well, I just feel it was years ago. Maybe for young people reading it, it might help. But I don't want people thinking, "Poor Johnny".' Fat chance. Secure amid his gorgeous 25 acres alongside The Curragh racecourse, with wife Orla, three children and a very small dog called Tito, not many people would consider sympathy the appropriate response. He can even watch MTV on television from his sauna. 'I sit there for an hour watching Geri Halliwell dance about,' he said, and I don't think he meant it as a penance. 'I'll tell you what,' said Orla, clutching four-month-old Lauren in one hand, doing the ironing with the other and grinning with mischievous conspiracy. 'Last year he was kissed by the Queen Mother, kissed by Naomi Campbell, and I got pregnant again. So he must be doing something right!'

So all is well for the builder's son from County Meath, even if he is not on Sir Michael Stoute's favourite, Golan, for Saturday's Derby, that privilege falling to Pat Eddery in the wake of Kieren Fallon's fall-out with the stewards at Ayr and subsequent short, sharp ban. You might think that Murtagh would be spitting private furballs of fury that he is not on the horse he calls the new Nijinksy. Instead, he teams up again with Dilshaan, on whom he won the *Racing Post* Trophy last October, and is expressive of nothing but pure pleasure. 'I am sure delighted for Pat and delighted for myself just to get a ride, especially on a horse as tough, consistent and rock-solid as Dilshaan.' The burning eyes betray not a flicker of disagreement with the words. This is either polite lying or generous truth, and the latter is not as unlikely as you think.

Murtagh is a man who has seen beyond the parameters of a horse's backside. Last year, in the wake of his Midas-touch success, when he might have basked in his new-found wealth and contentment, he went instead to Zambia as part of a Catholic charity mission.

'It changed me. It was a humbling experience. When you're on a bit of a high, when you think you're a bit special, you realise how many things you take for granted.' Like food. Fresh air instead of the smell of death. Fresh water instead of their malarial supplies. 'I'm religious. God's been good to me. I wanted to go out there as a kind of "thank you". What we were trying to do was not just to feed them for a day or two, but to establish a school to educate them, a workshop with sewing machines so the ladies could make clothes for their kids, crops to grow their own food.'

The education, however, went both ways. 'The first night, we stayed at the Lusaka Hilton, and then we went to stay at the mission. Lying on the bed was like lying on that.' He pointed to the table in his sitting room. 'Hard. I saw things that made me very sad. We visited a hospice. Ten men and ten women who had just gone there to die, on their last legs because of Aids. What really struck me is how much we take for granted. Just to have a chair would be something to these people. We complain because we think we have a TV that's not wide enough, or a car that's not big enough. These people have nothing. And yet they were happy. That's one thing that really shocked me. They were very happy and yet they had nothing. People in the Western world have everything and they are still not happy. I now realise I'm very lucky. I've a nice job, nice family, nice house. I couldn't wish for anything else.'

This sounds like a dangerous contentment for a professional aggressor. Perhaps coming second doesn't matter any more. 'Coming second matters,' he replied. It was a statement of fact. Competitive instinct, the one he thought he had lost, is a natural phenomenon in his case. He had two younger sisters for a start, which develops mettle in a boy, and swiftly became fiercely good at football, boxing and basketball. Basketball? 'They were all my size when I was ten.' It was boxing, however, at which he became schoolboy Irish champion. There is no trace of this bloody heritage on his youthful face today. No broken nose, no nibbled ear, all his teeth intact. He met Frank Bruno once at an awards reception and the former British heavyweight was genuinely amazed that he should have escaped unscathed. 'He said, "Jeez, you don't look like a boxer. No scars". I said, "I was a good boxer, Frank".'

All this time growing up and barely a horse in sight. His cousin had a pony that they might ride bareback for a lark ('you didn't have saddles where I came from'), and his father once took him for one lesson (unrepeated). But until he arrived at jockeys' apprentice school, aged 15, he had no contact nor affinity with the sport that would make him famous enough to have his picture taken alongside Sir Alex Ferguson, Steve Davis and the Queen Mother (see noticeboard in his household gym). He clearly remembers his first ride, out of John Oxx's Killarney stable in 1987 at Phoenix Park. Perhaps clearly is not quite the right description. 'Keen Note. Filly owned by Sheikh Mohammed. The whole day was just … it's all over before you know it. It was a sprint. Six furlongs. Seventy seconds. It takes the first ten or 12 rides before you realise what's going on.'

And to be thoroughly shaken by the senior jockeys, who take unkindly to whippersnappers clipping their heels and trying to barge through spaces that are the figments of their youthful, excitable imaginations. 'It used to be the unofficial disciplinary system but it's not there any more, because the apprentices are as big as the jockeys.'

He regards it as a tough life, but mentally rather than physically. It is the fear of not winning that drives him, not the potential damage to his looks. 'It's pretty ruthless, everyone's out to get what they can. If the hunger goes away, that's when you're gone. I'm a family man but when you put on those colours it's every man for himself. But I'm not a ruthless exterminator, I don't think. I always try my best. But I wouldn't do harm to anyone else. It's too dangerous. Behind all this rivalry are very good friendships and respect. If you don't look after the guy beside you, serious things can happen. It can be fatal. At lot can happen at 40 m p h. It's not just a kick in the ankle, like a footballer. It's a bit like being in the trenches together.'

You gain a glimpse of why his best friend in the sport is Frankie Dettori, fellow sparklers, high achievers and diet victims. Murtagh is probably the only man who has been to Africa and put on a stone and a half, so stringent is his starvation during the season. He yearns almost permanently for steak, chips, beans and onion rings. But the discipline is as iron as his muscle these days. He would love to vault into an orbit similar to Dettori, for his own and racing's sake. 'Frankie gets people interested in the sport. It's not all doom and gloom. It's not crooked. It's not gangsters. Sure, people had to pull a few tricks in the old days, but now the prize money is so good they don't have to.' With this ringing endorsement, he leapt to his feet. I thought he was going to make a speech. Instead – and it is a tribute to his good manners that he hadn't mentioned it before – he announced: 'I have to go to the toilet,' and ran from the room like Nijinksy.

---

21 JUNE 2003

I NEEDED HELP YEARS AGO

Sue Mott

Kieren Fallon is living a fairytale. But a gothic fairytale, full of as many trolls and gargoyles as it is of the sparkly types waving magic wands. He won the Derby earlier this month, the Ascot Gold Cup on Thursday and, given the places he has been, the life he has led, the fierce battles he has fought, the victories constitute a pretty good impersonation of happy ever after. But his history isn't history. For every streak past the winning post, the hard, sharp face relaxing into a smile, there is a commentator reminding the world that the champion jockey is recovering from a stay in a treatment centre in Ireland early this year for alcohol dependency.

That recovery looked near completion yesterday when he won the big race of the day, the Coronation Stakes, on the favourite Russian Rhythm. The day before he had steered Mr Dinos to victory in the Gold Cup, coming home six lengths clear in the afternoon Berkshire sunshine, followed by a round of golf, two cokes, half a steak and a late-night phone call from his wife, Julie, reporting on their children, Natalie and the twins.

The family man: sober, successful and fed. It wasn't always like that. Over dinner, ironically, he remembered his County Clare childhood in the west of Ireland where dinner barely figured at all. 'We came home from school then went out to work in the fields until it was dark. We had a family meal on a Sunday. The rest of the time we looked after ourselves. Toast, I remember. Toast on a long fork in the fire.'

It was the extraordinary grounding of a champion. His school was three miles away, up in the mountains. Maybe hills we would call them, but to a tiny, primary schoolboy they loomed like mountains. 'With boulders,' he said. School was 'two rooms and an outside toilet'. The schoolmaster was fine, fierce and adept at thrashing. 'There were four of us in my class, two clever, two thick. I was thick. But I was good at woodwork.' There were no horses. He rode the cattle on the farm. 'It wasn't too comfortable,' was the verdict. His dad, Frank, once acquired a Connemara pony – 'I don't know how, you know' – when Fallon was about ten or 11 and he would ride it bareback across the fields, hanging on to the mane, until the inevitable moment he was dumped on the ground. Then the pony disappeared and that was the end of his riding.

He has no sense now of the life being hard. 'We'd go down the fields, fishing, swimming. It was exciting. Country life,' he said, in Irish tones so soft you almost have to read what he is saying from his eyes. His father used to drop him and his brother at the bog a few miles away. They would cut plugs of peat out of the ground, lay them, dry them, stack them and leave them ready for collection by the side of the road. That would be their winter fuel. And still no horses. It remains one of life's inexplicable mysteries that this finest of Flat jockeys appeared to create himself from nowhere. He had been to Galway Races once in his life. How did he know that racing was his fate? He, to this day, doesn't know how to answer this question. Perhaps it is simple: it was either that or woodwork.

Not surprisingly, the Irish trainers were unimpressed. He fetched up in their yards at the age of 17, weighing five stone and admitting he'd never sat on a horse. They told him to get lost. But Tom Fitzgerald, the famous head lad at top Irish trainer Paddy Prendergast's yard, gave him a chance. 'Can you ride?' he said. Fallon admitted that he couldn't. 'Can you muck out?' said Fitzgerald. Fallon thought he probably could. He was hired. That day Fitzgerald put him up on a horse, watched him jog around the yard and though a man of extremely spare praise, uttered the prescient words: 'You'll do.'

Fallon has done. He has done almost all there is to do in a 21-year career, winning every Classic in British racing except the Doncaster St Leger. He fell in with, then out with, Henry Cecil. He was hired by Sir Michael Stoute. He married Julie and had three children. He has been crowned champion jockey five times. He would drink a bottle of vodka a day, eat a scrap of food and then throw it all up. And then have a drink. All this constituted his life. Not to mention many appearances before the disciplinary panel of the Jockey Club and, by way of alternating the problems in his life, he has also suffered chronic injury. A terrible fall at Ascot three years ago had many people questioning whether he would ride again.

It's funny the way things work out. It was during a visit to Paula Radcliffe's physio in Ireland, Gerard Hartmann, that the medical man took one look at Kieren's body and told him he was drinking heavily. It was that moment that may have changed the course of Fallon's professional and personal life. 'It was a lot of pressure. A lot was expected, you know,' is his gentle, euphemistic explanation. But perhaps that is truly all it was. Stress. His wife, Julie, points to his innate shyness. 'It was difficult for him to deal with everything that came with the job,' she said, a straight-talking girl from Wigan to whom Fallon pays the ultimate tribute. 'If I didn't have Julie, I wouldn't be racing today. I was a wild man. I needed help years ago. You know what it's like in racing. One big party, so it is. So you need to have somebody there to let you know that you have another life. Because you could get carried away. Julie is my rock.' And he, for a long time, was the hard place.

He is open about his break in the Irish clinic. 'I needed it myself or I wouldn't have a job. Probably quite a few in the profession, they have to look at themselves. You can't see the road you're on, the effect it has until it's too late. You don't realise the damage the drink is doing to your health. Most days you'd go through a bottle of vodka. No problem, after racing. Then you'd eat, you'd throw up and then have a drink. I wish I'd had someone to tell me ten years ago. But racing is such a social thing. Everybody's drinking. I couldn't see what was wrong with it. It's not normal to me anymore. I think, "How did I do it?" Now I'm in bed at ten o'clock and golfing. Then I was up two, three, four in the morning. Getting no sleep and going to work.'

It is a little like reincarnation, though possibly not the right image for a man of Catholic upbringing. No doubt, though, he has been stunned by the refuelling of his drive. 'I can't believe how good I feel. Like starting all over again. But knowing a lot more now. I'm going to keep going as long as I have the feel of the horse, as long as I'm fit, as long as I'm enjoying it.' And even when he retires, that may not be the end of the Fallons. His son, Cieron, the male half of the twins, is racing mad, hyperactive and never sleeps. That may remind a few people of someone. The twins are aged four, but Cieron has never yet slept through the night. 'He does fall asleep but then he gets up again. Midnight is his favourite time. He likes to bulldoze his way between us, you know. But Julie does everything, you know. I'm never there.'

This is not entirely true. Julie's much-loved father died two weeks ago and while she travelled north with Natalie to be with her mother, Fallon took the twins to Yarmouth races. His mother and sister looked after them while Fallon plied his trade, then he took them home again. Cieron insists on joining his dad. 'He thinks he's great. Thinks he's a jockey. He goes round the weighing room with a saddle and whip in his hand.'

It is hard to believe the man speaking is the same one who has fallen foul of the Jockey Club on innumerable occasions and once hauled a fellow jockey off a horse after a buffeting race. 'He did nearly put me on the floor. But I had a silly temper then. I wish it was under control now, but I'm better. At the Irish clinic they gave me a book on anger management. To be honest, I didn't read it.' He is dyslexic. He left his school barely able to read and write. 'I've only read one book in my life.' It turns out to be *Cane and Abel* by Jeffrey Archer.

Fallon is a privileged man. He has looked at himself. 'Very hard. I looked at the life I'd been leading. Lots of money, praise, fame. It's hard really for people to handle. It would be easy to fail, but if you fail in this sport, you're not going to get a job as a bouncer.' He still cracks jokes without smiling. Of course, he will never be as demonstrative as Frankie Dettori. 'He goes overboard. He does go overboard,' said Fallon quietly and he will not be trying a flying dismount either. 'If I tried that I'd break me leg. That's how I see meself: curled up in a ball, holding me fecking ankle.' Still shy after all these years.

CHAPTER 5

FOUR-LEGGED ATHLETES

Horses don't give interviews. Not even mighty Arkle could manage that. So there is no better way to gain an intimate insight into their characters than to get up on their backs and ride them out. Not every journalist is able to do that, so the Telegraph *was fortunate to be able to partner Lucinda Green, the three-day event champion, with some of the best horses of the age, and then publish her analyses. Among the horses she was invited to ride over the years were winners of the Grand National, the Champion Hurdle and the King George VI Chase, as well as Gold Cup favourites. She was not alone in knowing her hocks from her fetlocks, though. John Oaksey and Frankie Dettori, among others, all show they are good judges of bloodstock, even if they were not always able to give all the horses in question a test drive.*

---

7 JULY 2001

THE LEGEND OF ECLIPSE

John Oaksey

At midday on Sunday, 1 April, 1764, a mare called Spilletta, belonging to the Duke of Cumberland, gave birth to a chestnut colt, from whom, more than two centuries later, 95 per cent of all modern thoroughbreds are descended in the male line. The colt was named after the annular eclipse with which his birth coincided, and we shall be honouring him at Sandown Park today. Eclipse's extraordinary influence on the breed has inspired the learned racing historian Michael Church to write a definitive history, not just of the horse himself but also of the race named after him – and of the Racing Awards which, since 1971, have marked outstanding achievement by horses and humans alike in the United States.

Racing, and life in general, was very different in the 18th century, but snobbery and social distinction existed then, as they do now. They seem to have ruled the lives of horses as well as people. Knocked down at auction, first to a grazier and meat vendor called Wildman, the five-year-old Eclipse was then spotted and bought (in two instalments) by Dennis O'Kelly, an Irish gambler, adventurer and soldier. If Eclipse had belonged to an upper-class member of the English Jockey Club, his stud career, and especially the mares he was allowed to cover, would surely have been very different and much better bred. Many of the mares he covered were not even in the Stud Book and, despite siring three Derby winners, Eclipse was never leading sire. Nor was his owner a member of the Jockey Club, much as he longed to be elected. Perhaps, in the circumstances, you can hardly blame the Club for that.

O'Kelly, born in County Carlow, came to England in his early twenties to chance his arm and 'do the best he could' in assorted occupations – as sedan chair man, billiards marker and, when sent to the Fleet Prison for debt, carrier of beer for other inmates. A harsh-visaged 'ruffian-looking' fellow, he was said to combine 'the most offensive brogue his nation ever produced' with 'the manners of a gentleman and the attractive quaintness of a humorist'. Many fine judges of horseflesh have Irish accents, mind you, and those with 'attractive quaintness and humour' often get on in life. O'Kelly had the courage of his convictions as well. One morning, he happened to see a chestnut horse work on Epsom Downs and, because of what his eyes told him, 'Eclipse first – the rest nowhere' became the bold foundation of his fortune. It meant that he backed the chestnut to finish at least 240 yards (a distance) ahead of his nearest rival. All horses go fast past trees but, as John Lawrence (no relation of mine but a noted judge in those days) once said of Eclipse: 'No horse ever threw his haunches with more effect.'

Jack Oakley rode Eclipse in nearly all his races, obeying the instructions 'Sit quietly. Make no attempt to hold him up'. Just as well, perhaps, since in most of his 18 starts, Eclipse 'took an early lead – and drew further away'. A horse called Bucephalus was said to have 'made him gallop', but Eclipse still won, and Bucephalus never ran again.

Though the Jockey Club never relented, the fact is that O'Kelly managed Eclipse's racing and stud career remarkably well.

---

2 JUNE 1968

SIR IVOR – THE NEAREST TO PERFECTION

John Lawrence

It is, I suppose, quite possible to paint last week in gloomy colours as one of almost unrelieved depression for British bloodstock – but to do so would give less than half the picture. Our best three-year-olds were, it is true, cut mercilessly down to size, but Epsom 1968 was nevertheless a happy place to be – made unforgettable by two superb examples of what horse racing is all about.

Comparisons between different Classic generations are both odious and pointless, but I honestly believe that Mr Raymond Guest's Sir Ivor must be about as close as man has come to success in his long search for the ideal thoroughbred. Ribot and Sea Bird II were till now the best I saw, and of course no one can say whether Sir Ivor would have beaten them. But he is better looking than Ribot and a far better ride than Sea Bird – a beautiful, well-oiled machine who handles like a London taxi and accelerates like an Aston Martin.

He is, in a word, perfection, and has in Vincent O'Brien and Lester Piggott the sort of accomplices that such perfection deserves. No doubt there are many trainers who could have won two Classics with Sir Ivor, and it would, as things turned out, have taken a pretty moderate jockey to get him beaten in the Derby. But the measure of Vincent O'Brien's achievement since he first produced Sir Ivor on a racecourse is that the colt, despite travelling thousands of miles in the meanwhile, has never stopped improving. Between the 2,000 Guineas and the Derby he had actually put on weight and the two great mounds of muscle over his quarters say more than any words of mine about this trainer's skill.

As for Piggott, the point about his tactics in the Derby is not just that they succeeded, for we know now that Sir Ivor could equally well have led from start to finish. But if the doubts about his stamina had been justified that single superbly-timed thrust would still probably have got him home. If, for instance, Tudor Minstrel could have been ridden as Sir Ivor was (and it was no fault of Sir Gordon Richards's that he couldn't) I believe he, too, would have won the Derby. It is the mark of a great jockey to expect and prepare for the worst and last week Lester Piggott left nothing whatever to chance.

Gerald Thiboeuf, by contrast, left a good deal to chance on La Laguna, but it is no criticism of him to say that few, if any, top-class English (or Australian) jockeys would have dared ride such a race on a hot favourite in the Oaks. Thiboeuf's tactics were based firstly on his previous painful experiences at Epsom and secondly on the assumption that La Lagune had at least a stone in hand. He took one grave risk to avoid another and if anyone wants to complain he need only call their attention to the result. And in any case Thiboeuf did us a real service for, by setting La Lagune such a formidable task in the straight, he demonstrated, as no more conventional tactics could have done, the full extent of her outstanding ability.

Almost certainly the filly had far less to do than Sir Ivor, but the extravagant ease with which she passed all her rivals on the bit in less than a furlong makes it impossible to say for sure which was the greater performance. There is, at present, no firm basis for comparison between these two in the form book, and the slow time in which the Oaks was run means nothing. La

Lagune's stamina is not in question, and the fact that they cantered for the first two furlongs was, if anything, a disadvantage. History shows, however, that when a great colt and a great filly are born in the same year, the colt is apt to come out on top. For what it is worth, my opinion is that Sir Ivor would beat La Lagune if they met tomorrow – and that, in fact, he will never be beaten again.

---

29 JULY 2001

GALILEO'S STOCK RISES TO NEW PITCH

Paul Hayward

Galileo is becoming one of those mythical beasts who outshine the tens of thousands of mere humans who come to see him run. But he is also big business on the hoof, which is why his owners are concerned as much with turning him into racing's first $100 million stallion as they are with the romance of this year's Breeders' Cup in New York. Belmont Park's proximity to Wall Street ought to remind us that neon dollar signs will wink when Galileo takes on America's Point Given in the $4 million Classic on 27 October, the most coveted prize in Flat racing's yearly Olympics. Galileo, described as 'the ultimate' by Michael Tabor, his joint-owner, after the King George VI and Queen Elizabeth Diamond Stakes at Ascot on Saturday, is the kind of equine athlete who stud owners and pedigree experts have spent centuries trying to engineer. Eureka. Here, for our delectation, is a beast of burden who manages to be both beautiful creature and commodity.

Wading through the superlatives after his two-length victory over the five-year-old Fantastic Light, Galileo's owners could feel his stud value swelling with every sweet stride on a day when the average racegoer must have felt as cool as a baked potato. Six slaps of Michael Kinane's whip and a second spurt of acceleration when Fantastic Light came alongside were enough for Galileo's worth to rise to around $70 million, and for hardened racing folk to acquire a dreamy look of fulfilment.

Those traditionalists who argue that the sport has become a factory for manufacturing over-priced Lotharios have no grounds for arguing that Galileo is already a hostage to greedy breeders. Saturday's race was almost certainly his last over the Derby distance of a mile and a half. Now he switches to mile-and-a-quarter races with the aim of advertising his versatility and high cruising speed to breeders, who, lamentably, have turned against natural 12-furlong pedigrees in favour of speed and more speed. Unable to cope with the banquet of a true middle-distance race, the modern keeper of the house of ill repute prefers the fast-food of the high-speed showdown. The change in emphasis as Galileo begins phase two in his quest for global domination is intended to entice the owners of A-list mares as much as it is to exploit his undoubted natural speed. If Aidan O'Brien, his trainer, can add the Irish Champion Stakes, the Breeders' Cup Classic and maybe even the one-mile Queen Elizabeth II Stakes to his CV, Galileo will have every blue-blooded mare on the planet applying lipstick while they queue at the door to his boudoir offering hundreds of thousands of dollars a throw.

If anyone was unwise enough to tell him about the life that awaits him, he would doubtless refuse to put one foot in front of the other again, even under maximum duress from Kinane, who reminded us how high the stakes have become by taking out a High Court injunction against the two-day suspension for careless riding which would have cost him his place in the saddle. Kinane not only rode a horse but a cart as well through the Irish Turf Club's authority, and the dangerous precedent thus created was the only dubious feature of Galileo's spellbinding win. While the Turf Club may want to ask again why two witnesses – the jockeys Niall McCullagh and Declan McDonogh – failed to appear at the original appeal on Thursday, thus causing Kinane's legal challenge to be compressed into one dramatic Friday afternoon, Irish racing will doubtless rejoice to see the O'Brien-John Magnier-Tabor team bullying Sheikh Mohammed's Godolphin operation in another showcase event. The winning connections are propelled by guile and cunning more than a desire to build bonfires out of money or to own All The Pretty Horses. Galileo's mission now is to finance all the fun that is to be had from dominating some of the world's most powerful men in a sometimes ruthless trade.

This is not the first time a Niagara of praise has been showered on an uncomprehending animal, but never has so much commercial value been attached to a horse's exploits. Twelve months ago, we gasped as Kinane steered Montjeu in a canter past Fantastic Light, and wondered whether there had been an easier King George winner since the great Nijinsky. 'Last year, Montjeu was very special,' Kinane conceded on Saturday, 'but this horse has no weaknesses.' When Fantastic Light joined him, and Galileo could hear the snort of nostrils alongside him for the first time at the end of a big race, the pessimist in the stands thought the game was up. The optimist in the saddle knew his mount would quicken for the second time in little more than a couple of furlongs. O'Brien, the doubter, thought his claim that Galileo has too much speed to be a true mile-and-a-half horse was about to be justified, but Kinane, the pilot with all that brawn and potency beneath him, was sure that the upstart would be flicked away like a fly that had annoyed a deity.

'So much power. And bags of courage. He's very, very genuine,' Kinane mused. And then more: 'He was idling a bit, and Frankie [Dettori, on Fantastic Light] came quickly. It took him about three strides to react to him, but when he did he cracked Frankie quite quickly. He's an amazing horse. I've never seen him tired. With that big heart he's capable of filling himself with air. In his races now he's very relaxed, he never pulls, and he's really become a great pro. He's not a big horse, but he's got so much length to him. He reaches for ground. Nothing is ever happening too quickly for him. In the States on dirt, it's early speed and tactical pace that counts, and he has it.'

To avenge Giant's Causeway's defeat in the Classic last year is one incentive for Ireland's foremost rider, but there is a much bigger one: to ride round Belmont Park on a $100 million conveyance who, in victory, would make history as the first European winner and raise a roar that would be heard on Broadway. That, to us spectators, is the point, not the money.

---

23 DECEMBER 1996

GENTLE ROUGH QUEST SHOWS HIS AUTHORITY

Lucinda Green

'Really, nobody ever rides him but me,' said Terry Casey, trainer of Rough Quest, winner of the 1996 Grand National. 'He's only just run at Folkestone and I don't want to interrupt his routine. It's only a week before the King George – but come down and you can sit on him for ten minutes.' Recalling the neurosis I felt with my own horses leading up to a big event I fully expected the ten minutes to be halved on arrival the following morning in the questionable-sounding area of Beare Green, Dorking.

Rough Quest stood tacked up in his stable, the doorway of which had been raised last year to prevent him banging his head. He's a solid, big and strong bay, 16-and-a-quarter hands high with a deep girth and a reasonably long back. By Crash Course, sire of Jodami, the Gold Cup winner, and Esha Ness, who won the void Grand National, he was bred by Michael Healey in Ireland. As a yearling he jumped a four-foot jagged stone wall into a yard when he galloped down for his food too fast to stop.

'When my trainer, Tim Etherington, and I went over to buy him as a five-year-old, he'd been fourth in a couple of bumpers,' said owner Andrew Wates. 'He was very, very headstrong, a gangly great horse with legs everywhere. He was found for us by Arthur Moore and he was a smashing mover with a lovely big old-fashioned stamp. Often, such horses haven't enough toe – but if they are fast enough then you've got something. It took a long time to settle him when he came home. Graham McCourt was brilliant with him and ran him gently in his first few races and got him anchored.'

Although he wears a white plastic bit at home he needs a ring bit racing [a snaffle with 'spoons' either side, and a ring – like a chifney, used for leading bumptious stallions].

Before winning last week's novice hurdle – the only race Casey could find for him when frost spoiled his plans – Rough Quest's last sighting of a race-course was Aintree's spruce massifs in April. He was still quite wired as he was hacked out by Bradley Morgan, former head lad with Nicky Henderson. He took short quick steps, head high, his skin and his body resonated health and fitness.

A little later I was hoisted on and carefully released, to my surprise, to trot and canter around the all-weather gallops. Rough Quest is well balanced with a marvellous front and an enthusiasm for life. He had a surprisingly tight stride ... Apparently, he only really lets go of himself when he moves into racing gear. After a half-hour's walk Rough Quest had given me an indication of his character. He is a gentle, kind horse, but he is the boss. If his accompanying horse showed insufficient deference, 'Questy' flattened his ears and snaked his neck towards him.

Rising 11, Rough Quest is an example of how long horses take to mature, particularly big ones and particularly for some inexplicable reason, Irish ones. He has run 26 times in this country in six years during a career speckled with the odd problem – and therefore time off, including the whole of 1993 for a tendon strain. Nature's sometimes maddening delaying tactics probably gave Rough Quest the chance to fill his frame sufficiently before he was asked the ultimate question six months ago: in the two greatest steeplechases in the world within 17 days of each other. 'He wasn't quite himself when he was second in the Gold Cup, you know,' explained Casey. 'He'd worked disap-pointingly, his coat was wrong and he hates the cold. He still ran a good race, but we did not expect him to run again so soon. A few days after the Gold Cup he was just so well that Andrew Wates and I felt he should have his chance in the National.'

No stranger to Aintree, Wates, a point-to-point rider since Cambridge days when he shared a pointer with Ian Balding, won the Foxhunters in 1970. A permit owner for some 20 years with 80 winners, he had trained Hard Outlook (another Arthur Moore find) to be second to Grittar in the 1982 National. Wates's family building business, started by his great-grandfather, was expanding into health and leisure clubs, leaving insufficient time for training pursuits. He does evening stables on Sundays with Casey, who has worked for him for two and a half years, rides out at weekends and together they discuss all the horses. 'Terry had some excellent references,' said Wates. 'He was apprentice to Aubrey Brabazon who, among much else, raided three Gold Cups from Cheltenham. He then spent three years as head man to Paddy Mullins.'

After a further 15 years as a self-described second-rate jockey, Casey then began training in the 1980s, eventually setting up on his own in Lambourn, but found he was losing money. 'It's his instinctive horsemanship that appealed to me,' said Wates. 'The situation at home gives Terry the freedom to use that instinct – he doesn't have to worry about the business side.' Casey, 51, has filled all 18 of Wates's stables, having 12 owners, eight Wates horses and six lads. Six hundred acres of pasture, an all-weather track and grass gallops and fences a short drive away have given the unassuming Casey an opportunity for which he is ceaselessly grateful.

There is no pattern to Casey's training. He thrives on being able to use his feel for every horse. He doesn't plan to gallop twice a week or to walk on Mondays. He knows how his horses are eating because he feeds them himself four times a day, starting at 5.10 a.m. With that knowledge he decides on the work, judging from their 'feel' when they are out exercising. 'Anyone can train a good horse,' he says modestly. 'But I am committed each day and I enjoy what I am doing. I don't bet – all the other vices, yes – and I've been 36 years learning the game.'

Though he would not acknowledge it, Casey's handling of Rough Quest is one of the training feats of the decade. 'The first race I ran him in was in October 1994 and I couldn't run him again till February,' he said. 'The night after his race there was cold sweat over his kidneys and he was like a dog with broken back legs – he was just dragging them along.' Faced with this muscle enzyme problem Casey experimented with feed and work. He was telephoned by 'Patsy from County Tipperary' who had seen Casey interviewed about the problems after Rough Quest had won at Kempton in February. 'She produced some daily powders that helped balance his system. His unexpectedly speedy recovery from the Gold Cup and the fact that he is much less stiff each morning now is largely due to them,' said Casey.

Mick Fitzgerald, his jockey, said: 'He'll always be quick over the first three fences, then if you bury him behind another he'll switch off and become an easy ride. At Kempton we'll need to be in touch turning into the final straight. He'll make up so much ground at each of the final fences, I only have to give him a bit of rein – there isn't a faster jumper in the country. But he mustn't hit the front too soon. Once his head is in front, he tends to think he's won.'

If Boxing Day's King George does indeed provide a battle between One Man, last year's winner and favourite, and Rough Quest, it will be a fascinating comparison of converse types of horses. The butty, bouncing ball of grey is half the size with half the length of neck. Rough Quest's stamina is unquestioned and he is giving note that he is ready. Usually, he devours a packet of Polos at a time; now he is only picking at them.

---

30 MARCH 1996

PARTY POLITICS THRIVES ON LIGHT WORK

Lucinda Green

Many horses are described as 'pulling like a train'. Party Politics, hero of the 1992 Grand National and last year's runner-up, merely sounds like one. He breathes with every stride directly through a hole under his neck. This gaunt yet enormous brown horse – a six-foot man cannot be seen the other side of him – is an object lesson of encouragement to all who suffer the incessant disappointments that dealing with horses entails. He arrived in Nick Gaselee's Lambourn yard six years ago. 'Four long legs and a pair of hip bones,' remarked 'Buck' Rogers, his lad since that first day. Despite winning twice in his first season he was 'a real embarrassment in the paddock', said Gaselee's wife, Judy. 'Hairy – he hated being clipped, foaming white sweat and with a great ugly head.'

But that was about his only hang-up. 'We used to call him Haircut,' said Rebecca Smith who, with her Whaddon farmer husband, Gerald, gave him his earliest education. 'We gave him three weeks' long-reining and he developed a lovely mouth before we backed him. He found jumping poles very difficult to start with. We spent ages on it and soon he was out hunting and proved a super jumper.' David Stoddart bred and owned him for eight years. 'The dam was a big fast mare who'd won eight races for me, mostly over two miles. I probably shouldn't have put her to Politico as he was big, too, but I loved him the first time I saw him at the stallion show. I bred a giant.' At the age of five, Party Politics was 18 hands high.

Johnny Rathall – who later died in a road accident – was the first to ride him in a point-to-point. He pulled him up two from home to give him an easy introduction, but he never forgot the horse he had felt that day. Second in the next, he then went on to the Gaselees and after his two wins it was decided to sell him. Destiny interrupted. Unexpectedly, the Doncaster Sales vet failed the horse on his wind and he returned home and underwent the first of three operations. The following season, 1990–91, the bushy-maned giant with the distinctively high-set tail won three out of five starts, including

Newbury's Mandarin Chase, but was pulled up in the Cheltenham Gold Cup with breathing difficulties. The hobday operation had broken down and the next stage, the 'tie-back' was performed.

By the following year the eight-year-old had grown into his head; always gaunt, he was no longer ugly. He ran second in the Hennessy and the Welsh National, fourth in the Greenalls Gold Cup and was entered for the National. His regular jockey, Andrew Adams, who had schooled and raced him since he had arrived at Saxon Cottage Stables, had broken an arm. Carl Llewellyn came to school him. He kicked him to tell him when to take off and the big horse immediately put down again, fiddled another stride and screwed over. The diminutive Adams had always sat quiet, leaving the horse to make the decisions. 'You don't kick him to take off,' said Llewellyn, 'you must hold him and squeeze.'

The new partnership won the National, beating Romany King. Only two days before the race Stoddart had sold his big home-bred to Mr and Mrs David Thompson, breeders of Flat horses at Newmarket's Cheveley Park Stud. Out of the blue they offered £80,000 and agreed to a further £15,000 should he win. However, despite winning, further wind problems became evident during that race. The 'tie-back' had broken apart and it was decided to cut a hole in his windpipe and let him learn to breathe through that, thus bypassing all the previous problems in his throat. A two-inch, open-ended metal tube was placed in the hole to keep it open. During the summers the tube is taken out and the hole heals over. 'Many people keep the plug in the hole to avoid dust going into the lungs,' said Gaselee, 'but we felt it would be better to keep the plug out so that he learnt to breathe naturally through the hole and let him live all day in the field.'

It is a weird sensation to ride Party Politics. The expected breaths and sniffs that are among horses' ways of communicating are not coming from his nostrils – instead there is a silence. But as you lead him out you are aware of these noises just above your ear as you walk beside his neck. Possibly the biggest surprise from this kind-natured horse was his exceptional movement. Most good horses I have been fortunate enough to ride walk well. Desert Orchid probably had the most powerful walk, even after he had retired. But Party Politics's trot was like a gymnast floating.

Constantly enthusiastic, the big horse is always at the head of the string, trying to leave them behind with his grandiose trot. 'At last he's moving properly again this year,' Rogers said as we had a few minutes' walk – a pace which gave Party Politics no reason to mellow his keenness. 'Two years ago he began to go wrong in his feet. First he bruised them badly, then he had a corn, then he cracked a pedal-bone.' He has flat fleet, tender soles with no heels. It is a clever blacksmith who keeps him right. Not long after that he hit his hock so badly it was feared broken. It took a year to overcome the problem. On his return last year he ran second in the Hennessy and third in the Rehearsal Chase. He was below par and pulled up in the Greenalls Gold Cup, possibly due, in part, to an infection around his tube. In the final days before Aintree he came right. Carl Llewellyn, claimed for third-fence victim Young Hustler, was replaced by Mark Dwyer who rode him into second place behind Royal Athlete.

In the light of last year's long and difficult campaign, Gaselee decided this year to give him the shortest fitness programme that he dared. The Hennessy was run while Party Politics was still holidaying at Cheveley Park. He came to Gaselee in December and his fourth tube was not inserted until January. This February's chilly weather gave him a cold in his lungs. Time off and the plug temporarily inserted meant that he had lost crucial work and was not fit enough to complete his only preparatory race five weeks ago.

Shortly after that, however, this happy 12-year-old, moving as if on air, transported me up a Lambourn canter. He had a very good mouth, felt unusually 'now on the bit', safe and reliable. Always hacking off the roads, for the sake of his feet, and spending all day in the field, gives Party Politics a different life to most racehorses. The patience and gentleness of Nick Gaselee, along with the care of his first and only head-lad, Jumbo Heaney, and vet Charlie McCartan, have already paid two big Aintree dividends. And nearly a third, for he was running far easier in the void 1993 National than he had been when winning the previous year. Big horses have wind problems. Big horses are less athletic. He may have confirmed belief in the first claim, but he has rubbished the second. 'He is awesome, but so dainty,' said Llewellyn. 'It was a brilliant bit of common sense to bring him up so late and give him a light season. I'm very happy with him. He loves Liverpool more than any place else – I tell you, he loves that race.'

---

12 FEBRUARY 2000

ISTABRAQ CHASES HURDLE HAT-TRICK

Lucinda Green

Istabraq has become a name synonymous with excellence, and many already believe he is the greatest hurdler ever seen. Few will doubt it if he flies in from Ballydoyle, County Tipperary, to win his third Champion Hurdle in a row at the Cheltenham National Hunt Festival. 'He thrives on his jumping,' says his jockey, Charlie Swan, 32. 'He'll never look for a way out. Riding him is certainly one of the reasons I haven't retired yet.'

Istabraq's power and brain combine to produce quite extraordinary speed and jumping prowess. The winner of 20 of his 23 races over hurdles and £850,000 in prize money, these qualities place him in a league of his own. He landed the Royal Sun Alliance Novice Hurdle at the Festival in his first season and has returned twice since to win, effortlessly, the top hurdling prize on the racing calendar. He has also taken the last three Irish Champion Hurdles, and his standing is such that trainer Aidan O'Brien's entire 120-horse operation revolves increasingly around the brown, eight-year-old gelding now that Cheltenham is little more than a month away. 'Look at him, see how intelligent he is? Watch his face,' said O'Brien, as he travelled alongside the string of seven jumpers in his four-wheel-drive Mitsubishi, liveried in maroon and black like all the Ballydoyle work riders. Istabraq does not miss a thing. 'The slightest change to his routine upsets him. He lives on the edge. If you shout at him in the stable, he breaks into a sweat.'

There is room for neither loud nor rough people, nor practices. Life at Ballydoyle is designed to relax and bring to peak fitness every inmate. Istabraq enjoys the full force of this intricate pattern and routine, with extras – for instance, he is never tied up in his stable. When the yard's chief minder, Tommy Murphy, crouches to put on Istabraq's leg bandages, he does not tell him to stand still, instead Murphy follows his legs around the stable. Closed-circuit television in his stable is a constant monitor, beamed through to the security office and to O'Brien's small family bungalow.

No reprimands are delivered to this high-tensile individual. 'That's probably why he bit you,' said O'Brien, referring to the nervous grab he had made at my hand when I interrupted his routine for barely two minutes on his way back from work, to meet him and have his picture taken. There was no question of being allowed to give him any Polos. 'We try not to spoil him. We try not to let him get too high an opinion of himself. He can do.' It is a subtle balancing act to steer a genius towards a goal of supreme mental and physical fitness without interfering with his routine.

The riders, uniformly quiet, are carefully selected and trained and agree to stay a minimum of two years at Ballydoyle. Pat Lillis, who has always ridden Istabraq, talks to him all the way up the gallops to try to maintain his equilibrium. The work for this equine Eric Cantona is the same every day – there is no rest day to destroy the routine. The lead horse, either Darapour or Theatreworld, both Cheltenham contenders, keeps pace with O'Brien's vehicle, three feet the other side of white railings. Istabraq takes up the next spot, his head constantly level with the leader's haunches, and close behind him comes

Yeoman's Point and then the others. For a mile up a gentle incline, the seven work in formation at anything from 35 to 43 m.p.h. depending on the day and stage of training. Somehow O'Brien manages to keep his speed absolutely even and negotiate a bend without seeming to take his eyes off his horses galloping beside him. With such proximity he can pick up any signs better than if watching from the usual distance of some hundred yards. When you stand next to Istabraq, who measures little more than 16 hands high, he does not appear the massive, powerful, king-figure he looks in public. 'He blows all his muscles up at the races,' agreed O'Brien. 'He seems to grow bigger.'

Built up by the legendary Vincent O'Brien (no relation), Ballydoyle produced revered Flat horses such as The Minstrel, Sir Ivor and the indomitable Nijinsky, whose life-size bronze statue watches the front gates. His successor is an unassuming man of understated determination. With the boyish haircut and thin-framed, round spectacles, he resembles Microsoft's Bill Gates. It would seem that the quiet intensity, the breadth of mind and the collation of data are used by both to further extend the parameters of possibility. Ten years ago, when a 20-year-old jockey, he joined forces with his future wife, Anne-Marie Crowley, a former model and daughter of trainer Joe Crowley. Anne-Marie became the first female champion trainer when landing the jumps title in 1992–93 and immediately handed over the licence to Aidan. He scored his first winner on his first day as a trainer when Wandering Thoughts won at Tralee on 7 June, 1993. He was champion amateur rider over jumps in the 1993–94 season and champion jumps trainer for each of the subsequent five seasons. He has gradually cut back his National Hunt interests to concentrate on the Flat, and has unsurprisingly been hugely successful, winning the English 2,000 Guineas and Oaks in 1998 to add to his haul of Irish and foreign big-race triumphs. 'We'll probably never have such a good National Hunt horse again at Ballydoyle,' O'Brien says of Istabraq.

Including ground staff, there are 80 employed at the training complex, near Cashel, all but four having started when O'Brien arrived in 1995, or later. There are five wood-chip and ten turf gallops (the English training enclaves of Newmarket and Lambourn would not have many more and they are shared by dozens of yards) and last year a five-furlong hill with a 60-foot incline was built. There are countless small and larger stable yards, some for isolation purposes, several enclosed round-houses for quiet individual work, an indoor perimeter ride and a low-ceiling exercise barn in which every support pillar is padded like the legs of a pylon on a ski slope. It must have taken a while for O'Brien to become familiar with the orchestra of facilities at his disposal. The speed of his success, though, suggests that it did not.

O'Brien feels that the biggest factor in success is having happy, healthy horses.

There is nothing cunning or original about that, but the lengths to which he and his team go in order to promote those basics makes you marvel. One of O'Brien's less-heralded abilities is his driving. Nerve-rackingly, he knows to the second where he should be during each training session. He speeds from one section of the string – usually 40-strong – to another, sometimes in reverse, ignoring the optimistic 15 m.p.h. signs as he swings along narrow strips between barns. At one moment the mobile phone goes. 'Mummy's stolen my sword, Daddy,' complains Joseph, at six, the eldest of four.

O'Brien arrives on time to drive slowly by the line of horses, issuing polite, undemanding instructions to each lad or lass, or asking each one if their horse went well. He always remembers to use their Christian names. 'I would talk to every rider about each of their rides three or four times in a day,' explained O'Brien. Many trainers do not set such store in their riders' input. No outsiders are allowed into the stable yards. No press are permitted except for an annual open day for the Irish media in April before the Flat season commences. The minutest detail is followed to avoid the spreading of germs. Each horse has its own allotted equipment. Any horse who spends a night away returns to an isolation box, except for Istabraq, who returns to his own stable while all the others are moved out.

John Magnier, Ballydoyle's proprietor, also owns the Coolmore Stud and the equine operation is the only one in the world that comes close to challenging that of Sheikh Mohammed. Yet for all this Istabraq came to Ballydoyle through tragic circumstance. John Durkan, assistant to trainer John Gosden at Newmarket, was about to start training on his own and thought the four-year-old by Sadler's Wells, with quite good Flat form, would make a fine hurdler. He asked his father-in-law, Tim Hyde, to find a buyer and J. P. McManus, the legendary Irish punter, bought the gelding for £38,000. Over the next 18 months Durkan's plans were put on hold as he battled with leukaemia. Istabraq was dispatched to Ballydoyle to await his recovery. It never happened and one of the most popular young men in racing died at the age of 31.

Istabraq stayed in Ireland and Durkan's wife, Carol, now manages McManus's string of horses. Five of the seven Ballydoyle jumpers belong to him. Istabraq, Le Coudray and Darapour are favourites for their respective Cheltenham races. The Magnier-owned Theatreworld, three times runner-up in the Champion Hurdle, and Yeoman's Point are rated not far behind. Even with all that is at their disposal, horses are fragile in so many ways that it is remarkable that, at this point, all five are ready to run at Cheltenham. It is a tribute to the most extraordinary team of experts who appear to have their roots in the surreal, so unbelievable do their achievements seem. Istabraq is a looking glass of those who surround him.

MOSCOW FLYER LIFTS A NATION TO VICTORY

Paul Hayward

In a new book on horses and the Emerald Isle, the American author Bill Barich meditates: 'While the English are fond of their racing, I soon discovered the Irish can't live without it.' This neatly explains the euphoria that swept over the Cheltenham Festival when Moscow Flyer won the Queen Mother Champion Chase. The difference between fondness and addiction was there in the flying hats, the whoops of pleasure, the jigging tricolours that greeted Ireland's favourite animal as he regained his crown as the winter game's champion two-mile chaser. In carrying his jockey, Barry Geraghty, to victory over Well Chief and Azertyuiop, this charismatic 11-year-old also carried a torch for Arkle, Dawn Run, Istabraq and all the four-legged icons of the Irish countryside.

'The Irish have an extraordinary way with horses, after all,' writes Barich in *A Fine Place to Daydream — Racehorses, Romance and the Irish*. 'The earliest invaders from England recognised it, and remarked on how a rider and his mount appeared to be inseparable, a single creature with nothing between them, skin to skin.' In the Otherworld — a place beyond death — the Celts believed 'horses transported souls across the divide'.

The Irish at Cheltenham form a single team — skin to skin, if you like. Owners, trainers, jockeys, punters and the odd priest merge into one organism. Sure, each has his own private dreams and fixations. But when the 'good horse' sweeps down the hill and into the cauldron of the home stretch, the green congregation unites to shout the winner home. Hence the 'Cheltenham roar' in the winner's enclosure.

'I really did want him to regain his crown — and he did that in style,' gulped his trainer, Jessica Harrington, referring to her horse's mishap in this race last year. Moscow Flyer had won the Arkle Chase in 2002 and the Queen Mother a season later. But the title was ripped out of his grasp 12 months ago when Geraghty was unseated and Azertyuiop stepped in to fill the void. With the talented six-year-old, Well Chief, staking his own claim, yesterday's rematch was widely billed as the best contest of the Festival. Moscow Flyer versus Azertyuiop turned out not to be Ali-Frazier. A bad mistake by Moscow Flyer's English rival at the water jump sucked the momentum out of the defending champion. Pity, but there was no shortage of dramatic resonance in the leader's charge up the Cheltenham hill as Well Chief chased him home. Seniority stamped its authority.

Some bookmakers now make Moscow Flyer 2–1 favourite to win his third Champion Chase next year – even though no 12-year-old has succeeded in this fast, exacting test since Skymas 28 years ago. The will to fight again is strong. A curious fact about Moscow Flyer is that he has won all 18 races he has completed over fences. The only horse who can beat him is himself. On his hurdling debut he ran into a dolled-off flight. On his chasing bow he hit the deck. If he stays upright he wins.

'The thing is, Moscow's very brave,' Geraghty told Barich. 'He just doesn't worry about it. His style isn't careless – it's carefree.' Trotting back to the racecourse stables after a morning canter, the horse's work rider told Channel 4 viewers: 'He feels like a fish on the line.' If anyone has come up with a better image to describe the tautness, the twitch of excitement, transmitted by a top horse before a big race, then it has yet to be seen in print.

If only time would stand still in the Irish fields where Moscow Flyer leaves his hoof marks between events. Only Badsworth Boy (1983–85) has won three Champion Chases – though yesterday's winner already joins a multitude of distinguished double-winners. Now that he has conquered his concentration deficit, it seems unjust that age will threaten his pre-eminence. 'We're all attached to him, we've had him for six years and he has been an amazing horse,' Harrington said.

After him, there will be others, of course, because National Hunt racing in Ireland has probably never been so strong. Economic strength and government support for the thoroughbred industry have stemmed the flow of the country's best jumping horses to rich English owners. Ireland is hanging on to more of its fastest and most powerful beasts. Through the lens of the Irish infatuation, Barich celebrates the moment when the likes of Moscow Flyer 'take flight and leave the earth, [and] hang for a half-second in a cloud of uncertainty before they know what the future will bring'. In Moscow Flyer's confident leaps here yesterday, the 'uncertainty' was done away with.

---

8 FEBRUARY 2002

PEARL BACK IN SPOTLIGHT

Lucinda Green

The most enigmatic of today's racehorses would have to be Ireland's original will-he, won't-he, push-me, pull-you Florida Pearl. Now ten-years-old, he is thriving on a return to 'public darling' status after outjumping Best Mate on Boxing Day in Kempton's King George VI Chase. This large bay gelding, nearly

17 hands high and with a gentle disposition, is back in the spotlight and favourite for tomorrow's Hennessy Cognac Gold Cup Chase at Leopardstown, where he is attempting to win the race for the fourth successive year en route to his third try at the Cheltenham Gold Cup for owners Archie and Violet O'Leary.

Also in the line-up tomorrow is a stablemate of equal proportions, Alexander Banquet. Willie Mullins trains the pair at Bagenalstown, County Carlow, 50 miles south west of Dublin. Alexander Banquet lives just across the passage from Florida Pearl in one of Mullins's six grey concrete stable buildings. Both these two bay geldings took me round Mullins's unusually small, two-and-a-quarter-furlong, circular 'gallop' in entirely different fashions. The gallop's shavings, sodden from so much rain, were hock deep, making it sufficiently hard work for every horse's usual quota of circuits to be reduced, along with the speed at which they travelled during them.

Florida Pearl went much as I remembered him go two years ago. Keen, kind, easily balanced and powerful. Alexander Banquet, however, was altogether more laidback and needed constant encouragement to keep going. And yet he is the horse who has the more rounded action and is at his best when conditions are as heavy as they will be tomorrow.

Last time I rode Florida Pearl, he felt lame behind in the brief few minutes before cantering started. Many racehorses are stiff and usually loosen up, but it had always intrigued me that Florida Pearl faded so often in the latter stages of his races, as if he were hitting some kind of pain barrier.

Last summer, former event rider Tracy Gilmour, his attentive carer and Mullins's left-hand woman – his right-hand being his Essex-born, distinctly un-Essex wife, Jackie – spotted a lump on the outside of Florida Pearl's right hind leg when he came back from holiday. X-rays revealed the relatively unimportant splint-bone had a double fracture. He was kept in his stable for a month and then Gilmour started walking him on long reins, a method of riderless exercise. Gilmour said: 'As he was sore in his back just under one side of the saddle, it seemed worth trying this way.' Very often if one part of the body is injured another will compensate for it, and then that part too will become overused and hurt. 'Maybe he had a single fracture on that splint-bone for some time,' pondered Gilmour. 'We knew he was not quite sound but we could never find where the problem was.' Whatever the problem, Florida Pearl is now, according to his trainer, in great form.

Mullins, a six-times Irish champion amateur rider, was giving nothing away on tactics for tomorrow's race. He said: 'Whether we let him make the running earlier, as he did in the King George, depends on how we find the ground when we walk the course on Sunday morning. He has had it soft at

Leopardstown before, but it will be a real test of stamina. Alexander Banquet will relish the ground.'

Adrian Maguire rides Florida Pearl again tomorrow, having proved an able partner at Kempton, where he was only third choice, prompting Mullins to say: 'I am not worrying about who the jockey is any more.' In five years, apart from one fall, Florida Pearl has never been out of the money in 22 races and has won 12 times. On first appearance, he does not radiate personality. However, he refuses to eat breakfast until he has been exercised; and he has to be turned out alone because he is a surprising bully. Gilmour explained: 'When he is turned out in company on his summer holidays, he only has to look at the others and they part like the sea.' Florida Pearl is his own man. With renewed soundness and stronger muscles, he may yet achieve his Cheltenham Gold Cup aim.

---

26 JULY 1999

MY ASCOT WINNER JOINS ALL-TIME GREATS

Frankie Dettori

I have rarely been as bullish before a race about a horse winning as I was about Daylami in the King George VI and Queen Elizabeth Diamond Stakes at Ascot on Saturday. I said in Saturday's column that whoever beat Daylami would win, but even I was surprised by the way that he did it. Until Saturday no horse had given me goose-pimples when winning. I have been privileged to ride some of the best horses of recent times – Swain, Singspiel and Lammtarra – but Daylami's performance on Saturday was as good if not better, up there with those modern greats. He retains the speed of a miler at the end of a mile-and-a-half race.

After Daylami won the Coronation Cup at Epsom, which was very tactical, people said he won because the pacemaker had slowed things down to suit us. But we never said Daylami needed a slow pace. We knew he would stay. He had been working well and the team, Sheikh Mohammed, Saeed bin Suroor and Simon Crisford, took the brave decision to miss the Eclipse, for which he only had to turn up to win, to have him peaking for Saturday. Apart from vindicating that decision, the result also put Godolphin's season back on track. We won the Guineas with Island Sands but have lacked a really top-class three-year-old, and despite winning several Group Ones they have, without wanting to sound complacent, been bits and pieces by the operation's high standards. This was the race we wanted. It is a classic.

My only worry had been the draw. Daylami always goes through a bit of a flat patch in a race and at Royal Ascot last year when I should have been rousting him along through his flat patch I was stuck on the rails. When I got out it was too late and he finished third because the straight is so short. About five furlongs out I was tracking Nedawi and Daliapour and hemmed in by Oath, who was going well. Here I took a quick look and saw that we had opened up a gap back to the fifth, so I was able to ease back and switch to the outside. Once I was in Oath's slipstream with only two lengths to make up I knew Daylami's turn of foot would see him home, but I didn't expect what happened next in a million years. Once he was balanced in the straight I gave him a smack and he took off. When I went past Gary Stevens on Nedawi he said: 'Go get 'em, Frankie.' I could hardly hear the last word because Daylami was putting so much distance between himself and Nedawi. Inside the last furlong I looked up to the big screen and saw a grey horse a long way clear of the others so I was able to enjoy the last five seconds of the race. It was a hell of a performance (to give 12 pounds to a Derby winner) and credit must be given to the boss for taking a step back and saving Daylami for the race.

It was great to get another diamond from The Queen. I told her about the race, Daylami and how I'd won it three times, but had some way to go before I equalled Lester Piggott's seven wins. She replied that she thought I'd won it enough!

CHAPTER 6

THOSE WERE THE DAYS

Time can put a different perspective on events. Anniversaries are always opportune moments to look back and recount, reminisce, review. And who can resist a slice of nostalgia? The Grand National, in particular, throws up stories of derring-do that are often better with the second telling. Over the years, the Telegraph *has revisited many of those famous moments as part of its big-race build-ups. For example, 50 years after, Bruce Hobbs recalled his pre-War National win on Battleship as a 17-year-old; 40 years on, Dave Dick remembered passing the stricken Devon Loch to win in 1956; a quarter of a century after the event, Bob Champion spoke about his fairytale win on Aldaniti that moved a nation to tears in 1981; 20 years on, Marcus Armytage harked back to 1990 and Mr Frisk's big day; ten years after, and on the Flat, Frankie Dettori talked about his once-in-a-lifetime seven-timer at Ascot.*

---

23 SEPTEMBER 2006

DAY THAT CHANGED DETTORI'S LIFE

Sue Mott

Off to Frankie Dettori's house (recently burgled) for the tenth anniversary of the magnificent occasion when he went through the card at Ascot. Seven rides, seven wins, a world record that propelled him from mere jockey to sporting superstar. It would be a quick chat: Frankie then, Frankie now and a couple of tips for today's racing. But it is never that simple with Dettori. Any conversation with the little Anglo-Italian, father of five and pizza chain proprietor, is like soaring away in a helium balloon. ''Allo, Sue,' said a voice, but all you could see were dogs. Then a figure appeared, in layers and layers of bright Italian blue tracksuit. He was going for a jog to lose weight. Postponed. One politely inquired about the goldfish. All gone, thank God, he said. And the hamster? 'In there,' he said, pointing to the smallest dog which looked like an animated carpet.

Of course, he remembered the Saturday that changed his life forever, but 'to be honest, I don't really remember what anybody said. It was like your wedding day. I was just going around with a big grin on my face, telling how great I was to everybody. Don't forget, it was on the BBC so I was getting dragged left, right and centre. Every race, a different interview. I just went with the flow, let it rip. I was in 'eaven. Floatin' along. Like a bird. It uplifts you, dunnit? You know, going through the card didn't enter my head till after the fifth race. Going to the sixth, I thought, "Hang on, if I put this one in it equals the record. For a small chap of 25, that's not bad, isn't it?" It was almost just a race between me and Pat Eddery. We were both equal favourites and the rest was outsiders.

'Mummy [aka his wife Catherine]! Can you sling the dogs out,' he interrupted himself – as doberman, boxer and carpet invaded. 'George [That was the boxer]! Out!' – 'But I beat Pat in that one by a good length and a 'alf. I mean, 'orses are different. Is not just you and a car, or you and a bike. Is you and the 'orse. You equally important as each other. They have the ability of feeling your mood. I think the 'orses catch my mood that day. I wasn't even on the ground, I was flying and they were just running that little bit faster.'

It came down to the last race, the Gordon Carter Handicap on a dear old horse that hadn't won for a year, Fujiyama Crest. Getting on a bit, one-paced and lazy. On paper, not a chance even though he had won the self-same race with Dettori exactly a year before. But he was carrying only eight stone eight pounds then. This time he loaded up with nine stone ten. 'I'm no fool, no dreamer, I realised Fuji was an outsider. I said to myself, "I'm not stupid, this can't win and I'm not going to let this last race spoil my day". I didn't want to be deflated when it lost. So I just decided to go out and enjoy it, no matter what. I had a big smile on my face and as I cantered past the grandstand to the start I got this huge standing ovation. I thought: this is fabulous, fantastic! And I remember looking at the betting boards. And it was something like 2–1 favourite and I'm thinking, "You're mad. MAD!" But everybody was joyous and laughing. At that stage I didn't feel anything. I was numb with joy. Absolutely. The lads was slapping me. Big chaos. So I got to the start and I knew what to do. He's a relentless galloper. He's got one rhythm and that's it. So I kicked him out the stalls and my main concern was to get him as close as I could to the front, and then I threw him the lot. I'm sitting there like those Hawaiian surfers riding a wave. I was sitting there like that' — he leapt out of his kitchen chair and demonstrated a surfer's crouch plus invisible reins and a grin — 'wind through your 'air, like that.' Only Dettori could feel wind through his hair underneath his jockey helmet.

'I was in fantasy land. But then I saw the five-furlong sign and I thought, "I got to get serious now". I passed the five, past the four and I thought, "I better stretch these 'orses behind me. I want to get their legs tired because I don't want a sprint". I remember Derek, the lad that looked after him, told me beforehand, "Don't forget. He's extremely lazy so don't give up. The 'orse is getting older. You have to rouse him a bit more". So I fired him into the straight and the ROAR from the stand! But now I'm tired, he's tired, all the other 'orses are tired. Is like the Grand National. The last furlong takes forever.

All I could hear was the crack of Pat's whip and his whistling noise he makes. And I'm thinking, "Where's the frigging winning post?" And we pass the line and I punch the air, but I almost fall off I'm so tired.' Some said the other jockeys let him win that last race to give the whole sport a day in the lime-light. 'Hah!' he said. 'You should see Pat Eddery's face. That long! I not even comprehend what I have just achieved. Don't forget, I only been in this game two minutes. Historians realised what I did, but I didn't know. I walked back into madness. It was great, but too much for any 'uman being to accept. It was like Freddie Flintoff did the great Ashes, or Michael Owen with the goal against Argentina. It just gave me that extra boost.

'Then nobody wanted to go home. I weighed out, did interviews, got presented with Champagne and everything, 30,000 people wanted me to sign their race card because it was 'istory. I was there for hours. Madness. It was almost dark when I got in the car to go home. I just could not really under-stand the emotions. By the time I got home, I was in a bad mood. It was very 'ard to be in that position. Anyway, Catherine had me sucked into going to one of her ex-boyfriends' parties. I didn't want to go and we ended up on the greatest day of my career going to bed, not talking and sleeping back to back.'

The next morning he was reading the papers in his office in his underpants when the *Daily Mirror* walked in unannounced. That was the beginning of fame. He entered a different life from that moment. 'Because of that day a lot is expected of me, day in, day out. Everyone expects a smile, a seven-timer and 100 per cent commitment. Unfortunately, I'm only 'uman. It's great what I did, but prior to that day life was less demanding and easier. I'm still the same person. I'm 'appy. But life's circumstances have changed me. But racing isn't a novelty any more, it's a responsibility.'

Dettori does not strike you as a man weighed down with responsibilities, especially where fathering is concerned. Tallulah comes in, the fourth of his five children. 'Daddy's going to chase you,' Dettori said, leaping up, driving the little thing in pink instantly hyperactive. 'Actually, I'm the sixth child in the house. I make them over-excited, oh yes. I'm the one who messes every-thing up. Maybe they're not allowed sweets and I'm giving them sweets. Maybe they have to say "please" and "thank you" and I'm not even asking them. I'm always asking for kisses. Leo [the eldest] is at the stage where he says, "Dad, don't kiss me any more. You can cuddle me. That's it".'

But there is no such thing as 'That's it' to Frankie. Nothing is neat, finished, controlled, unless you count his riding style. His life seems to be a great, brimming vat of possibility, celebrity, affability, burglary and near fatality (the plane crash he suffered in 2000). His latest 'eyes and lows', as he calls them, are remarkable. Last season he missed the summer with a broken collarbone after a fall on Eclipse Day. 'Of all places, I had to go to this hospital in Kingston where, unless you got three bullet wounds or a machete round your head, they send you away with a pill. They sent me 'ome!'

This season began spectacularly. He won a very dramatic World Cup in Dubai, failed to win the Derby again, called Royal Ascot his 'nightmare' and then turned the season around with a win on Ouija Board at Glorious Goodwood. Since then Godolphin's horses have come back to form, and today he fancies his chances at Ascot with two of them. 'I don't like to tip horses in big races. I think it's bad luck. Bear that in mind. But Librettist in the Queen Elizabeth II Stakes is probably one of the horses that will turn Godolphin's season round. He won the Prix Jacques Le Marois in Deauville and the Prix du Moulin two weeks ago. He's lovely. A tremendous pro. We've slowly brought him from injury. He's actually come into the race like a true champion. The other horse I like is Desert Chief, in the first race.'

Busy time. Next weekend is the Prix de l'Arc de Triomphe at Longchamp, where Dettori could be riding Sixties Icon, even though some aficionados are wondering whether he might be persuaded on to the favourite, Shirocco. 'Whatever 'appens, it will be a decent ride. I've been riding the Arc every year since I was 17, when I rode the pacemaker for the Aga Kahn. I was watching the finish on the big screen, I was that far behind by the end.' He went on to win the race three times, on Lammtarra (1995), Sakhee (2001) and Marienbard (2002). That's form.

It must be curious to be riding with no Kieren Fallon around, presently banned in England pending a corruption court case. 'Ye-es,' he agreed, 'but I don't want to complain, because he's a hard jockey to beat. I do miss him, he's a friend, but he's so good, so cold, so difficult to beat. I haven't followed the whole shebang. I don't know what to think about it. We are kind of in a grey area. He's not allowed to ride, but he doesn't know whether he's guilty or innocent.' Racing and murk have always ridden together, but Frankie is resigned to human frailty. 'Is 'appening in soccer, it 'appens in cricket. What is this ball-tampering! What are they going to do? Have a cement ball so no one can touch it? Always somebody try. But, you know, wherever there is competition, money and gambling, there will be somebody trying to pull a fast one on somebody else.'

So, ten years after the Magnificent Seven, Dettori is the same and a different man. He knows where he will be in ten years' time. The dumps. That is when he wants to retire, at the age of 45. This is wishful thinking, probably, but he just cannot bear to contemplate The End. 'I am very nervous about the 'ole thing. Because I enjoy the racing, I get paid really well and all of a sudden I go from that to zero. No excitement. No adrenalin. Actually, the future is bleak.' By then his three daughters will be teenagers. 'Oh, I don't really want to tackle that bridge yet. I'll be retired and a right misery, a grumpy Italian pacing up and down outside the front of the house with a machine gun.' This, however, doesn't seem likely. He cheerily scooped up baby Rocco and took him outside to give Fuji (the same Fujiyama Crest, now an elderly family pet) a big pat and a chunk of apple.

---

26 DECEMBER 2003

THE DAY I BEAT ARKLE

Marcus Armytage

All horses are beatable, including Arkle. But that, says Stan Mellor, the first jump jockey to ride 1,000 winners and one of the few men who managed to lower the great horse's colours on a 25–1 shot in the Hennessy Gold Cup, does not make Arkle any less of a horse.

During his career Mellor weighed eight stone ten pounds, not much more than some Flat jockeys do now, so instead of using great strength he had to win races the way he found he could – by using his brain. 'If you win with strength people see it,' he says. 'And if you win with style people see it, but if you win with guile people don't see it. That's why I like the way Timmy Murphy rides, he thinks about it the way I used to. People say Arkle was beaten by the 35-pound weight difference in the 1966 Hennessy, but he could have won the race by 25 lengths; instead Stalbridge Colonist beat him for a turn of foot.'

Mellor can recall the race as if it was yesterday. It was Arkle's first run of the season (his last as it turned out, as he retired with a broken pedal bone after that year's King George) and Stalbridge Colonist was to beat him half a length with What A Myth, a future Gold Cup winner, back in third. 'Turning into the straight, Arkle was making his own running which he did for one very good reason – he had no big turn of foot. By going a good gallop all the way he'd stretch them out. I was on the outside in third and I wasn't at all happy because Johnnie Haine on Kellsboro' Wood was threatening to take on Arkle which is just what I didn't want for my own plan. At the ditch I got over on to the inside, got in behind Arkle, and then dropped about four lengths off him. If I'd so much as blown my nose he'd have been off.

'After the second last Pat Taaffe had a bit of a look and, bang in behind Arkle, he didn't see us. If I'd been at all bullish and not treated Arkle with the utmost respect he'd have seen us and gone. But I waited until about ten strides after the second last and gave my horse a smack to get him running. For two or three strides it felt like I would run into the back of him. I then hoicked Stalbridge Colonist out to his right and came wide of Arkle. I was flying into the last while Arkle was happily minding his own business, winning the race in a canter. The last was a blur but I landed running while he was still cantering. Pat then saw the danger and went from sitting to riding a big finish without giving Arkle a chance to get balanced. Getting the revs up in behind so he couldn't see was the most important thing.'

Mellor, who has now retired from training to Ashbury, near Lambourn, believes Arkle was a complete freak and, with the possible exception of Flyingbolt, that nothing has come near him, including Best Mate. 'Best Mate may prove a better horse,' he says. 'He hasn't beaten anything yet. He's a nice horse and I'd love to see him win another Gold Cup. He hasn't a turn of foot, but a lot of good chasers don't. That's not derogatory, Arkle didn't either, but they need riding positively. If you've got a horse with speed you can play around and if you know you're on the second-best horse you can influence the pace by pressing the leader or backing off him.'

---

9 APRIL 2010

THANKS MR FRISK FOR THE BEST TEN MINUTES OF FUN IMAGINABLE

Marcus Armytage

It is 20 years since I rode Mr Frisk to win the 1990 Grand National and realised a lifetime's ambition. Some of it seems like it happened yesterday, but my memories of the day are like a badly edited film of highlights interspersed with long blanks. Barely a day in those two decades has passed without someone, somewhere reminding me of the occasion. Strangers still come up and thank me because they backed the horse or light-heartedly cuss me because they backed the runner-up. The greatest irony of it all, however, is that while the jockey invariably gets all the praise and fame, it is the trainer and his lads who have done the hard work, the owner who has paid for it. The winning jockey just goes out there, has the best ten minutes of fun imaginable and gets all the plaudits.

Armytage family life revolved round an obsession with trying to land the National and I was not our prime suspect to win it. My father, Roddy, trained a succession of National-type horses, and spring in East Ilsley was announced not by the arrival of daffodils but by the preparation of another horse for another National. Without a runner spring didn't happen. The next most likely candidate in the family was my younger sister Gee. She had become jump racing's pin-up after riding a double at the 1987 Cheltenham Festival. She was a very different rider to me. I was cautious, she was fearless.

But if, through a lot of practice and endless patience on my father's behalf, I eventually became competent enough to win on a horse if it was good enough, she had the ability to win on horses that had no right to win. So you see, however Fate picks her National winners – and this may be some consolation to the numerous champions who have never won it – it's not done on merit; I was not even the best jockey in my own family.

Mr Frisk, trained by Kim Bailey, was long and low with powerful hind-quarters. He was a flamboyant jumper, frequently launching himself outside the wings and landing as far out the other side of a fence. He liked to make the running, but the absolute key to him was firm ground and in 1990 we were coming to the end of one of the driest winters on record. The course at Aintree was parched brown.

If National morning dragged on, the afternoon flew by. Eventually all the jockeys were herded into a room and a steward told us not to go too fast to the first. We laughed. Of all the pointless speeches made this was there up with them. The butterflies dissipated when I was legged up on the horse. My biggest concern was the first because if a brilliant jumper is going to come unstuck it is often there because they over-jump and get caught out by the drop. Having survived that I could relax a little and as we approached The Chair, with a circuit still to race, I was upsides Uncle Merlin in front. His rider Hywel Davies had been my mentor. He asked me to drop off him because our horses were taking each other on. I willingly obliged. It was the only chat I had.

At Becher's second time everything changed. I was wondering if I'd be able to get past Uncle Merlin when he pecked. As I went past Hywel was half on, half off and I assumed he would rejoin me shortly. I was unaware gravity won the argument. If I could replay one minute of my life over again, it would be the line of four fences from Valentine's. I challenged the horse and he responded with bigger and better leaps and, crossing the Melling Road with just two fences left, I looked up, saw the stands, felt I had a full tank of petrol, couldn't hear another horse – the *Racing Post's* Newmarket corres-pondent was ten lengths clear and they must have been having coronaries at the *Sporting Life* – and the first tentative thoughts of victory crossed my mind. I was being stalked by Durham Edition and Chris Grant, nicknamed Rambo because of his strength. That wasn't going to be a fair fight, but I thought it was Team Challenge, a plodder with no speed, and an inner calm set in. We only won by threequarters of a length but I never had to get desperate with the horse.

The first emotion was relief at not having cocked up. Though I began my Monday article in the Post with a corny line asking if I was dreaming, the enormity sank in before Mr Frisk had slowed to a trot. Here was an amateur rider, aged 25, with about 40 winners under his belt, none of any consequence, winning the biggest race in the world. It was only my fifth winner of the season. It was, frankly, ridiculous. We were swamped by well-wishers, four police horses escorted us in, and they tried to beat Kim Bailey out of the way until I told them he was the trainer. Then it was one interview after another. Brough Scott insisted I should write my *Racing Post* article that evening while it was fresh in the memory. I said I wouldn't get too many chances to celebrate winning a National. For that one day of my life I was a jockey and not a journalist.

No one told me that the winner buys a crate of Champagne for his fellow riders, which embarrassed me, and my National trophy was a bit of a letdown, a carriage clock with a plaque saying 'Grand National — winning jockey' which was glued on cockeyed. When I took it to a jeweller in the belief it must, at least, be worth insuring he merely pointed to half a dozen identical ones on a shelf. I offered it to the Aintree museum and even they turned it down. But Mrs Duffey, Mr Frisk's American owner, made up for it commissioning a bronze of us jumping The Chair.

It really sank in when I pulled up in a Liverpool petrol station and a local asked me to sign his receipt. I picked up Gee, who had broken her leg the previous Monday, from Shrewsbury Hospital on the way home, and by the time we got back to Richard Dunwoody's house for the 'party', they had eaten all the Chinese takeaway, some had gone home and, exhausted, I fell asleep in a chair watching a replay. From that day on life was never going to be quite the same again.

---

7 APRIL 1988

THE START OF AN AINTREE LOVE AFFAIR

Peter Scott

Youthful stamina, allied to outstanding skill apparent since boyhood, were the assets shared by England's two chief sporting heroes of 1938. Len Hutton batted more than 13 hours at the Oval for 364 runs that beat Don Bradman's record Test match score a few months after a lanky teenager became the youngest jockey to win the Grand National.

Bruce Hobbs – no relation to J.B. – will be at Aintree again on Saturday, remembering his triumph with Battleship 50 years ago and once more savouring a race always close to his heart. Hobbs, now a Jockey Club member, was only 17 years and three months old when Battleship, standing 15 hands and one and a half inches, became one of the smallest Grand National winners. At six feet two, he remains one of its tallest winning riders, and went to the scale at just ten stone.

Successful young sportsmen had their heads kept well below cloud level in the 1930s. Reg Hobbs, Bruce's stern father who trained Battleship, allowed him to attend the victory dinner in Liverpool, but packed him off to bed at 10.30 p.m. 'The Grand National was on a Friday in those days. I was riding the next afternoon and my father insisted on business as usual. He remained strict with me long afterwards,' recalls Hobbs. Reg Hobbs, a martinet in the stable yard, also insisted that his son attended Aintree and other major meetings in a blue suit, blue overcoat, bowler hat and gloves. One wonders what the old man would have thought of John Francome's turnout.

Reg never wanted to run Battleship in the Grand National, feeling he was too small. Battleship was also an entire horse – most top chasers are geldings – and brushing the tops of those big fences might have pained him. Battleship, like Red Rum, began his career on the Flat. Bred in the United States, he won sprints there before the American Grand National. Mrs Marion du Pont Scott, who owned Battleship and was once married to the film star Randolph Scott, then sent him to England with Aintree in view. Reg Hobbs talked her out of running Battleship in 1937, but she insisted on his taking part a year later.

Bruce, whose horsemanship was shown early in the Leicestershire hunting fields and show rings, rode his first winner aged 14 and had his first Grand National ride on Flying Minutes, a 1937 faller. Injury to Flying Minutes caused Bruce to ride Battleship a year later. Most Grand National winners need some luck and Battleship's came at the small, angled, fence after Becher's first time round. 'Battleship turned with the angle, but I did not turn enough. I was falling off when Fred Rimell grabbed me by the seat of the pants and pulled me back into the saddle,' says Hobbs.

'Royal Danieli, one of those big, old-fashioned chasers, led Battleship over the last. A loose horse then carried me across to the stands side, but Battleship's courage and finishing speed enabled him to get up close home and win by a head. Dan Moore, who stuck to the far rails on Royal Danieli, felt sure he had won. We later became great friends and always enjoyed a drink together on his visits from Ireland. I was delighted that, before Dan died, he trained L'Escargot to win the 1975 Grand National from Red Rum.'

Battleship retired to stud in the United States and Bruce travelled over with him for a 1938 summer holiday, but the luck changed that December. Hobbs fractured his spine in a fall at Cheltenham, his unlucky course. Bruce never rode in another Grand National, but recovered for War-time service and won an M.C. in North Africa. He took a few rides after the War before laying the foundations of a successful training career which centred on Newmarket, and it was there that Hobbs finally met Hutton at a charity cricket match.

Bruce retired from training towards the end of 1985. He was soon made a Jockey Club member and later became a director of the National Stud. Busy with the present, he still enjoys a look back at the past.

---

25 MARCH 1996

AINTREE ANTI-HERO SAVOURS LUCKY LIFE OF UPS AND DOWNS

DAVE DICK RECALLS ROBBING QUEEN MOTHER OF WIN IN THE GRAND NATIONAL

Robert Philip

'Go on then, you lucky devil,' thought Dave Dick enviously as Devon Loch galloped off towards the distant roar at the winning post. Under Dick's gentle guidance, the gallant ESB had jumped Aintree's 30 fences with the agility of a circus flea, but now, as they kicked for home a hoofbeat behind the leader, Devon Loch sprinted away from them in search of Grand National glory.

Exactly 40 years on, what happened next remains steeplechasing's greatest mystery: 50 yards from the finish line and with victory seemingly assured, Devon Loch pricked up his ears as if distracted by the cheers of the nation, prepared to jump a phantom obstacle, then belly-flopped to the turf, his four legs splayed out beneath him. A million sighs issued forth for horse, rider and, most of all, owner – the beloved Queen Mother.

Perhaps inspired by the inexplicable events of 24 March, 1956, jockey Dick Francis, forever remembered as Aintree's unluckiest loser, bought a typewriter and wrote his first thriller (becoming the Queen Mother's favourite author in the process), earned countless millions and moved to celebrity-conscious

Florida. Dave Dick, in contrast, the ultimate Aintree anti-hero, gradually slipped into blessed anonymity.

Now 72, he enjoys the life of an English country gentleman in a sprawling manor – 'the end bit is Edwardian, the middle's Victorian and this new extension we're sitting in is Dave Dick' – complete with swimming pool, croquet lawn and set amid 14 acres of rural bliss in Berkshire. The shelves of antique books, walls of original oil paintings, rooms full of stuffed sofas and an entrance hall crammed with walking sticks, waxed jackets and riding boots are deceptive, however, for this is not the residence of Lord Snooty. He may like to go shooting, but he loves a game of poker.

He also sounds unnervingly reminiscent of Tommy Cooper, which may explain why just five minutes in his company are sufficient to understand why back in the Fifties – a glamorous era when Grand National owners, riders and trainers stayed in Liverpool's Adelphi Hotel and took dinner in evening dress each night of the Aintree meeting – friends could pinpoint the exact whereabouts of Dave Dick's table simply by following the sound of boisterous laughter. 'He always reminded me of a swashbuckling pirate,' recalls one contemporary. 'With Dave around you just knew there would be another funny story along in a minute.'

A funny story like the one surrounding the immediate aftermath of ESB's unwelcome triumph when a jubilant Dick was presented to a disappointed, but gracious Queen Mother in the unsaddling enclosure. 'Well, I made a bit of a cock-up of that, didn't I?' laughs Dick at the memory of his tactlessness. 'When I met her after the race, she said, "What did you think when my horse fell down?" And without thinking I replied, "I was absolutely delighted, Ma'am". But I felt very sorry for the old Queen Mum because she's a smashing person. She's a star . . . she is. I'd love to see her win the National, but she's leaving it a bit late now, isn't she?' And does that make him feel guilty? He scoffs at the notion with a joyful 'Naaagh . . .' Just like that.

The signed card bearing Her Majesty's photograph sitting on the table by the huge open fire in the Dick family drawing-room (a treasured memento sent out to friends to mark her 400th success as an owner) suggests the many winners he subsequently rode for the House of Windsor finally earned him the royal seal of approval. Indeed, the man who coaxed ESB around the stricken Devon Loch and into Aintree legend should have been a guest of honour at the official Royal Ascot lunch celebrating the Queen Mother's quadruple century. 'But that was another cock-up, wasn't it? My invitation went to a Dave Dick in Scotland – some hunter bloke or something – and he pitched up instead. Sat right next to HM he was. "Who are you?" says the Queen Mum. "Dave Dick," says he. "Oh, no, you're not," says she. "I am," says he. And, of course, he was Dave Dick. But not the right Dave Dick.'

Married to the serenely regal Caroline these past 26 years and father of Alexander, once of Eton and now a captain in the Royal Horse Guards, and Daisy, training in the fields beyond the French windows in the hope of securing a place on the British three-day event team, Dick's journey to this pastoral paradise was as convoluted as ESB's trip to the winner's enclosure. It was in 1910 or thereabouts (Dick tends to be a tad vague on the subject of family history) when his father left the Fife mining town of Cowdenbeath nursing the dream of becoming a professional jockey. 'He was just 12 years old yet he walked from Scotland to Epsom, well over 400 miles. There was no such thing as hitch-hiking in those days so he went on foot did my father. And he bloody well achieved his ambition. He rode on the Flat and over jumps before becoming a trainer. I was born and raised among horses so there was never any question what I was going to be.'

And so, before his 13th birthday, Dick left school (where he shared a desk with life-long crony Fred Winter) to become an apprentice jockey at the yard of Epsom trainer Stanley Wootten. 'It was a tough life as an apprentice back then in the Thirties. You got one pair of jodhpurs a year plus your working clothes. Your lodgings were free and you were fed, but you were only paid two bob – 10p now. If it was your job to make the mash [horse feed] in the copper stove, you'd stand there all day. Five in the morning till half past five at night stirring the friggin' thing. And if you let it burn you were dead. You'd get a bleedin' hiding.

'I didn't get to sit on a horse the first year I was there. I used to stand at the end of the stables with a duster and a knife. I'd help the stable lad into the saddle – and he'd be wearing a jacket and tie in those days – then scrape the manure from the soles of his boots with a knife and polish them with the duster. They'd walk the string up the road and the guv'nor would watch them go by like he was inspecting the Blues and Royals on parade. Then, to keep me out of trouble in the afternoon, I'd be made to walk the gallop on Epsom Downs picking up every single stone. A mile and a half. It was like being in the nick.'

At 15, Dick was signed by the most successful trainer of the day, the Honourable George Lambton, for whom he would eventually ride 1941 Lincolnshire Handicap winner Gloaming. But first, there was the small matter of a period of probation to be served. 'When I first went to Lambton's I was allowed to live in digs provided I was in bed by half past eight every night. Anyway, one night I'm gaily marching up the High Street with my arm wrapped round this bird [a lady of indeterminate age, let us say] when a car pulls up at my side. It was the Honourable George and Mrs Lambton.

'That was it. Next morning I'd packed my case and was given a room in the attic of the big house. I was taken to the tailor's and fitted out with a dinner jacket and every night I'd be made to sit and have a formal dinner in the great hall of Mensil Warren with the guv'nor and his wife before being sent upstairs to bed. That stopped me galloping around, I can tell you. I was stuck up there on the top floor where there wasn't even a drainpipe to shin down. They didn't want me to get heavy so I was never given much to eat. Thankfully, there was this marvellous German cook who took pity on me and she'd smuggle me up great plateloads of sandwiches and a glass of milk each night.'

The Second World War and his call-up to the Army were 'four years in Butlin's after the stables'. Dick served with the 52nd Highland Regiment in Ballater where he became an instructor on the use of pack mules. Having lived on his considerably sharp wits for most of his 20 years, Sergeant Dave Dick was exactly the type of man you would want alongside you in a crisis. 'We used to be sent up into the bloody mountains in the depths of winter to learn about survival. We were supposed to exist on water and biscuits. I thought "sod that". First farm we passed I'd requisition a sack of potatoes. As soon as we were out of sight, I'd sling a ruddy grenade in the river and get a couple of salmon. Then – bang! – I'd knock over a young stag. So we'd sit round the fire at night roasting the potatoes with the fat from the venison and with salmon steaks for starters.'

Such was Dick's prowess as poacher and al fresco chef, that he entered the Army at the age of 17 weighing seven stone four pounds and was returned to Lambton's from his final posting in Palestine four years older and five stones heavier. 'In those days racing was great fun and I always enjoyed eating and drinking or a bit of a party, didn't I? So my second home became the steam room of the Savoy Baths in Jermyn Street.'

After retiring in his mid-40s with a serious knee injury, Dick became a bloodstock agent, then stud manager for a Kuwaiti sheikh before settling into mischievous retirement. 'I've had the best life anyone had. Wouldn't swap a day to be honest. I've been so lucky.' Never more so than 24 March, 40 years ago? 'Listen, ESB was only one second off the course record and that was after being brought to a standstill by a fallen horse at the first fence after the Canal Turn. But for that, he might have won properly.'

After a morning of unremitting laughter, reluctantly, it was time to leave. We stood for a moment watching Daisy trot by, idly savouring the birdsong and the crisp spring air. 'Be lucky,' says Dave Dick with a wave of farewell. From the Grand National's luckiest winner it sounded like a benediction.

20 JANUARY 1985

HAMEY HOLDS CENTRE STAGE

John Oaksey meets the oldest surviving Grand National winner

The Aintree paddock is full of memories, but on Grand National day this year it will hold a uniquely distinguished gathering when Seagrams celebrate their rescue and sponsorship of the world's greatest steeplechase by presenting replicas of its Trophy to all the 35 winning jockeys who are still alive to tell the tale.

Only three won Nationals before the War, and Fulke Walwyn (Reynoldstown 1936) and Bruce Hobbs (Battleship 1938) are still active near the centre of the racing stage. But they won't top the bill on 30 March, and it was both a pleasure and an honour for me to take news of Seagrams' gesture to the man who will – Tim Hamey, now 79, winner on Forbra in 1932. That was the seventh of 12 consecutive Grand Nationals in which James Henry Hamey rode. 'Someone once called him Tim and it just stuck,' says Mrs Hamey, who married him in 1926, the year of his first National ride on Koko.

Tim had won the Gold Cup at Cheltenham that year on Koko, but the Cup, first run in 1924, was still just one of several possible 'preparation races' for the only jumping prize which counted. Despite having only 11 stone 11 pounds at Aintree, 20 pounds less than the top weight Silvo, Koko started at 100–8 with Silvo second favourite at 7–1. Both fell behind Jack Horner.

But even before 1932, Tim Hamey several times played a significant part in the National's history. He and Ardeen escaped the Canal Turn traffic jam caused in 1928 by Easter Hero, only to fall themselves independently as Tipperary Tim came home alone. Hamey, in fact, was retained by Tipperary Tim's owner Mr Kenyon. 'But he wouldn't give me anything extra for the National and I didn't fancy the horse anyway,' said Tim. So Bill Dutton got the ride; and 14 years later, he and Hamey met in Egypt, putting up dummy tanks behind the lines at Alamein and then organising horse transport to supply the 8th Army!

In 1929, with the help of the special crossed noseband, now known as 'a grakle', Tim Hamey got the horse of that name round to finish sixth behind Gregalach and Easter Hero. 'Grakle tried to run out passing the stands first time,' he remembers. 'My left arm was numb.' The 'worst fall I ever had', cost Hamey the ride on Grakle before he won in 1931, but a picture of the horse still hangs on his wall. 'It came from the owner with £50 and "thanks for showing him the way round in '29",' says Tim.

He made an even bigger contribution to Grakle's victory on the day. Riding Solanum, Dorothy Paget's first runner in the race, he fell at Becher's, knocked over Easter Hero – the hot favourite – and so hampered Ballasport that this jockey Dudley Williams had to ride the rest of the way with one stirrup. So the change of luck was hardly out of turn when, making only one slight mistake at Valentine's, Forbra beat Egremont and 34 others in 1932. 'Just look what the fences were like,' Tim says, proudly pointing at a picture, and sure enough they look brand new. 'Bloody, great, green stone walls' without any of the chunks you see knocked out of them nowadays.

Though quickly too heavy for the Flat, and forced to go jumping at 16, Tim Hamey is understandably proud that in his two winning Flat race rides 'I beat Steve Donoghue a short head at Leicester and Charlie Smirke a neck at Brighton'. Then, from the 1920s to the Second World War, he joined that cheerful, battered, underpaid fraternity who rode at 'a pound a mile. It was £3 a ride and £5 a winner,' he says. 'So although for six or seven years only Billy Scott and Gerry Wilson had more rides, I never looked like getting rich.' Training a small string after the War at Cheltenham was no better path to wealth, but now even if Yewtree Farm, between Stroud and Gloucester, is more comfortable than luxurious, Tim Hamey is not complaining.

His eyes still twinkle as he remembers the happy, hectic days at Bishops Cleeve when Scotty (Bill Scott), Specky (Bill Speck), Len (Lefebvre) and he used to drive all over the country, often to meetings now unheard of. 'Bungay, Bournemouth, Torquay, Totnes and Tenby,' Tim recites. 'I was always the chauffeur and we used to average 35.'

Sadly, Tim remembers the day Bill Speck had the Cheltenham fall which caused his death. 'We could all see it was bad and I came back refusing to ride again that day. But then Mr Anthony said you must ride Thomond. So I did and he was brilliant. But it made no difference.' Another picture shows that Scott and Speck were a full head shorter than Tim Hamey, who is not a tall man himself. 'But they were great men,' he says. 'I've never forgotten them.'

Well, no doubt Bill Scott, Bill Speck, Fred Rees and many others will be looking down at Aintree on 30 March. They will be glad, but not, I think, surprised to see that the slings and arrows of a long, hard, busy life have failed to stop Tim Hamey smiling.

7 APRIL 2006

ENDURING LEGEND OF AN ALL-TIME CHAMPION

Robert Philip

Once upon a time, a horse aptly called Lottery won the first Grand National in 1839. Not quite so long ago, in 1904, Moifaa was shipwrecked off the coast of Ireland en route to Liverpool from New Zealand, swam ashore after being given up for lost by the crew, was found contentedly strolling along a beach by fishermen, then strolled to an eight-length victory at Aintree. Once upon another time there were three horses known as Devon Loch, Foinavon and Red Rum; aye, for 167 years, the Grand National has been spinning fairytales.

But no legend has been quite so romantic as that of Bob Champion and Aldaniti, who rode into the valley of death together and out of the other side into a wonderland of bright sunshine and into the hearts of the nation. When Champion was diagnosed with testicular cancer in 1979, one fantasy kept him going through the months of harrowing treatment: passing the Aintree winning post aboard his beloved Aldaniti, who, for his part, had cheated the vet's bullet on three occasions by recovering from serious leg injury. 'Two broken-down, old crocks. You couldn't write it, could you?' Champion grins. But, of course, write it they did, turning the story of Champion and his wonderhorse's famous victory against the most outrageous odds 25 years ago into a movie, with John Hurt playing the jockey and Aldaniti starring as himself.

Champion's fascination with the Grand National started in childhood when, the week after the race – there being no live TV coverage until 1960 – he would rush to his local cinema in Cleveland, Yorkshire, to sit spellbound before the Pathé newsreel pictures of the event. 'Dick Francis and Devon Loch ... Mr What ... Oxo ... even from a very young age I realised the National was a one-off, the 'people's race', and I dreamed of being part of it. When I was about seven, my two best friends – Howard and Derek Thompson, who you'll know from Channel 4 – and myself bunked off school to go to a meeting at Redcar. Having run out of people to interview for the BBC, John Rickman spotted us three scallywags and hauled us in front of the camera. "And what do you all want to be when you grow up?" he asked. Howard told him he wanted to take over his dad's steel business, I told him I wanted to be a Grand National jockey and Derek wanted to be a horse-racing commentator on television. All three of our wishes came true, and that doesn't happen very often.'

When he reached the age of 23, Champion made his National debut in 1971 aboard Country Wedding; it was a less than auspicious introduction to Aintree. 'We were brought down at the first fence by Gay Trip, who'd won it the year before, so I never got the chance to jump Becher's Brook, the Canal Turn or Valentine's. As I lay there on the turf all I wanted was for the race to start all over again. The first time I got round was in '73, the year of Red Rum and Crisp, when I jumped the last in third place and eventually finished fifth. For me that was fantastic. I was over the moon, especially because my horse, Hurricane Rock, was a 250–1 outsider who ran the best race of his life. We were a long way behind, but as I watched Brian Fletcher and Rummy being led into the winner's enclosure, I was even more determined it would be me one day when I found the right horse.'

That horse was Aldaniti. 'I knew the type of horse I was looking for because I'd won races on Highland Wedding and Rag Trade, and ridden both Corbiere and Rubstic, and Aldaniti gave me exactly the same feeling. I remember winning on him at Leicester when he was just a young horse, and as I dismounted I told the owners, Nick and Valda Embiricos, "He'll win a National one day".'

But Champion's hopes of climbing into the saddle again, let alone winning the Grand National, appeared remote when, at the age of 31, he was diagnosed as suffering from cancer, with only a 40 per cent chance of survival provided he underwent immediate chemotherapy, then a new form of treatment. 'Eighteen months earlier it would have been a death sentence, because before chemo there wasn't a cure for my cancer,' he recalls. 'But I still didn't think much of my chances and my despair deepened even further when I left the Royal Marsden Hospital to see a front-page headline announcing the news that Steve McQueen had died of cancer.

'To be honest, my first reaction was that I'd simply carry on riding and be killed on the racecourse, but a friend said, "You're a decent jockey and if you were offered a 6–4 shot you'd give it a ride, wouldn't you?" And I thought, "You're right, 6–4 is not a bad bet", so within the first week I'd had two operations because the cancer had spread into my lungs and what not. The chemo was not pleasant, not pleasant at all, in fact it was horrendous, but every time they started pumping it into my body, I imagined Aldaniti and me soaring over the Aintree fences. A quarter of a century on, the side-effects are not nearly so ghastly these days, but you learn to put up with anything when you don't want to die.'

And so, once upon a time, after a year of treatment and recuperation, Bob Champion and Aldaniti, who had spent four months in a plaster-cast recovering from a third serious leg injury, came under starter's orders in the 1981 Grand National. 'Because of all the publicity surrounding us, the pressure to win was incredible, but I was supremely confident that given the usual bit of luck – a riderless horse causing a pile-up and the like – I just couldn't see

anyone beating us on such a beautiful sunny day. So what happens? We nearly
went at the first; he paddled along with his nose on the ground, but we got
away with it. Then we nearly went at the second. "Hmm, things aren't going
as well as I anticipated", I told Aldaniti. But from the moment he sailed over
the big ditch at the third, he gave me a dream ride.

'When did I know we'd won it? At the winning post. The plan had been
to hold him until the last fence, but he was going so well we hit the front
at Valentine's the first time round, which is still three-and-a-half miles out.
When we cleared the last and came to the Elbow I thought Royal Mail was
the only threat, then John Thorne and Spartan Missile started eating up the
ground. They got within threequarters of a length until we pulled away again
to win by four. As we passed the post there was an explosion of noise. It's
funny but all the way round I'd been cocooned in what I can only describe
as a private silence, in which the only sound I could hear was Aldaniti's
breathing. But as I raised my whip in triumph, I was suddenly aware that
the cheers of the crowd were absolutely deafening.'

Aldaniti died, aged 27, in 1997 after helping his two-legged sidekick launch
the Bob Champion Cancer Trust, which was initially launched from dona-
tions the jockey received while lying in the Royal Marsden and has now
provided £13 million towards battling the disease. 'Cancer touches every
family, but the survival rate for my form, for instance, has risen from 40 to
90 per cent. I also had a heart attack five years ago, so every day is doubly
precious to me. I still go back to the Royal Marsden every year for a check-
up and I can smell the chemo when I'm still five miles away from the hospital.'

Champion will be at Aintree tomorrow when he fully expects another
fairytale to unfold. 'Ginger McCain, maybe, who's having a fantastic season,
or a third win for Ruby Walsh and second successive victory for Hedgehunter,'
Champion mused. 'One thing's for sure, the winning horse, jockey, trainer
or owner will have a story to tell. That's the magic of the Grand National.'

---

7 APRIL 2006

MISSILE'S BOLT FROM THE BLUE

Marcus Armytage

The Grand National nearly always produces a good story and very few have
come close to bettering the amazing tale of Bob Champion and Aldaniti in
1981. However, in Spartan Missile, who finished four lengths back in second,
there was a story of equal if not greater poignancy.

John Thorne, who bred, owned, trained and rode Spartan Missile, was a 54-year-old amateur rider who had already retired once from riding with a broken back to let his son, Nigel, take over. Nigel had even ridden Spartan Missile's dam, Polaris Missile, in the 1968 National before falling at Becher's Brook. A year later, however, after a day's drag hunting, Nigel was killed in a car crash while driving back to Newmarket. With his twin sisters Diana (later to become Henderson) and Jane (Sloan) too young to take over, their father returned to the saddle.

In 1978 and 1979 Thorne had ridden Spartan Missile to victory in the Aintree Foxhunters. The pin in one of his leathers came undone at Becher's Brook in '78 and the only thing to do was kick his other foot out of the iron and ride the remaining eight obstacles without stirrups. It proved no hindrance as he came home in front, beating Peter Greenall (now the racecourse chairman Lord Daresbury) on Timmy's Battle and Nicky Henderson (subsequently his son-in-law) on Happy Warrior.

After a year out with an injury, he trained Spartan Missile for the 1981 National and insisted that one of his daughters ride because they could do the weight. He even threatened, according to Diana, never to put them up again on one of his horses if one of them did not oblige. He had always had two ambitions in life: to have a horse good enough to ride in the National, and to swim the Channel. Here, the girls insisted, was the opportunity to fulfil at least one of those dreams. Normally a strapping 13 stones, he trained with soldiers at the local barracks to get fit and wasted down to ride at 11 stone five, just three pounds over weight.

Spartan Missile was running a great race until he landed on the first fence on the second circuit and lost his position. It was an uphill struggle to get back into the race from that point, but, when Champion appeared to have the race in the bag, Spartan Missile and his 54-year-old rider came from nowhere with a wet sail. 'He was so pleased for Bob and said it was the best result, but he always asked himself what he could have done to have made up those four lengths,' Diana recalls. 'It played on his mind. When you're second, other people think it's wonderful, but, actually, you think it's terrible and regard it as a failure rather than a triumph.' She should know, having finished second at Badminton and Burghley.

That night Thorne's wife, Wendy, drove the horsebox home to Stratford and they gathered at the Westgate Arms to celebrate, where they were joined by Champion. Having wasted so hard, Thorne could only eat *hors d'oeuvre* and figs. The story, alas, did not end there and it was not happy. The following season Thorne was killed in a point-to-point fall. Meanwhile at Aintree, the National was won by fellow farmer Dick Saunders on Grittar. In doing so, he became the oldest winning jockey at the age of 48.

8 APRIL 2006

McCAIN STILL DANCING DESPITE SAD END OF THE RED AND GINGER PARTNERSHIP

Sue Mott

Ginger McCain caused a phenomenon. He turned the whole of Britain into a one-horse town. That horse, of course, was the champion Red Rum, three times winner and twice runner-up of the Grand National in the 1970s. The horse was a national hero in every sense and McCain was his trainer. He was also a second-hand car salesman at the time, who never dared even dream of winning the greatest race on earth. Red Rum made Ginger McCain just as surely as Ginger made Red.

'D'you know what a stupid, stupid reporter once said to me? Red Rum was part of our life for 23 years, a very important part, the kids grew up with him. He said it must have been like losing the wife when he died. What a stupid bloody man. There's 25 million women in this country and if I lose the wife I could certainly get another woman. But I could never get another Red Rum. He was a one-off.'

Yes, and this is the other McCain phenomenon. He lobs outrageous comments into conversations like hand grenades, blazing with political incorrectness, then grins with huge pleasure as they explode round his inter-locutor's ears. As soon as the mist clears, he is on to the next one. 'Conk!' he is forever calling. This is a summons to his wife, Beryl, with whom he performs a remarkable double act. They are endearingly rude to one another and consummately happy about it.

'You lied on the phone,' McCain challenged the moment we walked into his yard on Cholmondeley Estate, near Nantwich. 'You said you were good-looking,' he added in explanation. No one had said anything of the sort. This is merely his welcoming sally to make you feel at home. And you do. Among a thousand pictures, portraits, models and mementos of Red Rum, plus Amberleigh House, the McCain-trained horse who won the National two years ago, to silence forever the persistent accusation that he was only a one-horse man. That is why his phone has barely stopped ringing this week. And last. McCain is part of the Grand National, its folklore, its furniture, its phenomenal grip on the sporting imagination. Beryl instructs you fiercely not to bother him for more than half an hour. But try stopping him. He is 75 and his memories flow like the Mersey to the sea.

'I remember my first National like it was yesterday. I was nine years old, thereabouts, and I never actually saw a horse until after the race. There were a quarter of a million there and, being so small, I couldn't see over the crowds. I just heard the crash when the horses hit the fences and I saw the jockeys' caps gallop past. We used to stand right out in the country of the racecourse and we didn't even know who'd won because we didn't have a radio. But what did stick in my mind, being a lad, was the turf after the horses had gone. It was all torn up where they had skidded. Spruce from the fences was kicked all over. It almost looked like a battlefield after the fighting was over. And then, they didn't have ambulances for the jockeys in those days. You'd see three sat on one horse, slowly walking back to the stables. Then one jockey riding this horse and leading two others. Being a kid, it was very exciting. Like watching what happened after the charge of the Light Brigade. I was a bit brainwashed by all that.'

He wasn't a rogue, Ginger, but he was a lad. Naming him after Just William's sidekick, as well as his matching locks of red hair, was a masterstroke. He was named Donald originally, but that wouldn't do. He was Ginger, good with a catapult and poaching the odd duck from Hesketh Park for tea. He grew up, took all sorts of jobs, joined the Army and somehow fetched up in a yard in Southport, selling cars out of the front and training racehorses at the back. He trained his string on Southport beach, swearing by the minerals in the seawater and swearing at the do-gooders who said he was disturbing the wildlife.

'It was a Cinderella story, our life with Red Rum. No question. Our yard was on a side street in Southport, that's all. Across the road there was the Chinese chip shop, the off-licence, the paper shop. It was all as simple as that. And Red Rum himself started from the most humble of beginnings. In a five-furlong seller as a two-year-old. That was his first race at Aintree. In those early days, winning the National was way, way beyond my hopes and imagination. Then he went through all the phases, through hurdles, novice chases, until finally he became the best Grand National horse ever. That is unquestionable fact. Throw in a Scottish National for luck, which he won. Then throw in getting beat a short head in the Hennessy Gold Cup with top weight. He was very, very special. He was a magical horse.'

McCain has seen too much to be a sentimental old fool. Times were hard during the War and he knew many families whose sons, fathers, brothers never came home. Even so, you can't help wondering how he took it when Red Rum finally died. 'Never bothered me a bit. Not one tiny, tiny bit,' he said, lying through his teeth. 'Well, maybe just a little bit. He was dying. We all knew that. We're all horsemen. We know what happens then. Horses get shot. Bang and they're dead. It's as simple as that. We knew the job had to be done. So all the boys went into his box and gave him a Polo mint. Then I went in and what happened next is unforgivable. I said to John, the vet, "D'you mind if I go outside?" He said fine. But that was unforgivable. I was a coward. I went outside. Pop. The job was done. I was wrong going outside. I should have been with him. I don't cry easy. Never have. But I think I did then. I had to walk away on my own. I was choked.

'You see, he never really belonged to us. He belonged to everybody. I'm known off the back of his fame. We met everybody. Royalty, actors, sportsmen. The entire cast of *Coronation Street* came to see him. Liverpool when they were European champions. He had such charisma, such character. Always bright and cocky, he was such a showman. I'll tell you a story. We were in Ireland at a big show and we needed to get away to another event right down in the West Country. Now Jonjo O'Neill had been riding him and he was like a god in Ireland, so we couldn't get through the crowd. We got to this place and lying in our way is a great big fat man, purple in the face, being treated by ambulancemen. One of the organisers said, "You've got to be getting away. Don't worry about dis fella. Dis fella's dead. Let the horse step over him." So we let the old horse have a good look and he popped over this big fat dead man and away we went. Now that is perfectly true. It could only happen in Ireland.'

This reminds McCain of something that annoys him. 'These bloody footballers now, they get a tap and they're carrying them off on stretchers.' He is thinking about horses and racing and the sport's durability compared to namby-pamby sportsmen in headbands. 'It's Amberleigh House's first National. He's gone to the Canal Turn in the first five or six. Warren Marston rode him. Next minute, a big thing with blinkers on that was loose hits Amberleigh midships and Marston's fallen off him. Then the field's gone by. This was something out of a cartoon. All the spruce has fallen off the fence and sticking out from a big pile of the stuff is . . . two . . . legs . . . two . . . boots . . . with . . . the . . . toes . . . turned . . . up.' He can barely speak for laughing. 'It was Marston. Another jockey who's had a fall runs forward and drags him by the feet to the side rail while horses are still going over the top of them at 30 m.p.h. I've often thought about that when I see bloody footballers keeling over at a tap.'

Beryl pops in, with instructions to hurry up and get to the best bits. 'What are the best bits, Conk, oops, Beryl?' I hastily corrected but it was too late. 'There's nobody else allowed to call me that,' said Beryl, scandalised and laying her hands, quite firmly, round my throat. McCain is vastly enjoying himself. When she lets go (quite some time later) I ask Ginger if it was love at first sight. 'Not on your life,' he said. 'I could have had better than her. The only reason I married her, she wore me down. Simple as that.' Beryl takes no notice whatsoever.

So we turn to a safer subject. Animal rights protesters. Predictably, McCain is not for them. 'Talking about Aintree, if I've got one serious, serious regret it's this. Before the start at the National one day, the horses lined up to jump off and the starter stopped them. A group of protesters had sat down across the course. Now, you've got 40 horses, all fizzed up, and 40 jockeys, equally fizzed up — and drunk some of them. No, I shouldn't say that — and they've all got to stop for a load of people with rings in their noses, and rings up their — no, I shouldn't say that either. Well, I would have loosed the horses off. I would definitely. It would have been like facing the charge at Balaclava and if someone had got killed, so be it. They shouldn't have been there. I sincerely mean that. Who do they think they are?

'There's no cruelty involved in racing horses. The work and dedication that goes into them is amazing. People say I prefer horses to people, and that's true. Thoroughbred horses are far, far better bred than your average human being. We're breeding idiots to idiots as far as humans are concerned.' None more idiotic, in his book, than EU lawmakers who have said that you cannot bury animals on your property. He takes no notice. He buries his horses round his yard instead of sending them away to be incinerated. Not the remains of Red Rum, they were reverently laid at the winning post at Aintree, but all the rest. McCain is none too worried if an EU employee comes calling either. 'I'd set the dog on them,' he said.

And so to this year's National. He has three runners: Amberleigh House again, now 14, Ebony Light and the recently-acquired Inca Trail for Amberleigh's owner, John Halewood. 'You know, Ginger, this is too good to stop,' Halewood said one day, acknowledging that Amberleigh's age was against him. So they looked elsewhere. McCain tried to buy the chaser, Joly Bey, first of all. That caused consternation among his friends. He was at the Doncaster Sales bidding £200,000, instead of his usual £5,000, when two Irish pals spotted him. 'For feck's sake,' said one to the other, 'let's get hold of Ginger, I think he's pissed.' He wasn't. Just intoxicated by the racing life that has held him in thrall for nigh on 60 years. His son, Donald, takes over his training licence this year and McCain sees the day, far, far into the future when he is content to be laid in the same earth as his horses, and to hell with the EU.

'Look, I'm not a European, I'm not a Briton, I'm an Englishman. I'd like to think that every Englishman is entitled to at least six feet of England. If I get that, it'll satisfy me. And if I get it in a nice spot where possibly an old fox or hound runs across it occasionally, or an old herd gallops over it, that would suit me down to the ground.'

MAYHEM MADE FOINAVON FAMOUS

Marcus Armytage

All Grand Nationals are remarkable in their own right, but tomorrow's race marks the 40th anniversary of one of the most remarkable, Foinavon's National. Today a sign beside the innocuous seventh/23rd fence, the smallest on the course, proudly proclaims 'Foinavon's Fence'. If you walk past it you'll probably hear the birds twittering. But like the site of an infamous World War One battle, which is now a municipal car park in some French commuter village, it is hard to imagine the mayhem of its moment in history, of that damp day 40 years ago when every horse standing was brought to a standstill – stand, perhaps, not being the operative word as a good number of them were upside down in the fence – with the exception of Foinavon.

That year, of the 44 starters, 18 finished. But that does not tell the whole story, 17 of them were either remounted or had more than one attempt at jumping the remnants of the 23rd. In the nation's sporting conscience the episode has come to represent triumph against the odds and it enhanced the National's reputation as more lottery than horse race.

Naturally, over four decades, parts of the story and myth have become indistinguishable. It is often said Foinavon's hopes of victory were so forlorn that even his trainer, John Kempton, did not turn up. A trainer-jockey whose lightest weight was ten stone ten pounds, he rode most of his own horses. With Foinavon allotted ten stone he, instead, went to Worcester to ride Three Dons, a 5–1 winner. 'It's not a great regret that I wasn't there,' recalled Kempton, 68. 'I had a winner at Worcester which was a great thrill in itself, then we came in and watched the National in the weighing room in amazement. It was a massive thrill.'

Kempton recalls buying Foinavon from Anne, Duchess of Westminster, after he had fallen four times in succession in Ireland. By the time Foinavon had been endlessly lunged over a fence at Kempton's yard in Compton, Berkshire, and hunted, his reputation was not as the fastest but the safest chaser in the country.

Hardly a day has passed during those 40 years when John Buckingham, his unassuming jockey, has not been introduced to someone as 'the man who rode Foinavon'. 'I remember it like it was yesterday,' said Buckingham, who became a jockeys' valet when he retired in 1971 and 'looked after' 14 National winning jockeys in 30 years. 'It was my first ride in the race. I was almost first out of the gate, but they were going such a strong gallop that from then on I was struggling and had to keep noshing away at Foinavon.'

There were an unusually large number of horses still standing at Becher's second time. Well down the field Honey End, the favourite, and Josh Gifford were about three lengths in front of Foinavon as they approached the 23rd. The riderless Popham Down, a first-fence casualty, was leading the field. 'Foinavon was running a respectable race,' continued Buckingham. 'He definitely wouldn't have disgraced himself and although he was 100–1 he'd only been beaten three lengths by Honey End earlier that season. The leaders had gone such a gallop they'd have come back to us. With Josh and Brian Fletcher [Red Alligator], both good judges of pace, near me I was quite happy at the time. I didn't know it was happening until I was in it. Popham Down stopped and ran down the fence. Horses were coming back to us loose, whipping round, at a standstill. There were more jockeys than horses running about on the landing side. Three strides out I was side-ways on to the fence. Honey End came back past me in the opposite direction to have another crack at the fence [it took him three goes]. I turned Foinavon in and show-jumped it. Pat Buckley was upside down in the fence, Johnny Haine had got over the fence but came off doing so. It wasn't until the Canal Turn that I knew I was on my own. From then on I was just concentrating on keeping him going. He was a lazy old bugger but I knew he wouldn't fall.'

Gifford, on the eventual runner-up Honey End, also recalled being happy with the way things were going until the 23rd fence. 'I was still in no hurry,' he said. 'But in the mayhem my horse just froze underneath me. I was taking a turn when John came past. He was the lucky one who got through. If I'd been able to follow him then I'd have won – that was the unlucky bit for me. It seemed like ten minutes. I used him up trying to catch Foinavon and I was actually closer to him crossing the Melling Road [between the third and second last] than I was at the line. My horse was knackered from the second last.'

'Josh was brilliant,' recalled Buckingham. 'We got the Champagne out and he opened the first bottle, split the cork, stuck a half crown in it and gave it to me saying, "Here, I hope this brings you a bit of luck!" – I've still got it.' Foinavon was actually running much closer to the pace the following year under Phil Harvey – Buckingham had a broken arm – when, ironically, he was brought down at the water. Maybe it is right what they say about using up all your luck.

Kempton gave up training when he stopped riding in 1970. 'When I couldn't race-ride any longer I lost enthusiasm for training,' he said. For the rest of his working life he ran a cruise boat delivering divers around the west-country coast and the kicks he used to get from race-riding he still gets from scuba diving, flying his own light plane and touring France on a 1100cc Honda Pan-European motorbike. 'It's quite lively,' he conceded about the bike.

CHAPTER 7

AT THE RACES

Occasionally, Telegraph writers step away from their laptops, and the comfort of the press box, and join the milling throng at one of our racecourses. Instead of training binoculars on the horses, they turn them on the Great British Public enjoying a day out. They watch them as they dress up to the nines for Royal Ascot, totter on their vertiginous stilettos at Aintree, sink or swim in a river of the black stuff at Cheltenham, and mix with Gipsy Rose Lee and her friends on Epsom Downs. Their reports always add a colourful, often humorous aside to the regular items on the racing agenda.

On a different tack, there is also a tour around Towcester, one of the smaller, homely tracks, where Lord Hesketh allows the public in on racedays for nothing, then recoups in the bars and hospitality areas. Surprisingly, no one has yet followed his entrepreneurial largess.

---

7 JUNE 1924

OAKS DAY SCENES ON EPSOM DOWNS

GIPSY AND THE BOOKIE

A Special Correspondent

I am not a confirmed racegoer, as I was careful to confess after making my debut in this capacity at the Derby; so that a second visit to Epsom within three days represents a new experience in my life which may be considered either a sad lapse from grace or a salutary part of my education, according to your point of view. Be that as it may, I am glad to have been to Epsom again, because now I really can lay my hand on my heart and say that I have seen a race. To visit the Oaks after the Derby is rather like going on an ordinary day to Piccadilly Circus, never having previously seen it except on Boat Race night. The place is still full enough, but it seems by comparison quiet and deserted; and you have a new sense of space and leisure in which you can take in its details. The chief difference is that in Piccadilly Circus they do clear up the litter overnight, whereas the relics of the vast hordes which got soaked so cheerfully on Wednesday are still lying about on Epsom Downs. I imagine that the contrast between the two scenes must always be pretty striking, but this year it has been especially so because of the change in the weather. About the weather on Derby Day I have already expressed such of my thoughts as were not too deep for words or too lurid to print; yesterday was a pleasant day, with quite a satisfactory amount of sun and a fresh breeze blowing – all very delightful.

The chief difference that forced itself on my attention was the greater prevalence of the gipsies whose caravans line the road that runs from Tattenham Corner to the paddock and the grandstand (which haunts of the aristocracy were looking rather festive except for a memento mori in the form of a Black Maria all ready and waiting for possible criminals). I attributed this increased activity partly to the simple mathematical fact that, as there were fewer people present yesterday to be pestered, there must be more gipsies per head to pester them; but there were no other reasons in the weather and (to take my own case) in the fact that this time I had a lady with me. It was about her welfare that the gipsies were chiefly concerned. 'Buy the lady a favour, sir,' pleaded one merchant whose stock-in-trade consisted of hundreds of disgusting little celluloid dolls. 'Buy the lady a favour.' Hardly had I finished explaining to him that the lady would not thank me if I did — a sentiment heartily endorsed by the lady herself — when another (thinking, I suppose, that she looked hungry) suggested that I should regale her with a depressing form of fish which had the appearance of stewed brown-paper bags. This temptation, likewise, I avoided. Thank goodness, I saw no eels. I can't bear eels, as I told you the other day; they take my mind back to the days when I used to learn about the Diet of Worms in my history book — and I have always hated history. The only member of the gipsy fraternity who hadn't got some suggestion to make how I might brighten the lady's life was one who was himself preoccupied with a lady. She was a very young lady — about two, my companion diagnosed her — and she was lying upon a space at the end of her parent's barrel organ, and was being nourished with stout, to her own, and her father's, obvious satisfaction.

My own lady, however, had only one desire — the same desire, as I had so lamentably failed to fulfil on Wednesday — to find an attractive and courteous bookmaker whose wealth was such that he would not mind parting with a little of it to her after the Oaks was run. I related my Derby experiences to her, but she was not cast down. She seemed, like most women in such circumstances, to rely upon some mysterious pricking of her thumbs to warn her when she found the right man. And, like so many women, she was justified in her ridiculous faith. Miles away, among a score of other boards, she descried one belonging to a bookie with a name suggestive of bones and charnel houses — we will call him Alf Coffin. 'That's my man!' she said, and was off like a flash, I toiling after her. We inspected Mr Coffin from every view, and liked him. We liked the car he operated from, we liked the empty beer bottles arranged neatly in rows beneath his stool, we liked his wife and her friends, and we liked his face. In fact, we liked him enough to try to ruin him, if Fate so willed.

We made our bets, and then found a nice empty space on the rails nearby to watch the race from (a thing which we could not have thought of doing at the Derby). We had both backed Straitlace – I because Hotspur had spoken well of her, and the Derby had left me with a touching faith in his judgment; my companion because she liked the idea of a horse with such a name having a mother called Stolen Kiss. In addition, I was on my colleague's other choice, Plack; while she had picked Mink, for some strange feminine reason: she had a friend whose uncle had once had a dog of the same name. When the big race was over, we gazed at each other in awe. Between us we had managed to pick out the first three horses! This was obviously too good to last. Our course was plain. We collected our winnings from Mr Coffin – who remarked in a resigned sort of way that this was 'a body blow', and we caught the first train back to town before the gambling fiend should tempt us to less happy adventures.

---

20 JUNE 2007

ABSENCE OF TOFFS AND TOP HATS SPELLS FUN

Andrew Baker

There has been a lot of fuss about viewing problems in the poshest areas of the course at Ascot, but what many commentators have failed to mention – or perhaps notice – is that the Royal meeting, for all the trappings of finery, is a surprisingly democratic event. There is no question that if you want to go the whole hog, with a table in the new grandstand, a hired morning coat and a new hat for the missus, plus all the Champagne you can guzzle, you can spend the thick end of £5,000 and still see not much more than the back of someone's top hat.

But not far away from the land of silk and money exists another social event, with its own codes and traditions, that is every bit as much fun and a whole lot more relaxed.

Basic entry to the smart bit costs more than £50, but for just £15 you can enter the adjacent Silver Ring and have a fine day out for a fraction of the toffs' expenditure. Remember, you will be watching the same horses. A small percentage of the crowd here are standard racing punters, in T-shirts and jeans and clutching battered copies of the *Racing Post*. On any other day they might be at Redcar, or Ripon, but here they are watching a better class of racing. Most of the Silver Ring crowd, however, have made a sartorial effort. The ladies are immaculate in party frocks and little silly hats, while their consorts wear shiny business suits. The rules of the dress code are subtle: high heels must be worn to walk through the gates, ties should also be at full mast. Thereafter, the heels are discarded revealing an astonishing array of ankle tattoos – and the ties are lowered along with inhibitions.

Competition is fierce for the plastic tables next to the three-furlong pole. Barefoot ladies scatter to collect the right number of chairs for their party, while others lay out dips and crisps, and the loudest and gaudiest member of each group yells and semaphores to gather any stragglers. These base camps have to be established before 2 p. m. and the processional arrival of The Queen. Support for the monarchy is gratifyingly widespread: everyone clambers on to a table or chair for a good view, digital camera in hand, as the first carriage trundles into view. 'Look, there she is! There's Queenie! Aw, don't she look lovely in pink?' 'That's never pink. That's cerise, that is.' 'Whatever. Ooo look, there's Camilla. Good on you girl!'

Loyal duties done, it is time for serious business. The men head for the bookies, while many of the ladies are drawn to the shade of the food marquee, where a competent rock band are bashing out covers of Eighties hits. A large group of ladies dance in front of the stage, waving their hats. It looks like the aftermath of a rather successful wedding. Two favourites fly home in the first races, and now most are betting – and drinking – with the enemy's money. For those who wish to watch the racing, there are plenty of unreserved seats in temporary grandstands next to the two-furlong marker, a fair way from the finishing line, but the big screens mean that you don't miss a thing. And there are no top hats to obscure your view. Later in the day, men join the dancing and things become more intimate. Sun, booze, sociability, great racing. The Silver Ring is just like the Royal Enclosure, really. Only with a lot more snogging.

---

28 MAY 1977

ONE RACE YOU CAN'T WIN IN FINERY

Elizabeth Benn

If you are off to the Derby next Wednesday, or to Gold Cup day of the Royal Ascot meeting, I wish you luck. These are the two great party-days of the summer racing season when people are far thicker on the ground, food and drinks harder to scrum for, and your chances of seeing the horses more remote than at any other Flat racing occasion. Personally, I hate bumping and boring, and would cheerfully exchange them for any ordinary day's racing at Newbury, Goodwood or York – three particularly picturesque and well-run racecourses.

My husband insists that we study the horses for each race in the saddling enclosure before they go into the parade ring and at Ascot this seems to mean walking to Bagshot. It certainly feels that far by the fifth race. To try to get there from one of the private lunching boxes and back again in time to watch a race is an exercise that has to be tackled like a cross-country obstacle course. It is almost impossible to achieve in a dignified manner, wearing elegant finery. A tracksuit and plimmies would be more suitable gear, but I don't see the green velvet-coated stewards allowing me to take a short cut by nipping across the lawn in front of the Royal Box.

York, the Ascot of the North, is my choice for atmosphere and pampered comfort. There are always masses of colourful flowers surrounding the criss-cross mown paddock, everyone is terribly friendly, and the walk-way around the back of the stand enables you to move about and avoid the crowds. From here, too, you can see the horses being led into the winner's enclosure and get an aerial view of the paddock.

The food is better than on any other track I know (we don't all go racing to see whose horses are running the fastest). Some of us regard it as a pleasant day's outing away from the chores. The crab and salmon sandwiches have more filling than brown bread, the raised pies are freshly made. And if you want a three-course lunch, Fawcetts (the local caterers) provided prawns and celery salad, cold turkey and ham with salad, and green figs – all for £2.80, earlier this month.

Should you lose your escort in the 'ring' – that is where the bookies generate all the excitement over fluctuating betting prices – you can always wander to the Museum of Racing at the top of the stand. Here, among old weighing scales, saddles, silks and torturous looking farriery and veterinary implements, you find a leaded waistcoat once worn under a jacket by a trial jockey to mislead touts, early photographs, and mementos of the match on the Knavesmire in 1804 between Mrs Thornton and Captain Flinton Brown.

Racecourses are invariably several degrees colder than anywhere else and I have learnt the hard way that it is worth taking an extra jersey, coat, or mac to leave in the cloakroom. York, like most tracks, boasts palatial ladies' loos and cloakroom.

---

9 APRIL 1990

NO FAVOURS FOR THE PRIVILEGED RACING FANS

Tony Stafford

Corporate entertainment may be the inevitable accompaniment of present-day major sporting occasions, but the Grand National on Saturday showed that even the privileged may be forced to suffer some of the indignities borne so stoically by Joe Public. Almost 70,000 people crammed into the archaic racecourse just up the road from Liverpool town centre, and most must have been appalled by the abject misery of facilities offered for a minimum £15 a head in the enclosures.

Apparently, heads were about all you could see in most places, unless you were seven feet tall. The alternatives were to pay £27.50 for a 'place' – no seat guaranteed – in the County Stand or, for £50, a more definite spot on the roof. Other vantage points at more competitive rates give only a fragmental view of proceedings, especially the thrills and spills of the big race.

But to return to the privileged few. Firms, clubs and enthusiasts bent on enjoying 'A Good Day Out' have latched on to British Rail's package at £85, without admission to the track, of course, comprising breakfast and dinner and 'transfers' to the course. Colman's of Norwich, who have a viewing box with rows of brightly painted seats opposite the winning line, annually take a coach in one of the private charter trains and provide their guests with a lunch to enable non-stop eating and drinking from breakfast till dinner-time. There was a slight contretemps when the immaculately dressed managing director noticed that there was no mustard to accompany his breakfast, but his disappointment, nay annoyance, was assuaged when the staff promised to buy some in Liverpool. Frank Cooper's Full Grain mustard duly appeared on all the tables going home.

Two-and-a-quarter hours from Euston to Liverpool is pretty good, but it was here that the group were to experience the vicissitudes of life. The convoy of buses set off in dilatory fashion from Lime Street, but still reached the County Stand entrance around midday. What the unsuspecting passengers did not know was that Liverpool's trusty police force did not sanction any disembarkation before the official coach park, which happened to be in the middle of the Grand National course, about six furlongs from the stands. That part of the journey took a further 45 minutes.

From the coach park, the guests had to scramble up and then down a four-foot bank of crumbling turf before legging it up to the course crossing point via the big iron bridge over the Melling Road. This smacked more of peak-time Japanese television than relaxation and it was not until the horses were in the paddock for the first race that Colmans' box was inhabited.

Mark O'Connor, whose last-minute acquisition of Thinking Cap was one of the first Grand National casualties, then had to put on a metaphorical one of his own to provide alternative transport after the entertainment had finished. He saw there was no way that the exhausted party could re-trudge their way back to the coach and he arranged for ten of the city's taxis to meet the group near the course. When they had not materialised at the appointed time, he hijacked a sparsely-occupied coach.

Liverpool as a racecourse has plenty of faults, but these so often are magnified by unintelligent stewarding, often from people who seem to have been recruited by accident in a midnight round-up after the pubs turn out. Despite those and many other more justified grumbles from, no doubt, the majority of the massive crowd, Seagram Grand National Day is still unmissable.

---

15 MARCH 2003

THREE DAYS IN MARCH

WIN OR LOSE, THE PLACE IS JUMPING

Andrew Baker offers a personal view of the Cheltenham Festival

Tuesday: Thirty-seven hours, 17 minutes, two taxis, two aeroplanes and three trains brought me from Melbourne, Australia, to Prestbury Park, Cheltenham, with 30 minutes to spare before the first race of the 2003 Festival. I feel weak-limbed and giddy, which is the way most people finish their three days in the Cotswolds; no way to be starting out. The Gloucestershire taxi was driven by Brian Carling, who tells me all about a revolutionary design of manhole-cover that he has patented. He is hoping to find a wealthy investor. I tell him he'll never have a better chance as the town will be crammed with people dedicated to pouring money down drains.

The first assault on the senses at the racecourse is unwelcome: ugly, bellowing touts wanting either your money or your tickets. There must be a hundred such Cockneys and Scousers prowling outside the main entrance, and if you get through them with wallet unscathed you meet the second wave, the so-called gipsy ladies with their 'lucky' heather. I make for the See You Then Bar above the parade ring, squeeze, threaten and beg my way to the counter, and ask for a pint of bitter. The barman smiles, apologetically, and says 'Bitter?' in a strong Scandinavian accent. 'Yes.' 'I am sorry.' He shrugs. 'I don't know this word.' We get there, by sign language, and I gulp the pint while watching the first race on the big screen behind the parade ring. Tony McCoy finds the burden of my £2 each way too much to bear and tumbles off Lirfox – the start of a rotten week for him – while Back In Front makes it a winning start for the Irish. An extremely elderly man with a feather in his trilby sitting on a bench nearby waves his aluminium walking stick in the air like a shillelagh. 'What'd I tell you!' he cries, to no one in particular. 'Back in Front it is! Back in front we are!'

Strolling the lawns of the Club Enclosure, I am struck by the hordes of plain-clothes security staff discernible by their clumsy green ear-pieces. Must be to do with The Queen's visit later in the week, I reckon: impressive. Only in mid-afternoon do I twig that the hundreds of MI5 operatives are in fact racegoers listening to Festival Radio.

I greedily back an outsider, Santenay, in the Champion Hurdle, and am more indignant than I am entitled to be when it runs as the form book suggested it might, as if dragging an anvil behind it. Other slow-moving creatures spoil my enjoyment: I am boxed in behind a catering operative pulling a trolley of frozen chips up the concourse behind the main grandstand for long enough to learn that every chip sold at Cheltenham is made by a sinister-sounding firm called Gastrofarm, and that they average 14 millimetres in length. Later, I am stuck behind a poor girl trying to make her way into the Cottage Rake Bar under the burden of a huge bag of ice: no one moves out of her way.

Late in the afternoon I try to recoup some of my losses with an optimistic bet on the last race, only to find that the Tote system has collapsed. With tens of thousands of other would-be punters I battle towards the octopus-handed bookies on the rails, but there is no way through the throng. My horse loses anyway, so I have saved money, but the frustration lingers. Overcrowding is always the bugbear of the Festival; the Tote's technical incompetence only compounds it.

In the evening, the bar at my hotel is crammed with Irish tycoons and English chancers. One of the latter, Dan, a smartly-dressed middle-aged man with wonky spectacles who claims to have been drinking vodka since 10 a.m., discourses at some length on global politics before falling asleep on the sofa. Loose change dribbles gently from his trouser pocket to the floor.

Wednesday: A poor night's sleep: paper-thin walls and party-minded neighbours. At breakfast, I break a tooth on a dodgy sausage. The omens for the day are not good, so foolishly I agree to stump up for the heather sprig a harridan plants on me outside the course. 'God bless you, sor!' The entreaty of a tout reminds me that I have left my racecourse pass in my bedroom: half-hour walk there, half-hour walk back. The way the day is going, I am tempted to climb back under the covers. Instead, I opt for the hard-core experience of the Courage Enclosure, the cut-price party zone on the far side of the track from the main grandstand. It is mayhem: 20 minutes to get a drink, 15 more to put on a bet. Leather-jacketed thugs guzzle lager and leer at each other's girls; a squadron of security staff stand by, waiting for the inevitable flashpoints.

It is a resolutely unenjoyable experience, yet everyone seems to be having fun. I can only assume that there is some kind of macho pride in winning the struggle for a pint and a punt. 'See More Business?' a scarlet-faced goon yells at his girlfriend. 'No way. See More Barstaff, that's me.' 'You're worrying me,' his girlfriend responds. 'When you go for it, you go for it large.' Everyone has a credo, and wants everyone else to know it. 'Do your talking while you're walking, do your drinking while you're thinking.' 'Always look on the bright side of life. Always – oh God, I think I'm going to throw up.' A heavy-set skinhead with a livid abrasion on one cheek is hustled away in handcuffs by a posse of police, with his mates in pursuit. 'He's done nothing! He's done nothing!'

I need an antidote to all this, and ten minutes later I am on the weighing-room steps next to the parade ring, watching Princess Anne chat to a walnut-tanned Willie Carson. That's the democracy of Cheltenham: yobs on the one side, nobs on the other, each chasing enjoyment in their own way. In the evening I visit the Queen's Hotel in the centre of town, which is heaving with Irish punters (several of whom are heaving themselves). In the Gents next door to the Regency Suite, two of them are at the urinals. One tells the other: 'I've two grand on Best Mate.' His new acquaintance disengages his hand from what it has been holding and offers it in congratulation. 'Then you're on a winner.'

Thursday: So he is. The massed bellow that greets Best Mate as he runs up the hill ten lengths ahead of the field is Cheltenham at its best: non-partisan approval of greatness. Thousands of the visitors from over the water will have backed Beef Or Salmon, their brave young hope who fell on the first circuit, but there isn't one of them who doesn't applaud the English winner.

The Queen, resplendent in electric-blue tweed, presents the trophies, then strolls back through the parade ring, stopping to gossip with friends. She seems very much at home: strange to think she hasn't visited the Festival for 50 years. I wander among the trade stands: equine tat and sensible shoes, good-for-the-loo-wall watercolours of mini-skirted 'classy fillies', mock sheepskin jackets. There's a naff village green with a fibreglass blacksmith's forge and a fake post office with advertising cards in the window. 'Full-body massage with oils from mature lady,' one reads. Bet they didn't show The Queen that one.

I find an island of civilisation on the infield next to the first hurdle. There's a burger bar, a Tote kiosk and a loo, and no queues at any of them. Just a few hundred people stand on a knoll with a fine view up the straight to the finish: it is like being at a point-to-point, smack in the middle of the biggest jumps meeting in the world. Uncramped and unhustled, I relax enough to back two short-priced winners. Economically insignificant, but good for the psyche. Feeling flush, I gatecrash a box at the top of the grandstand to watch the last two races in luxury. The Tote system crashes again, and there are angry mutterings in the queues about the future of their monopoly. Everyone is convinced that they have been prevented from putting on winning bets, and naturally no one has been denied a loser. The French hurdler Never, carrying my fiver, leads over the last in the final race of the day, but then goes backwards faster than a rewinding video. Free Champagne more than compensates.

As the sun sets, the big screen says 'GOODBYE' and red brake lights glow from the slowly emptying car parks. Burgundy-jacketed sherpas push wheelie-bins down the concourses while their colleagues pick at mountains of rubbish with long-handled pincers. They make £5 an hour for a ten-hour day. Across the road from the main entrance, the students of Gloucestershire University have opened their bar to racegoers. The floor is sticky, and Bob Dylan is playing at enormous volume. 'How many roads must a man walk down?' a balding Irishman demands of his companion. 'What sort of a question is that?' 'Ah, shut up,' his mate yells back. 'Shut up and drink.'

---

12 MARCH 2009

WALKING COURSE AN ADVENTURE NOT TO BE MISSED

Jim White

This week I did something everyone should do once in their lifetime: I walked the course at Cheltenham. There is no special dispensation required, it is an opportunity open to anyone with a ticket for National Hunt's greatest meeting; the morning before racing starts, you simply slip under the rails and head off.

Since most Cheltenham-goers restrict their perambulations to the hard yards between bar and Tote, not many take advantage of this glorious stroll. On Wednesday, as three of us ambled round, reining ourselves in down the long, long slope, panting up the hill and agreeing that anyone who attempts to jump fences that substantial aboard a couple of tons of horseflesh should be referred to a psychiatrist, we had the two-and-a-half miles of undulating Cotswolds almost to ourselves. Apart, that is, from a steady stream of jockeys jogging round in sweat suits and a chatty Irish stable lad who told us he was walking off the effects of the evening before, when he 'had rather over-shot the runway' (and, judging by the evidence lingering on his breath, crash-landed in a Hudson River of Guinness). Plus, the official hole-filling team, a party of some 30 Sikhs patting at the ground with spades, who have cornered the market in smoothing out hoof ruts at every course in the country.

The most astonishing sight was reserved for the finish line. There, standing out against the green turf, we counted half a dozen patches of dust, seemingly marking the final resting place of racing enthusiasts. Course officials turn down requests to sprinkle ashes there, but still the patches arrive as regularly as a Ruby Walsh winner. This suggests that at least half the people walking the course must be doing so like characters from *The Great Escape*, with ashes of loved ones secretly spilling from the bottom of their trouser leg.

---

3 NOVEMBER 2005

FREE SPIRIT HESKETH ON A WINNER

Andrew Baker

It is difficult to miss the man in charge at Towcester racecourse. Lord Hesketh is six-feet-something tall and built proportionally. He wears Ray-Bans and a spectacular tweed jacket, and is shod in smart loafers and shocking lime-green socks. When he walks through the concourses the crowd parts in front of him and racegoers nudge each other and point. All the glances in his direction are friendly, and well they might be. More than 6,000 spectators attended the most recent meeting at the Northamptonshire course and not one of them paid a penny in admission charges.

Towcester's free entry campaign will be maintained throughout the National Hunt season, but it should not be misconstrued as aristocratic largesse. Nor is it, as other racecourse owners have suggested, a gimmick. It is part of a plan to revolutionise the way that this racecourse treats its customers and Hesketh believes that other venues throughout the country are going to have to take notice of what he is doing. 'Free entry means that we need fewer staff, for a start,' he explained, watching the teeming crowds from the balcony of his splendid private box. 'We don't have people tearing tickets, we don't have to have security men for the gate receipts. And I wouldn't be surprised to find that quite a few spectators in the past had simply hopped over the fence without paying anyway. So why not make it all simpler?' But surely it is costing the racecourse money? 'Absolutely not. Last year we made a profit, this year we're going to make a bigger one, next year bigger still.'

People arrive at Towcester, enter for free, park their cars for free, and march into the racecourse feeling that they already have got something for nothing, a particularly popular notion with racing folk. Thus buoyed, they can start to enjoy the new facilities, which are only likely to add to their good humour.

Towcester has always been a charming racecourse, and one where the seem-ingly interminable uphill finish provides one of the sternest tests anywhere of a National Hunt horse. But until Hesketh started his rebuilding programme, the facilities were inferior to those you might find at a number of point-to-point courses. Quaint, but tatty.

All of that has changed. Towcester now boasts two grandstands and a stable block that may be the finest in the country. There is a style about the place. The buildings are not flamboyant, but more dramatic than most punters might expect. 'The architect had never done a grandstand before,' Hesketh said. 'But he had done a lot of churches.' The gospel that Hesketh is preaching is that racing is not just a sport, but entertainment, and the style of the new buildings is part of the show, in the same way that architecture in Las Vegas augments the lure of the green baize. It may be a long way from the desert of Nevada to the wet clay of Northamptonshire, but a sense of style is inter-national. Even so, the basics have not been ignored. Loos are a test of any sporting venue and Towcester's are big and clean and plentiful. When punters are drinking beer all day, these things count. Within the grandstand build-ings, spectators can choose the kind of day out that they want. On the ground floor, spacious bars and hog roasts. One level up, table-service restaurants, and on top the private boxes. You can come with a Thermos® and a folding chair and spend nothing at all, you can bring beer money, get a table in a restaurant for £20 a head or get the Lordly treatment (fine wines and a particularly good steak and kidney pie) for north of £100.

Towcester is not the first racecourse to offer such a wide variety of options, but it is the first – how can we put it? – modest venue to do so. What Hesketh has realised is that the quality of the competitors is not the only factor that influences people to spend a day at the races. It may not even be the most important factor. On a day when only one of the races at Towcester was worth more than £5,000 to the winner (and only just), another fixture, at Wincanton, featured a high-class race worth more than £18,000. But the Tote's turnover at Towcester was higher.

Hesketh has a history of sporting innovation. In the 1970s he took on the Formula One motor-racing establishment with a team which ostensibly boasted more style than substance, but which also defeated Ferrari, McLaren and the other powerful and wealthy teams to win a grand prix and produce a future world champion in James Hunt. That effort cost Hesketh a lot of money and ultimately fizzled out. The development of Towcester, which lies at the heart of his ancestral estates, is a different order of project. 'With the racing team everything happened so quickly,' he recalled. 'We went from Formula Three to the top of Formula One in about nine months and we had a great chance of winning the first British Grand Prix in which we raced. This has taken more than ten years to come together, but I would say that I am just as committed to this as I was to Formula One.'

The development has clearly been a labour of love, but Hesketh is a businessman as well as a sportsman and he tries hard to maintain a sense of perspective about his creation. 'When it's something that you've built, it can be hard,' he said. 'But you have to be careful that you keep making the right decisions.' The racecourse is just one part of Hesketh's racing-related operations, which also include GG Media, who own the media rights for ten racecourses spread over the country, and a racing website. He sees great potential in all his racing involvements, but rails against the forces of conservatism (with a small 'c') still prevalent in the sport. 'There's a shake-out coming,' he said. 'No doubt about it. When it comes, those courses who have been thinking about the future will do well.'

Hesketh believes that the kind of developments he has been able to make at Towcester are the only way forward for the sport. He cites Ascot as an example of a larger racecourse that has been making similar changes. Indeed, there has been frequent contact between the two courses while they have been undergoing transformations. But managers of other racecourses with shabby facilities and little money for investment will look at Towcester and shudder. This is what the future of racing looks like, but it costs money to get there. On the way down to the rails for a photograph, Lord Hesketh scanned the horizon. 'Full car parks,' he noted. 'Good sign, that. And that is another good sign.' He indicated a young father pushing two infants in a double buggy. 'What do you see there?' Hesketh asked. Two babies? 'No, no, no. Two future racegoers.'

CHAPTER 8

FLAG-MEN, FARCES
AND FALLERS

Racing has its fair share of disasters and farces. The Grand National is an obvious case in point: who can forget the flag-man's vain efforts in the 'void' race of 1993? Or Glenside (1911), Tipperary Tim (1928), Nickel Coin (1951) and Foinavon (1967) tiptoeing around the carnage on the course to score unlikely wins? Or the mystery of Devon Loch's infamous 'splits' with the finishing post in sight?

Flat racing is not immune, either. In the 1962 Derby, Larkspur managed to avoid no less than seven horses that fell coming down the hill towards Tattenham Corner. And what about the 1913 Derby, when the suffragette Emily Davison threw herself fatally under The King's horse? Then there are those who fall to earth unintentionally from their magnificent beasts at speeds of around 30 m.p.h. There are graphic, first-person accounts of those, too. It's certainly not reading for the faint-hearted.

---

5 APRIL 1993

NATIONAL HUMILIATION

WORLD LOOKS ON AS RACE IS TURNED INTO A FARCE

J.A. McGrath, Racing Journalist of the Year

The 1993 Martell Grand National, the 150th to be run, will be remembered as one of the greatest of sporting fiascos. The alleged failure of a casually-employed flag man, paid £28 for a day's work, to signal a second false start – and the subsequent failure of seven jockeys to pull up their mounts before a second circuit of the course was completed, reduced the event to farce. The race was declared void, and yesterday at a press conference at Aintree, Peter Greenall, chairman of the racecourse company, said that this year's race would not be re-run. 'Trainers who have been consulted overwhelmingly say that it would not be practical from the horse point of view to run the Grand National again this season.'

The fiasco, which was televised live to millions of viewers worldwide, has cost racing, the betting industry, and the Treasury dearly. Yesterday they were still counting the cost, with bookmakers William Hill threatening to sue Aintree racecourse for losses they claim amount to in excess of £150,000 in their marketing of the race. Their lawyers and directors were meeting late yesterday to decide whether to take action. The no-race has also cost those involved in the racing fraternity much time and effort, and the heartbreak of the whole episode was hitting home yesterday. The outspoken John Upson, trainer of Zeta's Lad, said the atmosphere at his yard was as if there had been a funeral. The trainers, however, are right in saying that it would be impractical to run the Grand National again this year. Among those consulted were Toby Balding, Upson, David Elsworth, Jimmy FitzGerald, Nigel Twiston-Davies, David Nicholson, Simon Sherwood, Nick Gaselee and Martin Pipe. Racegoers who kept their badges from Saturday will be offered free admission at Aintree's November meeting. Owners and trainers of runners can look forward to being reimbursed their travelling expenses, while owners will also be reimbursed the jockeys' riding fees. All entry fees on the race will be automatically returned.

The prestigious name and reputation of the Grand National have taken an almighty battering this weekend, but Peter Greenall remained convinced that its reputation had not been irreparably damaged. Many associated with the animal rights demonstrators will possibly, with their twisted and bizarre outlook, view Saturday's fiasco as a victory, but Greenall pointed out how dangerous and irresponsible their behaviour had been. A group of about 30 rushed on to the course moments before the 3.50 p.m. start time. Climbing over fences and running back and forth across the track, with police in pursuit, nervous horses and riders were forced to wait while the intruders were removed.

This took time, and with several edgy horses, made all the more agitated by the volume of crowd noise, starter Captain Keith Brown called the field into line, but at the first attempt the tape stretched across the track and was broken by horses anticipating the off and a false start was called. The whole field pulled up before reaching the first fence. On the second occasion, when the field came in, the head of Formula One, ridden by amateur Judy Davies, was over the tape, and with Captain Brown shouting to the riders to 'Come on!', and then hitting the lever, the tape was caught under Formula One's head and then thrown backwards, wrapping around the neck of Richard Dunwoody, aboard Wont Be Gone Long. Dunwoody was pulled back, and for a few strides looked in serious danger of being strangled when horses behind trod on the tape as his mount continued forward. The top of his racing colours were ripped and his neck was bruised.

Captain Brown signalled a second false start, holding his red flag aloft, but this time it failed to unfurl. Whether the recall man, Ken Evans, a Lancastrian in his late 50s, was able to see the second signal is uncertain, but jockeys claim they did not see Evans waving his flag a second time. Thirty of the 39 runners – Just So having been withdrawn in the morning – set off towards the first fence, with almost all of them believing it was a real race. The fancied Royal Athlete was among the fallers on the first circuit.

While the riders set off hell-for-leather towards Becher's for the first time, panic-stricken racecourse officials were trying to think of a way of alerting the jockeys that there had been a second false start. Many trainers and stable lads rushed out in front of the stands, with the express intention of signalling to the jockeys to pull up. Nine horses were, at this point, left standing near the start, having taken no part.

With the racecourse commentary team indicating to the crowd that there had been a false start, the only people who seemed unaware of the situation were the riders of those horses still running as they approached The Chair. Jeers and boos from the crowd reached a crescendo as the horses continued up towards the biggest jump on the course, and in a brave, last-ditch attempt to get them to stop, Rodger Farrant, the assistant clerk of the course, waved a red flag, while a solitary cone was placed in front of the jump. But it was to no avail, and with Ken Evans now waving his flag frantically further up the course, there was mayhem, the magnitude of the disaster becoming clear when a large contingent of riders headed out for a second circuit of the course.

Rod Fabricius, the acting clerk of the course, was in consultation with the stewards as they tried vainly to untangle a catastrophe which seemingly had no chance of being halted. The scenes on the racecourse, in the betting rings, on the track and outside the weighing room were unprecedented. Chaos reigned. Tempers exploded and emotions ran high as angry trainers and bewildered jockeys, as well as disgruntled racegoers, became caught up in the turmoil. Captain Brown, at one stage, suggested that the race could be re-run, with only the nine horses who had not jumped off with the rest not being allowed to compete. This was met with incredulous anger by onlookers, with John Upson shouting: 'I'll see you in court.' The stewards eventually declared the race void. Captain Brown, who was officiating at his last Grand National, along with Mr Evans, had to be protected by police as they made their way back to the weighing room.

In the weighing room Jenny Pitman, who trained the first-past-the-post Esha Ness, was in tears after pleading with officials to stop the race. Mrs Pitman shouted: 'What are you doing? My horse has already gone one circuit; I don't want to win the National like this!' John White, who partnered Esha Ness, later claimed he was unaware that it had been a second false start, but for whatever reason, on the second circuit, both he and Norman Williamson, who partnered The Committee, looked around, giving the impression that they sensed something was amiss.

Yesterday at Aintree, and all around Liverpool for that matter, it was like a wake. But Greenall, who said there would be a full inquiry, both by the racecourse and the Jockey Club, stressed that his overriding consideration was the long-term prestige of this international event. When the inquiries commence, two issues need to be addressed. First, why the riders did not realise the second false start had been called; and, secondly, why the attention of seven jockeys could not be attracted in order to warn them of the false start.

It should also be noted that when the 1994 Grand National is staged, the race will come under the authority of the newly-formed British Horseracing Board, who will take over control from the Jockey Club later this year. In this age of modern satellite links and mobile telephones, it is hard to comprehend why there was not something far more sophisticated than a man waving a red flag down the course in front of a 39-runner field charging towards the first fence.

---

5 JUNE 1913

SENSATIONAL RACE FOR THE DERBY

DISQUALIFICATION OF CRAGANOUR
THE STEWARDS' ACTION
UNPARALLELED INCIDENT
100 TO I WINNER

Hotspur

The most unsatisfactory, sensational, and lamentable Derby in the history of the race was added to the records at Epsom yesterday. The horse to finish first was the favourite, Mr C. Bower Ismay's Craganour. He passed the judge a head in front of the extreme outsider Aboyeur, while a neck away was Louvois, and next to him was Great Sport.

Half a mile from the finish a dreadful thing had happened. As the horses were swinging at a tremendous pace round Tattenham Corner, the negotiation of which was charged with some additional risk as the ground was hard and the turf glazed by the sun and footwear, a woman with deliberate design flung herself at Anmer, the horse carrying the colours of His Majesty the King, who, with Her Majesty, was looking on. Horse and rider were brought down heavily, the jockey, Herbert Jones, being flung clear, but striking the hard ground with his head. He lay prostrate. So, too, did the wretched creature who had caused the terrible fall, while the horse rose again and galloped after the receding horses.

Let me return to the finish of the race. As Craganour's number was hoisted in the frame there was plenty of cheering, and Mr Ismay, obviously influenced by the overwhelming excitement of the moment, went out to meet his horse and returned leading him in. It was a great moment for him, as it is for few men who have experienced the fierce emotions of leading the winner of the world's greatest race. He was smiling and happy as he turned to left and right to acknowledge congratulatory words from friends. There was another cheer, a hurrah three times given proceeded from an adjoining stand, and Johnny Reiff, the jockey, touched his cap as his name was sung out.

All this was happening in that narrow strip, a few yards in width, which is reserved for the placed horses when they return to scale. It is in the nature of a well, overlooked by a small stand, which is occupied only by members of the Jockey Club. Suddenly there occurred a distinct lull in the buzz of conversation. We who had been in a position to see had noticed some scrimmaging and squeezing among the leaders, and one was warned by instinct that trouble of a kind was looming ahead. But an objection in the Derby! Why, the thought had only to occur to the mind to be instantly banished. It was impossible. Such a thing, apart from one case of fraud, had never been known in the history of the race. Would any owner dare to break from precedent and tradition in this unheard-of way?

The Stewards were the interveners. They are the constituted guardians of the Turf morality, so far as the administration of its laws are concerned, and they stepped in to inquire into what they regarded as grave infringement of the first rule of fair play, and, if necessary, to right a wrong. Just for one brief moment was the suspense ended. A loud voice called 'All right!' It is the ancient verbal signal which announces to everyone within hearing – and beyond that the word is passed on from mouth to mouth with lightning-like rapidity – that the jockey of the winner has passed the scales, and that all formalities have been complied with without demur.

I saw faces of backers who had great sums at stake change their expression as when glad relief follows on grave anxiety. Craganour's trainer, William Robinson, a man steeped in the varied fortunes of the Turf, relaxed his serious features, smiled gratefully, and mopped the perspiration from his brow. The winner of the Derby was just on the point of passing out of the gate, when there was a sharp and authoritative shout of 'Stop! Bring the horse back!' Everyone guessed what this meant. The sinking feeling returned with an awful rush to the Craganourites. It could mean nothing else than that the horse was being objected to. The fact was that some unauthorised person had dared to give the signal. The 'All right' was all wrong, so far as the officials were concerned, and, as I have related, the audacious trick cruelly succeeded for the moment.

Picture if you can the bitter disappointment of those associated with the horse, to say nothing of his intimate admirers nearby. The hundreds of thousands crowded and scattered over the course and the Downs had no knowledge of these dramatic events. All this time Craganour, fierce of eye and over-wrought with his great effort, was in a state of intense excitement in the narrow, little enclosure. He kept kicking to right and left, and would not stand still while his presence was required. The object of keeping him there was not quite clear, and the Honourable F.W. Lambton, one of the Stewards of the Jockey Club, gave permission for him to be taken away.

Meanwhile, the Stewards of the meeting – Lord Wolverton and Major Eustace Loder (Stewards of the Jockey Club) – were sitting in judgment. The Earl of Rosebery is a Steward of the meeting, but I am unable to say positively whether he took part in the inquiry, though I understand his sanction was obtained to the issuing of the official statement. The Stewards had seen certain things happen through their own glasses, and their view was fortified by what the judge (Mr C.E. Robinson) and several jockeys said in their evidence. I understand on high authority that the judge's evidence was particularly strong, and thus it was that at the end of half an hour of intolerable suspense, during which the world was kept in an agony of doubt – for the news of the original result had been flashed far and wide – the following official statement was issued by the Stewards:

'The Stewards objected to the winner on the grounds that he jostled the second horse. After hearing the evidence of the judge, and several of the jockeys riding in the race, they found that Craganour, the winner, did not keep a straight course, and interfered with Shogun, Day Comet, and Aboyeur. Having bumped and bored the second horse, they disqualified Craganour and awarded the race to Aboyeur.'

To say that the dramatic sequel to the finish of the Derby of 1913 created a feeling of consternation is to apply quite a mild description. The greatest sensation was caused. For it meant general rejoicing being swiftly turned to bitter lamentation. A raging hot favourite, a popular horse with the people, had won the Derby at 6 to 4 against, and here he was deprived of the honour, and, instead, the one enthroned in his place was an animal whose starting price was 100 to 1. Jeddah and Signorinetta were 100 to 1 winners, and there was sensation about their victories, although they were deserved and straight-forwardly gained. But about this unthought-of Aboyeur, whose name had not even been bandied in jest as a possible winner, there was real tragedy in the manner of his exaltation to Classic honours.

What a Derby to go into history! Once upon a time a winner was disqualified because he was proved to be a four-year-old, and therefore an impostor. Once also there was a dead-heat, and many times the best horse has not been returned the winner. But only once, and that yesterday, has the winner been deposed for unfairly interfering with others. This result is too far-reaching, and altogether beyond comprehension, to be written in words. The public are poorer, and the bookmakers are indeed richer. How jealously do the gods watch over them, so that they shall come to no harm! They would have been stricken had the judge's verdict been allowed to stand, and had the name of Craganour been added to the scroll. But theirs is a clean sweep. They sweep into their coffers every wager, win or win and place, on Craganour, as also they do those made in respect of every other horse barring the winner. And the few who chanced to write the name of Aboyeur in their books were woefully unlucky.

You will have noticed that the Stewards have not introduced the name of Craganour's jockey into their statement. Presumably they exonerated Reiff from blame, and we are left to conclude that the horse alone was responsible for the erratic course he steered, and the 'Wild West' incidents that were the outcome. Perhaps, in the circumstances, it was natural we should look for an expression of official disapproval with the riding in general in the race. There never was a more disgraceful illustration of the depths to which modern jockeyship has sunk when a number of horses are concerned in the Derby with a scramble and scuffle altogether unworthy of the traditions of the English Turf. It is all very deplorable.

The official statement shows clearly enough that the ground for action did not only lie in the last furlong of the race. There were incidents further away from home, or how could the names of Shogun and Day Comet have been introduced? They were conspicuous a quarter of a mile from the finish to the distance. I dare say Frank Wootton's evidence would not modify the case against Craganour, for the trainer of Shogun, who is the father of that jockey, alleged that a bump which the favourite gave Aboyeur caused that horse to bore on to Shogun, and practically extinguished his chance when going particularly well.

On the other hand, a distinguished general officer, who was in D'Arcy's Stand, a most favourable position from which to view the oncoming horses as they finish close to the rails, assured me that he twice saw Aboyeur attempt to savage Craganour in the last 50 yards. This statement was confirmed by other highly credible witnesses, who were in a place which entitled them to pass an opinion, and if this really happened it would account for Craganour throwing up his head near the finish, which he most certainly did do. It might also indicate that the horse was running unkindly as the result of great pressure, and being run beyond the distance of his powers. Personally, I much incline to this latter view. All this, however, is surmise, but I have not hesitated to give the statement of the general officer referred to, because there was a strong feeling entertained that Aboyeur was contributory to the unsatisfactory finish of the race. If there was any doubt at all what a pity that the Stewards could not see their way to give the favourite the benefit of it! However, it was ostensibly demonstrated to the Stewards, as their statement makes clear, that the chief cause of the trouble was Craganour, and no amount of discussion and argument now will alter the decision, which stands irrevocable.

I must pause here to point out that Aboyeur and Craganour were always prominent in the front of the 'fighting'. The former, a well-grown horse, but wearing blinkers, which are usually taken to indicate that the wearer of them is an animal of doubtful courage and uncertain temper, drew out with a clear lead before they had gone a furlong, and it was at the distance that Craganour seemed to deprive him of the lead. This was taken to mean that Aboyeur was done with, as was only to be expected after the great pace he had set, and the force he must have taken out of himself. It was then that Craganour seemed to resent his task, for instead of coming on he sulked, as it seemed, for a stride or two, and Aboyeur drew level again. Then did the two race home locked together, and though I was not far removed from the winning post, I thought that Aboyeur had won by a short head. Craganour, however, must have spurted in the last stride or two to have caused the judge to hoist his number in the frame.

Poor Herbert Jones, usually vivacious and richly endowed with good nature, was brought back in a pitiable plight as the result of the outrageous act of the woman, Emily Davison. He lay pale and unconscious on a stretcher, the King's colours disordered, and blood showing from a wound on his face. The sight of him was a painful shock to all in the reserved enclosure who gazed at him as he was borne by police into the jockeys' dressing-room. Deep in the hearts of every onlooker was a feeling of fierce resentment with the miserable woman who had overwhelmed this innocent jockey with such an injury. It was a mercy he had not been killed outright, and I have rarely known men so intensely moved as they were over the circumstances of this tragedy of the day.

His Majesty witnessed him being brought back, and expressed sympathetic solicitude for his welfare. An equerry of the King and Lord Marcus Beresford, the manager of the King's racehorses, with Mr Richard Marsh, the King's trainer, attended to him, but there were no conveniences in this ancient grandstand, and, therefore, as quickly as could be in the circumstances, he was conveyed to the Epsom Hospital. I am, indeed, glad to say that last night a fairly favourable account of him was forthcoming. He has concussion of the brain, and is generally much shaken, but his condition is not really serious.

Walter Earl, who rode Agadir in the race, described to me what happened. At the place where the diabolical attempt was made there are double rails. The crowd is kept back behind the inner rails, and the woman, therefore, could not be said to have accidentally fallen over them. She dashed under both rails, as showing that her design was deliberately conceived. Furthermore, it is clear that she intended to bring harm to the King's horse. For Earl says she dashed right under the head of Agadir, with her eyes fixed on Anmer, who was slightly behind and on the outside. Earl then saw her deliberately throw herself in front of Anmer, with the dreadful result that the horse struck into her, knocked her senseless, but was himself brought down through being unbalanced. Of course, the horse fell, and poor Jones was flung heavily on the bone-hard ground.

I have spoken with several eye-witnesses, including an attendant on the Pullman car, which left the Downs Station for Victoria at five o'clock. He had a place near the spot, and he confirms the statement that the woman's action was deliberate, and was such as to give the impression that she waited for the King's horse to come. When he did come, Craganour, Aboyeur, and several others had passed, but the jockey of the French horse, Nimbus, had to check his mount, which action must have interfered with any chance he may have had of winning the race.

Well, the fiasco of the 1913 Derby is over, and it will not soon pass from memory. The few fortunate people, apart from the bookmakers, are those connected with the Druid's Lodge stable in Wiltshire, which shelters the winner. Mr Cunliffe, who owns Aboyeur, has not hitherto won a Classic race, though he has achieved some notable success in handicaps, notably the Jubilee Handicap, which his horse Ypsilanti won two years in succession. Time will show whether Aboyeur's victory is a great fluke, as it seems to be at present.

---

7 JUNE 1962

NO CHEERS FOR LARKSPUR IN CHAOTIC DERBY

DEBACLE ON THE HILL SHOCKS CROWD TO STUNNED SILENCE

Hotspur (B. W. R. Curling)

The Derby, run in perfect June weather, was wrecked yesterday by the falls of seven horses on the long hill down to Tattenham Corner. Victory among the survivors – and it seemed rather a hollow one – went to Larkspur, owned by the American Mr Raymond Guest, ridden by the Australian Neville Sellwood, and trained in Ireland by Vincent O'Brien. Larkspur, a 22–1 chance and the outsider of O'Brien's two runners, was out clear a furlong from home and won comfortably by two lengths from Arcor, who came from almost last to take second place close home from the fading Le Cantillen, with Escort fourth. The sight of six riderless horses passing the stands stunned most of the vast crowd to silence, and there was more concern for the missing jockeys, lying perhaps seriously injured on the course out of view of the stands, than excitement over the winner.

There have been some sad stories to report in the 183 years' history of the Derby – the favourite Angers breaking his leg two years ago, and the race spoilt by a suffragette in Aboyeur's year (1913) – but there has been nothing as ghastly as the debacle on the hill on this sunny June afternoon. It seems probable, but by no means certain, that Romulus, runner-up in the 2,000 Guineas, struck into the heels of a horse in front of him, bringing down Crossen. The favourite, Hethersett, was certainly brought down by the prostrate Romulus, and Pindaric in turn by Hethersett. The others to fall were the rank outsiders Changing Times, Persian Fantasy and King Canute II, who broke a leg and had to be destroyed on the spot. The other six horses did not appear seriously hurt, though Hethersett and some of the rest had superficial cuts.

Six of the jockeys were taken to the local hospital, and four were kept there – W.H. Carr, rider of Hethersett, T. Gosling (Changing Times), S. Smith (Persian Fantasy) and W. Swinburn, who rode Romulus. Only the day before, Carr had brought off a brilliant hat-trick, and yesterday – certainly through no fault of his own – he was brought down and seriously injured, not for the first time in a long and successful career. How quickly do fortunes wax and wane in this racing game.

We shall, perhaps, never know if the pile-up on the hill, five furlongs from home, affected the result. Going up the hill on the far side of the course neither Hethersett nor Pindaric appeared to be going particularly well, but both in fact were improving their positions when brought to the ground. R.P. Elliott, the rider of Pindaric, was back in the stands unscathed later in the afternoon and told me that Pindaric had really taken hold of his bit, and was improving steadily when brought down. Elliott's impression was that Hethersett was going well, too, though from the stands he looked to be off the bit and being driven by Carr to improve his position.

Of the survivors, there can be no doubt that Larkspur won on merit and it is clear that it was only very quick avoiding action by Sellwood, and some luck, that enabled him to steer clear of trouble. Sellwood, telling his story to me after the race, said: 'I was badly placed early on, and then, after nearly half a mile, I began to improve, moving up from one of the last ten to about 12th. When I got to the top of the hill I was tracking Hethersett. I saw Carr take quick avoiding action to his right when a horse came down in front of him, but he just failed to avoid Romulus. I swerved to my right, and by sheer luck scrambled over or through, I don't know how. I then began to improve steadily and coming to Tattenham Corner was just behind Sebring. I struck the front rather more than a furlong from home.'

The stewards started an inquiry into the pile-up immediately, but adjourned it to hear evidence from some of the injured jockeys. I doubt if any clear picture will emerge. Things happen too quickly when horses are racing flat out. One jockey told me that he sensed there might be trouble coming down the hill, with many horses going well, tightly bunched, and inclined to close in on the rails. When one of the leaders begins to tire quickly, and a tired-running horse is pocketed, there is always the risk of a horse striking into the heels of another in front of him, and it seems that this is what happened.

---

26 MARCH 1956

UNSOLVED MYSTERY OF DEVON LOCH

UNLUCKIEST NATIONAL LOSER OF ALL TIME

ROYAL CHASER, OUT CLEAR, STOPS 55 YARDS FROM WINNING POST

Hotspur

With 55 yards to go and the Grand National at his mercy, Queen Elizabeth the Queen Mother's Devon Loch, clear of all opponents, stumbled, skidded, tried to keep his legs and stopped at Aintree on Saturday. It was, I think, the saddest and most dramatic event I have seen on a racecourse. So ESB, ridden by D.V. Dick, strode on past him to win by ten lengths from the mare Gentle Moya with the 1954 National winner, Royal Tan, a further ten lengths away third.

It is unlikely that anyone will ever really know exactly what happened to Devon Loch. It was all over in a matter of seconds and occurred on the run-in from the last fence to the winning post exactly opposite the water jump. Some held that Devon Loch might have run into a patch of false-going. I do not think so. My impression was that the horse was in pain. One of the racecourse vets who examined Devon Loch immediately after the race thought he might have had a sudden attack of cramp. Another felt his behaviour might have been due to a small blood clot in a hind leg. The latter is known to cause paralysing pain and would explain the fact that Devon Loch appeared for a few moments to have no strength in his hind legs. Indeed, one's immediate reaction was that he had broken down.

Though the result cannot show it, this was in all but name Devon Loch's National and one cannot but feel extreme sympathy for his owner, his rider Dick Francis and his trainer Peter Cazelet. I can think of only two other National incidents of a comparable nature. One was in 1936 when Cazelet's great friend, the late Lord Mildmay, appeared to have the race won on Davy Jones two fences from home when the reins broke and the horse ran out; the other when Reavy took the wrong course from the last fence on Zahia in 1948.

There was no doubt, however, that Devon Loch was the unluckiest loser in the 120 years' history of the race. I shall long remember the picture of the Queen Mother, as ESB was being led triumphantly in, going quietly towards the racecourse stables with a smile on her face, to see if her horse was all right. A few minutes later, after the vets had examined Devon Loch, The Queen and the Queen Mother were congratulating Mr and Mrs Leonard Carver, owners of ESB, his rider, Dick, and his trainer, Fred Rimell, on their victory. It was just as if nothing untoward had happened.

Though Devon Loch's fantastically bad luck blighted the race, ESB's victory was that of a game, thoroughly exposed horse, now the winner of 17 chases out of 56 races he has run. A Warwickshire farmer, Mr Eric Binkstad, of Knowle, near Birmingham, bought him as a young horse in Ireland and later passed him at a profit to another Warwickshire farmer, Mr Rowley Oliver. After he had won for him, Mr Oliver sold him for 2,500 guineas to two Warwickshire owners, Mrs Leonard Carver and Mrs Geoffrey Kohn, who raced him for a time as a partnership horse. The partners decided to split up and ESB was offered for sale at Newmarket, where Mrs Carver bought him outright for 7,100 guineas. Mrs Carver, who is a fine horsewoman and has done well in the show ring, for a time trained ESB with her husband, but they had little luck with the horse. They then sent him back to Rimell, who had nursed him back to the form he showed as a young horse when he ran well in the Cheltenham Gold Cup. Dick, the winning jockey, is one of the tallest and longest legged of all the National Hunt riders of his generation. He had to waste hard to ride ESB at 11 stones three pounds, and it is hard to realise that as a boy he won the 1941 Lincolnshire Handicap on Gloaming, who carried only seven stone four.

As they had come to the last the race lay between Devon Loch and ESB. Devon Loch took it well (about a length in front), and so did ESB. At the 'Elbow', in the long run-in, Devon Loch had increased his lead over ESB and 100 yards from the post, Dick on ESB had accepted defeat and was looking round to see if was likely to lose second place. Francis was riding Devon Loch out with hands and heels, all set for victory when the unbelievable happened. It was bitterly disappointing. It remains to add that ESB's time was only four-fifths of a second outside the record of nine minutes 20 and one-fifth seconds set up by Reynoldstown in 1935. Devon Loch, had all gone well, would certainly have beaten it.

---

25 MARCH 1911

THE GRAND NATIONAL

A REMARKABLE RACE
GLENSIDE'S VICTORY

Never in its lengthy history has the Grand National provided a tamer race or ended in such an extraordinary and unsatisfactory way as it did yesterday afternoon. One might well ask if the steeplechaser is degenerating. The query is justified by yesterday's experiences. It is significant that the two top weights remaining in the handicap were both animals bred in France. One of them, Lutteur III, had won the prize as a five-year-old. Of the 26 starters only one, Glenside, actually completed the course without mishap, and he had been amiss, and was so hopelessly beaten when he was left all alone in his glory that his rider had to use his greatest powers of persuasion and all his most skilful knowledge of horsemanship to get the old fellow over the three last fences. He blundered at the final obstacle, but, happily, kept his balance. It was nevertheless far from an edifying spectacle to see Glenside, full of distress, crawling along to achieve the greatest triumph which falls to the snare of any steeplechase horse. The old horse, who has only one eye, could scarcely stand when he was pulled up, and he must, in the circumstances, be accounted one of the luckiest animals known to win the Blue Riband of cross-country sport.

The race was altogether disappointing. After going little more than a mile the field presented an extraordinarily long tail, and with competitors falling all over the course, and the loose horses galloping on and bringing down others, the spectacle was one which has rarely, if ever, been seen at Aintree. Mr George Hodgman, who has witnessed nearly 60 Grand Nationals, averred that he had never seen anything like it. In this contention he will, I have no doubt, be supported by all the veteran sportsmen who were present.

It was a magnificent day for the celebration of the great race, if the prefix is admissible in this case. No more glorious weather has been associated with past Grand Nationals, and it was pleasant to contrast the delightful sunshine and the absolutely perfect light with the experience of the years when Drogheda and Grudon respectively won the race. The attendance was enormous, and the general impression was that a larger crowd has rarely been seen here. Twelve months ago, the present King was the guest of the Earl of Derby for the meeting. Yesterday Royalty was represented by Prince Arthur of Connaught, who drove up with the Knowsley party just before the first race, attended by an escort. There was a large and brilliant gathering, particularly of people devoted to hunting, and it is gratifying to observe that, in spite of the laments which we hear about the decadence of National Hunt sport, the Grand National retains its pristine popularity. The scene in the stands and in the paddock during the intervals of the races was strikingly impressive, and so overwhelming was the crush that it was difficult to move about with any degree of comfort.

The first sensational incident was the downfall of the favourite at the fence after Becher's, though before this there had been considerable grief,

Trianon III having fallen at the very first obstacle. It appears that Lutteur III, in trying to avoid a loose horse, took off too soon, and landed in the middle of the fence, where he was hung up until his jockey could extricate him. This was terribly bad luck, for there is no safer fencer in training than Lutteur III. Carsey and Roman Candle had fallen at the fifth fence, and Pedlar's Pride at Becher's. Valentine's Brook was fatal to Bridge IV and Schwarmer, the latter of whom was knocked over by a loose horse, while Vix was placed *hors de combat.* Caubeen settled down with the lead from Precentor II, Rathnally, Jenkinstown and Glenside. Two fences before reaching the water, Jenkinstown came to grief, and at the water Rathnally blundered so badly that he shot Chadwick on to his neck. The jockey made a wonderful recovery.

Caubeen, who was jumping well, continued to lead from Precentor II, Rathnally, Shady Girl, Glenside and Mount Prospect's Fortune, of whom Mr Noble's horse fell before reaching Becher's the second time. At the obstacle after Becher's, Caubeen ran clean into the fence, and in doing so baulked Rathnally, who shot Chadwick out of the saddle on to the opposite side of the obstacle. The jockey had to run round and catch the horse and remount. He then followed on at a respectful distance. About a mile from home Shady Girl fell, but was quickly remounted. Glenside had established such a long lead that, although he was terribly tired, he managed to struggle on and win as above stated. Rathnally finished second, and Shady Girl third, the only other to complete the course being Foolhardy, who had fallen early on, but was remounted.

It was, of course, an immensely popular victory, owing to local connections; but, unfortunately, Mr Bibby, the owner of Glenside, has been ordered abroad for his health, and amid the hearty cheers of the crowd the horse was led back by Mrs Bibby. Mr Anthony, who is one of a family of celebrated jockeys, is an accomplished horseman, and he is to be heartily congratulated upon joining the select band of amateurs who have won the greatest steeplechase in the world. Doubtless it was a proud moment, and also a pleasant and unexpected surprise. Mr Anthony, who is only 21 years of age, had his first mount in the Grand National yesterday. He had got off something like ten pounds at comparatively short notice in order to do the prescribed weight. He is a farmer's son, and belongs to a Welsh family. He, like his brothers, has been used to the saddle since his earliest years, most of his experience having been gained in the hunting field. In spite of the numerous falls, there was no serious mishap to horses or riders, but Driscoll, the rider of Mount Prospect's Fortune, had his ear lacerated.

31 MARCH 1928

100 TO 1 WINNER OF THE NATIONAL

AN AMAZING RACE
HOW TIPPERARY TIM WON

Hotspur

Something awful was bound to happen. Forty-two horses went to post for the Grand National Steeplechase at Liverpool, and only one stood up to the end. That horse, of course, was the winner. Yesterday morning Mr H.S. Kenyon's Tipperary Tim was practically unheard of. In the afternoon he became world famous. He came in alone for a steeplechase worth over £11,000. Only one other, the American, Billy Barton, was placed by the judge, and that after the horse had been on the ground through falling at the last fence when holding a short lead.

A great massacre had occurred during the race, making it amount to something far worse than a mere debacle. Fiction cannot compete with the cold facts of this latest celebration of burlesque steeplechasing, for the winner of so much money would scarcely be ranked as a humble selling plater else-where. He has a tube in his throat because he was a rearer, and could not possibly have done what he did without this resort to artifice. Need it be added that his starting price was 100 to 1, which means that scarcely anyone had considered him worthy of a passing thought.

Yet it says something for the sportsmanship of our people when, though they had lost their money on others, they rushed to the paddock to meet the horse and give a rousing cheer to horse and rider for what, after all, had been a display of gallantry and endurance, though aided by that all-powerful ally we call luck. The young rider, Mr W.P. Dutton, touched his cap and smiled his joy. Not long ago he passed his final examination to become a solicitor at Chester. He had occasion to forget all about the law yesterday.

My story begins with the crowding in the paddock of all these 42 competitors. One of the spectators at close quarters within the parade-ring was the King of Afghanistan, who appeared to be much impressed with Trump Card. This commanding horse was halted for a few moments in front of him. The long line seemed unending as it filed out of the paddock for the short parade, and yet some brave people were accepting as little as 5 to 1 about Master Billie, and only a point longer odds about Trump Card. Even allowing for the painful facts we know, it ought to have been longer odds against either completing the course with such a swarm taking part.

They lined up, and three times the single line of tape was broken because some of the jockeys were even more anxious than the starter to get this detail over. Amberwave's rider was content to hang behind, and when, at last, they were sent on to the battlefield, which was so soon to become a sort of shambles, Amberwave was the last to get away. He may have missed the seething excitement of the front line, for after jumping awkwardly at the first fence – where, by the way, only one fell, he actually refused at the fourth fence. This, truly enough, was humiliating, and was the last thing expected. One felt he would have done so much better had he been among the front-rankers. Mr O'Brien set him at the fence again, and they went on with the hopeless job. It was the end of his feeble enterprise.

Another shock came rapidly. Sprig was on the ground. He had hit the fence just before Becher's. It was another unbelievable happening. The nightmare, however, was only just beginning. I should point out that the light was far from good. It is true that the race had the luck to be decided between the showers, but, away in the remote distance where is the Canal Turn fence, there was a screen of haze which made observation extremely difficult. Becher's did not seem to gather in its usual toll. The holocaust happened at the Canal Turn, which makes a sharp left-handed move necessary. Almost invariably it is the scene of alarming trouble, but nothing to compare with what happened now. My eye-witness, on whose evidence I depend, is Mr Harry Brown, the well-known amateur rider, who occupied a position in that crow's nest stand in the vicinity of the Canal Turn and overlooking Valentine's Brook. He said that the mischief-maker-in-chief was the £7,000 horse, Easter Hero.

I have written on previous occasions how this horse has jumped awkwardly to the right at these National fences. It was for this reason that I would never entertain his chance of winning, notwithstanding Mr Loewenstein's ideas when he gave that extraordinary price for him. Anyhow, he distinguished himself now by jumping on to the top of the fence, and there he remained until finally he fell back into the ditch. Meanwhile, events were happening rapidly. Two or three horses following immediately on his heels stopped for the simple reason that they could not jump, and they, in their turn, stopped others, so that in a few seconds there was a crowd of our much-discussed National horses baulked and prevented from getting on with their business.

It was an appalling situation, and the thing which had to be realised in a flash was that there was no help for it. Those out of it included Master Billie, Trump Card, and all the rest, so to say, of the horses we have been so conscientiously discussing for weeks past. What vain and wasted effort, to be sure, and what a cynical ending! The lucky ones to avoid the melee were the American, Billy Barton, the French mare, Maguelonne, De Combat, May

King and Tipperary Tim. It was the first time Tipperary Tim was even noticed. But there he was, going well, though last but one, as they went over the water jump in front of the stands. The last over was the French mare, and so they went into the country for the second time.

I ought perhaps to interpose a line here recording the fate of Koko, who was the expensive purchase made by Captain the Honourable F.E. Guest and Mr Grisar on the eve of the race. He made a bad business of Becher's, failing so completely to tackle the steep drop that he landed in the ditch, finally having to be hauled out. It was just one little episode in an inglorious story.

Let me continue with the narrative of the actual contest from the time they had passed out into the country. It was easy now to concentrate on these few survivors, and possibly the first sharp impression was of Billy Barton and the bold way he was going. Here was one who had been discarded and given no chance because of his feeble displays, and yet at the moment the despised one was shaping like a winner. Of course, they had a long way to go, but they crossed fence after fence safely, showing how most proved jumpers will not fail if given a fair chance.

They came to the Canal Turn of evil fame, and were watched by the riders of those who a wretched fate had bundled out of the affair. Still no one had given a thought to Tipperary Tim, though he was still standing up and going well, to all appearances. It was at the first open ditch beyond Valentine's that Maguelonne ended her part. Mr Brown tells me that she was going strongest of the lot, and, in his opinion, would have won had all gone well, but in landing over the fence she kicked back at it. It brought her down. Simultaneously May King fell, and there were only three left in it – Billy Barton, still going strong and still showing the way; Great Span, jumping safely but showing, I thought, some signs of distress; and Tipperary Tim, last of the three, but plodding on.

Now did we give him a thought for the first time, for at least he was going to be sure of a place, those last two fences permitting. They came to the second last fence. The question then was: would the English horse, Great Span, overhaul the American? It was answered dramatically enough. Great Span collapsed in a heap on landing, and a groan went up, mingled with sharp cries of elation from many Americans looking on and almost frenzied with excitement. Great Span's saddle had slipped and some think it was the cause of his fall. It may have contributed to it. My opinion is that he was dead beat at the time.

So now there were only two left. On came the Yankee, and it seemed a million to one on him, though he was beginning to labour, like tired horses will. He had only the last fence to cross safely, and the Americans would begin their rooting and cheering. He rose at it, or tried to measure off the right height, but hit it with his forelegs. He was tripped and trapped and on the ground. A length behind him came Tipperary Tim, the only one standing up out of the record field who had gone to post. Amid an amazement which left onlookers staggered and too astonished for expression during those moments, the tubed 100 to 1 chance galloped on to win from the remounted Billy Barton.

There is little to add. Lots of people rejoiced that the winner had been so capably ridden by a young amateur who acquired the arts of horsemanship in the Cheshire hunting field. He told me how he had seen the trouble at the Canal Turn, but missed it through having purposely been riding wide on the outside where there was not a hoof-print on the turf. He had benefited because of his prudence. I asked him if his horse had made any mistake at all, and he replied that Tipperary Tim never put a foot wrong. Well, he is a gallant horse who can complete the Grand National course and win without making a mistake, and so we must try and detach ourselves from the sharp disappointments of the race, and give this humble chaser and his plucky rider full marks.

We shall be told that it was due to an accident altogether exceptional that so many horses were put out of the race. Personally, I shall maintain that when nearly 50 horses go to post for a Grand National the race is robbed of its sporting character through those enormous risks of interference which would not be present were, say, a score of the best steeplechasers in the world bidding for what should be the Blue Riband of steeplechasing. It would be childish to argue that Tipperary Tim is not entitled to that Blue Riband today. Yet, he has profited by the calamitous misfortunes of others.

Until a solution be found we shall have scores more Tipperary Tims entered and sent to post. The trouble will be to find jockeys rather than riders in future. Mr Kenyon, the owner of Tipperary Tim, is a brother of Mr C.F. Kenyon, who had a big stable of horses at the time of his death a few years ago. Actually, Tipperary Tim, now ten years old, was one of them, and at the sale he was purchased by the late owner's brother for around about £400. He has been trained in a small stable at Whitchurch, Shropshire, by J. Dodd.

---

9 APRIL 1951

NATIONAL DEBACLE STUNS AINTREE CROWD

29 CRASH IN FIRST QUARTER OF RACE

Hotspur

After a race reminiscent of the fiasco of Tipperary Tim's year, three out of 36 horses finished the Grand National course on Saturday. In 1928, Tipperary

Tim alone did not fall; Billy Barton, the only other to finish, was remounted. On Saturday, the only two who remained standing were the winner, Nickel Coin (40–1), and the runner-up, Royal Tan (22–1). Derrinstown (66–1), brought down at Becher's second time round, was remounted and finished third, long after Nickel Coin had passed the post.

After such high hopes of a thrilling race it was desperately disappointing to see only a handful of horses still on their feet after Valentine's first time round. All the giants had gone – Finnure and Land Fort with nine others at the first, Freebooter (brought down by Gallery) at the second, Shagreen (a victim of his own carelessness) at the fifth, Arctic Gold (his attention distracted by a loose horse) when leading at the Canal Turn, where Armoured Knight, Cloncarrig and Pirate Brownie also met their fates, and finally Roimond at Valentine's.

I did not see Tipperary Tim's victory, but there can seldom have been such a debacle in the Grand National. Certainly I have never witnessed such a one. The perfect light one sometimes gets after rain, the reasonable going and the best National field since the War, all pointed to a thrilling tussle. Who could have expected 29 victims in the first quarter of the race? It was so staggering that the crowd was silent as the handful of horses came on to the racecourse for the first time, Russian Hero leading the seven survivors, jumping like a stag and apparently going the best of the lot.

With the seven were half-a-dozen loose horses and as they came to the redoubt-able Chair fence, the loose ones had either to jump it or run across it and turn on their tracks. They all chose not to jump, three or four going across Russian Hero and slowing him down. McMorrow on Russian Hero had to ride him into it at the last moment, and the 1949 National winner hit the top and came down – as for the same reason did his stable companion Dog Watch. George Owen, their trainer, must before this fence have had high hopes of winning a second Grand National. The dreaded Chair and loose horses put paid to them.

Now there were only five standing – Nickel Coin, Royal Tan, Gay Heather, Broomfield and Derrinstown. Gay Heather went at Becher's, bringing down Derrinstown, Broomfield at the next, and that left only Nickel Coin and Royal Tan to fight it out. A good race between the two it certainly was. There was nothing to choose between them coming to the last fence, with Royal Tan, if anything, going the better. But it was Royal Tan and not the gallant little mare who hit the fence. Nickel Coin leapt over it as nimbly as ever, Royal Tan hit it hard, and it was then 'all Nickel Coin to a China orange'. Derrinstown, remounted, trailed in long afterwards, a bad third.

All praise to Nickel Coin's Staffordshire rider, J.A. Bullock, former para-trooper, captured at Arnhem, and now in his middle thirties. It was his first Grand National ride and only the second time he had ridden over fences at

Aintree. Though attached to T.F. Rimell's successful stable, Rimell preferred to put up B. Marshall, a more experienced Aintree rider, on the stable horse Land Fort. Full marks also to Mr A. O'Brien, rider of Royal Tan, and younger brother of the horse's trainer, Vincent O'Brien, who has done so well with Cottage Rake, Hatton's Grace and others. Mr O'Brien, riding at Aintree for the first time, might well have been thrown when Royal Tan made his two mistakes – the first four from home, the second at the last.

Nickel Coin belongs to Mr John Royle, young son of Mr Jeffery Royle, of Jury Farm, West Horsley, Surrey, a well-known point-to-point rider in his day. Mr Royle gave Nickel Coin to his son as a present. It was Mr Royle, senior, who started Nickel Coin's trainer, J. O'Donoghue, as a trainer three years ago. O'Donoghue also was a good point-to-point rider, coming over from Mallow in the south of Ireland three or four years ago in search of rides in point-to-points and steeplechases. Mr Royle sent O'Donoghue two or three horses to train at his stables near Reigate, Surrey, and he now has over 20 in his yard.

---

9 APRIL 1967

NATIONAL 'FELL APART BEFORE MY EYES'

John Lawrence, who rode Norther in the race

The Grand National fell apart before my eyes yesterday. In ten ghastly seconds one loose horse tore the heart out of the race, and at the fence after Becher's second time round, the hopes of millions (mine among them) lay in a tangled, struggling heap of men and horses. But even disasters like this – the worse since 1928 – produce their hero. Somehow John Buckingham, on an unconsidered outsider, Mr C.P.T. Watkins's Foinavon, scrambled bravely through the carnage.

And a moment later, looking round, he saw a sight beyond his wildest dreams – an empty racecourse. No other horse had survived without at least irreparable delay, and alone in his glory, Foinavon plodded dourly home. In his wake, Josh Gifford, on Honey End, was the quickest to recover. Approaching the fatal fence some 20 lengths behind the leaders, he saw it all happen, steadied Honey End, went back 50 yards to get a run, then drove him through in gallant but unavailing pursuit. He made up all but 15 lengths of the leeway, but Foinavon was gone beyond recall.

Not for the first time, but I hope for the last, history had repeated itself in a Grand National. For it was barely 50 yards from the scene of yesterday's disaster that in 1928 the great Easter Hero fell into the ditch which then guarded the Canal Turn and decimated his opponents, just as the loose horse (I think it was

Popham Down) did yesterday afternoon. Then, it was Tipperary Tim who survived to come home alone the only horse to finish without being remounted.

It seems incredible now that a race which for me and for so many others had been going with dream-like precision should explode so suddenly into total chaos. But that is how it was. Going out on the second circuit, Norther was giving me the best ride I've had at Aintree since Carrickbeg. Up in front I could see Roy Edwards on Princeful, Terry Biddlecombe with Greek Scholar glued to the inside rail, Stan Mellor on The Fossa, Nick Gaselee on Kapeno (who was to confound the prophets by passing Becher's twice without the slightest difficulty), Johnny Haine still having his arms pulled out by Rondetto, and David Mould, who moved up alongside me just before Becher's, going like a train on Different Class.

No doubt there were others, too, but not more than a couple in front of Norther as we slanted down over Becher's Brook. The next fence, one of the smallest on the course, was only a few feet high in places where holes had been knocked in it first time round. I was just thinking that this was the moment to move over to the inside for the Canal Turn when suddenly from the left – apparently from nowhere – the blinkered Popham Down tore crazily across our path.

Greek Scholar, Princeful and Rondetto were, I think, the first to go, but Terry Biddlecombe stayed with Greek Scholar and got over at the second attempt to finish fourth. But as Norther reached the fence a horse lay directly in front of him. He did his best, but it was impossible, and I jumped the fence without him. Looking back from the ground, the sounds and sights were those of a defeated cavalry charge. Horses were everywhere, heads and heels appearing through and above shattered birch. If my description sounds incoherent, the only excuse is that that was precisely how it felt.

Jockeys who had the time were turning round to have another go, but when I got back to the take-off side and scrambled on to Norther's back, the leaders were gone far beyond Valentine's and he decided, probably wisely, that discretion was much the better part of valour. So back we came, bitterly disappointed, but no more so than at least a dozen others.

This National was, of course, one big hard-luck story, but from what I saw a moment before the end the unluckiest were Rondetto, Princeful, Different Class, Kapeno and The Fossa. And yet unseen by me there may have been even worse cases of misfortune. Honey End, after all, made up so much ground that he would surely have been concerned in the finish, and the second of Ryan Price's three runners, What A Myth was, in the words of his jockey Paul Kellaway, 'kept waiting for what seemed like five minutes'. Getting over at last he, too, made up an incredible amount of ground to finish ninth.

Price's third runner Vulcano was the only fatal casualty of the race, killed, alas, two fences before Becher's second time round.

And how must Peter Cazalet be feeling? Robbed already three times in his life by sheer bad luck in a National, he now saw both his runners, Different Class and Kapeno, taken out at a single stroke. Though I do not put it any higher, Norther, too, was desperately hard done by. I had asked him for no sort of effort and as we cantered back he was still full of beans, almost running away.

About a million years before, Mr Alec Marsh had sent us on our way in the old style – by flag – because the Grand National starting gate was not in working order. And almost at once the Fates were laughing, for Bassert, my own principal fancy, jumped the first fence perfectly only to topple over as he landed. He brought down Moon Valley on whom poor Andy Turnell's first race at Aintree lasted the minimum time.

But for most of us, the first circuit was, as I say, all that one dreams of in a National. There seemed to be masses of room and Terry Biddlecombe and I, choosing the 'unfashionable' outside lane, galloped down to Becher's together and congratulated each other as we landed over it. Norther hit the next fence quite hard and Terry said with a broad grin: 'That's a bastard of a fence.' Neither he nor I could know just how big a bastard it was going to be next time.

Last year's winner, Anglo, had, as I half-feared he might, remembered the place and decided that once was enough. He tailed himself off after a mile and got stuck on top of The Chair when already well out of it. Freddie, too, had got a long way behind, but according to Pat McCarron, was just beginning to get into the race when the heavens fell in after Becher's. Like the good hoofer he is, he got through somehow and finished the course, but never held out any hope to his many supporters. Third to finish was Red Alligator, who got over the fatal obstacle at the second attempt, and Greek Scholar, trained like him by Denys Smith, was fourth.

Of all the horses in yesterday's field, I suppose Foinavon would have been in most people's half-dozen least-likely winners. He once carried the Arkle colours when owned by Anne, Duchess of Westminster, and trained by Tom Dreaper, and perhaps his chance yesterday is best exemplified by the fact that his trainer, John Kempton, was at Worcester where he rode the first winner! But that's the National. Not for nothing was the first winner called Lottery in 1839 and let no one detract from Foinavon's triumph. His young jockey, John Buckingham, 26 years old, had never ridden in a National before, yet he and his equine companion did what none of the rest of us could do and therefore earned their triumph. Another hero of the race must have been B. Fletcher who, like me, Stan Mellor and others, crossed the crucial fence without his horse, but managed to get back aboard with such miraculous speed that he was able to finish third.

And now I remember an odd footnote at the start of this season when Foinavon's trainer, John Kempton, asked me to ride the horse in a four-mile amateurs' cross-country race in Germany. The venture never came off but judging by yesterday's events the Germans might have found us hard to beat! Foinavon's original owner, Anne, Duchess of Westminster, was at Aintree yesterday, and greeted those who sympathised with the words: 'If he was still mine he probably would have been running the Mullingar.'

---

31 MARCH 1996

PERFECT RECORD BITES THE DUST

Marcus Armytage, a past winner riding Mr Frisk, describes his severely abbreviated race this time around on Bishops Hall

Until about 3.05 yesterday afternoon, I thought I was pretty much invincible round Aintree. About a dozen rides over the big fences and I'd never hit the deck, though, all too aware that pride precedes a fall, it was not something to boast about. The prospect of falling, and falling at the first, had never occurred to me, didn't even cross my mind, as Bishops Hall, a picture of health, circled in anticipation at the start, and as we lined up between Chris Bonner on Sir Peter Lely and Charlie Swan on Life Of A Lord.

I should think Jason Titley, who won the race last year on Royal Athlete, thought the same. However, after the noise of horses crashing and the cheers of the crowd had died down and the dust had settled on the landing side of the first fence, Titley and myself, two National-winning jockeys in the past, found ourselves sitting on our arses, Titley, near the inside rail in some pain, gasping for breath, too sore to be miserable or downcast. Just getting his next lungful of air and checking his toes worked was occupying his mind.

My father, a trainer who tried to win the race numerous times with his best staying chasers, only gave me two pieces of advice about the Grand National. The first, in 1990, had been not to hit Mr Frisk until we got to the Elbow. The second was that the race was, for all but one of its competitors, invariably the most disappointing in the world. Sitting at the first, his second piece of advice came home to roost. In a family newspaper I couldn't tell you my precise thoughts.

When Chris Maude, having his first ride in the race, fell at the first on Bishops Hall last year he described the run to that fence as the 'most exciting 200 yards of my life'. I'm afraid I can't even rate it that highly. Everything, I thought, was going to plan as we approached the fence. I wasn't in the front rank, but didn't want to be. Bishops Hall was settled, not keen as he had been going to the start, and had plenty of daylight. He couldn't have met the obstacle better, but what exactly happened on our descent is hard to tell.

Caught out by the drop? First, his front end went, then, as he scrambled to keep his feet, his hind end went, like losing a car on ice. Any chance of the partnership being retained went out the window when he then started turning sideways. It felt like it was happening in fast forward, too; there was no slow motion about it. Technically you'd call it 'unseated rider', but I'd defy anyone to sit out that sort of mistake.

The abject disappointment lasted a few minutes. I was fine, the horse, who led the field loose for a while, was fine. We were both feeling a lot better than Jason Titley; it puts your own disappointment in some sort of perspective. I went over to Jason, who was shouting with pain and wanted his goggles removed. As soon as he mentioned his back, the paramedics made him lie still, put him in a collar and summoned a scoop stretcher.

He was being loaded into an ambulance by the time the others were jumping Valentine's. I watched bits of the first circuit on the big screen opposite the first and then saw Jason's mount Barvard Dieu and a bridleless Party Politics belting up the tarmac of the Melling Road in the centre of the course. They'd come to the races in the same horsebox and were still together. I hopped on Barvard Dieu for a lift back to the finish. I think Nick Gaselee, his trainer, was surprised to see me riding his horse and he had a double take. So the 1996 Grand National for your correspondent started on one horse, ended on another, with nothing in between. The only injury I picked up all week was a cut to my face while shaving.

It may have taken you longer to read this than I actually spent on Bishops Hall, but with the disappointments forgotten now, I can count my blessings. To win the race on Mr Frisk was a fantastic feeling, and last year I had a great ride on Romany King to finish fifth. But just now, I am beginning to think that I just might not win it again. Still, at least there is always next year.

---

1 MARCH 1970

ALL RACING FEELS TERRY'S BLOW

John Lawrence

Whatever else it may lack at the moment, British racing is lucky enough to have two superlative champion jockeys. Their excellence is a priceless asset, and last week when one of them, Terry Biddlecombe, fell – on the flat of all places – at Kempton, the blow that smashed three of his ribs was felt throughout the sport. Or if it wasn't, it damned well should have been, for we are far too apt to take for granted the sacrifices made daily throughout the jumping season for our entertainment.

Even at £13 a ride Biddlecombe is, in my opinion, still ridiculously under-paid, and such an injury at this important stage of the game is a cruel reward for the sort of life he has been leading. A week ago at Chepstow, with blood pouring from his nose and his body wracked by savage wasting, the 28-year-old champion rode as fine a race as was seen on an English jumping track to win the Welsh Grand National. For any comparable masterpiece, a top-class boxer or golfer — or for that matter Terry's Flat-race counterpart, Lester Piggott — would have earned several thousand pounds. Terry got a few hundred and would have been entitled to only his bare fee had French Excuse finished second instead of first.

Then, on Thursday, after suffering nothing worse than disappointment on Coral Diver at Wincanton, he hit the ground at 30 m.p.h. for the umpteenth time this season when Fearless Fred landed six inches short of the water. It was by jumping standards a relatively easy fall, but to this man at this moment no fall is easy, and as he walked slowly back, chalk-faced with pain, an almost tangible wave of sympathy went out from the stands to meet him. 'Why not call it a day and go home?' someone asked in the weighing room. But sympathy pays no dividends and half an hour later Terry was calmly getting up on a novice chaser who had never run before over fences. 'It's best to keep going,' he said. 'Otherwise you just get stiff.'

Now for the moment even he won't be able to keep going. Of all the ills a jumping jockey has to bear, broken ribs are perhaps the worst. There's nothing to do but wait until they heal. To breathe is agony — to cough or laugh, a flick-knife in the chest. For any man, convalescence from such an injury is horrid, but at least the rest of us can eat and drink to ease the pain and boredom. For Terry Biddlecombe, who is a natural light-heavyweight and puts on weight like a good Hereford steer, every mouthful has to be paid for later in the Turkish baths where in a single night I have seen him, with my own eyes, lose the better part of a stone. Unlike Lester Piggott, Terry has never let the demands of his profession interfere with his natural *joie de vivre*. Life, he believes, is meant for living, and if a glass of Champagne means an extra hour sweating blood in a rubber suit, well, he just makes it two hours and has another glass.

Such a life, in the nature of things, can't last for ever. The dreadful calls it makes on health and strength inevitably see to that. It is the measure of Biddlecombe's extraordinary mental and physical resilience that after half a dozen years in the very top flight he is, without any doubt, riding better than ever – sitting even further up their necks, driving tired horses even harder and showing no single trace of strain or loss of nerve.

So if, alas, as must at least be on the cards, we have to go to Cheltenham without him, just spare a thought for what that means. God knows, he deserves a holiday, but jumping jockeys don't take voluntary holidays in March – least of all when another championship and another century of winners is well within their grasp. Terry's many friends and countless admirers can only offer heartfelt sympathy and say: 'Come back soon, but not too soon. In your absence jumping may seem dull and colourless, but a man, even an iron man like you, can only take so much. Take it steady then and let the bones heal quick.'

If you want an example of how capricious fate can be, just consider the difference between two incidents last Friday afternoon. From one, a simple slip-up on the flat, the champion jockey got three broken ribs. From the other, one of the most horrific accidents I have seen, George Lee escaped without a scratch. At the first fence of a novice chase at Fakenham, a horse called Flush of Diamonds chose for some unknown reason to take on the wing and converted George into a human cannon ball. Cars are parked at that particular fence at Fakenham (though I hope they never will be again), and George, pausing briefly in mid-air with one foot on the running rail, flew on like Nijinsky in *Le Spectre de la Rose* to land with his head under the bumper of a prosperous-looking limousine. I don't know what the insurance company will say to the claim for 'damage caused by flying jockeys', but miraculously it was the car that came off second best. George's only comment afterwards is worth recording. 'That's a really nice young horse,' he said. 'I just hope it hasn't spoilt its confidence.'

---

19 JANUARY 2008

I WAS STRUGGLING TO BREATHE

A.P. McCoy

I wasn't expecting to have to write this week's column confined to my new barracks – the fifth floor of the John Radcliffe Hospital in Oxford. Still, look on the bright side, it might give some respite to those of you who follow my tips week in, week out. I am making good progress after an operation on Tuesday to secure my T12 vertebra with two small pins either side of the bone, and I'm in good spirits. On Wednesday, I couldn't get out of bed. On Thursday, I just about got to the bathroom on a Zimmer frame, but yesterday I was walking round my room and along the ward corridors – looking for escape routes! At the current rate of progress I'll be jogging home to Lambourn tomorrow.

The fall, from Arnold Layne at Warwick a week ago, was not a bad one and I was totally conscious at all times. I knew on impact that I had landed awkwardly. Lying on the ground I was never in too much pain, but I was finding it hard to breathe and, though I could move my toes and wave my arms about, I couldn't wiggle my upper body and I told the doctors if I could just lie still for three or four minutes it might go away. The doctors were first class. They put me on a spinal board, put my neck in a brace and didn't let me move. The surgeons here said that if I'd been helped to my feet it could have been an altogether different story, so I can't praise Warwick's doctors highly enough, though – and I apologise for this, but I had to blame someone – I spent half-an-hour doing nothing but curse them.

I couldn't believe I'd hurt myself in such an easy fall. In the medical room the doctor felt my spine and said he thought I'd done some damage around T12 and he was spot on.

In hospital at Coventry the CT scan just showed up a couple of broken ribs and the doctor was surprised that they had already started to callous over – two hours after my fall! I suggested to him that they might not be as fresh as he thought and might even be a few weeks old. The staff were prepared to let me go home, but I insisted on someone taking another look because I was still struggling to move, and I've been injured enough now to know when I've done some damage.

Even the MRI scan the next day was pretty vague about any damage and Dr Philip Pritchard, the trainer/amateur/racecourse doctor, fixed up for me to be transferred to see James Wilson-MacDonald and Adi Zubovic here in Oxford. I think I'd have been lost without Philip. They gave me two options: three months in a plaster-cast or an operation, and I told them I didn't have time for option one. Afterwards, they were very pleased I'd taken option two because, they felt, it might not have knitted and I'd have been back in there within a week of being out of plaster. They were very pleased with the operation and Adi said he was sweating up drilling through my bone because it was like rock – which I take as a compliment. He said he thought that was why I didn't break bones very often.

James came up to see me and couldn't believe I was walking round the room. The physios just came, said they weren't needed, and walked out again! They are talking about letting me home tomorrow. I'll see how it goes and take as much physio and exercise as the injury allows – hopefully that will take up most of today. I've been told to do lots of brisk walking to build up the muscle around the injury and I'll take a lot of calcium and vitamin tablets in the hope that it all helps to knit the bone together. I've set Cheltenham, seven weeks on Tuesday, as my target and I'm sure I'll be there. I'll give it every chance, but at the same time I appreciate it is my back, that I need it in good working order for my job and that it's not something you take chances with, so I'll be guided by the specialists.

I won't really look at too much racing when I'm home. I'm not a great spectator if it's not me riding winners. There have, of course, been some positives. I'm lighter now than I've been for ages and there are worse things in life than to be bed-bathed by my two pretty nurses, Louisa and Branka – happy days! A few other nurses have been asking for John Francome and going on about how cute and curly-haired he is, but, unfortunately for him, they've been predominantly male.

---

12 MARCH 2001

FOOT AND MOUTH SILENCES CHELTENHAM

Paul Hayward

Today they would have gathered at Cheltenham: excitable squires in tweed, jockeys with churning stomachs, twitchy trainers with thousand-yard stares – the whole year come to this. Foot and mouth is upon us, and the Cotswold bells refuse to ring. We would have choked the roads around Prestbury with our hopeful convoys, horseboxes up ahead and wide-boy touts lining the route. Passes, binoculars, *Racing Post*, war chest, aspirin: the check-list would have been gone through in the car park, while the sages studied form and the bookies looked on slyly, awaiting the slaughter of the innocents. The London trains would have disgorged high-heeled packs of ladies dressed for Royal Ascot, and swaying men who had got stuck into their ale too soon. You rush into Cheltenham, and Cheltenham rushes into you. Combat is everywhere. Punter against bookie, horse against fence, jockey against self. Go there once, and the whole radiant vista leaves an indelible imprint on the brain.

At a push, Cheltenham is life's journey; boundless hope and stuffed pockets at the start, exhaustion and survival strategies at the end. David Lloyd, the former England cricket coach, remembers seeing a man lying on his back and talking into his shoe as if it were his mobile phone. Cheltenham is the shires at play, but also the towns gone mad. And it's not there now. They are burning animals instead of racing them. The non-convert to Cheltenham should hear the roar when the tape goes up for the opening race, and feel the slam and thunder of hooves as the field heads off into open country. Closed country, now.

At Plumpton on Monday they braved the rain and defied the protests of local farmers to keep racing's show on the road. The ears of racecourse officials were still stinging with late-night threats from indignant Sussex yeomen. 'We know where you live. We'll do you in.' Nasty stuff, not normally associated with the National Hunt game. The authorities say it is safe to race on (though not at Cheltenham, where sheep had grazed). The farmers count the corpses and the hours of lost sleep. The countryside turns in on itself.

The questions pile up. Why is it safe to race in Britain but not Ireland? Which set of vets is right? Why was there no mention of Cheltenham being lost when racing resumed at Lingfield last Wednesday (by the time that night's ten o'clock news came round, the Festival was off)? At a sombre press conference at Plumpton, Peter Savill, chairman of the British Horseracing Board, blamed 'leaks'. If you accept his logic, you think Cheltenham should have concealed the postponement from the public even longer.

In any other year Plumpton would have been a tiny dot on the calendar, a dull March Monday before the great Cotswold invasion began. Instead it became a road to nowhere. There was no packing to be done last night, no traffic to join this morning. Bank accounts rest easy. Human livers are safe from assault. The shock, at 2 p.m., will be nothing compared to the jolt of discovery on a newly infected farm, but racing will require its minute of mourning anyway, as the Festival's lost first day stretches out into nothingness.

Will it be rescheduled? Maybe, if the epidemic halts or slows, a clash with the Punchestown Festival can be avoided, and racing continues to steel its conscience against the cries of farmers. Today is officially a void. Silence, where Cheltenham's whisky roar would normally be.

---

4 NOVEMBER 2005

A VERY BLACK DAY

Henrietta Knight

Everything seemed right as we set off for Exeter on that fateful November day. Best Mate had come through a four-month training programme with flying colours and was exactly ready for his reappearance race on Haldon Hill. He had delighted us in his home work and his enthusiasm was at an all-time high.

During those warm and sunny autumn days we had grown accustomed to watching him glide majestically up the gallops as he worked his way back to full fitness. We had so often gloated over the faultless conformation of this breathtakingly beautiful horse.

'Matey' was our pride and joy – our lives had revolved around him for more than six years. His near-impeccable race record and third Cheltenham Gold Cup victory in 2004 had made him the country's favourite steeplechaser and, despite his absence from the limelight for more than ten months, his popularity had never waned. Even last summer there had been a steady flow of visitors and his personal fan mail had continued to swell the postbags. He revelled in the adoration he received and thoroughly enjoyed life. After his morning work he would relax in his paddock, which had been carefully chosen because of its close proximity to our house. I would often sit and watch over him from an upstairs window. He was special – the horse of our dreams and a racing icon.

As I leant over the rails and watched our champion lead the parade for the 2005 Haldon Gold Cup, I thought to myself: 'This afternoon he looks absolutely stunning' – no wonder he'd been given the best-turned-out prize in the paddock. The crowds, who had flocked to Exeter racecourse from many different parts of the country, had looked long and hard at their idol. On that sad afternoon, he walked with his usual effortless steps across the green turf. His ears were pricked and his head held characteristically high at the end of his proudly arched neck. It was as if he was in an oil painting – even the dapples showed up on his gleaming bay coat in the sharp sunlight.

Best Mate looked at home on the Devon racecourse; he had been there three times before and had, on each occasion, come away victorious. He surveyed his kingdom knowingly and excitedly. What an athlete! What a feel he must have given his new jockey as he cantered down to the start. After watching him from the side of the course, I made my way down to a peaceful spot between the last two fences. It was on the inner part of the track and I didn't have to talk to anybody. I would be able to see enough of the action without being among the huge crowds of racegoers, but I did cast a glance back at the stands – they were packed.

By now there was little time left before the horses would be under starter's orders. My nerves were tingling but I would face up to my responsibilities and watch the runners stream over the first obstacle. Matey looked happy, he was up with the pace and he glided through the air with his customary grace. Then the runners disappeared from my sight. I couldn't hear the commentary, so I anxiously waited until they approached the final bend.

I held my binoculars to my eyes, my hands were shaking. Would I see our beloved horse still close to the front? The year he had won the very same race, he had been well clear on the final turn. All of a sudden I spotted the runners and strained my eyes for the claret and blue stripes. The field were closely bunched, but where was our champion? At first I couldn't see him, but then I picked him out on the inside and pulling wide of the fences. Instantly I knew something was horribly wrong. My heart sank, this was not our Best Mate.

He had never run a race like this before and wasn't accustomed to being pulled up.

In a flash I was under the railings and making my way down the course. At first he approached me in trot and his stride looked normal, but as he got closer he faltered and his gait changed. He veered across the course towards the outer railings close to the last fence. There was a lack of co-ordination in his hind limbs and his eyes were glazed.

It was very quick. He staggered and gently keeled over on to his side. I knew immediately that his life was ebbing away. Fortunately, he would have felt nothing and was already in another world. A sudden numbness came over me. Was this reality, or a bad dream? But then the stark facts hit home – there was a surge of people, green screens and endless photographers. I walked away and Best Mate's jockey, Paul Carberry, walked with me.

We returned in a state of disbelief to the shelter of the racecourse buildings. It was not a time for words. In a matter of minutes I had lost one of my greatest friends and had just seen our Best Mate, everybody's Best Mate, die in front of my eyes. It was the end of the perfect racehorse, but was he was too good to live? I remember the words of Byron: 'Those whom the gods love die young.' Best Mate had been cruelly snatched from us on that unforgettable autumn afternoon, but I shall never forget his noble head and special eye. He will be sorely missed and gave so much pleasure to thousands of people. His popularity and fame knew no bounds. In five years he had won over the hearts of millions, but 'the love of horses knows not its own depth till the hour of separation' (Anon), and 'where in this wide world can man find nobility without pride, friendship without envy or beauty without vanity?' (R Duncan).

Best Mate's end will haunt me for the rest of my life, but there is no answer to the question: 'How do you ever thank a horse?' He was unique and the memories will live for ever. May he rest in peace.

CHAPTER 9

MASTERS OF THE GALLOP

They are the Alex Fergusons of the equestrian world. Indeed, that is a term which has been applied to many, not least in the Telegraph to Paul Nicholls, the trainer of Denman and Kauto Star. It is a fitting analogy: both have to send out their athletes, on two legs or four, at the peak of condition to win, win, win.

There are trainers every bit as successful in their field as Sir Alex is in his: just think of Vincent O'Brien, his unrelated successor Aidan O'Brien, Fred Winter, Henry Cecil, Fulke Walwyn and Jenny Pitman, not forgetting the lesser known, but no less hardworking, Jim Old and Robert Alner. But no longer is it enough to turn up in the yard in Hunter wellies and waxed jackets, or in top hat and tails at Royal Ascot: training racehorses has become more scientific. Martin Pipe, for one, was testament to that.

---

7 OCTOBER 1994

SAINT OF TIPPERARY BOWS OUT QUIETLY AFTER 50 YEARS OF CLASSIC SUCCESSES

Paul Hayward

Towards the end of a career that ended quietly this week he was like some shy professor, those wise eyes turned moist with age. In his short blue raincoat and trilby, Vincent O'Brien would slide almost unnoticed through the realm he once dominated. The greatest trainer of this or probably any era was learning to let go. The farewell was a long time coming – too long, some said – but was no less sobering for that. 'No, no,' O'Brien's brother Phonsie said gently yesterday when asked if there would be a party. 'I really don't think so.' There would be no appearances on breakfast television, no tearful valediction. Ireland was on its own to work through half a century of memories. There was symmetry, as well as sadness, in O'Brien's quiet exit. It is exactly 50 years since he received his first trainer's licence. He was in the autumn of his career, a man who used to withdraw a horse if he saw one wintery whisker too many on its chin was unlikely to mis-time his own departure.

In the village of Fethard, County Tipperary, O'Brien is regarded as a local saint and symbol, the creator and custodian of the region's pride in its horses and their myriad triumphs on the race tracks of the world. In McCarthy's bar in the High Street, a yellowed portrait of O'Brien hangs beneath the optics. The walls are a dimly-lit gallery of framed black-and-white racing photographs from the 1950s and 60s. It is a tranquil, almost windowless shrine to O'Brien's art.

It is no exaggeration to say that O'Brien has been one of the pivotal figures in Irish history. His achievement in winning four Cheltenham Gold Cups, three Champion Hurdles and three Grand Nationals in his first ten years helped create for his country a modern, multi-million pound blood-stock industry at a time when the Republic of Ireland was still groping for a national identity. In Tipperary, he was as important to local morale as the Rock of Cashel, the monastic ruin that rises craggily from the rich southern soil.

They revered him so unerringly because he was one of their own, and because he led so many of them to temporary riches with his metronomic sequence of Classic successes. O'Brien was the son of an impoverished farming family from Churchtown, County Cork, and was steeped in the equine traditions of rural Ireland. It was a world far from the military and aristocratic bastions of Newmarket and Lambourn. As Jim Bolger, who trains in County Carlow, said on Wednesday night, O'Brien was 'the Christopher Columbus' of Irish racing who set sail for, and conquered, the equine world.

Peter O'Sullevan, the BBC commentator, recalls that it was almost unheard of for a car to be seen in the lanes of Tipperary when O'Brien was setting out on this odyssey. Later, when he joined forces with Robert Sangster and assorted industrial tycoons, O'Brien became an altogether more cosmopolitan figure, flying by private jet, securing lucrative deals and mixing with the Gucci-shod party crowd with whom Sangster surrounded himself. But O'Brien's primary concern was always the horses, the pedigree charts and stride patterns of the endless yearlings who would be paraded before him at the Kentucky sales. He spent fortunes, but only when his eyes told him to strike. 'Attention to detail,' Phonsie O'Brien, who was Vincent's former jump jockey, says when he is invited to assess his brother's gift. 'From the moment he got up to the moment he went to bed, details was everything.'

Away from the yard and the minutiae of horse husbandry, most of us saw something else. It was in the stare, the tilted head, when O'Brien was examining a young horse. Sangster remembers that in Kentucky in July he would stand for more than an hour examining a yearling in the brutal midday sun. This was his legacy: the sifting out from the equine masses of a line of elite performers who included Nijinsky, Ballymoss, Sir Ivor, Roberto, The Minstrel, Sadler's Wells, El Gran Senor and Alleged. These are names that turn on lights in the mind, and in the void opened up by O'Brien's retirement, it is easy to believe that there will never be another such dynasty.

It was in the Northern Dancer line of runners that O'Brien hit the genetic jackpot, and with Lester Piggott that he established his hegemony on the Flat. They have grown old together, as friends, with Piggott still addicted to the thrill of race-riding, but O'Brien no longer willing to sustain the hunt for champions. His attempt to revive the old formula of splashing out for the best yearlings failed when Classic Thoroughbreds produced too few top-class horses to justify their expenditure. Sangster and O'Brien had long since lost the great bidding wars with the Arab oil sheikhs.

There are only 12 horses at Ballydoyle to disperse. The days when McCarthy's bar hummed with the tales of work riders have subsided. There would always be one O'Brien champion to follow. The names of supposedly world-conquering two-year-olds would buzz through Tipperary and beyond. Why did he hang on so long? 'Horses are in his blood,' says Phonsie O'Brien. 'He just liked to go out and see them every day.' He waited and waited for another good one, but this time none came. The famous O'Brien name will remain at Ballydoyle with the announcement that Aidan O'Brien, the emerging force in Irish training ranks, will be based there next season.

It seems to add to the sense of loss that this has been a Flat season without the kind of equine luminary O'Brien used to produce as a matter of course. John Reid, another of his former stable jockeys, was probably right to say: 'He was quite simply the best we will ever see.' Piggott added his own tribute: 'I rode my first winner for him 40 years ago and he has been part of my life ever since. He was the man who gave me the most encouragement to return to race-riding. I would not have thought about it otherwise.' The professor will still be with us, appearing unannounced on the racecourses of Ireland and possibly England, shunning attention and praise. But he is no longer teaching.

---

4 MARCH 1979

WINTER THUNDER

TELEGRAPH SUNDAY MAGAZINE FEATURE

John Oaksey

The first time I saw Fred Winter off a horse he was walking round a room on his hands. That was 25 years ago and he says he cannot do it nowadays. But even if some of the muscles have got a bit softer you would still need to be a very short-sighted mugger to attempt the removal of his wallet. The short, wide-shouldered body, which in his riding days used to 'do' ten stone (including breeches, boots, colours and saddle) without much strain or dieting, is only a few pounds heavier. The lines are cut a good deal deeper into his face and there is some grey in his hair. But these are no great changes for a man who has, for quarter of a century, almost without a break, been an outstanding figure – often *the* outstanding figure – in a hazardous, highly competitive sport.

The sport in question is 'jumping', or National Hunt racing as it used to be called until the Jockey Club swallowed up the old National Hunt Committee. Either way, the description includes all the steeplechase and hurdle races which are run under Jockey Club rules on 44 different courses all over the British Isles for nearly 11 months a year from August to the beginning of June.

Even 25 years ago, to anyone struggling to find a place on the fringes of the sport, as I was, Fred Winter was already a hero. Between August 1952 and June 1953 he had just ridden 121 winners – a total which was then a record and which easily established him as champion jumping jockey. Any holder of that title was – and for that matter still is – a hero in my eyes. The title goes to the man who rides most winners in a season so, quite apart from all the gallops and schooling (teaching young horses to jump) he has to ride at home, its holder must, in those 11 months, have ridden between 450 and 600 horses in public on a racecourse. He will have ridden for more than 1,000 miles at 30 m.p.h. or thereabouts – leaving the ground several thousand times to jump, or attempt to jump, hurdles or birch fences four-and-a-half-feet high. And between meetings, on top of all that, he will have travelled around 50,000 miles by road, much of it in the dark. The number of times he actually hits the ground himself will have depended on his own skill, the agility and education of the horses he rides – and, most of all, on luck. Leading jockeys reckon to average at least one fall every six or seven rides and, of course, what happens then depends even more heavily on luck – on how you happen to bounce or roll and on where the hooves of your opponents land.

In 1952–53, for instance, Fred Winter had about 50 falls without suffering a single injury worse than bruises. Then, falling at the very first fence of his first race the next season, he broke a leg so badly that he could not ride again all year. That shattered leg was only a brief interruption quickly brushed aside. He was champion jockey three more times, he won two Grand Nationals, two Cheltenham Gold Cups, almost every other worthwhile British jumping prize – and the Grand Steeplechase de Paris on Mandarin, riding for three and a half miles with neither brakes nor steering, the bit having broken in Mandarin's mouth after only four fences. For the ten years before he finally hung up his boots Fred was, by common consent, the best, the strongest, the hardest to beat and the most consistent jockey riding in the British Isles. All his contemporaries freely acknowledge that; and one day, towards the end of his career I remember how, after riding four winners at Newbury he was cheered back into the changing room by his colleagues – something neither I nor anyone else who was present had heard before.

So, when Fred walked into the unsaddling enclosure at Cheltenham last April to welcome Midnight Court, the horse who had just won him his first Gold Cup as a trainer, there was far more than the usual warmth and affection in the applause which greeted him. Racing can be a jealous, bitchy business. But the Gold Cup had been a chapter of disasters for the stable since Fred started training, and even his closest rivals were glad to see him break the spell.

What else can he do now having proved himself to the hilt as a jumping trainer (his horses have won more prize-money than anyone else's for seven of the last eight seasons)? Like Vincent O'Brien and Ryan Price, he could switch to the far richer, better rewarded field of Flat racing. A trainer on the Flat even half as successful as Fred would now be a rich man. Flat-race prize-money is much higher and the international bloodstock market offers even greater rewards. Midnight Court, for instance, being a gelding, was worth very little more the night after winning the Gold Cup than he had been that morning. But a three-year-old colt with a future as a stallion becomes worth at least £1 million the moment he passes the Derby winning post at Epsom. Fred Winter senior was, and Fred's younger brother John still is, a Flat-race trainer, so Fred knows the disparity as well as anyone. But he has no intention whatever of changing to the richer world. 'Jumping has been my life for 30 years,' he says. 'I love it – and anyway what would be the point of taking on all those experts at their own game. Even if it came off it is just money. You can only have so many television sets and motor cars and I'm getting all the food I need.

'Ambitions,' he smiled. 'My ambition is just to carry on as we are – only better . . . I don't mind *how* many more Gold Cups we win.' They are the words of a happy man and you don't have to spend very long at Uplands, Fred's flourishing yard in Upper Lambourn, to understand why. Fourteen years ago, having decided to give up riding, he was not even all that keen to become a trainer. 'I had seen so many jockeys try and fail,' he says. 'All the money we had was in our house and we were happy there.' So Fred applied for a post as a starter – 'I thought it would keep me in racing and let me see my friends.' But, strangely, whoever was responsible turned him down. 'He seemed to think I was still too close to the jockeys,' says Fred. 'He didn't think I would be able to control them.' But whoever made the decision unknowingly did both Fred and racing a service. 'They did offer me a job as a judge, but I didn't much fancy that,' he recalls. 'So the only thing left seemed to be training. We sold the house and bought this place – though it wasn't much like this in those days, I can tell you.'

Uplands is tucked away under a shoulder of the Berkshire Downs – both the stable yard and the trainer's house have been far more altered by success than their proprietor. The yard where Fred started with only three lads and five horses is now crammed with 25 men looking after 65 of the best, or at least most promising, jumpers in the world. Richard Pitman, later Fred's stable jockey and now a television commentator, was one of the original three-man staff. 'We slept in a caravan standing in a clump of nettles,' he remembers. 'The woods were the only lavatory. I suppose it does seem a bit rough now, looking back.' The life of any stable lad is still some way from luxury by normal modern standards, but now more than half Fred's lads live far more comfortably, in a hostel at the top of the yard. The rows of wooden loose boxes, 50 of them in the main yard now, are terraced up a bank above the house. Less than a mile away uphill lie the rolling gallops and lines of schooling fences around which Lambourn revolves. The back of Fred Winter's house looks out on 'Millionaire's Row', the select block of boxes which owes its nickname to a golden period when it housed, simultaneously, Crisp, Bula, Pendil and Lanzarote – each in his own way a champion.

The house at Uplands, which the Winters had to gut almost completely when they first moved there, is now a warm, bright place, always seeming full of small, tough dogs and pretty girls. Of Fred's three daughters, two – the twins – are both expert riders, ex-members of the British junior three-day event team. His wife, Diana, supervises their careers and their horses and does not go racing all that much. But anyone foolish enough to suppose that she is not passionately involved in the fortunes of the stable needs only utter a critical word in her hearing to learn the error of his ways.

In terms of worry and responsibility there is a huge difference between a jockey's life and that of a trainer. 'You just had to ride the horses as best you could and then go home,' Fred says, looking back on his early years. 'All you had to worry about then was tomorrow. But for the poor trainer the worry has only just begun when you pull up. In fact it never stops.' It is the measure of his double achievement that, unlike so many successful jockeys, he took the switch to training in his stride. He turned out to have some, if not all, the other essential qualities — notably judgment of men as well as horses, and something else which is hard to describe without sounding pompous — a combination of leadership, man-management and personality, or call it what you will.

Perhaps Brian Delaney is the best to describe it. He was at Uplands from the start, and after only two seasons Fred picked him as head lad — by far the most important man in any stable, apart from the trainer himself. 'We've never had a cross word since,' Brian says. 'And although the lads come and go, I don't think we've had two sacked since we began. He *talks* to them, you see, listens to their opinions, even the youngest. Mind you, he only reckons to tell you once. If anyone makes the same mistake twice, there is trouble.'

Much the same rule applies to Fred Winter's stable jockeys. But though they get their share of criticism, Fred — who rode for the same man, Ryan Price, almost throughout his career — reckons loyalty the first essential between a trainer and his jockey. John Francome, Fred's present jockey, is almost certainly the best he has employed — apart from perhaps Bobby Beasley at his peak. Last year, when John was called before the Stewards of the Jockey Club to explain his alleged association with bookmaker John Banks, Fred's loyalty was put to a new kind of test. He passed with ease. 'It just never occurred to me that John might have done anything wrong. I know it's against the rules for a jockey to have 'punters' [backers who give money in return for information about probable winners]. But nearly everyone does it. John may possibly have chosen the wrong man, but I don't think he'll do it again.'

Since his marriage to Diana, and even more since he took up training, Fred has been too busy to have much spare time of any kind. He rather dreads, and by no means always enjoys, his summer holidays; at home the garden is his chief preoccupation apart from the horses. He does play golf — though not too well, and it can be a real nightmare to be his partner (the famous competitive spirit comes out in all its fearsome fury: 'You watch the bloody thing and I'll look where it goes,' he once told me through gritted teeth as I addressed a particularly crucial approach. The result, I need hardly say, was an air-shot).

But that kind of tension is the exception not the rule at Uplands. An evening spent going round Fred Winter's yard can be the best antidote to the pessimistic theory that nothing in England can nowadays be both happily and efficiently organised. When frost had produced spells of ground too hard for the delicate legs of valuable jumpers, the place was practically bursting with frustrated energy. But patience is another of Fred's virtues. 'I want him in one piece three years from now,' he said, looking proudly at one of the many gleaming coats, 'and I'm not going to chuck that away by running for peanuts on concrete.'

Many of the stable's best horses had not even been out once at that stage earlier this year – an infuriating situation for stable lads eager for action, and a desperately expensive one for owners who have to go on paying training fees and entries even if their horses are not running. But both owners and lads reckon that The Guv'nor knows best. Looking back on Fred Winter's two interlocking careers – one of the longest and most impressive success stories in sport – the odds are that the future will prove them right.

30 NOVEMBER 2002

PIPE KEEPS WELL AHEAD OF THE PACK

Sue Mott

This is a very surreal experience. Most recuperating invalids, when supplied with an electric buggy from social services, make serene and sober progress along the pavement. Enter a post-operative Martin Pipe at the speed of sound, electrically-powered, cornering like Michael Schumacher and brimming with exuberance because one of his horses, Villa, had just won the 3.05 at Chepstow. 'Have a kiss,' he said, from beneath a ramshackle old hat that his wife, Carol, would happily put on a bonfire. 'We always kiss everyone when we win.' At that rate, Pond Farm, near Taunton in Somerset, might resemble an orgy this afternoon.

Pipe, the champion National Hunt trainer (recurring), has four runners in the Hennessy Cognac Gold Cup at Newbury, with his stable jockey, Tony McCoy, opting to ride Bounce Back ('lovely horse, won the Whitbread, jumps and stays,' said the oracle). Does this mean I should rush to the bookies? The bookie's son shook his head. 'I couldn't tell you which one of the four has the least chance. I'm not bluffing.' He laughed and smiled and remained as impenetrable as the Bornean jungle.

He is a living legend, Pipe. 'I don't know about that,' he said, roaring on ahead on the buggy supplied following ankle surgery three months ago. 'Well, living anyway,' I said breathlessly, running to catch up. 'I don't know about that either,' he said, before dismounting and limping at a gallop into the house.

The lounge explains everything. There is a bank of five huge screens, each transmitting race meetings or the betting upon them. The only exception is on Saturdays when Pipe loves to watch *Blind Date*. 'I love Cilla,' he said. Every shelf is groaning with crystal and silverware, the accrued spoils from more than 3,000 winners in his remarkable and controversial career. If you didn't know better, and especially in that hat, he could be a fence for a light-fingered antiques gang. A vast, low wooden table is covered in videos, TV controls, photocopied sheets of a horse's skeleton, a bunch of grapes, a walkie-talkie, books on horses, magazines on horses, his own set of notes on horses, the *Racing Post* and a stopwatch.

'Thirty-one minutes,' he said, consulting the last item. What? 'We've been talking 31 minutes,' he said pleasantly. I was thoroughly unnerved. 'Sorry,' he said, smiling again. 'I time everything. Habit.' The other habit is winning horse races, one that swiftly became so galling to his rivals that Pipe has found himself all too often mistaken for the Prince of Darkness in a horse blanket. He appears bemused about this. 'It's horrid and wrong. People call me ruthless, accuse me of blood doping. *The Cook Report* on television was very bad about me. It's utterly bizarre and stupid. People couldn't believe we've been so successful without doing something wrong. I know I've become more careful, more suspicious because of it. But you love your horses. You really do. From the little ones who win sellers to the great champions. We love them all. We give them a kiss and cuddle, we wag our fingers at them when they're naughty.'

'It's jealousy,' interceded Pipe's son, David, primed to take over when his father retires. In which case, he may have longer in the wings than Prince Charles. 'I'll probably give up when I'm 90,' Pipe said. He is 57. The easy description of Martin Pipe would be workaholic, but that scarcely does credit to the full range of his obsession. From the moment his father, David, sold his West Country bookmaking empire and bought Pond Farm, a mess of pig sties, to train horses, his son was spectacularly, completely, sometimes dangerously, involved. He smashed up six cars before he was 20, one of the accidents involving a Volkswagen Beetle and an Exeter lamp post to such an extent that he was rendered unconscious and broke an ankle. It was the pain of the arthritis in that left ankle that finally drove him to hospital again for an operation that fused the bones. 'I've wasted three months of my life because I haven't been able to go racing,' he grumbled, somewhat ungratefully for someone who will be able to walk without pain for the first time in years. Why didn't he do it before? He laughed. 'I was the same with marriage. We were courting 11 years, you know, Carol and I, before we got married.' His wife looked upon him benevolently. 'Fear of the unknown,' she said. And yet, it was the unknown world of horses into which Pipe pitched himself and promptly caused a revolution. When he started out, 'we'd have a winner a year and go to the bar to celebrate with a few bottles of Guinness and a trip to cloud nine'. That was the extent of the science.

As a child, Pipe had barely seen a horse, let alone ridden one or fallen off one. That was swiftly remedied. He persuaded a local trainer to teach him to ride, climbed aboard a thoroughbred that was smart enough to sense an entire novice on its back and carried him, possibly screaming, at full gallop into the Taunton. 'I don't think there was a single day I didn't come back to Carol covered in blood,' he said. 'As a jockey, I was useless. Totally useless. But it was exciting. I liked the thrill.' The thrill was somewhat dimmed when a horse called Lorac carried him through the wings of a jump and broke his thigh. 'I was in one hospital in traction. Carol was in another having a baby.' So he diverted his prodigious attention to training. 'I had an inquiring mind. I like finding solutions to things. I used to be very good at jigsaw puzzles and that's what horse training is. Putting all the pieces of the puzzle together. We take the horses' temperatures here twice a day. I have all the reports by 7.30 every morning. I know how they are, what they ate the night before, if they have a runny nose, a cough, for all 160 of them.' I sympathise with the necessity of absorbing so many facts. 'Don't be silly,' he said.

He doesn't think like the rest of us. He admits that himself. He even welcomed the pain he used to feel from his leg injuries because he thought it might give him a greater insight into his animals. 'Every stride I took really hurt. But it helped with the horses. I'm sure God gave me these problems to understand the racehorse.' Humans are another matter altogether. Particularly the unusual humans he tends to employ as his stable jockeys. He and Richard Dunwoody were two unbridled perfectionists whose state of perfection did not necessarily coincide. A.P. McCoy – 'I don't think we're disagreeing at the moment,' said Pipe disingenuously – was in a fair huff two weeks ago when he watched Pipe's Cyfor Malta win the Thomas Pink Gold Cup at Cheltenham while riding stablemate and favourite Chicuelo. 'Am I difficult? Definitely not!' Pipe proclaimed. Then added: 'I'm winking!' He knows he is. Or rather, is told he is. To celebrate this fact with a complete lack of contrition he once sponsored a race day at Taunton, featuring the 'Am I That Difficult' Novice Hurdle. 'As for Tony McCoy, we get on pretty well when he wins. Not so well when he loses.' Pipe is now positively twinkling with laughter.

But it was not ever thus. In March this year, he and a number of other stables were greeted by a sort of veterinary SAS team making an unannounced dawn raid to – according to the Jockey Club – maintain the high standards of purity in the industry. Most people assumed it was an anti-blood doping exercise. 'Oh, yes, the dawn raid,' said Pipe, still quietly livid. 'That wasn't the right thing to do. I was brought up to be polite by my father. I let them in. I wouldn't do it again.' The swoopers found nothing untoward. 'You've seen my laboratory. It's just there for the health and welfare of the horses.' We had indeed visited the lab, where blood tests from all the horses are analysed every day. Pipe even proudly displayed a glass bowl of congealed red with what looked like a culture of lichen growing on it. 'Marvellous, isn't it?' he said proudly, while the rest of us were trying not to be revolted.

Everything is horses. Every minute of every day is devoted to them. What else does he think about? 'Nil,' he said. What does he spend his money on? 'Don't know,' he said. 'Ask Carol.' His bedtime reading consists of books called things like *Equine Gastroenterology* or the cards he has drawn up for every horse in the stables which record every last relevant detail about them. 'Their breeding, their pedigree, their health, the ground they like, whether they like right-handed tracks or left-handed, absolutely every conceivable detail down to the very smallest. There is no such thing as too much detail.' And it is true that one of his champions, Gallant Moss, has a large mirrored wall in his stable because he tends to get lonely.

But two things happened in March to jolt the world of compulsive order that he inhabits. His father died after a long illness and a horse, a potential champion called Valiramix, was killed after a fall at Cheltenham. After the race, McCoy, who had believed this to be the horse of his dreams, went back to the weighing room, put his head in his hands and cried. 'We did the same,' said Pipe. 'To lose a horse of that calibre was so upsetting. And then my father. It was so sad. It makes you wonder whether it's all worth it.' In the end, his wonderment did not last. His solution was to saddle more winners. If the detractors cannot resist hinting that he cheats, his answer is to go on winning. 'You just carry on. It makes them madder,' he said, not without a mischievous streak. 'Funnily enough, I thought I was becoming more accepted until the raid happened.' That was the signal that the traditional, jolly-hockey sticks, band of brothers and sisters in National Hunt racing, who prided themselves on being a fun sport not an industry, still resent the scientific leaps and bounds Pipe has gained on their patch. But then would their spouses have given them a horse's scapular for Christmas? Probably not.

'One hour 13 minutes,' he said, at the conclusion of our discussion, having consulted his stopwatch again. That was a long time to talk to a legendary horse trainer without getting one single decent tip, I thought. So if the Hennessy was too close to call what about another of the races at Newbury?

'Deano's Beano,' he offered without hesitation. It took us to one hour 14 minutes, but you never know, it might have been worth it.

---

21 SEPTEMBER 2002

TRAINING GENIUS FIGHTS AGAINST ADVERSITY

Sue Mott

Henry Cecil sits in his study, light pouring through the leaded windows behind him, wreaths of smoke from his Marlboro Light curling round him. It lends him a distant, mystical air, so that questions asked across the rug-strewn divide (past the cabinets filled with toy soldiers and painted knights, beyond tables of lilies and carved wooden ducks, round the walls bedecked with ceremonial swords and Neanderthal weapon heads dating back to 250,000 BC) seem to shaft through the mist like impertinence. Yet there is so much to know. Here is a man who reached the very pinnacle of his sport, ten times the champion trainer of Flat racing, winner of almost 3,000 races, 32 Classics, a seriously beloved aristocrat of the Turf, a character they called 'Old Gucci Shoes' in affection and, often, 'genius' in awe.

But slowly, it seems, the lush rug of success has been pulled from under him. A catalogue of misfortunes and tragedies has beset him in the last few years. His last Classic victory was with Love Divine in the 2000 Oaks, his second marriage fell apart with salacious tabloid interference, his twin brother David died of cancer, he was convicted of drunken driving and banned for five years, his horses were beset by a lingering virus and the number of horses in the yard at Warren Place, Newmarket, has dwindled from 200 to about 140. 'I've had a couple of not-too-exciting years, yes,' he said in magnificent under-statement. 'But things don't always go right, do they? It's probably good for the character. You can't expect everything to be marvellous all the time. I've just got to look ahead. And see if it works out.'

The 'it' in question is his new venture, a scheme to form his own racing club, offering owners the chance to invest £30,000 in up to eight horses over two years, all expenses included. If it seems a little like The Queen's travel secretary turning bucket shop, Cecil is not in the least snobbish or repentant. 'I can either sit here and do nothing or take the initiative. There are some very nice people out there who would like to get into racing but they haven't been encouraged. This is their chance to get an insight into the world of racing and have some fun at a sensible price. It's £15,000 a year. You could spend that in a casino in five minutes.'

Perhaps he has. Cecil always talks about his 'wild' youth, when the twin sons of Henry Senior, the father they never saw who was killed in North Africa during the Second World War at the age of 28, began to enjoy life after public school. His brother David suffered a life-long addiction to alcohol. Henry was deflected by ambition. 'I was always very ambitious. Always wanted to be at the top of the tree. I used to have charts to work out how I was doing. Lists of my winners, making sure the graph was going up, not down.' You can imagine how the recent hard times must have hurt, though all traces are hidden behind a benign and courteous facade. 'It's so frustrating,' is all he will say. 'I don't seem to have the ammunition. My three-year-olds have been disappointing, my two-year-olds are a bit behind. I went to Southwell the other day, convinced we had a winner and we came fourth.

'Coolmore and Godolphin are very, very powerful,' he confessed, in reference to the empires of Aidan O'Brien in Ireland and Sheikh Mohammed Al Maktoum's operation in Dubai. 'I can probably turn them over on occasions when I play my ace card. But they have got a few more decks than me. I can still come up with a good horse, but it's more difficult. I'm not sad or bitter about it. I get frustrated I can't compete in a lot of the big races. But I have a good history, great winners. We can rebuild.'

Cecil is 60 next year. There were many during his terrible tribulations who took the trouble to retire him from the sport. He smiled at the suggestion. 'It's a way of life. I don't feel ready to retire.' A little black pug-nosed dog, Lillie (after Langtry), detached herself from the rug and charged about as though demonstrating the vigour of her owner's intentions. 'I don't intend to go on forever. But now it's too soon. I'd like to win a Classic again. But you've got to have the ammunition.' In a study filled with weaponry and war trophies, it seemed an appropriate metaphor. There was an atmosphere, not of pessimism and failure, but of martial valour and hope.

His loneliness following the departure of his second wife, Natalie, with their son Jake, has been eased by a new relationship. His secretary, Jane McKeown, is his new partner in more than a mere business sense. I double-check I can report this as a fact. 'If you like,' he said gruffly, but not unkindly. He is understandably wary of his private life becoming a matter of public perusal following the various marriage upheavals he has suffered in the past. His benedictory dealings with animals and children may grant him a monastic air, but it hasn't quite worked out that way in practice. Now, however, he is on good terms with Natalie and sees his son during holidays and every other weekend.

Cecil lights up, even through the cigarette fog, in discussion of Jake. 'I used to worry about everything, but as you get older your priorities change. When I was working very hard, I never had enough time for children. When Julie, my first wife, and I were together we drove 60,000 miles in our first year. But now, if I've a horse running, I'm just as likely to see it on TV. I take Jake to cricket instead. And he's a great Arsenal fan. He flew in a Jumbo jet from Gatwick last season to watch them in the Cup final. There he was, a little thing in red yelling away, surrounded by depressed people in blue.' Did you go, too? I asked. 'No,' he said, followed by silence. 'He's eight and a half now,' resuming his thread. 'Knows everything, of course. He was even teaching me how to bowl spinners in the garden the other day,' said his father, who knew how 50 years ago.

These are huge advances from his state two years ago, when his brother was dying from pancreatic cancer and he himself suffered a terrible back injury following a fall from his horse, a 20-year-old Hanovarian, Impresario. 'He broke his bridle, it fell over his eyes and he panicked. Set off at a full gallop straight towards a tree at about 40 m.p.h. I jumped off and jarred my vertebrae so badly I couldn't sleep for 17 weeks for the pain. I couldn't lie down, couldn't sit for more than two minutes at a time. One night it was such agony I had 17 hot baths one after the other to try and distract myself from the pain.' A side effect was Cecil's inability to ride out for three months, his four-hour prologue to every day except Sunday. 'The day I can't ride out any more is the day I retire. It is the way I tell whether my horses are happy or not. I have always done things basically by instinct. Certainly not judged by the form book. If my horse is right I just seem to know by feel and instinct.'

This is why Cecil has been called a genius. Why Slip Anchor won the Epsom Derby in 1985, followed by Reference Point (1987), Commander In Chief (1993) and Oath (1999). 'I should have won it seven times,' is Cecil's response to the roll call of his talents.

Amid the lime oak panelling of his study, he seems more exhausted by his past achievements than excited. 'I remember them. My first Derby, the King George and Queen Elizabeth, Ascot Gold Cup. But it's more a relief when it's over than anything else. You bring so much of yourself to it. So much can go wrong. It's like an examination. When it's over, win or lose, I'm just a damp squib.'

Cecil never liked examinations. As he is happy to admit, he and David were the first boys at his prep school, Sunningdale, to fail the Eton entrance exam. 'We were late developers, very backward. We had tutors in the holidays. In the end, we were sent to school in Dorset where my stepfather's brother was a governor. But they wanted to know why in our exams, David and I made exactly the same mistakes.' He smiled. 'David used to freeze in exams.'

The benevolent elder brother (by ten minutes) must have lent a helping hand. In fact, Cecil's schooldays seem characterised by some failure or other. The school football team, for whom he was both vice-captain and goalkeeper, did not win a match all season and once let in 14 goals. 'Eleven,' he corrected, 'but you can say 14 if you like. We used to go to away matches in two old taxis. The team always returned during supper time. The tradition was that the taxis would sound their horn all the way down the drive if we'd won. They never tooted once while I was playing.'

You wonder if this catalogue of let-down planted the burning ambition in the elder Cecil boy. 'These things have their effect, don't they?' he responded obligingly. But there is something restrained, even gently sad, in his manner. His five-year ban from driving has been a hardship. He was even threatened with a custodial sentence at the time, for injuring an elderly couple in a road accident. 'I thought the sentence was very harsh but I was responsible and that was that. Now I have to rely on Jane to drive me about. Unless Jane takes me somewhere I'm a prisoner here. It's very restricting. It's not easy to function. I don't drink now, not really. I'm not very good at it. Too much is poison to me. At the time David was so ill, I was on medication, it was horrific. You get over it to some extent. Never completely. I hate the thought of death. I'm not ready for it yet.'

One day, when he gives up the house, the horses, his rose garden and his fierce ambitions, he would like to settle in, of all places, Marrakech. 'I've been twice and I really like it. You can sunbathe in the winter with the Atlas Mountains in the distance. The people are nice and there are miles and miles of shops. I love shopping. My mother loved to shop. Most men don't. I've probably got some female hormones.' He smiled again, then rose up decisively from behind his desk, cutting a swathe through the cigarette smog. 'That's enough,' he said.

---

24 DECEMBER 1996

RESILIENT TRAINER BATTLING HIS WAY BACK THROUGH A WAR ZONE

Paul Hayward

They could run a lorry over Jim Old and he would get back up. 'It's the only way I know,' he says. Outside in the mist, the charred girders and singed straw provide a ghostly intimation of the fire that destroyed half of his racing yard and four of his precious horses earlier this year. It is as if a war has swept through his land and on across the Wiltshire plains.

Old is a misnomer. It ought to be Jim Young. For all the misfortunes that have pursued him through 24 hard years of training, he is fresher than the cold winter fog enveloping his dismembered stables. As workmen huddle in the remains of his racing office – scorched copies of the *Sporting Life,* the scent of fire and terror – there is the sense of a career and a life saved yet again from calamity. In the 1980s a virulent equine virus tore the lungs out of his string of horses. The fire – on Monday, 16 September – was like a Biblical holocaust coming to finish the work of nature.

It nearly did, but it picked the wrong target. Brian Simpson – a neighbour of Old's – was charged with arson, but the case against him collapsed and the charges withdrawn by the Crown Prosecution Services. For Old there is nothing to be done but rebuild his covered ride and boxes from the ashes high on the Wiltshire downs at Barbury Castle. He gives the Champion Hurdler, Collier Bay, a special look of gratitude and respect before attending to his team for Boxing Day and beyond.

The gallops are gloomy and cold yet ineffably beautiful. Old's yard is so high it seems to scrape along the underneath of the sky. Ask him about the night that nearly wiped out his string and the tears still form around the rims of his eyes. He stops, hesitates, and recounts the story as if hypnotised. A still night, early hours of the morning, the horses supposedly snug in their hay . . . He remembers every detail. 'I pulled on a pair of trousers, no pants, and a pair of leather slippers, because they were the easiest thing to get on,' he says, leaning forward over the wheel of his Jeep. 'I ran, not wanting to believe what I was hearing. Four of the staff had been woken up in their bungalows. They were arriving bleary-eyed [Emma, one of the sleepy walkers, is below us now guiding a horse through exercise]. Our neighbours [the Simpsons], who raised the alarm, were there, too.

'The side of the barn where some of the horses were was a ball of fire. Dear Emma said, "What about those two horses?" I said, "Don't worry about them, they're dead". She said, "What if they're not, we . . .".' Old's voice rises a notch. 'I told her, "FORGET IT, if they're not dead now they will be in a minute". The neighbour went diving in. Two of my boys followed. They managed to grab him and we all rushed over and pulled him out. "What do we do now?" we all said. And that's when I shouted, "Get them [the horses] out. Turn them loose". That's when the lights went out. There was thick black smoke from the hay and tyres around the covered ride. You couldn't see six inches in front of your face. Noise and flames and chaos . . . We let 42 horses out into the night.'

By 4 a.m., Old's yard was a war zone, and his horses, in heaven knows what condition, were spread across one of the remotest stretches of Wiltshire.

Old, his friends and staff, exhausted, traumatised and afraid of what they might find, set off into the dawn for the second phase of their ordeal. Two horses had already died in the fire. Old told his staff: 'Be prepared for something worse than what we saw last night.' He says, sadly: 'They'd all gone into barbed wire and God knows what. They were cut to ribbons. If you can't imagine it, think of one of these old films: a cavalry officer going round looking for horses after a military engagement. Bits hanging off them. That's what it was like. Each time we got to one, we thought, "Oh, God not him, please, not him". The vets arrived and shot two. We started stitching up the others.'

Wretched, awful memories. An extreme manifestation of the kind of things that have been happening to him since he took out a licence in 1972, at the age of 25. Most of the horses are back now, and in good form. He is one of the most popular men in the game, and the racing public have followed the vicissitudes of his career with a kind of agonised concern. He is a man of broad tastes and intellect, who collects old films and loves to be thrust into good conversation. Most of all, though, he craves the early-morning thrill of being with his horses, and has stuck with his obsession when accountants and members of his family were telling him not to bother.

This is racing's spell, the part the punters never see. And it finally brought salvation for Old that day last March when Collier Bay surged up the Cheltenham hill, under Graham Bradley, to beat reigning champion Alderbrook, and Pridwell. Cima (second to the brilliant Dawn Run, in 1984) and Mole Board had both gone close to winning the race for Old, but Collier Bay finally crashed through in triumph. After a couple of prep-races he will defend his title next year. In honour of Old's victory and his courage in fighting on through the fire and all its effects, the racing press elected him National Hunt Trainer of the Year. Recognition was a long time coming and maybe some scars do remain. Old remembers his string's struggle with a rare strain of the equine herpes virus with more pain than he recalls the fire. He talks of 'suffering horrendously through the virus' and 'loads of lovely horses being wiped out'. When that happens, he says, 'the knives and the knockers come out. You have a fire; you knock it down and start again. People say, "poor Jim" and want to help and give you things. When it's the dirty old virus you don't get any of that.'

Old has ridden out just once today. He normally rides out all three lots. 'Stiff as a board,' he says, wincing. Why? 'Mole Board,' he says. 'Rolled over on me when he died last week.' The sky, so damp and wintry, looks like it's steadily falling in on us. Jim Old is still holding it up.

3 APRIL 2009

PAUL NICHOLLS: THE ALEX FERGUSON OF HORSE RACING

Ian Chadband

Paul Nicholls sounds like Jim Bowen ticking off the prizes on Bully's Prize Board as he points in turn at the treasures peeping out over the doors on the righthand side of Manor Farm's old brick stables. 'In box one, Kauto Star; in two, Denman; in three, Master Minded; in four, Big Buck's.' Good grief. In the space of a few yards, more magnificent champion horseflesh than most trainers could dream of moulding in a lifetime. It would be like Nicholls's mate Sir Alex Ferguson taking you round Manchester United's dressing room and parading Ronaldo, Rooney, Rio and some new thoroughbred called Messi.

Then Nicholls turns to the boxes on the left. He introduces a placid black beauty called My Will, the favourite in the Grand National. 'Now if we could get a National winner over this side to go with the Gold Cup winners on the other, that would be just the job, just fantastic.' He smiles, appearing to daydream for just a second. Except Nicholls doesn't really do daydreams. He doesn't have the time. The champion trainer deals only in unsentimental, 24/7 business. He calls it the business of 'just trying to keep being successful'; to outsiders, though, it looks like the business of fashioning a jumps dynasty.

They once called Nicholls the Jimmy White of racing, so often did he finish runner-up in the trainers' championship to his Somerset neighbour Martin Pipe. At 46, though, he has become *the* man now, a serial winner so pre-eminent in his trade that he must be about the only bloke around who can tease Fergie, one of his owners, down the phone: 'Hey, Alex, bad result for United today. Sure you don't want me to come and sort it out for you?' Certain of a fourth successive trainers' crown and rumoured to be under investigation from the Monopolies Commission after a mind-blowing Cheltenham, there ought to be white flags going up in yards all over the country if the affable lord of Ditcheat village were to land the National with one of his four entries.

That is because the greatest of all steeplechases is supposed to be the last defence against the Nicholls tsunami, the race which has mocked him for 24 years, since he was a hungry jockey who, instead of riding the hopeless 100–1 Roman Bistro, rather wished he was eating in one. His record has been so ill-starred, he just has to laugh. He never did get round as a jockey. 'I rode Another Duke in the colours of Des Lynam as well. Cleared Becher's like a dream. Fell at the next, a little one. We still have a laugh about it.'

But it has only got worse as a trainer. Nicholls saddles, on average, a winner once every four runs; in 17 years at the National, it's none out of 40 and only one in the frame – runner-up Royal Auclair in 2005. Of those 40, just eight have got round. What with Denman's nasty fall in Thursday's totesport Bowl, Aintree remains a stubborn foe.

'It's extraordinary, really,' Nicholls concedes. 'It's the same with A.P. [McCoy], too. Champion trainer and champion jockey and neither of us get a look-in. Maybe we should get together. But that's the National for you. No point getting annoyed. The Gold Cup? The best horse always wins. The National? Could get brought down at the first. Of course, I'd love to win it, but, honest, it is not top priority to me. I would far rather win the Champion Hurdle or a fifth Gold Cup. Mind, this is probably the best chance we have had.'

His strong quartet includes Big Fella Thanks, a well-fancied novice, Eurotrek, a winner over National fences before, and Cornish Sett, 12th last year. But all eyes are on My Will. A well-handicapped, consistent battler who was a fine fifth in the Gold Cup, Nicholls promises that it is the first horse he has targeted specifically for the National. Once the blessed Ruby Walsh had offered his royal assent, declaring it on Monday as his mount, the bookies ducked for cover. 'So after all that hard work, it's bound to go and fall at the first, isn't it?' chuckles Nicholls. But nobody is fooled any more by that self-deprecating burr and clubbable air. Nicholls's career history also informs them that he is such a determined, try-and-try-again perfectionist – 'Yep, probably I am,' he concurs – that if he does not get it right today, he will next time.

How else could a policeman's lad, whose only connection with racing was his grandad's love of the ITV Seven punt on a Saturday afternoon, go on to create one of jump racing's most remarkable production lines, with his retired dad Brian now looking after his two all-weather five-furlong gallops? Nicholls stands in this one-time domain of dairy cows where, having pumped the ten grand he had earned as a jockey into an all-or-nothing gamble, he first started off mucking out and training eight horses and can hardly credit how it has mushroomed into a multi-million pound champions' realm. 'Building a dynasty? Nope. Never enters my head,' he says. 'There's no great secret. We just try to keep it simple: work 'em hard, treat 'em well, keep 'em well, get them super fit, run them in the right races. I've worked bloody hard but I've been incredibly lucky too.'

His best bit of luck, strangely, came as a jockey in 1989 when he had his leg broken by a horse's wild kick. 'At the time, however much I starved myself, I just couldn't get the weight off – and if you look at me now, you'll know why!' grins Nicholls, who actually cannot quite believe he is so well-padded when he burns off so much nervous energy all day. 'Anyway, I just remember my only thought waiting for the ambulance that day was "for ****'s sake get me to hospital so I can have something to eat!".' When he was finally discharged, he had ballooned to 13 stone. His riding days were done and, instead, he became assistant to trainer David Barons. 'If not for the accident, I may never have been where I am now. I'm going to call my auto-biography Lucky Break!'

There's nothing lucky, though, about an operation which he reckons bears some comparison with Ferguson's United. It's no coincidence that they prefer to talk about their 'great' teams rather than themselves. 'It's fascinating to talk to Alex; there's a lot of similarities. Like a football team, you've always got to be offloading a few and bringing new ones through, always moving forward. That's what we both do.' And like Ferguson, underpinning all the success is a hopeless passion for his sport. When you watch Nicholls in his office, madly cheering on one of his charges in the televised 3.55 at Fontwell, it is like seeing a besotted punter betting (and losing on this occasion) his last fiver. His fan's enthusiasm gives a lie to the idea that it is only business to him.

Pre-eminence has not changed him, he reckons. Where once he had the odd war with Pipe, he still gets on with his pursuers now he is the hunted. 'I'm not champion trainer; I'm just P. Nicholls, trainer. I'm just me. I don't really think about what I've achieved – it would be nice to have the time – I just enjoy what I do and want to keep on winning them big races.'

---

29 DECEMBER 1968

NOTHING COULD KEEP FULKE DOWN

John Lawrence

On 19 April, 1939, a horse called Grosvenor Bridge fell in a novice hurdle race at Ludlow. It was a real gravedigger of a fall, and his jockey, a 29-year-old by the name of Fulke Walwyn, woke up in hospital five weeks later with a badly fractured skull, a pronounced stutter and no very obvious future. With the War only months away, it would at that moment have taken an exceptionally clear-sighted crystal gazer to predict that this somewhat part-worn ex-cavalry officer would become one of the most successful National Hunt trainers there has been. And yet, in only the second post-War season, the third in which he held a licence, Walwyn headed the trainers' list. He has done so four times since, and, as I write, is £5,000 clear of his nearest rival in this season's table.

Not a bad record, you may say, for a man who, six months after Grosvenor Bridge's little misdemeanour, still had difficulty in writing his own name. By 1939, however, Fulke Walwyn had already spent quite long enough in National Hunt racing to know that where the difference between victory and the first-aid room is so often measured in split seconds, despair and over-confidence are equally pointless emotions.

He had, for instance, seen Anthony Mildmay carried powerless past the second last fence in the 1936 Grand National – and remains, perhaps understandably, one of the few people not convinced that Davy Jones would have beaten Reynoldstown that day. Having watched a film of the race recently, I am inclined to agree that it would at least have been desperately close. Reynoldstown lost many lengths by blundering horribly at Valentine's and had made up all but a few of them when the buckle of Lord Mildmay's rein came undone and disaster intervened. Anyway, even if luck was on Walwyn's side, he had blundered it by surviving that dreadful blunder. It was, he says, the only mistake Reynoldstown made, but for nine jockeys out of ten one would have been more than enough.

Later in 1936 Fulke Walwyn turned professional, but was then still an officer in the 9th Lancers – the only regiment to have produced three winning Grand National jockeys: David Campbell won on The Soarer in 1896, Frank Furlong on Reynoldstown in 1935, and Walwyn the year after. If they count mere conscript soldiers, Carrickbeg nearly made it four in 1963! Having already cracked his skull once, Walwyn broke an arm so badly in November 1936 that he missed the whole of the following season. The day before, however, though beaten by Royal Mail in the Becher Chase, he had succeeded in getting Golden Miller round Aintree safely – a feat only one other man (Gerry Wilson, in the 1934 Grand National) achieved.

And this 'failure' may well have been worth more in the long run than many victories. For it, among other things, fastened Walwyn's name in the mind of Golden Miller's owner, Miss Dorothy Paget, and after the War it was this eccentric, legendary figure who gave him his greatest chance as a trainer. She wasn't the beginning, though, for when Walwyn set up at Saxon House in 1945, his first winners were mostly owned by Mr Tony Colmore. Everything he bought for Mr Colmore seemed to win, and it was in fact a victory which ended their association.

Walwyn had noticed the promise of a then almost unheard of jockey called Bryan Marshall, and asked him to ride Mr Colmore's Leap Man in the Cathcart Challenge Cup at Cheltenham. The owner had wanted Frenchie Nicholson instead, and taking the view that this unknown Marshall was certain to make a nonsense of things, proceeded to back something else. Bryan, needless to say, made no mistake whatever, and Leap Man, started, due partly no doubt to his owner's apparent pessimism, at 100–8.

It was the beginning of a long and brilliant partnership between Marshall and Walwyn – but Mr Colmore's horses left Saxon House soon afterwards. Their place, however, was soon much more than taken by Miss Paget's growing string, and there followed eight eventful, arduous years during which Walwyn sent out nearly 400 winners in the famous blue and yellow colours. The word 'arduous' is used advisedly, because in return for the wonderful top-class raw material with which she supplied her trainers, Miss Paget demanded – and got – top-class service.

Walwyn, who had heard all about her nocturnal habits, made it a condition from the start that there should be no telephone calls after 9.30 in the evening. That promise was faithfully kept, but, before 9.30 no telephonic holds were barred. Whenever Miss Paget had runners, the trainer was expected to give 24 hours in advance a detailed summary of their prospects and of the probable dangers. And, if she didn't go racing, an equally detailed post-mortem was called for afterwards. Her famous racecourse conferences – ending long after the last race and sometimes not till around midnight – were another occupational hazard involved in the job.

Walwyn remembers sitting for hours drinking endless cups of tea in the ladies' cloakroom at Windsor. But all this, of course, was infinitely well worthwhile, for the privilege of training horses like Mont Tremblant, Happy Home, Prince of Denmark, Legal Joy and many others. And Walwyn recalls with pride that, despite their many furious differences of opinion, he and Miss Paget parted in the end by mutual consent and without ill-feeling. There were those who said it would be the end at Saxon House – that without the Paget horses the stable would never be the same. Just how wrong they were can be seen from the records since.

For long before Miss Paget left him, Walwyn had built up the team on which his success is so securely founded. And he built it originally around one man, Joe Lammin, his first head lad in 1939 when the stable consisted of four moderate horses, and still head lad today – a wise, firm, kindly despot who had forgotten more about the art of stable management than many so-called experts will know. Joe served his time with Fred Darling and 'did' the 1931 Derby winner Cameronian – two years after Walwyn had his first ride under National Hunt rules. They met in 1937 when Joe was working, and Fulke riding, for Dick Warren, and, apart from the War years, have been together since. The stable lad is apt to be a bird of passage, shifting easily from job to job. But Walwyn has always managed to keep a skilled nucleus of 'old soldiers' round whom the yard revolves. One of them, Darkie Leatham, died last year, but Tommy Turley, who took his place as travelling head lad, had also been at Saxon House as long as I can remember.

Nor is this long service achieved by soft soap or soft talking. Riding out – particularly schooling – at Saxon House is no job for the thin-skinned or faint-hearted. When I first ventured there my style was tersely described as 'a fine example of the old English lavatory seat', and when things go wrong – as for instance when Mandarin used to disappear over the hill towards Wantage at a relentless unstoppable half speed – the air around Fulke Walwyn turns very blue indeed. But, as everyone who knows him soon realises, Walwyn's bark is far worse than his bite. And those who don't realise it don't stay long. Far more appreciate that a few words of criticism, probably well-deserved, are a small price to pay for working in a superbly-run stable with good horses and a steady supply of winners.

The master of this remarkable establishment looks, at 58, remarkably like the 29-year-old who hit the ground so hard off Grosvenor Bridge. The same smooth brown hair covers the same much-dented skull, and if there are any grey ones I've not seen them. The smile is the same and so are the occasional explosions. Some years ago, for instance, Fulke was in some danger of taking on Willie Pastrano, then the light-heavyweight champion of the world. After Pastrano had disposed of some unfortunate English hopeful, Fulke, meeting the champion in a night club, inquired how much he had paid the referee! But all was well – as it always is on such occasions. And, as always, whatever the night before may have involved, this supremely dedicated man was up at the crack of dawn when the first lot pulled out. Whether he ends this season with another championship or not, he long ago proved – at least to my satisfaction – that there has never been a better trainer of high-class steeplechasers.

10 JUNE 1995

'FORGOTTEN MAN' WALWYN BACK IN GLAMOUR STAKES AT EPSOM

Paul Hayward

In the distance he waves a stick at you amiably and ambles along with that famous rolling sea captain's walk. You evade death by a thousand dog-licks on the path to the early Georgian masterwork of Windsor House, stop to read an inscription from the Koran on a stable wall and then follow history's tunnel to the time, 20 years ago this week, when Peter Walwyn won the Derby.

Past and present tenses are at last rejoined for the trainer who once described himself as the sport's 'forgotten man', but never stopped joshing his way through a richly enjoyed Lambourn life. How appropriate it seems that the man they nicknamed Basil should be back with a front-rank Derby contender at a time when the BBC has turned on the lights again in *Fawlty Towers* and all things Seventies have been recalled from the deep freeze. Walwyn, for the short of memory, was the Martin Pipe or Henry Cecil of the glam-decade and was pretty near invincible at the top of the trainers' championship. In 1978 his yard was struck by the equine herpes virus EHV1 and it has taken until the last few seasons for the stable to regain its power.

In today's first Saturday Derby since 1953, the languid and long-striding Munwar will attempt to complete his master's resurrection with a surge round the Epsom course Walwyn so unfailingly adores. An audience with the unofficial mayor of Lambourn (he is a tireless benefactor and leader of the Valley of the Racehorse movement) is one of racing's most lasting pleasures. Walwyn would gain automatic selection for England in an international eccentricity tournament and talks in sparkling free-form about life both on and off the turf.

The drive through the gates of Windsor House is a passage into a world most of us had assumed had vanished and is a precursor to the tricky walk through the massed ranks of the family's dogs. 'Only one of them bites,' says Walwyn's wife, Virginia, otherwise known as 'Bonk', in a gallant but failed attempt at reassurance. By now you are in the inner sanctum of one of the most colourful and deeply-rooted training fiefdoms. Walwyn is that most intriguing of English countrymen: the reformist, or enlightened conservative. In matters equine he is a traditionalist who has no time for 'gimmicks', like fancy training techniques, and is a self-proclaimed downland man (like Dick Hern or John Dunlop) carrying the torch for racing's past.

But put him on a stool on Channel 4's *The Morning Line* and he will entertain you as skilfully as John Cleese himself, and is every inch the modern PR man, attracting owners and sponsors into the misty dip of the Lambourn valley. Walwyn recalls a time when racing would have raised its muskets at a besuited sponsor or marketing executive who wanted to defile the playgrounds of the aristocracy with billboards and hospitality tents. He says, with superbly-crafted understatement: 'One regrets that when I first went to Newmarket I looked down the Rowley Mile and the only landmark was the bushes. Now there's banners all the way down, advertising Durex and everything else. I'm afraid we've had to go off and sell ourselves.'

Outside in the courtyard there is budding, and that music of hesitant bird-song that marks out early summer in racing yards. Asking Walwyn about his many big-race triumphs prompts a compendious outpouring of form notes stored over three decades. 'I only have to see a race once and I remember it,' he says proudly. From this stack of mental records it is still Grundy's piercingly emphatic victory in the 1975 Derby which rushes most speedily to mind. The symmetry is perfect. Though Munwar, winner of the Lingfield Derby Trial, lacks the raw acceleration of his predecessor he has a fine each-way chance of reminding the world that Walwyn is still a force in the game. Meridian, Central and Channel 4 have been breezing through his yard this week and the nerve endings are twitching nicely as Walwyn retires to his study for a midday glass of vintage Moet. The questions and the expectations are mounting, yet here is a man resolved really to enjoy the bumpy last week leading to Epsom.

Each Derby day Walwyn travels to the track early on a kind of mini social safari. 'We go round the fair in the morning and walk the course,' he says excitedly. 'We look at the amusements and call in on Gypsy Rose Lee, Lee Rose Gypsy and Rose Gypsy Lee – all with their caravans with tinted windows.' This amuses him. Even the gypsies have designer caravans these days. 'The Derby is a day for everybody, it doesn't matter whether you're wearing a singlet or a top hat. You go into the centre of the course and people have had a few beers at lunchtime – they never watch the racing at all. If that's the way they want to enjoy it, fine. I hope I'm going to be there when I'm in my wheelchair.'

The miracle of Walwyn's good humour is that it endured the long nights of the 1980s when owners slipped away as if from a listing ship, and the quality of his horses fell dramatically. He never panicked. He kept rowing away with diminished resources and discovered a new cause in the Lambourn Trainers' Association, with its ubiquitous Valley of the Racehorse banner, which seems to hang from every tree on the leafy approach to the village. On arrival in the cramped and cheery office at Windsor House (where he moved from the larger Seven Barrows stables) Walwyn wears a Valley of the Racehorse sweatshirt and sees to it that you drink coffee from a Valley of the Racehorse mug. 'We've raised nearly £600,000 in six years,' Walwyn says with bulging pride. 'We're buying land to build housing for staff, we've given a £1,200 computer to the local school, we've even helped the bowls club. We had 800 horses here four years ago and now we've got 1,500. The whole village benefits from that.'

Already this year Lambourn has captured the 1,000 Guineas, Grand National, Gold Cup and Champion Hurdle. Today every last neutral soul in the village will be hoping that Munwar's prodigious galloping powers can carry him away from the speed horses up Epsom's cambered stretch. If he can, victory will be shared by an Arab oil tycoon (Sheikh Hamdan Al Maktoum, Munwar's owner), the elfin Willie Carson, son of a Stirling banana packer, and Walwyn himself, whose benevolent presence through so many difficult cycles and seasons seems to be inviting further reward.

Comparisons with Grundy, whose struggle with Bustino for the 1975 King George VI and Queen Elizabeth Stakes is still regarded as 'the race of the century', are quickly curtailed. 'Grundy was champion two-year-old. This one was late maturing. A very different cup of tea.' It is somehow comforting to see that the Derby, so often maligned as a fading tradition, can still induce such fretfulness and fervour in those condemned to pursue its seductive light. For Walwyn now, that light is a little closer once more.

---

8 APRIL 1995

SIX OF BEST WILL HURT PITMAN

Paul Hayward discovers how a National institution will be paralysed by fear during the great Aintree race

Jenny Pitman is recalling the moment her horses step on to the track for the Grand National. 'Oh God,' she says, with a rumbling laugh, 'I go into a coma. Once they've left the paddock I don't feel good. I think to myself, "What is the matter with you? Why do you do this? I don't want to be a trainer no more and I don't want me horses to run".'

It would be pointless to start a National without a Pitman runner. Through Corbiere's win, Garrison Savannah's gallant second and Esha Ness's non-victory in the void race of 1993, the stable has written so many of the plot lines for Britain's most compelling race. Jenny Pitman *is* the Grand National. But with the joy of taking part comes the most acute torment and fear of loss. 'I get into this cocoon,' Pitman says. 'This hard shell I can see through and hear people from. It feels like one of those Perspex bubbles that I'm walking along in. You have to be like that. You couldn't cope otherwise. My owners have stood next to me at the races and said, "Look at her shaking". I wish I didn't. If I didn't care about the horses and the jockeys my life would be a lot easier, but I can't help the way I am.'

Pitman has half-a-dozen runners today. As she stands in the parade ring with her six jockeys, fighting off fear, she will look like a teacher leading a school outing to Aintree. But it is all a good deal more serious than that. The trance-like state that Pitman enters is evidence of the National's unique appeal, its manifold dangers and the almost eerie bond between the trainer and the event. In 1993, before the race collapsed in farce, Pitman had a kind of premonition. 'That day,' she recalls, 'I said to Dave [Stait, her assistant and partner], "There's something wrong here". This was in the car on the way into the racecourse. He said, "What do you mean?" I said, "I don't know. It feels wrong, there's something wrong". Dave said, "Oh, you're just wound up".

'When we got out the car, I walked on with our friend. I don't like talking about funny things in front of Dave because he thinks I want certifying. I said it again. I thought there was something wrong with one of my horses, so I went to look at them, and said, "Well, I don't know what it is, doc – they're all right". It makes me feel very uneasy when I get like that. It's creepy, it is.'

Pitman is a superbly eloquent witness to the attractions of Aintree. She says: 'It's the atmosphere there. It's just different, innit? It's real life up there, d'you know what I mean? The fish and chips, mushy peas. It's real. You go to Cheltenham and it's all a bit unreal. You've got all the hospitality tents and so on and everything's a great deal grander than it is at Liverpool. Everybody don't walk around Liverpool with fish and chips and bowls of mushy peas, but it's the north and the north is very different. The warmth and welcome of the people is different. I think the National's about tough people and tough horses and that's what they are up there. They can see what it takes.'

Pitman's Grand National recollections could run to at least ten volumes. If it was Corbiere's victory in 1983 – the first by a woman trainer – which propelled her to the peak of her trade, the narrow defeat of the Gold Cup winner, Garrison Savannah, four years ago and Esha Ness's empty win two years back dragged her to the other end of Aintree's pain-and-pleasure spectrum. When she climbs out of her car at Liverpool, the drama goes with her.

'My younger son laughs at me,' she says, sifting these memories. 'He says, "Mum, whenever anything like that's gonna happen, why are you always sat in the front row?" I said, "I dunno, Paul. I wish I was sat in the back row in the stalls".' Any suggestion that the new, less-forbidding National has lost some of its mystique is quickly punctured. 'You tell me one person in racing who could have even foreseen a void National. Whatever people'll tell you, mate, it can happen up there, and that's the long and the short of it.'

Chances this year? The contenders, from the top, are Royal Athlete, Lusty Light, Garrison Savannah, Superior Finish, Esha Ness and Do Be Brief. Pitman is not one to grade and analyse her horses' chances in the hours leading up to such an ordeal, but she does say: 'I've got as good a chance of winning as I've had. People say to me, "Why six runners?" An owner's dream is to have a runner in the National and then take it one step further and have a winner. I've got entries in the Scottish and Irish Nationals and I suggested to one or two of our owners that they might prefer to go there – but they're not interested. Why do people buy a Lottery ticket? Why do they do the football pools? National Hunt people want to win the Grand National or the Gold Cup and most of them, from my experience, would prefer to win the Grand National.'

To her six jockeys, some of whom are young and probably petrified, Pitman will simply say: 'Go and have a good ride.' She says, laughing again: 'We go through the usual bit. The clerk of the course tells them every year not to be in too much of a hurry, the ground's very fast and all the rest of it. Everybody just says, "Up yours, we're gonna do what we want to do". To the younger jockeys I just say that if anything goes on around you, just put it out of your mind and concentrate on what's ahead. On statistics, half of mine won't finish, which means one'll probably fall and one'll make a bad mistake or something. I don't say this as a load of cobblers, because it's the gospel truth. All I want is for my horses to come back sound. That's the most important thing to me and always has been. Everything else is a great big bonus.'

With the race looming, and her favourite television programme, *Coronation Street*, coming up, Pitman is still in reflective mood as she ends the conversation. 'There are benefits from perhaps being sensitive, and I'm very lucky in being able to pack away the past,' she says. 'I'm very lucky to have David, too. He came back one night and sat across the room looking at me. I watched the TV and pretended not to notice. Then I started thinking, "He's found another woman. He's gonna leave", and he said, "I've been thinking about you. When I was going to Fontwell today, I was thinking about how you started, and I thought – don't ever change the way you are". And that's the nicest thing anyone's said to me.'

NO AIRS AND GRACES FOR A THOMAS HARDY NATIVE

Marcus Armytage

When Robert Alner was a young lad his father, a hunting farmer who trained the occasional point-to-pointer, had more working cart horses than tractors on his Dorset farm and still employed a carter to look after them. Even as late as the 1960s the family used a cart horse to feed the cattle in winter because tractors would get bogged around parts of the farm while the horse wouldn't. His father's views on training were also of an earlier era. He would saddle up his horse at lunchtime, gallop it twice round a field and then see to it in the evening after milking. 'It makes me sound about 80,' says the lean and greying Alner, 61, reflecting on an upbringing that evokes images of a Thomas Hardy novel. Generations of Alners have lived off Dorset's most abundant natural resource, grass. Originally they produced milk from it, now they are galloping on it and hoping to harvest a second Gold Cup for Locketts Farm when Sir Rembrandt lines up for racing's Blue Riband today.

'I well remember taking hay to the cows on a cart and several times being run away with when one of the straps came undone or broke,' adds Alner. The term 'to be carted' is still used by jockeys to describe a hairy ride on a runaway horse. After he left school his mother thought he should, like a lot of other farmers' sons in the area, have a point-to-pointer. It was, Alner recalls, trained with the free advice of farmers they would meet at the weekly market in Sturminster Newton, then the largest calf market in Britain. When it won its first race well at a local point-to-point it provided the young jockey with the first of 212 winners between the flags and sowed the seed for a career in the saddle that would span 33 years and another 55 winners Under Rules. Only a badly broken leg at 50 brought Alner's career to a 'premature' end and forced him to concentrate on training.

But the farmers' next advice was bitter sweet for Alner. So impressed were they with its win they suggested his parents run the horse in a hurdle at Wincanton and replace the young and inexperienced jockey with David Mould, advice his parents readily accepted.

It is jump-racing's grassroots, the point-to-point field, which has served Alner well in his 12-year professional training career and been the hallmark of his success. Typically, he brings on young, usually Irish, strongly-built store horses of a certain stamp, purchased from Tom Costello – the man who produced previous Gold Cup winners Cool Ground, Best Mate, The Thinker among others – and Alner's first Gold Cup winner, Cool Dawn. Three of his best four horses, Cool Dawn, Harwell Lad and Kingscliff, a late defection from this year's race, were brought primarily to give their owners a bit of sport round lesser known racecourses like Badbury Rings and Larkhill, where a good picnic is as much a part of the day as owning a winner.

'They start off pointing, hunting stands them in good stead, and they'll go back to it when they've finished Under Rules,' Alner says. 'Hunting teaches them to cope with hullabaloo, where to put their feet and how to handle different ground. We don't go in for hurdling in a big way. I don't tend to buy horses off the Flat, and the year we won the Gold Cup with Cool Dawn I think we had just one hurdle winner.'

Until six years ago, when the operation started losing money and he sold it, Alner and his wife, Sally, who runs the point-to-point yard, still combined training with a dairy herd and quota to produce one-and-a quarter million litres of milk annually. Now the milking parlour has made way for more stables. But you could forgive Alner for a sense of déjà vu before today's race. Three days ago the shorter-priced of his two intended Gold Cup runners, Kingscliff, worked badly and was ruled out of the race. Last year he was pulled out three weeks beforehand. 'It was devastating,' admits Sally Alner, who rides the horse daily, 'but it's no good trying to kid yourself it would be all right on the day. Aren't we lucky to still have a runner in the race?'

So it is all down to Sir Rembrandt again. Last year he chased Best Mate up the hill and only failed by half a length to peg him back. Stamina, the guts for a battle and a love of mud and left-handed tracks are the nine-year-old's principal qualities but, unlike his trainer, he is no gentleman. 'If he were a human he'd be a lager lout,' says the trainer's wife. 'He's in great form but we'd love some more rain.'

Alner is one of racing's most unassuming men. There are no airs and graces about him and another Gold Cup won't change him. Today, just as he did in 1998 when Cool Dawn won the race, he will leave Locketts Farm at the wheel of the horsebox. Behind him will be Sir Rembrandt and Free Gift, who attempts to emulate Kingscliff's Foxhunter win of two years ago and is a couple of rungs behind his stable-mate on the progression from point-to-point to Cheltenham winner's enclosure. From transport by horse to horse transport, Alner is still in the driving seat.

1 MAY 2004

CLASSIC CHANNON

Sue Mott

Memories of Mick Channon are dressed in red and white stripes. In your mind's eye, you remember him endlessly scoring for Southampton (229 times, actually), slim as a wand and wheeling his arm, all grin, hair and super-lavish sideburns. Like Bisto, a little thickening has gone on since. A face has emerged from the fuzz, one upon which the grin is still plastered even if the hair has receded from the margins. It suits him. It just makes more dramatic the expression in his blue eyes that light up with rage, joy, disgust, excitement, anticipation and laughter at roughly five-second intervals.

His enthusiasm is vastly infectious. It must be. His West Ilsley Stables, once owned by The Queen, produced 141 winners last season and tomorrow we will know whether his filly, Majestic Desert, has picked up the mood to win the 1,000 Guineas at Newmarket. That would represent his first Classic victory after 16 years as a horse trainer. Beyond that, it would represent the first time an England footballer had graduated to the pinnacle of a second sporting career, unless you count Gary Lineker on television or Francis Lee in loo rolls. 'Sunday is a big day,' said Channon, removing his cap and running his hands through his stubbled hair in his excitement. 'I'm positive we go there with an outstanding chance.' The rain, pounding on the roof of the Portakabin that functions as his operation nerve centre, delighted him. 'Soft ground will suit our other filly in the race, Silca's Gift,' he added, in that Worzel-like West Country accent, renowned for pronouncing vigorously on any and every subject.

'I think there could be a party if we win,' he said. No 'could' about it. His staff of 60, assorted owners, his 82-year-old mum, very likely all 146 horses and almost certainly the entire complement of the 1976 FA Cup-winning Southampton team – they beat Manchester United – would be there to join the festivities. He will have to keep off the Champagne. 'My arthritis,' the 55-year-old explained. The bubbles seem to make it worse, but pure thrill might be an acceptable substitute.

But we are getting ahead of ourselves. He hasn't won it yet and may never win it. 'That's probably part of the attraction: the challenge. I think we must be masochists for the highs and lows we put ourselves through.' More head-rubbing. 'There are a million things that have to go right to win an 'orse race,' he said. 'Christ! I've got the solution for Gamblers' Anonymous. They should come 'ere and see all the things that can go wrong with an 'orse. They'd never 'ave a bet again. If you saw the problems, from sore shins, to dirty noses, to coughin', to sore girths. Ah, Jesus Christ, it goes on and on. Ringworm! We can't cure the common cold, can we? What chance 'ave we got of telling if a certain race 'orse is 100 per cent on the day?' His eyes widen with splendid rhetorical inquiry.

Don't mistake this for complaint. Channon loves and adores his second life, in the gorgeous surroundings (not including the Portakabin) of the yard that used to belong to The Queen's former trainer, Major Dick Hern. That a former footballer should acquire such a place was beyond everyone's reckoning at the time, including his own. The former council-house kid didn't begin to think he could afford it, and his wife, Jill, was not too enraptured either by the human skull found under the old spiral staircase. But when he was urged, twice, by Lord Carnarvon to put in a bid, the penny began to drop. Was Her Majesty keen to see the property stay within racing, as opposed to being sold as luxury flats? 'Ah, we'll never know. Lord Carnarvon's dead and you can't talk to The Queen. But that's the impression I got.'

The faith of the Establishment has been amply repaid. Channon, reared in a council house in the Wiltshire village of Orcheston, has proved to be a natural in the mysterious business of horse training. 'We had a trainer in the village and we just grew up with an interest. I remember as kids, a group of us boys would be kicked out of the house after breakfast with a bottle of orange pop and a bread roll and we used to go miles across Salisbury Plain. We'd find ponies and ride 'em. Hangin' on for a few minutes, till someone threw a stick at 'em and we were down on our arse.'

He was always tearing around, helping with the haymaking (probably in both senses) down on the local farm or getting up in the middle of the night with his two brothers, John and Phillip, to catch chickens. Catch chickens? 'Oh yeah. Catchin' 'em, boxin' 'em. Getting 'em ready for the market. I think we earned a fiver each. Good money. Work's not a problem. Never has been. It's enjoyment. If you've got time on your hands, you'll rob or steal or shag, won't you?' I rather hope this is a rhetorical question, too.

His boisterous childhood was tragically interrupted when he was nine by the death of his elder brother, John, in a tractor accident. 'I remember it but I don't dwell on it. I don't know when your character forms or how it would have affected me. I remember the sadness and that, you know, but I had a good upbringing. I was encouraged to play football. In the end, if you're happy and enthusiastic it comes out in you.' It came out in Channon, partly in the form of betting slips. 'I remember my first decent bet. Mr Sturdy's it was, won the Ebor. Tintagel II it was called. I had £6 on it. I was an apprentice at Southampton and £6 on a 'orse would have been a lot of money back in the Sixties. I was earning £7 a week and £4.50 on digs. I always remember. 40 Wilton Avenue. Mrs Fifer was the landlady. Used to frighten the s*** out of me.'

Hauling him back from this digression, it turned out he won £100 that day. 'I don't know what I done with it. Spent it, that's for sure.' He smiled in age-old remembrance. He is the type of man whose memories either bring vast amusement or fake denials. He claims it was only Peter Osgood and Jim Steele who used to jump on the back of a bus during Southampton's cross-country training, but it seems highly unlikely he would have foregone the lark. For all the joviality in his soul though, he became a favourite of Sir Alf Ramsey in the twilight of his England management career. 'He tried everyone else first. Osgood, Jeff Astle, Francis Lee. I came in after Rodney Marsh. It was 'ard to get in, but then it was even bloody 'arder to get out. Alf stuck with the people 'e liked.'

A lot of good it did him. Channon's reign with England (21 goals in 46 appearances) coincided with England failing to attend two successive World Cup finals in 1974 and 1978. 'I would say that game against Poland at Wembley was my most sickening sporting moment. The purists said we should have been more patient!' The eyes flashed like a neon sign, and Channon conducted one of his trademark combustible arguments with himself. 'More patient! F*** off, you daft bastard!' he scoffed. 'You know what I'm saying. We battered 'em for 85 minutes. We hit the post, the bar, the goalkeeper, knees, heads. So I don't say, "Cor, I regret it". We all gave 110 per cent. I regret not going to a World Cup, but I don't regret the way we all played. But there, that's history. We've all moved on.'

In England's case, to an appointment with France in their opening game of the European Championship in June. Channon is not a fan. 'I don't rate the manager to be honest with you. I'm a great believer. You get a team together that you trust. You all stick together. If anybody out there says anything against anyone of mine, I'll fight 'em. That's the way I believe a team should be. But all this changing about. He's totally degraded international caps. They're not worth a toss, are they? What's a friendly now? I mean, Jesus Christ, there's 26 players going to play in a friendly. What supporter wants to go and see it? I think it's taking money under false pretences. What a load of b******s. I think he's cheapened an England cap, that's what 'e's done. You can buy the f***ers in Woolworths now. It doesn't appear he knows his best team, going into the European Championship. He doesn't seem to know what he's doin', that's the annoying thing.' The trainer stopped and dropped his voice as though imparting a secret. 'He's Swedish as well. I'm very patriotic,' he added ruefully, then laughed. Storm over.

If Channon was a weather system, he'd be tropical. Thunder and lightning, chasing glorious sunshine. But beneath it all is a shrewdness and attention to detail that belies the old footballer image. The Jockey Club may have refused him a trainer's licence when he first applied, having tried and failed to imagine his 15-stone bulk on a horse, but they succumbed a year later and have no need to repent. His philosophy is nicknamed 'Kiss'. For Keep It Simple, Stupid. 'We all 'ave the same bridles, we all 'ave the same tack. Every 'orse is fed the same. 'Ey, I'm not that bloody clever to think that a little bit of garlic 'ere and a little bit of Guinness there and 'arf a dozen eggs, you know, will make a 'orse go any better.'

They are going well enough as it is. He has kept it simple. He is staying on the Flat, for a start. 'Jump racing's like an egg and spoon race. Drop the egg and you're out the race. Listen, it's hard enough for me to win on the Flat without putting jumps into it.' Even on the Flat, Channon has pretty well stuck to his six-furlong sprinter milers. 'I'd love to win the Derby but I 'aven't got a 'orse that would get a mile and a 'arf on a bus,' he said. Nevertheless, it is a dream. A horse called Tobougg is the nearest he has come. It finished third in the 2001 Derby, but by then it had already been taken back by the Godolphin operation. Channon had just been a foster father. People imagine he might be upset by this arrangement. 'I know the rules. I'm a big boy. It's not my job to fall in love with 'orses. It's my job to train 'em. At the moment, I can't see a day when I'm not doing this. It just gives me such a buzz. It's my fix. It's my drug. It's like a football manager trying to find the next David Beckham. In a stable like this, we want a 'orse to come through to be a star. The sort that makes a great season out of a good season.' Over to you, Majestic Desert.

---

11 NOVEMBER 2001

SUPERMAN WITH THE MIDAS TOUCH

Brough Scott

Clark Kent needed a telephone box to turn himself into Superman. Aidan O'Brien doesn't even take his glasses off. Soon he'll be teaching his horses to fly. He's certainly got the running sorted. In his native Ireland, this softly spoken 32-year-old tops the trainers' table for the fifth consecutive year; his £3,427,545 prize-money total being a mere £1,500,000 ahead of the redoubtable Dermot Weld, his nearest rival. While another £3,389,908 earned by his horses over here puts him a cool million clear of runner-up Sir Michael Stoute.

Two weeks ago at Belmont, he added another £630,000 to this not inconsiderable total when St Leger winner Milan ran a gallant second to Fantastic Light in the Breeders' Cup Turf and then the brilliant two-year-old Johannesburg whipped America's best in the Breeders' Cup Juvenile to become favourite for next year's Kentucky Derby. In all, the famous Ballydoyle stable, in Tipperary, has logged an unbettered 22-strong set of victories at Group One level this year, with Epsom Derby hero Galileo the star turn among seven European Classics; not bad for a trainer who has also knocked off the last three Champion Hurdles at Cheltenham with Istabraq. The greatest compliment you can pay him about this year's success is to say that, in hindsight, it seems inevitable. Believe me, it need not have been.

In March of '96 I went to see him at his then Piltown base, halfway up a mountain in County Kilkenny. He was already a phenomenon, having taken over the stable from his father-in-law, Joe Crowley, and his own wife, Anne Marie, and in three full seasons topped the jump list each time. In 1995 he recorded an accumulated Flat and jump total of no fewer than 242 winners. The farmer's son from County Wexford had always been serious about horses. He had thrived under the ultimate taskmaster Jim Bolger, at Coolcullen. He had raced against Ann Marie on the way to becoming a hard-hitting amateur champion rider. The commitment was there. But what about the wisdom?

He was lean, quiet and very focused, just like the ten-horse squad he was preparing to try and break his duck at Cheltenham. From 7.30 until 9.30 it was all uphill hustle with these tough and battle-hardened jumpers. It was a million miles from the manicured serenity and the fragile young minds and limbs of the million dollar two-year-olds at Ballydoyle across the river in Tipperary. But at 9.45, that's exactly where he drove to.

Fifteen years ago Robert Sangster hired Britain's jump racing genius, Michael Dickinson, to operate his wonderfully-ambitious Flat racing project at Manton. It didn't last a season. John Magnier has long been acknowledged as having the coolest and cutest brain in the thoroughbred firmament. The son-in-law of Ballydoyle's legendary creator, Vincent (absolutely no relation) O'Brien, Magnier had masterminded Sangster's stallion-making boom with the likes of The Minstrel, Alleged, and El Gran Senor in the Seventies and Eighties. Coolmore Stud had become the first truly global breeding operation, apparently above the passing storms in the economic weather. But with Vincent finally retired, to pick a 26-year-old to rush in part-time when his main job was over, seemed the most un-Magnier-like thing to do. Some of us prissily clucked our tongues and waited for the fall-out.

It cannot have been easy, but Desert King won Ireland's top two year old race that year, and in 1997 he took their 2,000 Guineas and Derby to top the table. In 1998 King of Kings came over to win our 2,000 Guineas at Newmarket and the new O'Brien legend seemed on the way. Yet a month later, when King of Kings and two other Ballydoyle runners got very publicly stuck in traffic on the way to Epsom before running abysmally in the Derby, there was an element of rushed-naivety about the arrangements, which left at least one of the top stables curling their lips in disapproval. Once again we watchers wondered. But Magnier was backing his man. 'What attracted me,' he says, choosing the words as carefully as he studies a pedigree in the sales ring, 'was how Aidan trained lots and lots of winners from ordinary horses when he started. That was a very good sign. And,' John added with typical approval of the publicity-shy ethos established by the new master of Ballydoyle, 'he still wears the same size of hat.'

Today the head inside the hat is having to cope with 150 of the most expensive, carefully chosen young stock that any trainer has had led out before him. Last summer I rode out on Glyndebourne, a handsome son of Galileo's sire Sadlers Wells, who a month later finished second to Sinndar in the Irish Derby. It was a gorgeous morning, rooks calling in the trees, the sun shining on the distant green-clad Galtee Mountains. Alex Ferguson was a guest beside Aidan in the Jeep. The trainer was quiet, but not content. For, every bit as much as Ferguson, he has an operation for which winning trophies is not optional. Magnier and his partner Michael Tabor have amassed funds which can actually outbid the Sheikhs at the Sales. Classic victories and stud value are what the trainer is paid to deliver and the way Aidan has approached the challenge is to narrow his responsibilities not widen them. Vincent O'Brien created and was in charge of all the developments at Ballydoyle. Today Sir Michael Stoute would be the utterly-dominating centrepiece of the currently most effective single-person training operation in the world. But for Aidan, the buying, selling, even the most simple glad-handing, is to be avoided whenever possible. He is head coach, not manager.

When the triumphant team had dinner at The Cashel Palace on the night of Galileo's Derby, Aidan stayed just for a bowl of soup before heading home to Anne Marie and the four children. At Belmont, after the Breeders' Cup, a taxi was ticking in the car park so that he could race to the overnight plane at JFK and be back on the gallops at Ballydoyle by eight o'clock next morning. The plain, but well-appointed family bungalow at the bottom of the gallops is his absolute sanctuary, the gilded training track his workbench. Out there, for all his softly spoken, Christian-name civility, he can be ruthless to the point of destruction. But this season in particular the top horses have lasted right through the year. It is because the coach cares. It is about focus. After Glyndebourne had given me that golden canter last summer, we filed past the trainer and for a brief moment those glasses homed in as hard as any Superman laser throw. 'He seems fine,' says Aidan. Yes, Clark Kent has X-ray eyes.

CHAPTER 10

BRASS IN POCKET

Wouldn't it be nice to have enough money to own a racehorse? Imagine it: standing there in the parade ring, rubbing shoulders with 'the connections' of other runners in that day's feature race. Then, once your horse has thrashed the opposition, it's off to the winner's enclosure, pat the horse, thank the jockey and trainer, collect a big fat cheque, and possibly another glittering trophy for the mantlepiece, and order another magnum of Champagne for your entourage. It must be a great life — if you've got the money to fund it. Among those featured here are Anne, the Duchess of Westminster, owner of Arkle, the Aga Khan, the Earl of Derby, Lady Beaverbrook and Jim Lewis, of Best Mate fame. Brough Scott also provides an inside perspective on the corrosive quarrel between John Magnier and Sir Alex Ferguson over Rock of Gibraltar. Owning a race-horse isn't all fun, it seems.

---

6 APRIL 2001

A PRIZE GEM AMONG OWNERS

Sue Mott

It went from bad to worse. Anne, the Duchess of Westminster, is the doyenne of regal steeplechase owners. The Queen Mother may have had more winners and tiaras, but 'Nancy', as she is known to her many friends and admirers, had Arkle, not to mention a stunning victory in the Grand National in 1985. (His name was Last Suspect. And he was indeed the least suspected. 'Everything else fell,' said the Duchess accurately.) She has three gloriously polished Cheltenham Gold Cups in the dining room, ditto three Hennessys (all courtesy of Arkle) plus plates, plaques, portraits, photos on every wondrously waxy surface and square inch of luminous wall commemorating a lifetime's devotion to horses. The fourth wife of the late Duke of Westminster, she is, at 86, a grande dame in tweeds and pearls, and the trouble was I was sitting on her *Racing Post.*

'You're sitting on my *Racing Post,*' she said, producing an electric leap from me such as I had not experienced since gym club 30 years ago. I flustered about, offering to move it. 'No, leave it alone,' she uttered sharply. I left it alone, sat down (or rather felt my legs give way underneath me) and ploughed on.

She has a close association with the National. 'Yes, it's a great test.' The voice is a Doberman's bark softened by majestic elocution. She goes every year to Aintree, drawn as everyone else in National Hunt racing to the show-piece event, and often as not because she has a runner of her own. Not this year, however. Radiation, her horse in training with Jonjo O'Neill, did not make it to the starting tape, jockeyed out by higher claims among his rivals. It is a shame. He might have won at whatever odds through the sheer Niagara force of his owner's personality. The Duchess is a monumental character. Arkle knew it too. 'When he was out in the field and you shouted to him, he came galloping for his sugar. He knew one's voice. When I drove into the yard at Tom Dreaper's, he knew my voice. He'd go bang, bang, bang on the stable door. But I think he knew my car as well. He'd go thump, thump, thump – knowing there was a sugar lump, y'see.'

She would ride him in their mutual summer holidays in Ireland, where she was born. 'He took great care of me. It was as if he knew who I was. He was a friend.' And so she was, having discovered the greatest steeplechaser of the century ('well, I think so, but I'm prejudiced') in Goff's Sale, Ballsbridge, Dublin, in August 1960. She bought him for 1,150 guineas on the spot. He retired eight years later having won 27 of 35 races and the Duchess, necklaced in binoculars and topped off by sensible hat, attended all of them.

She approached Dreaper to train the legend-in-waiting the day of his purchase. He was not entirely won over by the prospect. He went home and told his wife: 'We've got another horse coming.' 'Good. I hope you like him,' said his wife. 'Haven't seen him,' he replied. 'Do you like the pedigree?' she asked. 'No,' he answered, 'but I like the look of the girl.' The 'girl' was 45, already widowed by the death in 1953 of her husband, Bend'Or. Unusually, he had been named after a horse, a portrait of whom (dated 1886) hangs on a wall in the dining room. 'Your husband was named after a horse,' I said, conversationally, over delicious shepherd's pie. 'Yes,' she said, betraying no surprise or alarm whatsoever.

In her prime, the Duchess hunted, stalked and fished. Wild salmon fishing, on her own river in Sutherland, and backgammon are now the limits of her sporting activity, to her intense annoyance. 'I gave up riding not very long ago. I think it was at the end of my seventies. I enjoyed being young and going hunting and racing. I don't like being old. It's dreadful now. Not remembering things. But I'm nearly 90 so it's no wonder,' she chuckled. 'Nearer 90 than 80 anyway.' Looking quite remarkable, she could pass for 20 years younger and bears an uncanny resemblance to The Queen.

The memories are gently jolted by her books and albums. There is one for Arkle, a huge, leather-bound black book with his name in gold lettering, stuffed full of an escalating legend. Headlines trumpet 'Arkle the Magnificent', and photographed beside him endlessly is a radiant woman in a hat, joyous in victory, generous in rare defeat. 'Mouth open again,' censured the Duchess of her younger newsprint self. 'No wonder The Duchess Looks Overjoyed,' says the caption because Arkle had just won the President's Handicap Hurdle at Gowran

Park, earning £432, largely by-the-by when his owner was married to one of the richest men in the world and formerly lived in Eaton Hall, Ecclestone, near Chester, where her private wing alone ran to 30 bedrooms. We were meeting at the Lodge instead, much more manageable for dusting, to which she repaired two years after her husband's death. It is cosier and about a 50th of the size. Indeed, her snug is no bigger than an average family house bathroom and it takes some effort not to tread on Penny the Dachshund snoozing on the floor by the log fire. This would have been terrible. 'She's 112,' said the Duchess.

The mantelpiece presents the family gallery: father, mother, brother and herself in uniform on a motorbike. 'That's me winning the War,' she said. 'Oh, you during the War,' I replied stupidly diluting the content. 'That's me winning the War,' she restated with due emphasis. I was succumbing to a discouraging, slow-burn, ongoing terror. But there was nothing for it but to keep going, like Last Suspect, doggedly over every hurdle until I either collapsed or staggered to the post. 'Oh look, there's you receiving the Hennessy Gold Cup from the Queen Mother,' I said. 'Oh good,' she murmured politely.

She is, by all accounts, a wonderful owner, perhaps by virtue of being a wonderful horsewoman. Her view was that the trainer should train and the jockey should ride. 'Exactly. Mind your own business,' was her philosophy. Everyone worked to their maximum. 'Best I ever rode,' said Arkle's jockey, Pat Taafe, in the *Irish Independent* in 1964. 'I should jolly well hope so,' commented the Duchess. That was the year Arkle won his first Cheltenham Gold Cup, the Irish contingent so excited that a report from the time described 'noisy leaping fans, as if he were a Beatle'. The Duchess, of course, was not among that number. She would conduct herself calmly. 'I was so much more worried about him being hurt.' She never would allow him to race in the Grand National, fearing for his extremely precious life in the rough and tumble of the race. 'I was so afraid he'd be hurt through no fault of his own because it's such a big field. Anyway, I knew he could win it, so what's the point of running.' Friends in the racing world occasionally tried to persuade her otherwise. I doubt there has been a more fruitless enterprise. The Duchess's 'no' is spectacularly final.

The daughter of Brigadier General Edward Sullivan, she was born and bred with military backbone. The bomb scare year at Aintree, 1997, put no fears into her. What did she do? I asked, eager for breathless tales of a great escape. 'We left,' she replied. There was no hiding place. You do wonder if her horses have experienced similar feelings. It is an incredible fact that Tom Dreaper's yard gave her 97 winners (27 of them Arkle). She had no idea. 'Cor blimey,' she said elegantly. I thought it provident at this point to make a timely run to the lavatory. They tell you a great deal about people and sure enough there was a rollicking cartoon from Giles, featuring the dreaded 'Grandma' of his imagination and a politician on the hustings. Grandma has mistaken this hapless candidate for the far more socially telling character of a bookie. 'Ten shillings to win. Arkle,' she barks at him. It is signed: 'To Anne, Duchess of Westminster. And Arkle. Giles 1966.' It is a tribute to her humour and the warm esteem in which her sensitive ownership was and is held by everyone, within and without the racing industry. She is, you suspect, a bit of a lad and the Grand National will be more than infinitesimally poorer for the lack of a runner in her black and yellow colours today.

'What time is your beastly train?' she asked suddenly. And I really do see why Last Suspect thought it prudent to carry on running round Aintree when all around him were falling down, despite the fact he'd pulled up at Warwick a month earlier through lack of commitment and boredom. Perhaps she had had a waspish word with him. I knew about this. At one point I had asked her about the non-running Radiation, his character and provenance. 'He's got four legs, a head and a tail,' she said. I blustered about some people investing animals with human characteristics. 'Do they? Sounds a bit daft to me,' she said. She made a hefty prod at a log on the fire and I prepared to take my leave. Her Grace does not bet, but I felt a general salutation in order with the Grand National in such imminent view. 'I wish you luck,' I said. 'As you wave me goodbye,' sang the Duchess lyrically.

---

20 JUNE 1995

THE AGA KHAN STORY RESUMES

John Oaksey

Whatever his fate in today's St James's Palace Stakes, the mere presence at Ascot of the Aga Khan's Adjareli must surely mean the end of a sad, unnecessary interruption to a famous racing story. From 1921, when the present Aga Khan's grandfather asked George Lambton to buy him the foundations of a stud – to 1990 when the Jockey Club belatedly disqualified the Oaks winner Aliysa – the name and colours of an Aga Khan have, almost without a break, played a leading role on the British racing stage.

The present Aga, like his grandfather, is a direct descendant of Mohammed. That makes him spiritual leader to more than 20 million Ismaili Muslims. I suppose the best-known picture of an Aga Khan is that one of a plump old man being weighed in gold, or maybe diamonds, to celebrate his jubilee. But, rich though the family unquestionably is, the impression is slightly misleading. There is a rule, obeyed by about half the Ismailis, that each shall pay the Imam between eight per cent and ten per cent of his income. But almost all that money – like the gold and diamonds on the scales – is spent on education, the relief of poverty and other charitable objects.

In any case, besides being a descendant of the Prophet, Karim, the Aga Khan also happens to be a tough, bright, conscientious Harvard-educated businessman who takes his duties as Imam to the Ismaili Muslims very seriously indeed. He also runs his studs and racing stables on the strictest possible lines. Which is why, having twice in the 1980s suffered the effects of misleading or inaccurate drug tests – Vayrann's Champion Stakes and Lashkari's Breeders' Cup – he is understandably sceptical of sample analysis as currently practised in racing. Holding that no single analyst should be exclusively relied on, the Aga summoned a group of international experts who – at least to my unscientific ears – threw sufficient doubt on the 'prosecution' evidence to justify a Jockey Club finding in Aliysa's favour. But all that, with any luck, is water under the bridge.

There is not much doubt that owner-breeders, however successful, need the exposure and merit-assessing opportunities which go with a presence in one or two top British stables. No bloodstock order has been better filled than the old Aga's to George Lambton. Two Classic winners, the original 'flying filly' Mumtaz Mahal and the dams of Bahram, Theft and Dastur were among the eight yearlings for whom Lambton paid a mere 24,250 guineas. No wonder that in only his third season racing, thanks mainly to Diophon's 2,000 Guineas and Salmon Trout's St Leger, the old Aga headed the list for the first of 13 times. Blenheim, Bahram and Mahmoud won him three pre-War Derbys and by the time Tulyar and Charlie Smirke made it four in 1952, the Aga's son Aly Khan had bought a half-share in his father's stable.

Partly, no doubt, because of his spectacular and sometimes sensational lifestyle, Aly Khan was passed over and the position of Imam went to his son. But besides his famous charm – which I am told worked on men as well as women (even cuckolded husbands often ended up liking him) – Aly Khan became a genuine expert on the Turf. Before his death in a car crash, he was taking a major part in the family racing operation, and in the last years of his life, had the great joy of breeding Petite Etoile. Beauty and speed, the grey filly had both the qualities Aly loved best and it was perhaps a blessing of sorts that he died without seeing her beaten.

Petite Etoile's last failure, in fact, came in the one race she was most wanted to win – the Aly Khan Memorial at Kempton. The young Aga, who had not then decided what to do about the family horses, was at Kempton that day. I remember the gloom and bewilderment on his face as this supposedly invincible wonderhorse came back. But, happily, it was not long before Aly Khan's son realised just how valuable the family's equine properties were, or could be made. 'Aly Khan knew every single horse by sight,' one old stud man remembers. 'But although Karim started from scratch, it did not take him long ...' He knows a good deal about it by now and I wonder whether Adjareli will remind him how sweet victory tastes today.

---

23 JULY 2004

A WALK ON THE WILDENSTEIN SIDE

J.A. McGrath

Just when there was a remote possibility the outside world might believe all was rosy in racing's garden, along comes Ascot's King George VI and Queen Elizabeth Diamond Stakes and the controversial Wildenstein family, once described by the great Lester Piggott as 'inveterate bad losers'. Alec Wildenstein, who took control of Ecurie Wildenstein on the death of his father, Daniel, less than three years ago, will be seen in his outsized pinstripes chatting with Olivier Peslier, the most recent in a long line of appointed jockeys, in the paddock prior to the feature race of high summer in Britain. They will be represented by the 6–1 second favourite, Vallee Enchantee, who, on paper, has an excellent chance.

Piggott could speak with some authority on the Wildensteins, having been sacked for a somewhat adventurous ride on a two-year-old colt named Vacarme in the Richmond Stakes at Goodwood. The legendary jockey found himself locked in a pocket, with the only way out being to barge through near the inside. This led to several rivals being knocked aside, an inevitable visit to the Stewards' room, and, ultimately, disqualification. Piggott was given the elbow shortly after.

The bigger the name, the more likely they are to fall out with the Wildensteins. In 1978, no less a jockey than Pat Eddery, 11 times champion and partner of over 4,000 winners, was given the order of the boot for his ride on Buckskin, who finished fourth in that year's Ascot Gold Cup, having been sent off 11–8 favourite. In what was called, in one report, an outstanding example of how to lose gracelessly, Daniel Wildenstein complained about Eddery – but trainer Peter Walwyn stuck by his jockey and told the French owner to look elsewhere for a stable. In May 2001, 42 Wildenstein horses left the equally difficult Andre Fabre (what an association that must have been while it lasted) despite the temperamental genius being responsible for a series of winners, including the family's outstanding Peintre Celebre, winner of the Prix de l'Arc de Triomphe, and, significantly, the sire of Vallee Enchantee.

But it doesn't end there – in fact, the tales become juicier and more bizarre.

This year alone, there has been the blatant transgression of the Rules of Racing by the misuse of ear plugs on a Wildenstein horse, a totally unfounded accusation that Godolphin had been doping their horses, and then the very public sacking, at Epsom last month, of former champion jockey Dominique Boeuf. When approached by one reporter, who suggested diplomatically that Vallee Enchantee and Boeuf may have been a trifle unlucky in the straight in the Coronation Cup, Alec Wildenstein replied: 'We weren't unlucky. She was ridden by an asshole who didn't follow instructions.' It would be very unlikely such an unsporting statement would be made publicly by an owner in this country, particularly about a jockey who had served the stable well. There followed the almost comical scene of Boeuf having to wait patiently outside the weighing room until Wildenstein had finished blasting him to the press – owner and jockey were booked on the return to Paris together, and if Boeuf had lost his job, he certainly wasn't going to miss his lift back to Heathrow.

The nastiest of the incidents involving Wildenstein this year came after Godolphin's Papineau won the Ascot Gold Cup, ridden by Frankie Dettori. Wildenstein's stayer, Westerner, had finished second, but looking over at the winner's enclosure, the French owner uttered: 'The dope-testing machine must be broken.' Sheikh Mohammed and his entourage were distinctly unimpressed. Simon Crisford, racing manager to Godolphin, said bluntly: 'We will make no response to statements of that kind.'

With the *entente cordiale* smashed into very small pieces, it remains to be seen just how the public will react should Vallee Enchantee cast aside the bad luck she endured in both her outings this year – she should certainly have finished closer at Epsom whether or not you believe Boeuf to be 'an asshole' – and win the King George VI and Queen Elizabeth Diamond Stakes. The Wildensteins have won the race already, with another very good filly, Pawneese, in 1976. Whether Vallee Enchantee is in the same league is another question, but in what appears a non-vintage running of the race, she might not have to be very good to actually win. Her trainer, Elie Lellouche, believes she has both the form and ability to pull it off – if so, the post-race interviews should not be missed.

---

2 JUNE 2007

RACING HERITAGE BREEDS SUCCESS

Sue Mott

You can't be too careful. Bearing in mind that I was a guest of the Knowsley Estate, home of the Earls of Derby, where the fifth Earl (Ferdinando) had been poisoned by arsenic, the seventh Earl (James) had been beheaded in Bolton, the 12th Earl (Edward) kept gnus and the 14th Earl (Edward) had become three times the British Prime Minister, it was with some trepidation that I accepted the invitation of the 19th Earl (Edward) to lunch of cottage pie and cabbage in the conservatory. Luckily, Ollie was there. Ollie is the youngest scion (aged five) of this particular wing of the noble Stanley family, his lineage directly traceable to Adam de Stanley (1125–1200), and if he could eat his food with such gusto, then it was obviously safe for all-comers.

This was a relief. The Earls of Derby have been in the thick of the action for centuries (one married the mother of Henry VII) and both the family and the estate are at the epicentre of high society still. Only recently, Brad Friedel, the Blackburn goalkeeper, held his wedding at Knowsley Hall, so did someone called Tracey from *Coronation Street*. There are concerts and charity events and the hugely popular Safari Park, but on this day of all days – Derby Day – it is the connection to one of the world's most famous horse races that becomes an issue.

It was the 12th Earl's doing. The current Lord Derby kindly showed me the Gainsborough portrait in which the famous old sportsman looked entirely proper and benign. No sign of his wild streak, which came out on his deathbed (among other occasions) when he insisted his favourite fighting cocks should be brought up to his bedroom. 'By winch, so that his wife couldn't find out and stop him,' explained his amused descendant. It was the 12th Earl who founded both the Oaks (in 1779) and the Derby (1780), the famous Epsom races. Was it really a toss of coin over dinner that decided whether the Derby would be called the Derby, after his lordship, or the 'Bunbury' after Sir Charles Bunbury, who also put himself forward for the honour?

You have a feeling the 19th Earl has been asked this before. 'We're not going to find a photo taken at the dinner party of them tossing the coin, but it's done the rounds enough to have entered folklore and legend, whether or not it's true.' He is charmingly unwilling to dismantle popular history and that is as it should be. For this particular Lord Derby, whether by accident or design, became part of horse race history himself.

'It was a bizarre quirk of fate that began it,' he related, settling himself down in an armchair in his study, apparently not the slightest inconvenienced by a small dog, resembling a roll of carpet, leaping on his knees. 'It was pretty expensive having horses in training, so I cut back a little when I took over the title when my uncle died in 1994.' As a result Lord Derby only had one horse in training in 2003. The 12th Earl might have been scandalised, until he saw the horse in question. Ouija Board was astounding, one of the greatest racing mares in the long, lavish history of the sport.

'She was born on 6 March, 2001, and I'd be a liar if I said there was anything remarkable about her. She was nice enough. But she was neither staggeringly beautiful nor startlingly crooked to make you think anything was special about her,' he remembered, well-versed, having just finished his book, *A Mare In A Million,* the story of Ouija Board. Some people might have wondered about the slightly satanic connotations of the name, but Lord Derby was not one of them. 'It was my wife's idea. I am not a great expert in ouija boards because I think they're more a girl school sort of thing.' (He went to Eton himself, where he was hugely popular among the junior boys for inventing a device that switched off forbidden radios and record players when a house-master opened the door.) 'I don't think the name is so much satanic as spiritual. We're delving into the beyond, not down to the devil. It never worried me anyway. Some horses can go awry whatever you name them. I have one called Buddhist Monk who I've nicknamed Borstal Boy because it was the most awkward thing to train.'

So the filly, bred by Lord Derby at his Stanley House Stud in Newmarket, went into training with Ed Dunlop as, nominally, nothing special. She did not stay that way very long. She came third at Newmarket in her maiden race and was due to run at Great Yarmouth on 21 October, 2003, coincidentally Lord and Lady Derby's anniversary. 'Yes, I took my wife to Great Yarmouth on our anniversary, but I did put a bottle of Champagne in the helicopter, which I hired for the first time in my life.' With cause.

'Ouija Board ran very convincingly and won. Goodwood next. The Pretty Polly. Kieren Fallon was riding and I remember my wife being rather worried. "What's she doing at the back?" she asked. A moment later she came roaring up and won by six lengths. That was the first moment when I thought, "Wow! Now we can look at the Classics".' For those not immersed in horse racing: to back a horse who wins a Classic race is as unbridled a joy as the human condition provides, resulting in adrenalin, yelling and money, in that order. To own a horse who wins a Classic, double the effect. And to breed and own a wonder horse who wins a Classic named after an old ancestral home, frankly that is just a ridiculous Disneyfied dream. Lord Derby lived a ridiculous Disneyfied dream, and then some. They decided to run Ouija Board in the Oaks. 'There was so much family history and sentiment about it. I was pretty excited but we had to keep a bit of balance. These things are not normally quite as happy as the fairytale you'd like to write.'

He does indeed seem to be the type of Earl, earnest, sensible and in his mid-forties, not prone to wild streaks of incontinent behaviour. You wouldn't necessarily say the same for Ollie, who, during the course of luncheon, ran several laps of the table at breakneck speed and kept everyone guessing, including his father, as to his future career. 'Fighter pilot?' 'No.' 'Farmer?'

'No' 'Teacher?' 'No' (Scorn) 'Footballer?' 'Nooo.' We gave up. He still wouldn't tell us, even with some wheedling involving rhubarb fool.

But Ollie's youthful spirits aside, this was a family trying to keep the ambitions reasonable on Oaks Day 2004. Ouija Board was only third favourite in a very small field. All Too Beautiful was the favourite, just in front of Punctilious. The race was being billed as the two superyards squaring up: Coolmore (Ireland) versus Godolphin (Dubai).

And yet there were omens. 'The first ever Oaks won by the 12th Earl was with a horse called Bridget, and my Aunt Bridget came along with us that day.' Admittedly that was a fairly limited omen. Lord Derby was trying to content himself with the thought that with prize money down to sixth place, all Ouija Board had to do was beat one horse and he could say he'd collected money at a British Classic. 'We weren't overly nervous. We had no serious thoughts of winning. We were just out to have a fun day. But as she came round Tattenham Corner, she moved through them all, took the lead two furlongs out and ended up winning by seven lengths, one of the longest winning margins in the history of the race. Well, we went completely wild. There's some very embarrassing BBC footage showing us leaping up and down like absolute lunatics. I can assure you that this peer of the realm gets pretty happy on a good occasion.'

There were plenty of good occasions that year. Ouija Board won the Irish Oaks, came third in the Arc and then turned her multi-national attention to the Breeders' Cup in America, a race of global prestige and significance being hosted that year in Texas. Ouija Board won and, remarkably, Lord Derby remembers going to bed. 'The thing is, it's quite stressful and nerve-wracking the whole business. You don't sleep too well on the eve of the race. I go for a run on the morning because I can't just sit there making small talk. I can't concentrate coherently. By the time you get to midnight after the race and one too many drinks, you're pretty knackered. So we certainly tried to have a good celebration but perhaps I failed to look like some of the binge drinkers we see being picked up on the streets of this country at unbelievable hours of the night.' Nevertheless, it was wonderful.

'But like all fairytales and movies, then something went wrong. We discovered a splint, a bony growth on her leg. Then she got a cracked hoof. Then we raced her in the Prince of Wales at Ascot, the year it was removed to York, but the ground was wrong and Ed couldn't get hold of me because we'd been lucky enough to be asked to join The Queen for lunch and I didn't have my phone on, for obvious reasons. It was the only race in Ouija Board's entire career where she didn't earn a penny in prize money. She lost a shoe and suffered a stress fracture.' But the Stanleys tend to come up trumps. Look at history.

Ferdinando may have been bumped off by poison but he was patron to a company of actors including Will Shakespeare. The 12th Earl may have had a soft spot for his fighting cocks, of which we strongly disapprove these days, but an estimated 100,000 people will gather at Epsom today to watch the running of 'his' race. The 19th Earl was down, but not out. Demonstrating a spirit in keeping with her heritage, Ouija Board returned to lustrous brilliance in 2006, winning the Breeders' Cup for the second time, the Nassau Stakes and the Prince of Wales's Stakes, while the family looked on from the Royal Box at Ascot. One presumes Lord Derby managed to maintain decorum in the company of his monarch. 'No,' he said simply, 'we went crazy. There was lots of shrieking. We had the trophy out on the table for tea and The Queen was delighted.'

It had been a truly remarkable career when Ouija Board retired the day before she was due to run her last race, the Hong Kong Vase, after her old injury flared up. Had she won, the wonder mare would have become the highest earning British racehorse in history, but her owner has no regrets whatever. 'She's been such a superstar. She's travelled 73,000 miles, won seven Group One races and I thought, "What else can she do, what else does she have to prove?"' She didn't, he concluded, and so his beloved horse was sent off to America to reap the romantic advances of the stallion King Mambo, the first of many, hopefully happy, occasions, which may one day give rise to Lord Derby's long-term ambition. Of course, to win the Derby.

Postscript: A day later there was a message. Ollie had finally revealed the secret of his future career. Nothing to do with horses you will be surprised to learn. He is going to be a rock star.

I FEBRUARY 2004

WATCHING MY TWO FRIENDS BECOME THE BEST OF ENEMIES

Brough Scott

It was enough to put a song in the heart, even the horse beneath me was called Glyndebourne. It was Ballydoyle, the golden heart of the Coolmore racing empire one late May morning just four summers back. In the car, his flushed face intoxicated by the sights and sounds of that heady Tipperary landscape laid on by Coolmore's mastermind John Magnier and their ubiquitous mutual friend, Mike Dillon, was Sir Alex Ferguson. How ironic that the song should now be 'Everyone loses when friends fall out'.

It had seemed a friendship made in some sporting heaven. Ferguson, the driven football man, relishing the different world – but the shared search for excellence – which sets Coolmore and Ballydoyle apart. John Magnier, the shy but all-powerful breeding and business genius happy to welcome such a winner to his circle. They shared Oscar Wilde's definition of 'very simple tastes' in that they were 'always satisfied with the very best'. They were destined to link up once it became known that Ferguson was seeking relaxation in the racing game. 'I need a hobby away from football,' he had said, 'something I can get involved in, something my wife Cathy can share.'

We were eating club sandwiches on the hotel terrace looking down towards where Rome lay resplendent in the autumn light. He was on a busman's holiday to see England's World Cup qualifier that October weekend in 1997. He was friendly, kind and clearly very keen on racing. 'What do you know about the two o'clock at Huntingdon?' he said. Total ignorance in this quarter did not dissuade him from pursuing the punt. That evening, before the happiest of meals in one of those glorious piazzas of the Eternal City, he had come across, eyes blazing with triumph, squeezed the arm, and said: 'It won, and at 7–2.' The born winner was getting his kicks on the racetrack, too.

The dinner, my own trip, and probably the Huntingdon bet, were organised by the tall, bespectacled, black moustachioed father confessor that is Dillon. Up until then, he had only been known publicly as ambassador on earth to the mighty Ladbrokes betting operation. Privately he had long done infinitely more than lay the odds. Without divulging the secrets of his confessional, and what a best seller that would be, he put people who needed each other together, arranged travel, helped the unfortunate, and oiled the wheels of many divergent elements in the racing game. We joked about Ferguson's enthusiasm. Dillon dismissed suggestions it should be stretched into owning racehorses. 'Oh no,' said Mike with an unwitting prescience he and the rest of us have come to rue, 'I have told him he is much better just following it and having his bets. Having horses will be a lot of hassle and will only lead to trouble.'

Such warnings were long forgotten when Alex turned up at Newmarket next spring to see his newly-registered scarlet colours carried for the first time on a racetrack. The horse was a Jack Berry-trained two-year-old called Queensland Star, named with true Ferguson clanship after one of the biggest vessels his father had built in the Clyde shipyard. The new owner was so welcome he even had a sponsor who held a press conference beforehand. Queensland Star started favourite and stuck on as gallantly as any United player in extra-time. He duly won again at Chester and ran on both Derby Day and at Royal Ascot. Ferguson and racing – could there be a happier match? For a long while it did not seem so. There was Candleriggs, who won twice with Ed Dunlop, a successful steeplechaser called Yankie Lord, a talented colt named Chinatown in partnership with Hong Kong maestro Ivan Allen, who ended with Sir Michael Stoute. Alex became a popular visitor, always happy to talk racing as an escape from the pressure cooker of Old Trafford. Enjoying the strange quasi-democracy of the Turf, where like monarchs, magnates and music maestros, he would be reduced to epithets like 'the guy with the red colours who has a runner in the fifth'.

Dillon would keep me posted on our friend's latest racing adventure. One day he told me how he had taken Alex to see Aidan O'Brien at Ballydoyle, how thrilled the young trainer and all his staff had been to have the great man around the place, how absorbed Alex was by Aidan's minute attention to detail as he brought his four-legged players to big-match pitch. I said that Ferguson would be joining the Coolmore team in no time. 'Not yet,' said Dillon. 'John says he wants to wait until he is sure he has a horse to suit.'

Just 'John', just the Christian name, the ultimate mark of respect, affection and fear, all three of which John Magnier commands in inordinate amounts, though not always from the same people. The Ferguson-Rock of Gibraltar dispute has brought to the wider world what the racing and bloodstock globe has known for some time. That this is the biggest, hardest, and coolest hitter of them all. If the 'Coolmore Mafia' is the derogatory term with which envious rivals brand his coterie, there is no doubt who the 'Godfather' is. Magnier is the ultimate example of generous, if demanding employer, loyal friend, ruthless competitor and, as Alex Ferguson is discovering, formidable foe. In his own circle he is every bit as much of an Alpha male as Ferguson is in his.

Watching Magnier over the years deciding on seven-figure bids at the yearling sales has been to see a broodingly intense, if slightly quieter, reflection of the gum-chewing manager in the dug-out about to make a substitution; the acolytes looking back for guidance, the 'big man' making the final decision. The core of the current ever-escalating row is that Alpha Male Ferguson has thought that he can outstare Alpha Male Magnier over the stallion fee arrangements that Magnier had offered him over Rock of Gibraltar. It is understood that while Rock of Gibraltar was officially registered as owned in partnership between Ferguson and Magnier's wife, Sue, so that he could carry the Ferguson silks, he was in fact what might be described as a 'celebrity loan' and in 2001 Ferguson was offered the choice of either five per cent of any prize money or two covering rights at stud – one in the northern hemisphere and one in the southern. Ferguson reportedly opted for the breeding rights. For a man who was already a millionaire, it seemed a reasonable bet, and when the horse took off towards greatness in 2002 it seemed even better. That is if you accept that two breeding rights were all that was on offer.

Exactly who said what to whom is officially destined for m'learned friends, though it would seem very much in both parties' interests to avoid going on the stand, the arcane nature of bloodstock deals being every bit as complicated and open to discussion as football transfers. Sometime in 2002, there was a blurring of the details of the deal. Dillon was even quoted as saying that Ferguson had paid £120,000 for half ownership of the horse at the start. But everyone was having an increasingly good time. Just for once the Coolmore operation did not make things clear and when Rock of Gibraltar finally retired with superstar status Ferguson believed he was entitled to far more than just two breeding rights, which with north and southern hemisphere coverings already amounted to more than £100,000 a year. In an increasingly heated row, it is understood that Magnier doubled the offer. Ferguson, used to forcing his way, rejected it and came back with a demand for all his future breeding rights up front, in effect a multi-million pound lump sum. Events suggest he has chosen the wrong man. Magnier and Coolmore are very bad people to cross.

The Coolmore empire now stretches way beyond Ballydoyle and the adjoining Irish stud from which they take their name. There is Coolmore USA and Coolmore Australia, where last year Rock of Gibraltar served 130 mares at a cool $A132,000 a time after doing the same thing to another hundred ladies in Ireland for stud earnings of over £13.8 million. In scope and commercial acumen there is nothing to match Coolmore on the planet. All over the world they have mares, foals, yearlings, and horses in training who they buy, sell, breed and race, always with an eye for excellence and for profit. They have several multi-millionaire investors, but everything reverts back to the unique instinct that Magnier has for how the bloodstock market will develop and his brilliant and often uncompromising methods of getting his way.

He has had it from the start. Back in the early Seventies he was a quiet, rather intense young Irishman staying at jockey Tommy Stack's draughty farmhouse near York. 'You should come in with John and me with a couple of broodmares,' said Tommy generously. 'John has a real touch for it, you know.' It has been a matter of profound financial regret to watch the young Magnier go upwards towards the stratosphere, teaming with Robert Sangster and his own father-in-law, Vincent O'Brien, to make bloodstock a major international commodity and himself into the most powerful player in the game.

Today, though the tastes and the locations are rather more expensive than was on offer in Stack's house, John is still publicly reticent. You can count the interviews given on one hand and it is strictly through lawyers and judiciously-placed 'sources' that he has conducted the Ferguson campaign. There are fine paintings on the walls of his homes, which include a beach house in Barbados where he and the legendary Irish gambler J.P. McManus are partners in the rejuvenated Sandy Lane Hotel along with that other shamrock heavyweight Dermot Desmond. McManus is also quiet, but he is happy to come on TV for interviews about his legions of jump horses – triple champion hurdler Istabraq was his star – which he conducts in a simple friendly country-boy persona somewhat at odds with the money world he now inhabits and in which he has joined Magnier in the business vehicle Cubic Expressions. McManus has a box at the Cheltenham Festival where he is a hospitable, if teetotal, host. Ferguson seemed to be getting very lucky with his friends.

They began to buy shares in Manchester United. There was even talk of them launching a takeover and Ferguson retiring from management to join the board. Come the summer of 1999 and Magnier had a horse for Alex Ferguson. It was a two-year-old called Yentsov Street, ran second at Leopardstown, won at Newmarket in September and finished third there a month later in the prestigious Dewhurst Stakes before being sold on to America. The exact details of any financial arrangements were never disclosed, but it seemed easy to assume this was much more a goodwill venture than a business one for all concerned, and when Rock of Gibraltar came on the scene in July 2001, the goodwill cup was soon overflowing.

In August the colt carried the Ferguson silks to win the historic Gimcrack Stakes at York, and after running second at Doncaster, embarked on an unprecedented seven consecutive Group One wins which only ended with an unlucky second in the Breeders' Cup at Arlington in November 2002. He was the best horse in Europe. A resplendent Fergie was pictured leading Rock of Gibraltar in at Longchamp, Ascot and all points west. He accepted trophies, gave interviews and, crucially, spoke eagerly of 'next year's stud fees'.

Somehow, somewhere this was either overlooked or not acted upon, and the exact expectations not clarified. Somehow Ferguson's team had forgotten racing's oldest adage that it is not enough to look a gift horse in the mouth, it is necessary to listen very carefully to what its owner has to say. Everything that has followed, the 'you must be joking' claims and counter claims, stems from this misunderstanding. What had begun as friendship was now a bitterly-disputed business deal. Poor Mike Dillon has been torn in two, but has reverted to the Coolmore camp. Racing, which had thought he had brokered that promotional marriage made in heaven, is staring at a divorce rising in acrimony.

So as the rest of the world looks on by turns appalled and gleefully fascinated by the meltdown of the Ferguson-Magnier quarrel, those of us who were there that Tipperary morning can only shake our heads wistfully and wonder at the morality tale of the gift horse that showed just what friends should not be for.

16 JULY 1999

GENIAL PILLAR OF BRITISH TURF AND BREEDER OF CHAMPIONS

John Oaksey

Lord Howard de Walden, whose funeral was held yesterday, was blessed throughout his long, eventful life, with a well-developed sense of humour. A member of the Jockey Club for 47 years, he may well have seen the funny side of the internal squabbles and all too public disagreements which have lately plagued the Club's 'democratic' successor, the British Horseracing Board. Lord Howard's father had always been interested in racing and breeding. It was he who asked Augustus John's advice on the best, most easily visible colour for a jockey's silks. 'Apricot' the great painter replied and, as Lord Howard notes in his delightful memoir *Earls Have Peacocks* he was absolutely right. As horses like Slip Anchor, Lanzarote, Kris and Diesis have so memorably demonstrated, apricot does stand out wonderfully well against a background of green grass.

When Lord Howard's father decided to send him racing for the first time he chose what most parents would consider an exceptionally unsuitable guide and mentor. Bob Sievier had, admittedly, been bold – or rash – enough to pay a record price for the yearling filly later to immortalise herself as Sceptre. He trained her to win four of the five Classic races in 1902 – but was not only a foolhardy gambler but also a thorough villain. Luckily the young John Howard did not catch his companion's gambling mania – but he did get a taste of just how exciting a race can be. Racing has always been popular at Eton (they used to stage special roll calls to discourage would-be visitors to Royal Ascot!) and, as it happens, John Howard fell in with the best – or depending on your point of view – worst possible company. Lord Halifax, Martin Gilliatt (later Queen Elizabeth, the Queen Mother's popular racing secretary), Clive Graham (The Scout on the *Daily Express*) and Bill Curling (Hotspur on *The Daily Telegraph*) were already all mad-keen – and sat together at the back of the class. John Howard (his father died in 1946) was a welcome addition, and as the results came in, the *Evening Standard* (Racing Edition) was in great demand. You can guess how much boring work got done.

But the rest of Lord Howard's youth does not sound boring at all. He travelled all over the world, especially to Kenya ('who will you be sleeping with tonight, sir?' said the butler), Australia and Germany – where he found his first wife. One of the many nice and extraordinary things about this splendid, many-sided man is that he enjoyed not one but two long happy marriages. Four years after the death, through leukaemia, of his first wife Nucci, he met (in 42 Portman Square, would you believe it!) a beautiful girl called Gillie Mountgarrett, to whom he was happily married until his death. I said 'many-sided' and meant it. At some stage of his life Lord Howard became an accomplished conjurer and his extra-sensory perception was well above the average. He was interested in sports and spectacles of every kind and had the great privilege of attending in 1963 the Mano a Mano duel between the two great bullfighters Dominguin and Ordonez. 'Never go to a bullfight again,' Ernest Hemmingway told Lord Howard. 'You will never see one like that.'

It was about this time that the racing and breeding luck began to improve – largely through the purchase of some ex-Sassoon mares. They included Soft Angels from whom, via the 'useless' Doubly Sure, are descended Kris and Diesis. The purchase of some German blood was encouraged by stud manager Leslie Harrison – and led, through Sayonara, to Slip Anchor and the Derby. Anyone might envy those racing achievements, though no-one in his senses would begrudge them. A superlative giver of parties all his life, Lord Howard created for his friends enormous pleasure.

---

3 MARCH 2009

JOHN HALES KNOWS THE DOWNS AS WELL AS THE UPS OF CHELTENHAM FESTIVAL

Marcus Armytage

Few men know the agonies and ecstasy of owning a racehorse better than John Hales. He will, as usual, spend four days at the Cheltenham Festival and it is one of the curiosities of his hobby that he will only truly enjoy Wednesday and Thursday – the days when he does not have runners. On Tuesday and Friday he will be, effectively, paying good money to put himself through what he quite clearly finds an emotional mangle, when I'msingingtheblues lines up for the Arkle and Neptune Collonges runs in the Gold Cup.

'I will,' he says, 'be a bag of nerves.' And it not just racing that does it to him. When his showjumper, Arko III, was set to jump for the gold medal in the Athens Olympics in 2004, he went and hid in a hut behind the grandstand – and missed the horse having a smashing time as the heat finally got to him. He and rider Nick Skelton finished 11th.

Hales, 70, runs Golden Bear, a company whose place among leading toy manufacturers was cemented by the Teletubbies, from an office in Telford. While he has no intention of retiring just yet, he is the only person at Golden

Bear without a computer on his desk. Only now, in the recession, is he finding his job more pressurised than his pastime. 'We've just lost our biggest customer in Woolworth's,' he points out. 'That in itself is a big challenge.'

His interest in racing stems back to the early Nineties when he was on holiday in Barbados at a hotel owned by the owner of the 1988 Grand National winner Rhyme 'N' Reason. One thing led to another until some money that he and his wife had put to one side for a holiday home in the south of France was spent on a horse instead. 'I didn't know anything. I thought you could buy a horse on Monday and run it on Tuesday,' he recalls. 'When Gordon Richards said the horse wouldn't be ready for six months we went with him to Arthur Stephenson's dispersal sale to find something ready a bit sooner with a limit of 7,000 guineas and ended up paying 68,000 guineas for One Man. The rest is history – if he'd been no good we'd have probably been out of racing.'

One Man's two attempts at the Gold Cup ultimately resulted in heroic failure – ten strides off the last bend he would hit a brick wall. In 1998 he was dropped back in trip for the two-mile Champion Chase, which he won. Two weeks later he suffered a fatal fall at Aintree. 'I sometimes ask myself what the hell I'm doing in this sport,' Hales says. 'If you win the feeling is euphoric, the bigger the race the greater the euphoria. It's fantastic. The tears for One Man didn't stop for a year. It hit the family hard. In the summer he'd be in the field in front of the kitchen at home. You miss that. You live in fear of anything happening to them.'

On the whole, though, Hales has been a lucky owner. He has had no more than 25 horses, and besides two Champion Chase winners – the other was Azertyuiop – it would surprise no one if Neptune Collonges, third last year, were to win next week's Gold Cup.

'I find it much easier to watch if we're not considered to have much of chance,' he says. 'I was very calm about last year's Gold Cup, which was all about Kauto Star and Denman. Although, actually, afterwards I was quite disappointed because I'd loved to have split the pair, we just didn't quite upset the party. It won't be quite so easy this time.'

---

26 DECEMBER 2005

JIM LEWIS'S DATE WITH FATE

Marcus Armytage

Jim Lewis, one of the world's luckier racehorse owners, has a good memory for dates but 2005, particularly the last two months of it, will go down as the worst of his 71 years. On 1 November Best Mate, his three-time Gold Cup winner, collapsed and died at Exeter. But the death of a horse was put into stark context five weeks later when his wife and childhood sweetheart, Valerie, finally succumbed to cancer. The last public outing Valerie made was to Huntingdon on 19 November where she collected the trophy for Impek's success in the Peterborough Chase. She had borne the illness so bravely that, until he was told, the winning jockey, A.P. McCoy, simply didn't realise she was unwell. The lilies he subsequently sent her as a get-well present still bloom above Lewis's kitchen sink.

Today, Impek goes for what would be, following the successes of Best Mate and Edredon Bleu, a third and most emotional victory for Lewis in the Stan James King George VI Chase. Knowing how racing loves to entwine itself in human romance, there are those punters whose hearts will rule their pockets in the expectation of the sport providing another happy ending. 'I had a winner at Fontwell last week called Wenceslas,' says Lewis in support of the theory. 'He wasn't entitled to win but the two dangers fell and he strolled home. How else do you explain a horse with that name winning at Christmas? I've backed Impek at 12–1, a realistic price for him. But if Edredon Bleu, who I didn't think would stay, could win a King George at 25–1 we've all got hope.'

Lewis lives in a small village outside Worcester and, apart from a business posting to Yorkshire, he has never strayed too far from his Birmingham roots. His garden, dominated by a 200-year-old oak tree is, under the surface, a mass of bulbs. It peaks, like Best Mate used to, during the Cheltenham Festival. The son of an engine driver for London Midland and Scottish Railways, racing was an integral part of his childhood. The family lived near Birmingham's Bronford Bridge racecourse and he remembers watching, intrigued, by the Shilling Shocker who would sell tips scribbled on a slip of paper for a shilling (5p).

His father, Frank, bet with backstreet bookies who were then illegal and the young Jim would look at the nap selections of the leading tipsters while he was busy delivering newspapers. 'To have a bet then,' Lewis recalls, 'you would write your selection down on a piece of paper with your *nom de plume* (so the bookie would know you but the police wouldn't) then wrap a coin in it and walk past the spot to see if the bookie was there. Then you'd walk back past him and surreptitiously slip the package into his hand. If he owed you any you'd make a second pass. My father's *nom de plume* was Frank 170, because we lived at 170. He might just have well have supplied his name and address had he been caught!'

The young Lewis was also a regular at Aston Villa – his claret-and-blue striped colours are a similar design to Villa's 1957 FA Cup-winning strip. Small boys would be lifted over the turnstiles so they wouldn't have to pay. He still goes ten times a year and paraded each Gold Cup. Doug Ellis, the chairman and a friend, keeps reminding him that he is the only man to have brought gold to Aston Villa recently. Lewis was also a useful sportsman himself. He played town football and he was a good cricketing all-rounder. 'I'd bat number six and was a first change bowler,' he says. 'It was quite a culture shock when we moved to Ilkley in Yorkshire. We liked a pint with the opposition, but up there the Ilkley captain said we shouldn't even talk to the opposition until we'd played them twice. The emphasis in those days was on natural skills rather than fitness. Now it's total fitness, it's gone the same way with horses and jockeys.'

In 1961 he joined the furniture trade with Slumberland Beds, becoming their salesman of the year in 1963. He then became managing director of Silent Night's upholstery division. About 25 years ago he left to start importing pine furniture from South Africa, Brazil and Zimbabwe. He soon became one of the biggest pine importers and five years ago sold out to Steinhoff International. When he began courting Valerie in 1950 he made that oft-quoted promise of his: 'If you marry me I'll buy you a house, I'll buy you a car and I'll buy you a racehorse.' On their 30th wedding (pearl) anniversary he fulfilled it by buying her Pearl Prospect who they sent to Henrietta Knight. His choice of trainer was pure fate. 'I walked into a coffee shop in Pershore,' he recalls, 'and on the front page of a magazine it said "Queen of point-to-pointing to take out a licence", and the story was of this woman who had trained Rolls-Royces against Minis in point-to-points! We met at Hereford. She took Pearl Prospect, who won at Wincanton and then Nottingham in 1988, though he hurt his back at Kempton and was never much good again.'

Since, Nakir, Camitrov, Edredron Bleu, Stars Out Tonight – named after the opening line of the song *I Only Have Eyes For You* which he sang to Valerie on their first date – Foly Pleasant, Best Mate and now Impek have carried the colours with distinction. 'When Henrietta faxed me saying she'd seen a horse she liked so much she would train him for nothing [Best Mate] we had to go and see him. But even when we bought him luck played a part. I asked one of Tom Costello's sons how impressive he had been winning his point-to-point. He told me he'd won by five or six lengths pulling up. Of course I never asked what he'd beaten like anyone sensible would have done. Two months later I found out it was a two-horse race. If I'd known that, I might not have bought him.'

Best Mate's demise at Exeter – he would have been retired there and then after pulling up – exacerbated an already bad time. 'It was tough and trying for us,' Lewis says. 'Losing Best Mate didn't help. There was enough stress around before that occurred. We knew because of Valerie's illness that we were having a time we might definitely not be able to repeat. You need a strong family around you and fortunately we have a very strong family unit. Valerie was an incredible person. She was as natural as the grass. In a way, Best Mate dying prepared us because we knew it would get worse.'

Having had more than his fair share of luck with his horses, Lewis is adamant that those with whom Lady Luck chooses to ride pillion should make the most of their passenger. 'We always said it was a dream, a wonderful romance that wouldn't last,' he points out. 'It will be someone else's turn for my luck and whoever inherits it should appreciate it in the knowledge that such good fortune is only borrowed. Embrace it and enjoy it.' Lady Luck may not have moved on to pastures new just yet.

———

3 JUNE 1991

IT DOESN'T MATTER IF MYSTIKO WINS AS LONG AS HE IS SAFE AND SOUND

John Oaksey

In 24 years as an owner, the Dowager Lady Beaverbrook has always cared less about winning races than about the health and happiness of her horses. The thing which will matter most to her in Wednesday's Derby is that Mystiko should come back safe. Lots of owners say that, I know, but with this one it is no exaggeration. Lady Beaverbrook worries so much about her horses that she is seriously thinking of giving up ownership altogether when her current two-year-olds have had a chance to prove themselves.

'People say I worry too much, but there it is,' she says. 'I just am a born fusspot and, if anything, it's getting worse. I shan't sleep much this week. The Derby is so *rough*. The more money there is, the rougher it gets. I don't mind about the jockeys. They are being paid and want to be there. But no-one asked the horses. I don't even like my horses going out in the rain and when Mr Brittain [Mystiko's trainer] said he had a lad sleeping in with Mystiko all night, I asked couldn't they put a chair or bed for him *outside* the box? Well, he's a very *proud* horse and I thought he might not like having someone in with him all the time. I know what a nuisance I am to my trainers, but I can't help it.'

For trainers, the wise ones anyway, I suspect there are many worse things in life than owners who worry too much about their horses – and the horses themselves are certainly not complaining. Lady Beaverbrook's great favourite,

Boldboy, for instance – 'He could be very naughty, but gave me so much joy' – lives in luxury with her Ebor winner, Totowah. Each has his specially-built retirement home, complete with paddock, on a stud not far from their devoted owner's Newmarket base. Bustino, Minster Son and Relkino are all enjoying themselves at stud, but Lady Beaverbrook's mares, one of whom, Madrigal, is a daughter of her very first racehorse, Rosebid, may not be asked to breed again. 'The two youngest might,' she says, 'but the others have done their best for me and deserve a rest.'

It was in 1967, three years after the death of her second husband, Lord Beaverbrook, that Lord Rosebery persuaded her to become an owner. 'He found me all alone here [at Cherkley, Lord Beaverbrook's Leatherhead home] and said, 'This is ridiculous. What on earth is the point of moping around in all this black cotton? Come racing'. Thirty years earlier, Lord Rosebery had made a less successful attempt to interest Beaverbrook himself in racing. But although this rich, talented and arrogant pair had many things in common, racing was not one of them. 'It always bored my husband stiff,' says Lady Beaverbrook. 'He could never see the point.'

But she soon could. Rosebid, named in honour of her purchaser, won at the first attempt – the Banstead Stakes at Epsom on 26 April, 1967 – and a few years later her daughter, Madrigal, won the very same race. By that time, the Beaver Brown, Maple Green cross-belts had become familiar to punters and judges alike, and the appearance of Lady Beaverbrook's handsome face beside a yearling sale ring was one of the two sights then most calculated to warm a commercial breeder's heart. The other, in those pre-Sangster-Maktoum days, was David Robinson, and the TV millionaire once rather wittily named a colt Breeder's Dream after he and Lady Beaverbrook had fought out a bidding duel to secure it. The record prices they paid sound like chicken-feed now, but in 1975, even for Million, a colt from Mill Reef's first crop, 202,000 guineas was an eyebrow-raising bid.

Unlike most price-record breakers, Million was not completely useless (he once beat Sea Pigeon) and Relkino, the top-priced yearling in 1974, was a highly respectable second in Empery's Derby. Two years earlier, Lady Beaverbrook had her biggest Derby Day disappointment when Bustino, finishing like a too-late train, ran fourth behind Snow Knight. He had beaten the winner at Lingfield and, after winning the St Leger, broke the Epsom track record in the following year's Coronation Cup – before his historic King George duel with Grundy.

With Relkino beaten and Minster Son injured, it is no wonder that Lady Beaverbrook has unhappy memories of Derby Day. 'Oh no. I *hate* Epsom,' she told Brough Scott after Mystiko's 2,000 Guineas victory – throwing an unexpected spanner into my old friend's 'How much you must be looking forward to the Derby' eulogies… Like so many owners (and racing correspondents), Lady Beaverbrook is superstitious. When I visited her at Cherkley last week, Hailsham had just won the Italian Derby. 'Great news,' she agreed. 'But I do wish Mr Brittain [all her trainers are given their full formal titles – Mr Nightingall, Sir Gordon (Richards), The Major (Dick Hern)] would not keep saying things like, "Hailsham is no match for Mystiko". It may be true, but I don't like him *saying* it.'

Born in Surrey – 'about 15 years ago' as she told the impertinent Scott – Marcia Christoforidi was the daughter of a Greek tobacco merchant. Much as she loved him, the most valuable lesson her father's life taught her was not to gamble. 'He would bet on anything,' she remembers sadly. 'But it was mostly cards. He ruined himself in the end. I remember all our beloved horses being led off down the drive.'

That is only one of the reasons why Mystiko's owner will not be backing him on Wednesday. 'I was once sitting next to another owner [who had better remain nameless] at Royal Ascot,' she told me. 'We both had runners in a big race. His, a huge great colt, was hot favourite and my little filly seemed to have no chance. Well, this horrible man kept bragging about his horse and spitting food all over me. So I made a pact with the Almighty. "God," I said, "if you will let my filly beat this disgusting man's horse, I will never bet again". And she did – so I haven't.' Lady Beaverbrook would not tell me what her side of the pact will be on Derby Day but, worried or not, she is a determined lady. My own bet is that Mystiko will have the Almighty on his side.

CHAPTER 11

OH, WHAT A NIGHT ... AND OTHER HORSEY TALES

It was like the Blitz, that old Dunkirk spirit still alive more than half-a-century on. Everyone in the city of Liverpool rallied round when the IRA warning call came through and Aintree had to be evacuated, the 1997 Grand National postponed. Marcus Armytage's brilliant sketch on the brighter side of another National disaster is just one of a collection of horsey tales that can be digested and enjoyed over a night cap after a day's racing. There's John Oaksey's involvement as an unlikely middle man during the Shergar kidnap saga, Jeffrey Barnard's touching tribute to Lester Piggott at 60, a madcap race at the Pegasus point-to-point, the wordsmiths who have become the 'Voices of Racing' for millions via the television screen, and some vignettes of the unsung people who work tirelessly in the background of the sport: the clerk of the scales and a jockeys' valet.

---

7 APRIL 1997

THE PARTY MAY BE OVER, BUT OH WHAT A NIGHT . . .

Marcus Armytage

Among the small crowd awaiting news, who had gathered outside the gate to Aintree's owners and trainers car park at noon yesterday, were trainers, officials, stable lads and a large number of Grand National jockeys, some in their breeches, boots and silks for the 24th consecutive hour. 'Do you want to know the rest of my Sunday?' asked Go Ballistic's jockey Mick Fitzgerald on hearing that the great race would definitely go ahead today. 'Bath, bath, sauna, bath, sauna, bath, bath.'

On Saturday he had been, like so many of his colleagues, trying to pare his 11-stone frame down to less than ten stone by a process otherwise known as desiccation. In the belief that the race was unlikely to be rescheduled, he had spent most of Saturday night bingeing. 'Two pieces of chicken was all I had for supper last night,' he said glumly. 'And four bags of chips,' added his light-hearted and light-weight colleague John Kavanagh, who partners Turning Trix. 'I daren't get on the scales,' said another of his colleagues. 'I'm not going to until tomorrow morning,' agreed another. 'As far as I know,' rejoined Fitzgerald, 'my saddle is still on the horse.' The whereabouts of 37 other saddles, one of which was left on Scribbler, who proceeded to roll with it, is another of the logistical problems that will have to be sorted out by 5 p.m. today.

The stories of this extraordinary Saturday night in Liverpool were already filtering into the annals of the world's greatest race's history. How jockeys, in their full kit, had to wend their way on foot into town with the crowds and find accommodation. No money, no credit cards, no clothes, but if you were in Liverpool on Saturday, 5 April, 1997, dressed to ride a racehorse, then the world was your low-calorie oyster.

In the weighing room, the Melling Road is no longer a gravel-covered lane which you cross four times in the Grand National, it's now a byword for Liverpudlian hospitality. Carl Llewellyn stood with us in a pair of loose-fitting jeans and shirt. He'd been passing a local house in Camelot Knight's green and white silks. A man had rushed out. 'Do you want to stay here for the night?' he asked. Llewellyn declined. 'Well the least I can do is lend you some clothes,' he added. The loose-fitting jeans were his, and the shirt. It's one way of losing your shirt on the horses.

Lester Manners, son of Killeshin's trainer, had spent the night on a couch in a front room in the same street. 'We were only allowed to stay there on one condition,' he enthused. 'That we didn't pay a penny. It was far better than the hotel we had the night before and they knocked up a grand meal.' Adie Smith had been paraded round town like a trophy. 'Do you want to come out with us?' Over The Stream's jockey was asked by a rough-looking bunch in the foyer of the Adelphi Hotel. He looked doubtful. 'We're not robbers,' they reassured him. 'But I haven't a dime on me,' contended Smith. 'We'll pay for you,' they insisted. 'The night of my life,' recollected Smith to his colleagues. At the first nightclub the bouncer had taken one look at him. 'You've had a bad day, mate, you can come in for free,' he said. Smith never had to pay for a single beer.

Llewellyn was one of 12 jockeys who slept in David Walsh's room in the Adelphi. 'Who was in there?' he was asked, and he began reeling off names: Carberry, Murphy, Hogan, Brennan, Whitely... before adding with a mischievous grin, 'Jane, Suzy, Amanda, Janet and two Traceys!' Was it comfortable? 'Ask Timmy Murphy,' he said. 'He kipped in the bath.' Russ Garrity, Valiant Warrior's jockey, had slept with 300 others in Everton Sports Centre. What was that like? 'En-suite,' he said before adding: 'The only good thing that happened to me on Saturday was that Tiffany from *EastEnders* signed my T-shirt.'

Francis Woods was last seen getting on a plane back to Ireland at Speke Airport – an ordinary everyday sight in his silks. Tony Dobbin, his car locked in the car park, persuaded a colleague from Cumbria to pick him up at a junction on the M57. He had to walk two miles to get there and called in at a McDonald's on the way. 'Got some pretty strange looks,' he laughed. 'Did you get lucky?' asked one jockey to another in the knowledge that breeches, boots and silks were likely to shorten the odds of such an occurrence. 'No,' replied the other. 'But I didn't stop trying until 7 a.m.'

Other jockeys went to the Post House in Runcorn which the Jockeys'

Association secretary Michael Caulfield had had the foresight to block-book on hearing of the abandonment. They included Richard Dunwoody, Paul Holley and Andrew Thornton, and had all got there via the only form of transport allowed to leave the course on Saturday, a horsebox. In another, Josh Gifford had taken Spuffington to be re-stabled at Haydock Park racecourse – along, of course, with 20 friends. The extra cost to owners, trainers and jockeys for the National's two-day delay is negligible. The cost of a good night out in Liverpool, which is nothing compared to the cost to Aintree Racecourse. 'An extra £19 a night for each lad, and a small transport surcharge,' suggested trainer Tony Balding. 'That's the least of it, though.' There will be some small loss in earnings for northern jockeys who were engaged to ride at Kelso today. 'I had four good rides there,' said Tony Dobbin. 'But I'm definitely coming back here. Unfortunately for us, Kelso is the only meeting in the north until Saturday.'

Some of today's runners, like Suny Bay, Master Oats, Smith's Band and Nahthen Lad, were re-stabled at Haydock where they were exercised. Dextra Dove also joined them yesterday. The Irish runners all remained at Aintree where hay from the nearest mounted police stables was shipped in when supplies ran out. Others, like Lord Gyllene, Go Ballistic, River Mandate, General Wolfe, Celtic Abbey and Don't Light Up were all tucked up in their own West Midlands beds.

Back at the gates to the car park was trainer Charlie Brooks. He asked the assistant clerk of the course, Ian Renton, if he was thinking of watering the course yesterday. How any official at Aintree had any humour left is beyond me, but Renton found the funny side of it. After a couple more hours of standing around, Carl Llewellyn's feet were beginning to hurt. Spending most of the night in a pair of thin-soled, tight-fitting racing boots is about as practical as a pair of ballet shoes for mountaineering. 'Could I have a quote about your evening last night?' I asked him. 'Tell them,' he said, 'we spent it in the gym.' I was left to ponder on whether or not that was Liverpool's hottest nightspot. After all the pre-race hype and tension of Saturday's events, the jockeys unwound in time-honoured fashion. Today, however, it will be back to deadly serious work.

---

20 NOVEMBER 2004

IT WAS TERRIBLE TO BE TOLD THAT THE QUEEN MOTHER WANTED ME TO RETIRE

Sue Mott

It is a matter of public record that Dick Francis is 84. But this is mere numerical pedantry. The man who sat sipping Campari and lemonade in a neatly tucked corner of the Goring Hotel in London, recalling a life riding horses for the Queen Mother, flying Spitfires during the Second World War, writing 39 mystery novels that made him a fortune and reciting a poem entitled *The Great Farting Contest At Stilton-on-Tees* – all demonstrating hugely varied individual skills – was nowhere near as advanced as his birth certificate.

For a while, as we sat amid the genteel din of denture on cucumber and rattle of teaspoon in saucer, he was a 20-year-old stripling again, nipping down to the Army recruiting office in Reading to join up at the start of the War. 'I said, "I want to join the cavalry". They said, "Oh yes? You join the Army, you'll go where you're sent". So I said, "I won't join the Army then". I joined the RAF instead.'

But he did join a cavalry later: the travelling band of certifiable madmen known as professional jockeys. He was ten years in the saddle, becoming champion jockey in 1954 and a national icon two years later when the horse he was riding in the Grand National, Devon Loch, owned by the Queen Mother, collapsed a few strides from victory. His fame, notoriety perhaps, opened the door to the rest of his life. Fascination with Devon Loch led to his autobiography, which led to his novels, which led to a house in the Cayman Islands with his beloved late wife, Mary, to whom he had been married 53 years when she died in 2000.

It also led to this moment: his arrival in London, immaculate, sparkling with understated wit and primed to present the Hennessy Gold Cup at Newbury next Saturday. Last year it was Ronnie Wood, the Rolling Stone, who made the presentation and a short speech. 'What blows my mind is that I'm still alive,' said the old rocker. This year it is Francis, whose own mind is not blown by his longevity at all. In fact, his mind is conspicuously all there, sorting times and places and conversations at ridiculous speed and with fiendish efficiency.

For instance, Mary learnt to fly a Piper Cherokee Arrow. Don't ask me how this came up in conversation. It just did. How old was she? I asked, picturing the formidable light-aircraft-flying woman to whom Francis was devoted. He worked it out. 'I retired from racing in 1957, wrote my first book in 1962, wrote my fifth book, *Flying Finish*, in 1967, which is when Mary learnt to fly and she was born in 1924, so she must have been 43.' (And this after the Campari.) He misses her badly and recalls with awful but unfussy clarity the morning of Mary's death from an asthma attack. He remembers shaving in the bathroom mirror and her shout for her inhaler. She died, her husband at her side, three or four minutes later. 'Not nice for me, but wonderful for her, to be so quick,' he said. 'I miss her a lot. If it wasn't for her I wouldn't have written the stories. She had an English degree and she used to correct my writing, my spelling.'

For years, Mary was suspected of being the true author of the equine mystery series, which must have irritated them both. 'It didn't irritate us,' Francis said equably. 'We thought, "What the hell!"' Indeed, they were happy, well off, the parents of two successful sons and fabulously connected (as well as the Queen Mother they knew the entire aristocracy of British theatre, since Mary began life as stage manager at Hereford Rep). They had to hold not one but three golden wedding anniversary parties — in the Caribbean, England and New York — to accommodate all their friends and relations.

But we were getting ahead of ourselves. It was time to go back to the beginning. Dick was born in 1920, the second son of a professional steeplechase jockey, Vincent Francis, who emerged intact from the First World War with the ambition to set up a horse-dealing business. Predictably his younger son developed a passion for horses, most particularly for riding them and was just settling into the job of 'nagsman' when Hitler invaded Poland and young Francis made his trek to the Army recruitment office. His War 'wasn't too bad'. He spent two years in the west African desert as ground crew, trained as a fighter pilot in then Rhodesia, flew a few sorties over the Channel in a Spitfire, trained again for flying gliders and then transferred to Wellington bombers. He joined raids, chiefly over Norway and Denmark, to attract enemy defences away from the Ruhr and flew many missions over the Atlantic seeking out U-boats.

Through it all, he was determined to become a professional steeplechase jockey like his father. Obviously, swapping horseback for cockpit had thwarted his ambition, but only for a while. In 1945, when Francis left the RAF, he resumed his quest. He moved up to Cheshire to work with the trainer George Owen as assistant trainer, dogsbody and amateur rider, and his luck turned. 'I was with him four days and I rode in a novice chase at Woore Hunt in Staffordshire on a horse called Russian Hero. I came third. After that, George put me up on everything. Finally, after I'd been riding for about 18 months, the stewards called me in at Cheltenham. They said, "Francis, we think you're taking the bread and butter out of the professionals' mouths".' He was instructed to turn professional. He said he would by the end of the season. They said by the end of the week. He turned professional by the end of the week.

'No sooner had I turned professional than I was offered the job of first jockey to Lord Bicester. He had a lovely string of horses. Then the trainer to the Queen Mother, Peter Cazalet, asked me if I would go and ride as first jockey for him. I said I couldn't accept because of my post at Lord Bicester's but then he died and so I was retained as jockey to the Queen Mother for four seasons, 1953 to 1957. I wasn't nervous. I was never nervous and she was entirely charming with a wonderful sense of humour.'

He and Mary had married in 1947. 'On 21 June and people always pulled our leg because it was the shortest night of the year.' Their social progress could be espied in their choice of car. In the courting years, it was an old Hillman that plodded the 90 miles between Cheshire and Hereford, followed by the green Wolsey his father gave them as a wedding present. Then, as the winners flowed (over 350 of them) they moved up through a couple of Rileys to, finally, a Jaguar.

However, there was another list being compiled at this time: his injuries, and they became increasingly significant. 'There was nothing serious. My worst was at the Cheltenham Festival when I fell at the first fence and the one coming behind put his hoof on my face. There were 32 stitches but I rode a winner two days later. Of course, I broke no end of ribs. Never counted. Broke my collarbone six times each side. My last fall broke my wrist.' He waved a hand, slightly contorted and wayward, as evidence. 'But when I retired it was with great reluctance. It was January 1957. I had hurt my spleen and I was at home nursing it better. I received a call from the Queen Mother's adviser, Lord Abergavenny, he lived off Sloane Street, asking me if I would go and see him. So I did.

'He said, "Listen, I'm going to tell you something now. You're at the top of the tree, you're leading the jockeys' table, why don't you get out now? The Queen Mother doesn't want you to ride her novice chasers any more". It was a terrible thing to say to me at the time. I nearly threw myself in the Serpentine on my way back through Hyde Park. But I was 36 and I knew I wasn't bouncing as well as I had done in the past. I had a troubled weekend, talking it over with Mary. On Monday morning I phoned up the producer of *Sportsnight* and said, "If you have me on tomorrow night, I've got something rather surprising to tell you".' They had him on; he duly surprised them by announcing his retirement.

But his stepping down as a jockey meant stepping up as a writer. John Junor, the editor of the *Sunday Express*, paid him £100 per article to become racing correspondent, a job he maintained for 14 years. He published his autobiography in 1957. 'It was called *The Sport of Queens*. You couldn't call it that nowadays,' he added as a gentle aside.

Then Mary had a brainwave. She said: 'We've got two sons to educate, the car's beginning to knock and the carpets are wearing out. You should write a novel.' Her husband sat down and wrote *Dead Cert*, and there began the next Francis incarnation as a thriller writer. But Mary's next brainwave – 'you must write Lester Piggott's biography' – proved slightly less easy to accomplish. Francis found himself gathering material for the tome for over 14 years, and you can hardly say the subject himself was a mine of information. 'I said to Lester once, "Now, I know Sir Ivor is your most favourite of your nine Derby winners. Tell me all about him". Lester thought for about five minutes. "Nice 'orse," he said.'

It might be some consolation that Francis's other books were eventually translated into 30 languages. He has received an OBE and CBE from The Queen, not to mention daggers galore from the British Crime Writers' Association. Clearly the organisers of the Hennessy Gold Cup, the big pre-Christmas steeple-chase won by such equine superstars as Arkle and One Man, could hardly have chosen a more warmly cherished character to present the trophy. And to any first-time visitors to Newbury next week, you can only say that Dick Francis is easily distinguishable from Ronnie Wood. He looks years younger.

And behaves like it. He attended a dinner at Cheltenham last week in honour of four National Hunt heroes: Tony McCoy, Toby Balding, Best Mate and Francis. But it was the last of that quartet who brought the house down when he recited all six verses of the poem he learnt 50 years ago about flatulence in the Stilton-on-Tees area. 'Don't write that!' he urged, but how could I resist?

'My ambition now . . . ?' he mused. 'I've got no ambitions left, I don't think. I've done all I wanted to do. What I wish is that I had my wife back to keep me company. We had a lovely time together. I miss her so much. But I believe I'll see her again one day.'

---

6 NOVEMBER 1995

LESTER PIGGOTT – MAN OF MEANS BUT NOT A MEAN MAN

Jeffrey Barnard

When I was a boy, November the Fifth meant fireworks. Now that I am an old boy, November the Fifth means Lester Piggott's birthday, and the great man is now 60. That is something to celebrate in itself, but he is a man whose existence is something I have celebrated myself almost daily since I became aware of the proposition that one horse can go faster than another. Lester Piggott is, and always has been, something of an enigma to me. I suppose I am lucky to have met him during the heyday of his freelance riding, and a photograph of the two of us together takes pride of place on the wall of my study.

It is fairly unusual to meet a hero and for that person not to be an enormous disappointment. Face to face, and in what is called 'real life' stars can be very ordinary people indeed. I feel almost lucky to have met the man and to know him even very slightly. I see his life as having been in three distinct phases. In the first one he was the chubby and cocky apprentice, then the young rider who had the cheek to describe the Derby as being 'just another race', for which he got a deserved rollicking from the press and his father, Keith.

Next there were the golden years with Noel Murless, before becoming a freelance. Finally there was the amazing partnership with Vincent O'Brien and the days of Robert Sangster and Charles St George. That was when I first chanced to meet him. I hung on his every word, and they were very few and far between, but I remember well how Charles St George used to tease him and make him laugh. It is typical of Lester that St George turned out to be one of his best friends. Lester has always liked big, expansive men, good with their hospitality, and outgoing. It was at St George's house that I used to bump into Lester when he was passing through London.

The man I met there in Brook Street, Mayfair, was never really much like the picture that he built up for himself over the years. For one thing he had, and has, more upstairs than most of the professional sportsmen I have met. He was also extremely witty and amusing in a dry rather cynical way. I never saw any signs of his legendary meanness, and I suspect Lester himself has always enjoyed playing the roles that other people have cast him in. He has, in his time, helped out many a jockey and racing pro who has fallen on hard times.

I miss him already, though he is still with us, and the daily lists of runners and riders in the newspapers seem strangely lacking without his name. Racing is now almost Marks without Spencer. It is going to be an extremely hard, if not impossible act to follow, and it must be odd for him to reflect that he was, in his time, the best in the world at what he did.

I first met him in 1970, when I began to write a column for the *Sporting Life*, and on the first occasion I spoke to him I asked him at Doncaster races if he could give me a lift to Newmarket in the hope that it would get me nearly to my front door, and that we would have a fascinating chat during the journey. As it happened he didn't say a word the whole way, but had his head stuck into *Timeform* the whole time, and at the end of the journey just inquired with a sardonic smile whether or not I was mad.

It's a great pity that Lester stories are mostly unprintable because of the libel laws, or the fact that they might offend his wife and daughters. They will remain so until the sad day he dies, if he does. It is quite interesting, though, to hear him talk horses without the usual caustic or amusing asides. Lester has always said that of the horses he rode, the three he liked most were Primera, Park Top and Moorestyle. Bought as a yearling by his wife Susan for only 4,000 guineas, Moorestyle was eventually syndicated at a value of £2 million. This is some indication of how incredibly shrewd Susan Piggott is and it means that their future will be a fairly rosy one.

Lester once claimed: 'I don't talk to horses. All horses are alike to me. They all obey the same orders.' This is hard to believe, and it is a fact that the horse he most admired was Sir Ivor, the 1968 Derby winner, who supposedly couldn't and wouldn't stay the Derby distance. Lester more or less kidded that horse and kept his stamina up his sleeve. The horse's sleeve.

With all the memories of those marvellous days, it seems a shame that there is no permanent memorabilia of Lester in our heritage at the National Portrait Gallery. Sadly, racing is for the most part run by men very like ex-military types, who don't know their arts from their elbows. Contemporary equine artists are a very mediocre bunch, and nearly all trainers and owners want a photographic likeness of a horse, never mind the jockey, and they sadly think that if a picture is painted in oils, then it is *per se* a good painting. Lucien Freud would desperately like to paint Lester, but the best painter in England today has hardly been heard of by anyone professionally involved on the Turf.

Anyway, Lester himself would be just about the only one able to afford to buy it. And what an awful, and yet occasionally wonderful, way he has become entangled with money. Forgetting the disaster with the Inland Revenue, it is said that when he was burgled in 1966 the thieves got away with £70,000 in readies. There have also been crafty windfalls of his own making. He rode Valoris for Sir Charles Clore in the 1966 Oaks (and won) on the condition that he would get not just ten per cent of the prize money, but the entire sum of the prize money plus a nomination to her on retirement.

The O'Brien horses, Sir Ivor, Roberto, Nijinsky and The Minstrel, made up a syndicate between O'Brien and Sangster worth £100 million. Who knows what Lester's share was? His money has always been well invested on good advice, though one wonders how much damage was inflicted on Piggott since Charles St George got him membership of Lloyds. He has worldwide investments in bloodstock and breeding companies, various share-holdings, gold, property and aviation, and perhaps others that he may have forgotten.

He will never starve, and for that matter neither will he over-eat and put on the enormous gains in poundage that other ex-jockeys have done. He has still great self-discipline and he told me that he doesn't intend to end up looking like a pig simply because he has retired. Lester hasn't just survived 60 years, he has been winning for 60 years. And, as he says, it is the *wanting* to win that is important.

I MARCH 2008

SIR PETER O'SULLEVAN GOING STRONG AT 90

Sue Mott

In America the voice of God is always played by Morgan Freeman. Fine actor as he is, we do things a little differently in this country. Omniscience is all very well but, to the British ear, it must be accompanied by a magnificent authority, mellifluous beauty, grammatical proficiency and a hint of drollery. There is no finer exponent of the art in this world (and mercifully not the next one) than Sir Peter O'Sullevan, who celebrates his 90th birthday on Monday.

It is not just the 'Voice of Racing' that meets you at the front door of his cosy flat in west London, it is the voice of voices. For more than 50 years, on a variety of airwaves, this glorious instrument has instructed us upon our victories and our losses (the latter, by far, predominating) with the accuracy of an obsessive and the compassion of a fellow sufferer. The sound of Sir Peter calling the horses should be one of our exports into outer space to signify the depth of our civilisation. In person, this paragon is the least stuffy companion imaginable, ever watchful for an opportunity to amuse, provide sustenance and, of course, back a winner. It is impossible to believe he will soon be 90. 'I can't believe it either. It's ridiculous,' he said. 'Particularly as I was so sick and feeble as a youngster. I had double pneumonia four times and you're not supposed to have it more than once really. I still have a letter – it's rather fun keeping things, you know – from the headmaster of my prep school to my poor, long-suffering mum saying he was sorry to hear I was ill and "certainly at school he holds the record for interruptions".'

How wonderful then that he should go on to hold the record for non-interruptions as a broadcaster. He commentated on his 50th, and last, Grand National for the BBC in 1997, a fittingly round number for an astonishingly robust career that included 36 years as a racing correspondent for the *Daily Express*. His longevity in a media world where the attention span of a distracted goldfish is the accepted norm, is testimony to his powers.

He would, however, be the first to admit that matters did not begin auspiciously. After one of his first outside broadcasts on black-and-white television, his mother commented: 'Darling, I saw you on television yesterday and you looked absolutely ghastly. I do hope you're never going to do that again.'

There had been other significant blockages to his path. Not only double pneumonia, but chronic asthma, which eventually demanded his 'export' to a school in Switzerland, followed by the desperate outbreak of a skin condition that receded only with time. 'It was a nervous complaint and much more inhibiting. I became reclusive and, during my early days racing, I would never go through the turnstiles. I always went on the "wild side", as it were, because I felt awkward.' But resoluteness was already forged in his character. Born in County Kerry, he was brought up by his indulgent maternal grandparents in a stately home in Surrey after his own parents, Colonel John Joseph O'Sullevan DSO, and his wife, Lady Henry, divorced. 'My father first put me on my horse when I was two, but whatever encouraged me to turn into an animal welfare freak at an early age, I don't really know.

'I remember once being grossly offended when friends of my grandparents came hunting for the weekend and brought their horses with them. My pony was turned out of its box in the pouring rain and loosed in a distant paddock. I went missing. When my absence was discovered, my grandfather got on to the police and reported the missing child. There was a huge area of land to search but it was eventually reported back to him two hours later that a child had been seen in a paddock adjacent to the Reigate road, holding an umbrella over a pony.'

Of course, that passion for horses and their well-being might have evolved into a gentle immersion into country life. Instead, he developed a complete crush on horse racing, fostered at the age of ten by a seminal experience. 'I had sixpence each way on the winner of the 1928 Grand National. Only two finished that year and one had to be remounted. That was Tipperary Tim at 100–1.' A year later he met Lord Beaverbrook, the newspaper magnate, at a race meeting at Lingfield. 'He asked me what I wanted to do when I grew up. I said I was going to be a racing commentator and correspondent for the *Sunday Express* because it struck me that it would be much better to write one day a week than six. He gave me a ten-shilling note and since I couldn't improve on that, I didn't have a bet all day.'

'I was 29 when I met him again, after I had joined his newspaper, the Express, at a party he was holding at the Trocadero. I told him the story of our first meeting and he gave an absolutely astonishing reaction. He said, "Don't think it will make any difference to your standing on the newspaper with me". I thought, "You stupid man", and the next time I saw him was 1958, when he invited me to his suite at the Waldorf in New York to congratulate me for an exclusive story I had come across in America. He couldn't have been more solicitous. "Have another gin. Come up and see my pictures in New Brunswick. Stay and have a holiday, then go home on the Queen Elizabeth". I was becoming more and more agitated because my flight was leaving shortly and the Cheltenham Festival was fast approaching. He started to realise he had a nutcase on his hands when I insisted on going home straight away. I just caught the flight and then the captain announced that due to a fuel shortage caused by a very adverse wind, we were going to have to go back to Newfoundland. "Ask them to take a chance," I begged. "I'm going to miss bloody Cheltenham". I only made it by five minutes in the clothes I stood up in. Touch wood, I was never late for a broadcast. And if you're doing it for over 50 years, that's not bad.'

Perhaps as a legacy of his childhood illnesses, Sir Peter had never taken mortality too seriously. During the War, being unfit for service, he joined the Chelsea Civil Defence Rescue Service and scooted about among the dropping bombs in west London effecting life-saving activities where possible and noting wry signs on closed-for-the-duration shops saying, 'No Business As Usual'. 'Wonderful spirit,' he said. This might be applied in particular to the young man who, amid the carnage, took delivery of his first racehorse to his flat in Chelsea, necessitating an eventful ride bareback to Richmond Park. A veil must be drawn over the subsequent career of Wild Thyme – alas more Elephant's Foot, by nature – and it marked a period of sustained optimism at odds with the unfolding events.

'I did have quite an arduous apprenticeship as an owner,' Sir Peter said. 'In 15 years, I had 16 horses and not one in the first three. They were all reasonably priced purchases or rescue horses who did not repay the compliment by rescuing my impecuniousness. But I was fortunate – twice. Be Friendly and Attivo were both stars really. Be Friendly was the champion sprinter of Europe. In 1966, as a two-year-old, he won an aggregate of £44,000, which was a record at the time. And I was lucky enough to breed Attivo because I bought his mother as a bride when she was carrying this potential disaster. He was as narrow as a plank with his feet turned out like Charlie Chaplin and the trainer said, "You'll be lucky enough to run this one at White City!"'

Yet Attivo was the horse who would give Sir Peter the most difficult experience of his commentating career. How he contrived to retain his poise and professionalism during the running of the 1974 Cheltenham Triumph Hurdle is a matter of mystery, but as Attivo crossed the line in advance of his rivals, the BBC commentator said in his usual, velvet, modulated tones: 'And it's first Attivo, trained by Cyril Mitchell, ridden by Robert Hughes, owned by Peter O'Sullevan.' Even the most sturdy of characters might have lapsed into a shriek of 'Go on, my son!' at that point, but Sir Peter looks positively horrified by the thought. 'No, no, there's absolutely no excuse for partiality because money's involved in horse racing. Murray Walker could crack jokes in his commentaries because there wasn't betting on motor racing in those days. Already I was the bearer of bad news 90 per cent of the time; to get things wrong would have been very serious.

'My great good fortune is that most of my mistakes in commentary were not made at a critical time.' He managed also to make friends of a legion of horse people, from royalty to roguery, from Leopardstown to Ladbrokes to Lester. While we talked the phone burst into regular life, illustrative of a man both popular and employed, most lately on the arrangements for his 90th birthday party at Berry Brothers. He has worried down to the last detail about producing the right outcome, which can best be described as merriment.

This acute attention to minutiae underpinned his entire career as a commentator, with his uncanny ability to read a race more or less unsullied by error. But it does have the unfortunate side effect that at least two rooms of the large apartment he shares with his wife, Pat, are simply festooned, stuffed and piled high with nearly every communication and memento he has received. Who else has letters from their former prep school headmaster?

When it came to writing his hugely well received autobiography, published in 1989, his forensic memory and accumulation of years actually caused a problem. 'I over-wrote incontinently once I got into my stride and a very nice guy from Random House had to spend the whole of Sunday here taking out 15,000 words.' You feel his pain. Sir Peter is a purveyor of felicitous sentences, both in speech and print, and their loss to mankind is significant. We, who are plagued by the post-match interview – that window on the gormless – truly value a proper thought process when enunciated by the voice.

I asked him about the upcoming Cheltenham Festival, in which the National Hunt Chase has been renamed in his honour. 'Appropriately, it's the oldest race at the meeting,' he said, smiling. He is relishing the prospect of the duel between Kauto Star and Denman, both trained by Paul Nicholls, in the Gold Cup, but is wary of predicting the winner. 'Kauto might be a little bit quicker in the decisive moments, but Denman – he's a big tank, isn't he – might draw the sting out of him.'

His principal business these days is with the Sir Peter O'Sullevan Charitable Trust, which works tirelessly for the protection of animals, especially horses. 'One of my obsessions is the way we abuse and exploit animals. I have this simplistic view that harmony is unlikely to break out among us until we accept our responsibility for the lesser creatures. But I have tried hard not to get labelled a crackpot because then you don't get anything done.' He need have no fear on that score. His 90 years have been fairly action-packed so far and show no sign of diminishing in activity. His stamina, on air, in print, in life, is splendid. He is, as they say in racing circles, a stayer. Happy Birthday, Sir Peter, and many more.

---

13 APRIL 2007

NOBODY CALLS THEM HOME LIKE McGRATH

Robert Philip

His admirers are convinced that had he been at Balaclava he would have kept pace with the charge of the Light Brigade in precise order and described the riders' injuries before they hit the ground . . . – Hugh McIlvanney's matchless description of Sir Peter O'Sullevan

When it came time for the master to retire after 50 years and 35,000 or so television commentaries for the BBC in 1997, Sir Peter pre-empted any discussions on the matter of his successor by announcing the identity of his preferred heir. 'Jim [McGrath] is brilliant, the best I have heard. Accuracy is the lynch pin of race commentary and he has no peers in that respect. He is a great caller. There's no question that he will take over from me.'

Thus did the journalist known to *Daily Telegraph* readers as Hotspur (J.A. McGrath) become the new 'Voice of Racing', a voice, incidentally, which after 21 years in this country, remains unadulterated Melburnian. Tomorrow's 160th Aintree Grand National will be McGrath's tenth as senior commentator and the most important thing experience has taught him is 'to expect the unexpected. I always go there with my newsman's hat on because you're very conscious of the fact that history is in the making. My first year as a commentator was '93 and that was the year there was no race. Then in '97 there was the IRA bomb scare. When Charles Barnett [Aintree's managing director] told Des Lynam that everyone must leave the course – 'and that includes you, the BBC' – they forgot about me because I was in the commentary box down at Becher's. The cameramen locked their cameras in position and I was on the air for 13 minutes 50 seconds being fed information from the studio. Eventually, a security guard clambered up the ladder and looked at me as though I was one of those Japanese soldiers who'd just emerged from the jungle 20 years after the end of the War. "You've got to leave now! You're the last one".'

His voyage from the suburbs of Melbourne to the suburbs of Liverpool has been a circuitous one, beginning in Ireland of the 1880s when three brothers voiced the notion of leaving the old country to seek their fortunes in the New World. 'One decided to stay, one emigrated to America and Frank McGrath, who sailed to Australia with his wife and sister on the Champion of the Sea, was my great-grandfather.' McGrath's fascination with the Turf was inherited from his late father, Brian, who left the family sheep and cattle farm in Charlton, Victoria, to be educated in Melbourne where he stayed with his maternal uncle, Jack Scallion, who, as fate would have it, was a bookmaker.

'My father got a very safe job as a clerk in the law courts, transcribing witness statements, evidence and all the rest of it. When he was about 16, great-uncle Jack took him to Geelong one day to act as his clerk and he was hooked. From the moment he walked on to the course he knew racing was going to be his life. He became a bookie at the age of 21 – which made him the youngest by about 15 years – even though it was considered a slightly risque occupation at the time. My grandmother wasn't too happy – she wanted him to become a lawyer or something similarly respectable – but my grandfather, James Henry, who was a great guy, said, "Do whatever you want to do and if you want to be a bookmaker just make sure you're the best".'

It was inevitable, therefore, that young J.A. (his middle name is Aloysius) should go racing for the first time at Pakenham at the tender age of four. 'Like any kid, I was just excited about going out for the day with my dad, but as I grew older and was allowed to visit the paddock by myself, I fell in love with horses and racing. Even better were the times Dad would take me along with his four clerks – Arthur Cuff, known as 'Screwball', George Maxwell, Jimmy Jones and Gerry Forbes – to a course somewhere. He had a big tan-and-white American Pontiac and with the five of them in their big hats and coats, it was very, very Runyon-esque. The tales, as you can imagine, opened up a whole new world to me, a world probably no-one else in Melbourne knew about. They were all knockaround guys with a great sense of humour, so it was the perfect initiation. I've never smoked and I have Dad and his friends to thank for that. They all smoked cigarettes and cigars, and in the middle of winter with the windows up you couldn't breathe. Actually, I'm not sure how Dad saw to drive through the wall of smoke.'

It was while working as a trainee reporter on *The Australian* that McGrath's abiding fascination with the Grand National was aroused when Crisp set off from Down Under for Aintree and his historic engagement with Red Rum in 1973. 'Crisp had captured the imagination of all Australia where he was all but unbeatable. People held Grand National parties all over the country – I was at one in St Kilda – at which we gathered round the wireless around a quarter to one in the morning to listen to the race.'

As history now records, had the Grand National been run over a yard shorter than the four-and-half miles, there might have been a statue of Crisp by the winning post today instead of Rummy. From the off, the huge Australian chaser hopped over Becher's Brook, Valentine's and The Chair as though they were mere toothpicks placed in his way. Partnered by Richard Pitman, Crisp produced the most devastating display of jumping seen over the National course, despite being saddled with the top weight by the handi-capper, and built up a lead of 30 lengths by the time he cleared the Canal Turn on the second circuit. Then at the 29th of Aintree's 30 fences, Crisp, at his best over two miles, suddenly began to show the effects of his front-running heroics; out of the chasing posse burst Red Rum, and the lead fast diminished from 30 lengths to 15 as they cleared the last, then ten, then five until, right on the line, Rummy poked his nose in front.

'We couldn't believe it back home because Crisp was a national hero in Australia, but it was the classic Grand National encounter between a brilliant front-runner and the horse who would go on to become Aintree's greatest champion. But I still believe Crisp is one of the Grand National's biggest heroes. I remember seeing slow-motion footage of him running at Flemington where he had to jump six fences in a row. I'm sure the fences were so unchallenging for him he got bored, but as he came to the sixth and final one, he completely misjudged it. He took off far too early and you could see his ears swivelling as he computed the information that he's in trouble. Flying in mid-air, he extended his front legs even further and tucks his rear legs under his backside to clear the fence with nothing to spare. That kind of thing – seeing a horse's mind twig that he'd made a blunder and then correct it – is uncanny and makes Crisp one of the cleverest horses of all time.'

A past winner of the Royal Television Society's Commentator of the Year award, McGrath will not sleep easily tonight unless he can look at the colours of all 40 horses and rattle off their names without hesitation. 'You always have to be conscious of the fact that one of the things that makes the National unique is that everyone in Britain will have a bet on or be part of an office sweep. And each and every viewer will want to hear his or her horse mentioned at least once.' As part of his meticulous preparation, he will also have walked the course at least once because 'you need to be reminded how big the fences are and what an enormous challenge Aintree represents. If you look at the Cresta Run on TV it never looks as steep as it truly is and it's the same how wide and tall the likes of Becher's is. That's why every jump jockey wants to ride in the Grand National – it's the ultimate test.'

And who does McGrath expect to see follow in Red Rum's hooves as first past the post? 'I think the name Carberry will figure very prominently [Paul will be riding Dun Doire, brother Philip will be aboard Point Barrow with sister Nina partnering A New Story].' Ah, but which Carberry, Jim? 'I think Point Barrow will go very well. An Irish Grand National winner and trained especially for this race by the very astute Pat Hughes. And a horse I've been following for a long time is Botha Na. That's two, so how about Zabenz, trained by Philip Hobbs and owned by Michael Watt from New Zealand who's been over here many years and is a good friend of mine? I'd love to be calling that home for Michael.' And as Sir Peter O'Sullevan says, no-one, but no-one, calls them home better than Jim McGrath.

---

11 FEBRUARY 1983

MYSTERY OF A MAN NAMED ARKLE

John Oaksey, Marlborough of The Daily Telegraph *and Racing Correspondent of the* Sunday Telegraph

At two o'clock yesterday I became, willy-nilly, one of the most improbable 'contact men' in the history of kidnapping – the nearest I expect to be to a

Dick Francis story. Fourteen hours later, 30 miles south of Belfast, the ransom being demanded for the kidnapped Derby winner, Shergar, had dwindled from £2 million to £40,000 – or £1,000 for each share. A ransom, of course, is still a ransom and even if the demand proved to be genuine, the Aga Khan and Shergar's 34 other shareholders may well reckon that paying it would set a precedent likely to shake the bloodstock world to its foundations.

The last thing we heard on Thursday night from a mystery voice, which may or may not represent the kidnappers, was a statement that no further instructions would be given until the whole syndicate had agreed to a £40,000 'reward'. But there was no proof that the voice (codenamed Arkle) is not a hoax. Danger was very much in my fuddled mind yesterday morning when the news first broke that a telephone call to the *Belfast Newsletter* and BBC had asked for negotiations to be started through Derek Thompson, of ITV, Peter Campling of the *Sun,* or myself.

We were invited to be in the Europa-Forum Hotel by yesterday evening. Since this seemed to be something of a no-stones-left-unturned situation, all three of us caught the 12.30 shuttle complete with toothbrushes, pencils and misgivings. There followed a series of those hectic and ridiculous airport scenes with convoys of cameramen trying to break the Olympic record for walk-backs while taking pictures. To Miss Sophia Loren it would, no doubt, have been old hat, just another day – but for Messrs Thompson, Campling and Oaksey it was something entirely new.

Before we boarded the almost virginal Boeing 757 one significant piece of news had fallen into my lap. Mrs Judy Maxwell, whose husband Jeremy trains near Downpatrick racecourse south of Belfast, called to say that a man using the Arkle codename had rung her at 1 a.m. His message, the first of several, was the same as that received by the *Newsletter* and BBC. But by 9 a.m. the Arkle voice (Irish, according to Mrs Maxwell, but neither deep south nor far north) had become a great deal angrier, infuriated by the publicity given to his original request.

By 2 p.m., when Arkle made his third call to Mrs Maxwell, our ill-assorted three-man embassy had run two more media gauntlets at Belfast airport and in the lobby of the Europa-Forum. Here, with recording machines and cameras snapping around him like piranhas, Derek Thompson himself took a call from Arkle. 'Ring the Maxwells,' the voice said, and rang off. But when we obeyed a brand new voice replied – that of an RUC Detective Inspector. Mrs Maxwell had told them of her early calls and now, following Arkle's instructions, had gone with her husband to a nearby hotel. The telephone was ringing as they arrived – Arkle again – but before they could get to it there 'the voice' had rung off.

Back in Belfast, our problem was to leave the Europa-Forum without a trail of media bloodhounds. With kindly guidance from the management we crept out, James Bond-like, through the back door. We finally arrived at the Maxwells 30 frightening miles later (driven by a freelance cameraman with a Fangio fixation) with two press cars still on our tail.

Out in the chilly Northern Irish countryside the presence of several large policemen was frankly reassuring. But patiently though we waited by the telephone, Arkle made only one more call – the somewhat optimistic hope that we three would, in ten minutes or so, contact the 34 syndicate members.

As I write, therefore, the £40,000 is the voice's last demand and there is still no news of where £10 million worth of Shergar is concealed. So as we swigged Irish whiskey and waited hopefully for the telephone to ring it seemed about time to spare a thought for the handsome, courageous horse all the fuss is about. In his all too-short career Shergar never did the human race anything but good. He made money for some, gave pleasure to many, and only disappointed once.

---

2 JUNE 2001

I'LL NEVER FORGET THAT NIGHT THE IRA LED SHERGAR INTO THE BOX WITHOUT A PROBLEM

Owen Slot

The fanfare of the Epsom Derby will reach a peak on Saturday afternoon with the second coming of Shergar. Twenty years after winning the race by a margin that no one had seen before or has witnessed since, the great stallion will arrive in the form of a bronze statue to be presented to the owner of the winning horse. As inspirations go, Shergar's Derby could hardly be bettered. The moment captured by the bronze has Walter Swinburn, his passenger that day, looking over his shoulder as they reached the final furlong. It is a moment Swinburn recalls vividly. The roar from the crowd that was ringing in his ears carried the words 'Come on, Lester' and the reason he glanced round was because he was terrified that he was going see Piggott making a charge on Shotgun. The reality, of course, could not have been more different, a point that was not lost on the BBC's Peter Bromley who celebrated Shergar's lead with a now-famous piece of commentary: 'There's only one horse in it. You'll need a telescope to see the rest.' Of such stuff are legends made.

Far from the madding crowd this Saturday, in a house in Newbridge, on the banks of the Liffey just a few miles from The Curragh, the sight of Shergar will unleash a surge of familiar emotions. Jim Fitzgerald will settle down to watch the Derby on his television and when he sees his old friend, he will feel a bewildering combination of deep pride and immense loss. Fitzgerald's whole life has been horses. He was brought up in the inter-war years just down the road on the Ballymany Stud where his father was the stud-groom. He started working there himself in 1946 and he had risen to the position of stud-groom by the time Shergar was retired back to the stud at the end of the 1981 season. And, 18 months later, on the evening of 8 February, 1983, it was he whom the IRA commandeered at gunpoint to lead them to the horse.

The arrival of armed men at his house, and their threat to kill his family if he spoke to the police, is a trauma that time has enabled him to live with. However, his last glimpse of Shergar – the last of anyone bar his killers – is one he believes he will never forget. Of the half-century he has worked with horses, Fitzgerald's favourite was Shergar. 'There were some great animals here,' he says gently, 'wonderful race horses, but Shergar stands out. A grand, grand horse. He has to stand out as the best.'

Fitzgerald has never before spoken publicly about Shergar, and still refuses to be photographed. He never enjoyed the interest of the media, but more significantly, he simply didn't want to go back through the ordeal. He is by no means alone in this, for Shergar has never really been allowed to rest in peace. As well as in almost every acre in Ireland, he has reported to have been found, either alive or dead, in such disparate locations as Sussex, the Channel Isles, Canada and Cleveland, USA. On the morning of the last significant sighting, four years ago, the Irish Equine Centre received 17 calls in an hour from international TV companies. 'If there was a quadruple murder, there wouldn't have been as many people involved – police, government, everything – as there was for this horse,' says Captain Sean Berry, the spokesman for the industry who himself started appearing on chat shows. 'It was talked about so much it was more important than an election.'

All that is certain is that it was a hopelessly embarrassing cock-up by the IRA, who only admitted it indirectly in the 1998 publication of *The Informer*, the autobiography of Sean O'Callaghan, the IRA member turned police informer. O'Callaghan writes that Shergar was killed within days and he also confirms the depth of the miscalculation. The thinking was that 'kidnapping a horse would never be viewed by the general public in Ireland as equivalent to kidnapping a person'. Yet this ignores the fact that by stealing so famous a stallion, they were threatening the extremely valuable Irish bloodstock industry, and perhaps more pertinently, the simple reality that when it comes to horses, the Irish are not exactly unemotional.

'I always believed that he'd appear somewhere,' says Swinburn, who would return to visit him in his retirement at the Ballymany Stud. 'We'd go back and see him and he'd be grazing in a field with a couple of cows, and you could just walk up to him. He had this terrific temperament, that's why he was so easy to kidnap.' Swinburn was in India when Shergar was taken and when he was contacted and informed by BBC World Service, his initial reaction was that it was a joke. 'Apart from being an amazing racehorse,' he says, 'he was the kindest horse I knew. I just didn't think anyone could hurt a horse like that and I held that belief for a long time.'

This character assessment, however, flies in the face of O'Callaghan's assertion that 'the horse threw itself into a frenzy in the horsebox, damaging a leg and proving impossible for the team to control. He was killed within days'. Swinburn says: 'It would really surprise me if that was the truth. The only Shergar I knew had this amazing temperament.' It is such speculation that has turned Fitzgerald away from the story ever since. He prefers to recall the triumphant stallion who was walked through the high street of Newbridge on his return from his victories. 'When he came back as a stallion, he was wonderful to work with. He had lots of visitors. I used to feed him in the mornings and look in at nights and, I tell you, it's a pity he had such a short life because he really was grand.'

Fitzgerald was hooked on Shergar long before he returned to the stud. When Shergar was racing, he would travel excitedly to Kildare to watch him at the house of a friend whose TV could pick up BBC. Even today, he has in his house a video of that 1981 Derby which he turns to when he wants to be reminded of the majesty of the beast. It is this image in particular that he treasures. 'When Walter is interviewed about him on the telly,' he says, 'you can tell that he still feels very strongly about the horse, too.' Indeed he does. He was, says Swinburn, undoubtedly the best horse of his career. 'Some horses get fazed by the big day, but not this one, not at all. Everyone expected him to win, including myself, but I never realised quite how good he was. It was amazing.

'Of the race, I remember jumping out and only ever seeing two horses in front of me. And he was so easy, it was like riding a piece of work in a gallop morning. It was the horse that got himself in that good position and then took me to the front. I just had to sit on and keep him going. When I looked round at that final furlong, it felt absolutely amazing. It was signed, sealed and delivered. If I hadn't eased him off, his record winning margin would have been doubled. Anyone could have ridden him that day; the only one who could have messed it up was me.' 'Jeepers, he was impressive, wasn't he?' says Fitzgerald smiling. 'You could tell he had the Derby won at Tattenham Corner, and it's not often you can say that.'

The final chapter of Shergar's life, however, is not so easy for Fitzgerald to recall and occasionally he breaks away from the narrative and looks away into the distance. Contrary to the accepted version of events, he says that his visitors that dark night were not rough and they certainly didn't pin his son, Bernard, to the ground. 'They were all right, they were all good to us. They didn't knock me about or anything. I'll always remember one of them — I hope he's still alive — because he was nice to me. Even when they took me away in the van, he put his hand on my shoulder a few times. But I'll never forget that night. I had to lead the horse into the box, it was one of those small ones. He went into the box all right, he was such a grand horse he went in without a problem. I remember one of them asking me if he'd been out that day, because he had clay on his back. The one glimpse I remember best was in the stable, when we were getting ready to get him out. He was relaxed and kind as ever, he didn't look concerned at all. Then I led him into the box. And that was the last I saw of him.'

It was then that they went their separate ways, Shergar in the horsebox, Fitzgerald in a van. Fitzgerald was dropped some 20 miles away, was told in which direction to walk and not to look back. Oh, and they wanted £2 million, too. 'It was a desperate time. I was so involved in the horses, for that to happen, it's very hard, it gets to you right in there,' he says, touching his chest. 'And it ate away at me. One of the detectives said to me, "It's a good job you don't drink, because you'd really hit the bottle".'

In the weeks after the heist, Fitzgerald also believed that he would see Shergar again. He will see his likeness again on Saturday afternoon, though, and that cheers him enormously. 'That's a grand thing, isn't it?' he says. 'Because that's how he was, a gentle fella and a real champion.'

----

3 JUNE 1979

WHY I WOULDN'T HAVE BET ON THE DERBY

The most famous horse race will be run for the 200th time at Epsom on Wednesday. John Oaksey, Sunday Telegraph racing correspondent and the former amateur jockey, looks back over the years, from its faltering beginnings to the establishment of the race as a great British institution

'Born 1780 and still going strong' — in the week of its 200th birthday, the Derby could hardly be blamed if it stole Johnnie Walker's slogan; but, for nearly half of those 200 years, any sensible betting man would have wanted good odds against the race reaching such a happy anniversary. In its first 70 years, in fact, the sporting institution of which we are now so proud tended more often than not to bring out the worst features of human nature in general and of the British character in particular.

Greed rather than generosity was its trademark and cunning played a bigger part than courage. The horses – when allowed to – did their best, but without a lot of luck and the efforts of one or two exceptional men, what is now the richest and most famous Flat race in the world might, before 1850, have sunk into disreputable obscurity – or even been abolished altogether by some high-minded Victorian politician.

It did not help, of course, that Lord Derby's 'roistering party', as Lord Rosebery later described it, thought up their bright idea during the American War of Independence, in which, incidentally, Derby's uncle, 'Gentleman Johnny' Burgoyne, had just presided over the surrender of a whole British army at Saratoga. As Michael Wynne-Jones notes in his book, a masterly account called simply *The Derby,* there is a nice irony in Burgoyne's connection with Saratoga – now one of America's oldest and most elegant racing centres – when you remember that it was he who sold Lord Derby the house at Epsom in which the race was invented.

But while Lord Derby and his friends (including Sir Charles Bunbury, after whom the race was very nearly called) were trying to get it established, one thing was leading to another in foreign parts. When Waxy (one of the best early winners) won in 1793, the tumbrils were still rolling towards the guillotine and, in 1806, Lord Egremont's Trafalgar was rather inappropriately beaten a short head by Paris only six months after the battle in honour of which he had been named.

Admittedly, unlike the Kaiser and Adolf Hitler, who both forced the Derby to be transplanted to Newmarket, Napoleon seems to have had surprisingly little effect on the racing scene. When Whisker won the 1815 Derby, Waterloo – only three weeks ahead – seemed to be less on people's minds at Epsom than the riding of the favourite's jockey (who was pulled from his horse and 'badly mauled' by an infuriated mob).

Nevertheless, these were hardly ideal years in which to establish a brand-new race. Luckily, to begin with, the general public neither knew nor cared much about either the horses or the race: there were never more than 15 runners (once as few as four) in the first 30 years, but this wasn't surprising since the only way of getting a racehorse from A to B was to walk. The journey from Newmarket took weeks, and, in 1800, when Champion became the first Derby winner to win the St Leger, too, he had to be led all the way from Epsom to Doncaster between his triumphs.

But at that time, the newspapers scarcely covered racing: the first racecard was produced (by William Dorling, whose family were the driving force at Epsom throughout the 19th century) in 1827 and only those closely involved knew even what was running in the early Derbys, let alone what might win. What brought the crowds to Epsom Downs was not so much the horses as the chance of a cheap day out provided more or less free by the moneyed toffs with whom otherwise they had little contact. All sorts of 'fun' was organised – cock-fighting, bearbaiting and prizefighting, which though still illegal was extremely popular – and a tumblerful of gin cost only one penny. That, too, not surprisingly, was popular and, in 1821, the happy crowd so encroached on the course that, according to his jockey, Gustavus (the first grey to win) had to 'wind in and out all the way from Tattenham Corner like a dog at a fair'.

The Derby could survive such little local difficulties and, by 1830, with the winner's prize up to £2,800, its pre-eminence in the racing world was pretty well established; but that pre-eminence now attracted such a galaxy of unsavoury and unscrupulous knaves that, for the first half of the 19th century, scarcely a year went by without an attempt to arrange or alter the result by one kind of foul play or another. The first bookmakers – then known as 'blacklegs' or 'legs' – had begun to cater for the rich, heavy-betting, mostly aristocratic racing 'fancy'. The Jockey Club's rule was still both weak and haphazard and some of the more successful 'legs' soon entered ownership in a big way and set about making sure that their horses either won or lost as the occasion demanded.

Most of these villains had little or nothing to recommend them, but one of the most famous, John Gully, had at least been heavyweight champion of England – a title he earned by lasting no less than 59 rounds with Henry 'The Game Chicken' Pearce. The fact that Gully ended up MP for Pontefract may or may not be to his credit: but there is no doubt that between these two achievements, he was a shark in the top rank. Gully's great rival, William Crockford, who eventually set up the famous West End gambling house on his ill-gotten gains, was a far less attractive character. These two were not, so far as we know, involved with Daniel Dawson, who was, quite rightly, hanged in 1812 for putting arsenic in a horses' drinking trough at Newmarket; but, poison aside, they had an almost limitless armoury of dirty tricks.

With a few honourable exceptions, jockeys were neither respected nor respectable in those days, stable lads were even worse paid than they are now and races were started in a casual way which gave ample scope for every kind of cheating. When Gully's horse, Mameluke, was favourite for the St Leger, for instance, Crockford and his gang entered half-a-dozen no-account animals specifically to cause so many false starts that Mameluke would exhaust himself. The starter had, of course, been squared and, despite rushing down to the start with an enormous whip, Gully lost £40,000. He got most of it back with an almost equally dishonest gamble on one of his three Derby winners, but he and Crockford were only two among a whole parasitic swarm who were sucking blood and money out of the sport.

'Victorian' morals had not yet encroached on those of the Regency and, by the sound of it, some of the well-heeled punters were amazingly easy 'marks' for such expert con men. Berkeley Craven, who shot himself after Bay Middleton's Derby, was only one of several who preferred death to the 'dishonour' of not paying and though the young Marquess of Hastings did not actually take his own life, his lunatic gambling and profligacy were almost suicidal.

So, you can see, that the Jockey Club and the Epsom Committee must have been both surprised and overjoyed when the young Queen Victoria lent the 1840 Derby the badly needed cachet of her presence: the visit was by no means a total success (The Queen's lunch failed to turn up), but she is said to have admired the winner, Little Wonder, who, standing a pony-sized 14.3 hands, was much the smallest horse to win. 'How sweet,' Queen Victoria no doubt thought; but she might have been less amused if anyone had been foolish enough to tell her that Little Wonder was a four-year-old whose lack of inches made it easy to conceal his age!

Quite apart from the bad catering and the fact that she didn't much like racing, it isn't at all surprising that Queen Victoria never went near the Derby again because, four years later, its biggest scandal of all time exploded when – thanks to the tireless (and sometimes fairly unscrupulous) detective work of Lord George Bentinck – it was proved that the winner Running Rein was, in fact, a four-year-old called Maccabeus. There was at least one other four-year-old in the race (in fact, he may have been six, but Running Rein struck into him and broke his leg on Tattenham Hill) and another well-backed horse was either doped or stopped.

So you can see what I mean by saying that in 1844 no sensible man would have bet on the Derby even reaching its 200th birthday – let alone becoming the richest, most famous, most universally respected Flat race in the world. That miracle was brought about by several heroic figures, some of them equine and some human. Lord George Bentinck was certainly one of the latter: he may have bent the law on occasion – for instance, by kidnapping the real Running Rein to prevent the other side producing him at a trial; but with men like Admiral Rous, he set in motion the long, hard process by which racing was gradually reformed, controlled and rescued from its least desirable hangers-on.

But that was racing in general. The prestige and glory of the Derby itself was built and reinforced in the second half of the century by several wonderful horses and one incredible man. His name, of course, was Fred Archer, and though he and Lester Piggott have a lot in common, no one, not even Lester, will approach, still less excel, Archer's record. Five Derbys, an unbroken 13-year reign as champion jockey and the unbelievable number of 2,471 winners from only 8,084 rides would sound miraculous now with evening racing, motor cars and aeroplanes to ease a jockey's life. But Archer had none of these. He travelled by train, coach or on horseback and throughout those 13 years was subjecting his five-foot ten-inch frame (it weighed 11 stone in winter) to unimaginable torture and privation. It is no wonder that when he stayed in an hotel there were crowds outside to cheer him on his way to the races, and no wonder that when he shot himself, aged 28, driven half mad by illness, wasting and depression, sporting England went into mourning. 'The punter has lost the best friend he had,' said Lord Marcus Beresford, and no one has given him an argument.

One of Archer's five Derby winners, Ormonde, was among the equine giants who adorned the second half of the century. He was never beaten and when he retired, his owner gave a garden party for him in London at which Ormonde walked among the crowd politely eating cakes, sugar and geraniums. Before him, the great northern pair Voltigeur and The Flying Dutchman had spread the Derby's fame (both of them won it) by their famous Yorkshire rivalry. The French-born Gladiateur had become the 'avenger of Waterloo' by winning the Triple Crown – despite a jockey so short-sighted that he could only see the winning post in the last half furlong. The brothers Perisimmon and Diamond Jubilee had won for the Prince of Wales, and when his mother finally died, Minoru gave the Epsom crowd the chance to sing 'God Save The King' as Edward VII became the only reigning monarch to lead in the winner. Perhaps it is too much to hope that Milford and Fred Archer's reincarnation will do the same for us on Wednesday afternoon. But who knows? There have been a lot of miracles in the Derby's long, eventful history.

I OCTOBER 1995

RIDERS IN SEARCH OF LOST ARC

Brough Scott

It's still Europe's most fantastic theatre, but do we have the stars and indeed the audience to justify the show? Arc de Triomphe day at Longchamp and the visiting turfistes have to think they have stepped into racing's Promised Land. But for France, and for Britain, too, it's time to take stock. Time to wonder how come this most brilliant of awaydays still makes so much more impact over here than over there. Time for the 10,000 fans crossing the Channel by plane, boat and, this year, by extremely well-lubricated train, to consider if the race will again anoint the champion they crave. To be blunt, can the Arc still be the crown?

All sports need an identifiable annual peak and since the mid-Fifties that one-and-a-half mile pitch in Paris has served European racing well. Forget the Derby, the King George VI at Ascot, to win the Prix de L'Arc de Triomphe on this first Sunday in October represented the ultimate attainment for owner, trainer and jockey. For Britain, especially so, for the seeming impossibility of it.

We saw the Italian superstar, Ribot, storm away in both 1955 and 1957 and register legitimate claims to be one of the horses of the century. In 1958 Vincent O'Brien saddled Ballymoss, the first Irish winner, to assert his own right as the greatest trainer to tighten a girth. In 1965 France's Sea Bird II slaughtered a brilliant field in the best Arc performance seen. They were the standard, and fine runners though we sent over, this most coveted of all prizes was the one that got away. Got away so memorably from Lester Piggott in those marvellous Arcs of 1968, '69 and '70: Sir Ivor couldn't match Vaguely Noble's power; Park Top's late run was too late to gather in Levmoss; and most controversially of all, Nijinsky's unbeaten reign ended as he swept up to Sassafras but failed to get home. Imagine then the triumph when Mill Reef, already the winner of the Derby, the Eclipse and the King George, dazzled clear under the gaze of President Pompidou in 1971. The Arc had been cracked finally and when Rheingold broke Piggott's duck two years later we began to think it was easy. It wasn't. Only Rainbow Quest in '85, Dancing Brave in '86 and Carroll House in '89 have won for Britain since. Lammtarra has some heavy hoofprints to fill today.

Dancing Brave's victory ranks for me as the greatest Flat racing moment of the last ten years and Generous's early capitulation in '91 as the worst. The Arc is what the game should be about, but can the magic still work? Certainly a first-time visitor there today will think that this has to be just about the most perfect site for a racecourse on earth. Set by the Seine on the edge of the Bois de Boulogne with the Eiffel Tower in the distance and the Arc de Triomphe itself but five minutes away, it's as if we had Epsom in Kensington Gardens.

What's more, Auteuil, France's premier jumping track, is but a mile and a half away: that's Cheltenham in St John's Wood. When the literati talk of Hemingway in Paris in the Thirties, few remember that it was the proximity of the racetracks that was for him one of its big attractions. But, nowadays, not big enough. For behind all the buzz and the bunting on offer this afternoon lies a public apathy of quite horrifying dimensions. A malaise we ignore at our peril, and which the French are only now fully equipped to do something about. Welcome though the British interest may be, it is nonetheless a symptom of the problem the French face. Imagine a crowd of 40,000 at a Kensington Gardens Epsom and 10,000 of them from across the Channel. Think of Gold Cup day at this St John's Wood Cheltenham and BBC or Channel 4 just screen the one big race while French TV network three. British racing itself faced the harsh facts of competition last Sunday when the best promoted Ascot day yet could draw just 13,000 to an empty-looking arena. In France they are starting from an even more difficult base.

The real irony is seen if you visit Longchamp on a weekday, as I did last month, and find – horror of horrors – it's empty. Yes, there's a race meeting on, but hardly a spectator in sight. We know watching on English tracks can be a solitary pursuit, but this was ridiculous. No-one knows that better than Louis Romanet, long-standing pillar of the old ruling authority, the Societe d'Encouragement, but now centrally placed in the newly formed France Galop which, as the name suggests, brings together the different racing disciplines around the country. 'Yes, Longchamp needs redesigning,' says Romanet crisply. 'The stands are now 30 years old, they were built after Sea Bird's Arc. We need to be able to cater for small crowds on weekdays and yet have the capacity for 40,000 on Arc day. It is not an easy track, but it can be done.'

That sums up Romanet's attitude to the problems of funding and public support which he faces at present and, as he talks, you realise that he has some huge advantages over his English equivalents. In Jean Luc Lagardere he has a president of France Galop who is one of France's leading owner-breeders at the same time as being an industrialist of awesome influence in a country whose cabinet now contains two members also deeply involved in the racing game. Think of that over here. Well, with the Labour Party sponsoring today's meeting at Brighton, perhaps we can!

More directly, think of the racing authorities in Britain owning not just the racetracks but all the betting facilities, too. France's Tote monopoly means that Romanet can put financial muscle behind all his high-sounding plans to make racing more accessible to a younger audience, to a wider ownership base. But many of those who today queue interminably at the Tote windows will hanker for the competition as well as the colour which bookmakers bring. Yet in the end, on either side of the Channel, the competition is of a wider kind. It is about making these two-and-half frantic, galloping minutes around the Bois as exciting as anything other sports can offer. For that there is one simple but nearly always unachievable solution. We need a star. A Nijinsky, a Mill Reef, a Dancing Brave. Worthy Classic winners though both Balanchine and Lammtarra may be, they have never yet progressed into that galactic status.

29 OCTOBER 2003

PASSIONATE OBSERVER WHO CAME SO CLOSE TO NATIONAL GLORY

J.A. McGrath

It takes a special type of reporter to ride in a steeplechase and then walk, mud-spattered, to a telephone and dictate copy describing his experiences. But for John Oaksey, who was simultaneously 'Marlborough' and 'Audax' to a couple of generations of readers of *The Daily Telegraph* and *Horse and Hound,* respectively, prior to becoming 'The Noble Lord' to a younger audience via television, this was common practice for nearly 20 years.

Geoffrey Lawrence, the first Baron Oaksey, a Lord Justice who presided over the Nuremberg war crimes trials, was John's father, and having paid for his son's rather expensive education at Eton, Oxford and Yale, he was probably expecting a little more of his offspring than a desire to write about matters of the Turf for the rest of his working life. But, thankfully, Baron Oaksey, then 76 years old, also displayed a masterly sense of judgment and understanding of life when he informed his son: 'If you can find someone prepared to pay you to do something you really enjoy, don't, for heaven's sake, let them out of your sight.' *The Daily Telegraph's* 'Marlborough', who never did, later wrote: 'Those were his words – some of the wisest and kindest I was ever lucky enough to hear.'

John Oaksey's life, within racing and without, has been remarkable. He has been the amateur rider who won a Whitbread Gold Cup and finished a close second in the Grand National; the racing commentator whose distinctive tones give impressionists enough material for a field-day; the writer whose style of reporting was consistently the most passionate and descriptive of his time; and the founder trustee of the Injured Jockeys' Fund, to which his personal commitment is still often displayed by selling Christmas cards and diaries in the chill of winter alongside his wife, Chicky, on racecourses throughout the country.

That John has chosen to record a wide selection of his best stories and experiences in racing in his latest book, *Mince Pie For Starters,* which was published this month, is fantastic news for anybody who has even a passing interest in horses and horse racing. His skills as a raconteur are well known in racing, and he has put the stories on paper in the same wonderful prose he would have filed from darkened press rooms from Warwick, Sandown Park or Ascot in the halcyon days of the riding journalist.

314 | *Kings, Queens and Four-legged Athletes*

John had 11 rides in the Grand National, but none is recalled more than his third mount, Carrickbeg, who was touched off by the Pat Buckley-ridden Ayala in the 1963 running of the great steeplechase. 'I had little time to feel the crushing disappointment of "so near and yet so far",' John writes, 'as I had to file my report for the *Sunday Telegraph* within minutes of returning to weigh in. I dismounted, rushed into the changing room to wipe the worst of the Aintree mud off my face, then, still in my riding colours, ran across the Ormskirk Road to the house from which I had made an arrangement to file the story.'

John likes to tell the story of being confronted by a scruffy little man in the summer of 1978, outside the 'gents' in Piccadilly Underground. It was late at night, and much the worse for wear, the grubby, shambolic punter looked sideways at Carrickbeg's rider (of 15 years earlier) and said: 'I know you! You're the booger who got tired before yer 'orse.'

Those pressmen who believe facilities at Aintree to be a little primitive these days would never have expected to find themselves having to strike a deal with near-neighbours to the racecourse for the unrestricted use of a telephone soon after the big race. For Oaksey and colleagues, it was all part of the annual Grand National 'experience', which was, and still is, unique. The disappointment of losing the Grand National was clear when Oaksey, as 'Audax', wrote several days later: 'At that bitter moment when Ayala's head appeared at my knee, I wished them both at the bottom of the deep blue sea. Now, with admiration and only a little envy, I salute them for winning, deservedly, a truly wonderful race.'

John had his own set ways when it came to filing copy. It was my great privilege to work alongside him in his last five years as a regular racing correspondent to *The Daily Telegraph,* and we experienced very enjoyable times. He was in the habit of writing his stories out in indecipherable long-hand before dictating the words over the telephone. When he had finished the call, he would always roll the writing paper into a little ball and throw it across the room, aiming for the rubbish bin. Even when laptops came along, he would happily tap away at the keyboard, complete his article – and then phone copy. He never mastered the last, crucial step that would have transmitted what was on his laptop screen to his office in a matter of seconds. But then, that was not the Oaksey style. A traditionalist, with old-fashioned values, he has always been happiest when admiring the great National Hunt athletes of the various eras, and riding some of the very good ones of his time. His life has been one of passion and commitment to racing in general, but jumping, in particular. It shows very clearly in this very enjoyable book.

A HELPING HAND COULD ALWAYS BE FOUND AT THE PEGASUS

John Oaksey looks back at the 1951 Bar point-to-point race, which began his addiction to the sport and deprived the legal profession of his services

I never much cared for the name, but it was a mare called Next of Kin, who, by winning the Bar point-to-point in 1951, gave me my first taste of a drug to which, given the chance, I would still be addicted. In those days, the Pegasus Club point-to-point used to feature two races confined to members, and would-be members, of the legal profession. Next of Kin did her best to live up to her name, by rearing and coming over backwards in the paddock, but in the race she jumped like a stag inspired. It was the others who fell over. So, home she sailed with a bewildered, blissful burden dreaming improbable dreams on her back. The distinguished judges and barristers responsible for the race had, quite unwittingly, deprived their profession of my services.

The Pegasus Club was responsible for another life-long addiction, because it was there that I backed my first winner. He was my sister Jenny's 18-year-old hunter Lohengrin, and he only ran because, when the Bar point-to-point was revived after the War, entries were hard to come by. My father, a steward and life-long supporter of the Club, pressed the old horse into service and my sister became, overnight, a dedicated, full-time trainer. Still at school, I was not allowed (or qualified) to ride, so she engaged a genial law student called Gerald Ponsonby.

Gerald, in the throes of the Bar exams, freely admitted that his fitness left a lot to be desired, but since he was just there to make up the numbers, nobody thought it would matter. The first six fences reinforced that view because, though Lohengrin jumped them like the good, safe, hunter he was, the others were soon two fields ahead. But Kimble was one of the few point-to-point courses with a water jump and what the poet calls 'a bird's-eye gleam of the flashing stream' was enough to make the leader stop stone dead. His rider, a sporting, but portly, County Court judge, cleared the fence really well – but lacked the momentum to negotiate the water. His Gaelic cries, the baby tidal wave caused by his immersion and the presence of his steed, cavorting nervously on the take-off side, had the disastrous effect on the morale of their pursuers.

One after another they, too, ground to a halt and, as 'those who cried "Forward" and those in front cried "Back",' there followed a distressing scene in which not all the language would have been approved in the High Court. To Lohengrin, arriving on the scene some minutes later, none of this seemed either strange or frightening. Quite accustomed to musical chairs at the Pony Club, he lolloped calmly through like a condescending grown-up making allowances for naughty children.

No one was immediately able to follow, so he and Gerald came to the second last in solitary glory. But now, alas, the strain of their exertions was beginning to tell. Lohengrin made only a slight mistake, but the sad words 'unseated rider' went down in the form book and, at that crucial moment, one preserving rival succeeded in getting over the water. Willing hands hoisted Gerald back into the plate, but Lohengrin was tired now, too, and, brushing wearily through the last, he dislodged his jockey yet again.

The lone pursuer was closing fast. Both Lohengrin and Gerald were exhausted – and my ten bob on the nose at 20–1 looked in deadly danger after all. But all was well. A huge farmer threw Gerald back aboard and, without stirrups, whip or hat, he rode for home like a hero. Threequarters of a rapidly-disappearing length was the verdict in the end – and of all the great finishes I have seen since, nothing, not even Crisp and Red Rum or Special Cargo's Whitbread, has meant more to me at the time.

Most of my point-to-pointing was done while at Oxford – which, at that time, had two meetings of its own. One was the Bullingdon, a Club of which my old friend Gay Kindersley, later champion amateur and owner of Carrickbeg, was one of the leading lights. Gay's father Philip had been president of the Bullingdon and in our last year we decided to give him a final, triumphant ride in the Past and Present race. A high-class hunter chaser called Cash Account was borrowed for the purpose and, with only four other runners, all of them in on the plot, the stage seemed set for a victorious farewell.

But we had, alas, reckoned without Robin Higgin, a fearless but extremely shortsighted sportsman, who has since, I believe, become a pillar of the Kenya Jockey Club. Without a thick and cumbersome pair of spectacles, he was as near blind as makes no difference and, charging at 45 degrees towards the first fence, he caught Cash Account amidships and sent Gay's father into orbit. There followed a scene unique in my experience – a five-horse race with one faller and all the surviving runners striving, in vain, to catch their riderless opponent. What the stewards thought is not recorded but, sadly, Cash Account was much too fast for us. So the only 'rigged' race I took part in ended in ignominious disaster.

Many brave things are done in point-to-points, but my personal award for gallantry would go to a 12-year-old girl who, on the day of her exploit, never went near the course. Owing to a marked tendency to fall off and break things at the time, I was unable to ride a horse of mine called Chinese Pact at the Old Berks. John Cunningham, a vet, took my place and through no fault of his own, parted company at the second fence. As so often happens in such moments, the bridle came off with him – so it was with double misgivings that I set off in pursuit down the precipitous hill which leads from Lockinge to Wantage. Every bend in the road seemed likely to reveal a horrid sight and even if Chinese Pact (no child's pony at the best of times) negotiated the traffic, he was clearly going to take a bit of catching.

So imagine my feelings when, approaching the centre of Wantage, we see Chinese Pact trotting calmly towards us – ridden by a girl who turned out to be the daughter of Mr Cottrell, a local butcher. She had, it seems, been riding her pony through the outskirts of Wantage when this riderless, bridle-less horse galloped round the corner. 'I was afraid he might get hurt,' Miss Cottrell said calmly, 'so I turned my horse loose (he knows his way home) and put his bridle on yours. I'm afraid it does not fit too well.' Spoken by a grown man, those three magnificently-understated sentences would describe no mean achievement. From a 12-year-old standing under five feet and weighing about six stone, they represent a masterpiece.

---

7 JANUARY 2001

TWESELDOWN HEADING FOR A FALL

Andrew Baker

Tweseldown racecourse, nestling in a woody nook near Aldershot, looks like a set from Camberwick Green or Trumpton: too picturesque to be believable. Smoke curls from the chimneys of the pretty red-brick buildings and drifts away against a bright blue sky, while in the distance horses gallop out of sight behind the trees. It would be no surprise to see Windy Miller toddle out of the tower on the hill and start stacking bags of flour.

But the tower is no windmill: it is the commentary point and race control centre for the Tweseldown Racing Club point-to-point meeting, one of two such events held yesterday on the first day of a new point-to-point season. The pretty buildings and pretty horses are real and functional enough, but the timeless charm of the picture may be misleading. Such a sight, as old as racing in this country, has an air of permanence in that the very landscape seems to have been designed with competing horses in mind. But point-to-point racing depends on hunting for its horses: all those who compete must qualify in the hunting field. And with hunting under threat, many aficionados fear for the future of the point-to-point.

The distant charm of Tweseldown is not diminished in close-up. The secretary's office, changing rooms and stewards' room flank a tiny courtyard where the movers and shakers of this little world meet to exchange the gossip of the holidays and speculate on the season's racing to come. Inside the corner office, a log-fire burned busily while Angela Cooper supervised the distribution of packed lunches for the security guards and ensured that the stewards' walkie-talkies were functioning. Mrs Cooper has been helping behind the scenes at Tweseldown for a decade. 'It's a beautiful little course, isn't it?' she said. 'Just like a time capsule of the way that racing used to be. There's really nothing else like it in the area, and on a beautiful day it's no wonder people want to come and spend the day.'

So they were, standing three-deep beside the parade ring to assess the runners before backing their judgment with the line of bookmakers in front of the grandstand. Come race-time, there were two options: crowd on to the little stand, no bigger than a semi-detached house, or head up the hill in the centre of the track. Here there is a comical routine which allows those racegoers with energy to spare to witness most of the action. To see the start and the first fence, one must stand next to Windy Miller's tower. Then begins a hasty perambulation up, down and around the hill to catch glimpses of the field between the trees. It's a slightly hazardous process made more so by the dogs who are such a trademark of a day's point-to-pointing, but good manners always prevail.

But the horses are the ones doing the hard work, and most of them are pretty respectable competitors. Call It A Day, for instance, tipped as a star of the Men's Open Event, won the Whitbread Gold Cup in 1998, was third in the Grand National in 1999 and sixth at Aintree last year. He has since qualified for this class of racing by hunting with the Farmers' Bloodhounds, and seemed to the uninitiated a banker bet. One for the mugs, as it turned out. Aintree experience is all very well, but Tweseldown experience proved more valuable yesterday, as Call It A Day was well beaten by the local course specialist, Rectory Garden. A similar fate befell Energie Sud, owned by the National Hunt grandee Martin Pipe and trained by his son, David, who started at short odds for the Ladies' Open, but was found out by Persian Butterfly, owned by Steven Astaire, who is chairman of the Tweseldown Racing Club.

The winning owner thus arrived for the presentation carrying not only the trophy and Champagne but the microphone for the post-race interviews. Having briefly parted with the cup, only to be given it straight back, Astaire then thoughtfully inquired if the sponsor had managed to have any lunch yet before dashing off again, walkie-talkie in hand. This is the charm of the point-to-point, where power and pleasant behaviour go hand in hand, where the members' car park sports well-used Subarus rather than shiny Rolls-Royces and where the top prize is £120. It would all be idyllic were it not for the imminent threat of anti-hunting legislation.

Tweseldown's event, unlike most point-to-points, is run by a racing club rather than a hunt, and the volunteers who staff it love racing rather than hunting (though many enjoy both). But there is no escaping the bond between the two pursuits, and were hunting to be abolished then the very least of the challenges facing point-to-point racing would be a radical restructuring and an administrative crisis. Hence the popularity of the Countryside Alliance tent where Randolph and Margaret Willoughby were dispensing stickers and badges, calendars and that latest must-have for the livery-yard office, the field sports-themed mouse mat. Randolph reported: 'Everyone is stopping by to say hello and do their bit. People here know how important it is.'

On the rails, Desmond Gleeson, whose sign has proclaimed him 'The Point-to-Point Bookmaker' for 40 years, was also doing a lively trade. Gleeson's sign also announces 'Courtesy and Civility to All', but it's a fair bet that this pledge would be strained if the Prime Minister stepped up to his pitch with a fiver outstretched. 'It's a disgrace and a bloody nonsense what the Government are up to,' Gleeson said. 'They don't know the first thing about racing and they don't know the first thing about agriculture.' What odds, then, on the Tweseldown Racing Club point-to-point meeting taking place in ten years' time? 'This meeting will be here when Moses comes back from the bullrushes,' Gleeson declared.

Astaire was more measured. 'This meeting is organised by a racing club,' he said. 'We're not political. But it's clear that if there is some sort of ban on hunting, then point-to-point racing as such may be in danger, and may be replaced by a sort of second class of ordinary horse racing.' And who needs second-class racing when you can have first-class point-to-pointing?

---

24 JANUARY 1971

THE TRUTH TO JOCKEYS ISN'T ALWAYS THE SAME

John Lawrence

As I stood in front of the Taunton stewards the other day (assisting them, as the police would say, in their inquiries) it occurred to me that a jockey's role in such proceedings has never been adequately defined. What exactly is his function and to whom is his first duty? Is he merely a witness bound to tell the whole truth and nothing but the truth – or an advocate whose duty to his client, the owner, is to put his case as strongly as it can be put.

Nowadays, of course, the patrol camera often decides such issues more or less without argument. But it isn't always available and even when it is the evidence of jockeys concerned in a disputed finish is still called for and may still be decisive. So what should they do? The obvious, morally impeachable answer is 'tell the truth'. But after an incident as brief, violent and controversial as the finish of a horse race (or for that matter, as any magistrate would tell you, a motor accident) there are apt to be as many different 'truths' as there are witnesses.

And in any case the truth can be put in many different ways. 'Our horses touched three times' may, in the mouth of a more enthusiastic observer, become: "E murdered me going to the last, guv'nor, 'e murdered me landing over it, and then 'e murdered me all the way to the bleeding post.' That, indeed, was the evidence once given by a jockey who had better be nameless. It drew from a kindly but sceptical steward the cool reply: 'Well, Jones, how lucky it is you can only die once.'

In fact, of course, considering the frailty of human nature it is asking the impossible to expect a plain, unbiased account from a man on whose brow the sweat of a hard-fought finish is scarcely dry and through whose veins the adrenalin of mingled fear, anger and excitement, is still pumping. Clearly no jockey should knowingly lie, but short of that it can at least be argued that he owes it to his owner – to say nothing of those who have backed his horse – to put the facts in their most favourable light.

That, after all, is the duty of every barrister – and the answer to the common question, 'How on earth can you defend a man when you know he is guilty as sin?' is that justice requires both sides of a case to be put with as near as possible equal force. This can have embarrassing results. My grandfather, for instance, once defended a burglar against whom the chief evidence was a footprint alleged to fit a pair of gum-boots found in his house. By a masterly piece of cross-examination my grandfather destroyed the prosecution evidence on this crucial point and, as he sat down rather pleased with himself, his client leaned from the dock saying in a hoarse, stage whisper audible throughout the court: 'Well done, young man. I wasn't wearing them that night.'

But racing cases seldom have such sensational endings, and in them it seems to me short of telling downright untruths a jockey is perfectly within his rights to act as advocate for his owner, his horse and himself. Obviously, since he is also a witness, the wise steward will take this into account, keeping a large salt-cellar handy. In fact, if these random reflections do nothing else, they should make us all realise the debt we owe to the inventor of the patrol camera!

In the Taunton case referred to above, the stewards, in case you were wondering, were both models of fairness and absolutely right in their decision. And personally I was much too relieved to get round in some of the foulest going I've seen to do much silver-tongued advocacy on Stradivarius's behalf.

The whole day at Taunton must have been a waking nightmare for the stewards and left me thinking, not for the first time, what a ghastly job they often have, particularly at the smaller, less well-upholstered jumping meetings.

The popular picture of a typical local steward, largely derived, I am ashamed to say, from cynical scribes like myself, is of a port-swilling retired colonel combining the perspicacity of the three blind mice with the disciplinary outlook of Judge Jeffries and the racing knowledge of a Lithuanian washerwoman. But even if this was anything like a true image – which in a vast majority of cases it certainly isn't – such men still have a thoroughly unenviable task.

At Taunton last week, for instance, the stewards had first to decide whether to race at all on ground resembling a badly-drained snipe-bog (rising at some unearthly hour to do so) and then, as the rain poured down all afternoon, whether or how long to stand by their decision. On one hand they had to consider the paying public, the owners, jockeys and trainers and the unseen millions waiting to have a bet. But on the other they knew all too well that should a man or horse be seriously injured, few of these interested parties would hesitate to put the blame on them, the stewards, for racing in 'impossible conditions'.

Even for a well-paid official such a choice would be horribly difficult and full of anxiety, and the only reward English local stewards get is a free lunch and plenty of brickbats when things go wrong. At Taunton, in spite of the worst the weather could do, they were right and the stewards, whose boldness enabled five races to be run, are heartily to be congratulated.

---

13 NOVEMBER 2007

ROB WOOD GAVE JOHN FRANCOME A FRIGHT

Marcus Armytage

A half-century in racing is a long time, so let's hear it for Rob Wood, one of racing's unsung heroes, who has recently clocked up 50 years as a part-time clerk-of-the-scales. He will be retired next year when he reaches 70, the age at which British Horseracing Authority part-timers have to leave the crease. But, ever since he was 19 – Newton Abbot couldn't find anyone else to do the job at their Easter Bank Holiday meeting in 1957 and he was roped in without a minute's training – it has been his passion.

In between, much has changed. Then, of course, jockeys weighed out on balance scales and the clerk had a helper to put 28-pound blocks on one side while the jockey sat on the other. Before long, the scales will be connected by computer to Weatherbys and all the information will be downloaded to Wellingborough, but the clerk of the scales is not an endangered species; a machine can't tell if it's raining heavily and that's why a jockey has weighed in three pounds heavy. Of course, just as poachers have tried to put one over on gamekeepers for centuries, so have overweight jockeys tried to cheat the scales with varying degrees of ingenuity. Rob can spot a pair of paper-thin 'cheating boots' from 50 yards and usually greets their arrival at his scales with the avuncular, but firm, inquiry: 'You are planning to ride in those boots, aren't you?'

'The camaraderie of the changing room has always amazed me,' he said. 'I remember one jockey, who retired shortly afterwards because of weight problems, who came to weigh out with three colleagues. They were trying to get their feet under the scales and lift it to make him appear lighter. In the end he had to weigh out a stone overweight.'

Rob has only once had to object to a 'winner' – when a euphoric jockey walked straight back past the scales into the weighing room at Towcester, thereby committing one of racing's cardinal sins: forgetting to weigh in.

Obviously, this was only his part-time job. His day job was flying planes. After 12 years in the RAF he spent the rest of his career in commercial flying and rose to be chief pilot for Monarch Airways, flying boisterous holidaymakers to places like Malaga. One day one of his hostesses told him that they had a 'celebrity' on board. 'Oh, who's that?' said Rob. 'John Francome,' said the hostess. 'Well, send him up,' he said. To this day, Francome has never really recovered from seeing the clerk of the scales at the helm of the plane taking him to Spain. 'Racing people and aviators are completely different breeds,' he says. 'And there's no comparison with flying a plane these days and riding a novice chaser down to an open ditch – 99 per cent of flying is incident free.'

---

16 DECEMBER 1988

JOCKEYS WILL MISS LORD'S HELP

John Oaksey talks to Robin Lord, a recently-retired jockeys' valet, who has mixed memories of his 42 years in the weighing room

A good jockeys' valet needs to combine the qualities of a psychoanalyst, a diplomat, Jeeves at his wiliest, an insomniac rally driver, a thick-skinned comedian and, above all, a comforter when things go wrong. Robin Lord, who was all those things, retired last month after more than 40 years.

No doubt, the weighing room was a welcome change when Robin came out of the RAF after more than 50 raids as a pilot-engineer over Germany and France. His father, Arthur Lord, had married a jockey's daughter and set up as a valet before the War. Then, in 1946, a cataract formed in one of his eyes and Robin was summoned down to help him at Newton Abbot, wearing his demob suit. 'I think our fee was ten bob a day then,' he says. 'But maybe it was a pound. Mind you, the jockeys were only getting a fiver and not many races down the West were worth much more than a hundred quid. As for the changing rooms, they were just tin shacks. For washing we had an old copper with a fire underneath and the loos were just Elsans. Imagine 60 jockeys in there on a hot August afternoon with half of them wasting to do light! By the end of the day, you knew you had been in a fight, I can tell you.' But those early post-War days had their consolations. 'The whole jumping circus moved down West in August,' Robin says. 'Newton Abbot, Haldon, Buckfastleigh – we never needed to go home and there seemed to be a party every night.'

Jack Dowdeswell – champion in the second post-War season and, at 71, still riding out in Lambourn until very recently – was one of the jockeys Robin and his father looked after in those days. 'Jack used to get some dreadful falls, but there was always a smile on his face,' says Robin. As I remember from my own riding days, there was very nearly always a smile on Robin's, too. 'He was the best in the world at cheering you up,' says Bill Smith, another long-time client and one of the great valet's warmest admirers. Bill lives in Hayling Island, and whenever he came back covered in mud or shrouded in the gloom of defeat, Robin had this standing joke about deckchairs needing painting on the beach. It may not sound so funny now, but when you've just ridden another loser or hit the ground at 30 m.p.h., it is the old ones which work best.

Some of Robin Lord's happiest memories come from Liverpool and the Grand National – and one of the oddest from Worcester, where he went on Grand National day in 1967 'because there were more runners – and more work'. The changing room was so packed with people watching the television that Robin could scarcely see the screen. 'But I saw it better than John Kempton [Foinavon's trainer] standing beside me,' Robin says. 'When I said, "Well done" he asked me what on earth I meant. I was the first person to tell him he had won the National!'

Of course, there were sad days, too – the melancholy task of packing up a jockey's clothes for his wife or girlfriend to take to hospital and, just once or twice, days when one of your jockeys is not coming back at all. Robin had just helped Richard Linley dress before his tragic road accident and though not actually looking after Jessica Charles-Jones the day she had her fall, he remembers fondly allowing her to change in the men's room when pushed for time one day at Worcester.

A jumping valet's winter day starts before dawn, loading up his car with 30 or 40 saddles, weight-clothes, breeches, tights, scarves and boots which are either his stock-in-trade or belong to the group of jockeys he regularly looks after. It ends as it began – in the dark, after yet another long drive, following yet another spell of hectic, bustling action. Somehow, even with four different jockeys shouting at him from different sides of the room, Robin Lord still managed to look and behave like a calm and cheerful bishop. If 42 years of strain have left a mark on him, it does not show. Many hundreds of jockeys, with good reason to be grateful, will wish Robin luck and tight lines (he is a mad keen fisherman) in his well-earned retirement.

CHAPTER 12

WEIGHED IN

It's the end of the race, the end of the road, and winners and losers alike must weigh in with the great clerk of the scales in the sky. The jockeys, the trainers, the owners and their trusty steeds. They have brightened our days, lightened our nights, and, if we were lucky, lined our pockets. Their past deeds have been remembered in death notices, obituaries and tributes in various parts of the Telegraph. *From champion jockeys like Fred Archer, Steve Donoghue and Sir Gordon Richards, owners like the eccentric Miss Dorothy Paget and the Aga Khan, trainers like Fred Darling, to the horses themselves, including Red Rum, Desert Orchid, Phar Lap, Mandarin, and MySilv, the filly owned and mourned by thousands of members of a syndicate. And we finish, as we began, with Arkle, arguably the greatest racehorse ever to be led into the winner's enclosure. Thanks for the memories.*

---

11 NOVEMBER 1986

SIR GORDON, THE BEST JOCKEY OF THEM ALL

John Oaksey

'The most beautiful sight in the world,' the late Quiny Gilbert wrote, 'is Gordon Richards two lengths in front and his whip still swinging, when you have bet twice as much as you can afford.' However large or small your bet, the news of Sir Gordon Richards's death yesterday at the age of 82, will bring a lump to many throats from which the cry 'Come on, Gordon!' welcomed that 'beautiful sight' between 1925 and 1953 – when the most consistently successful British Flat race jockey of all time hung up his boots for good.

Only three days ago, 8 November, was the 100th anniversary of another great jockey's death, the day Fred Archer shot himself at Newmarket, aged only 28. Archer was champion 13 times and rode over 200 winners in seven different seasons. Only one other man before Gordon Richards beat Archer's record total of 246 in 1933 and no one, repeat no one, has done it since Sir Gordon retired. The year 1933 was the seventh of his 26 championships, but this is no time for futile statistical comparisons. Unlike Fred Archer and Lester Piggott, Gordon Richards – never troubled by weight – could eat what he wanted throughout his riding career; but unlike them, too, he had neither racing nor riding in his blood.

Born into a family of eight (his mother had 12 children, but four died), he was the son of strict Primitive Methodist parents who might well have been expected to object when their son answered an advertisement for stable lads. But not a bit of it. Gordon's mother had already refused to let him go down the mines and his father, a mining contractor, said: 'Go and ride, if you want. If it does not work at least you'll have learnt a lesson.'

If you look to your left travelling up the M4 towards London, you can still see the two places, Foxhill and Russley Park, where Gordon learnt his first and most important racing lessons – at the feet of the great Steve Donoghue, then Jimmy White's stable jockey. It was there, too, that his genius first became apparent and from Russley, in his first season out of apprenticeship, weighing six stone 11 pounds, he first headed the list with 118 winners.

But just because he was a natural lightweight, let no one suppose that this extraordinary sportsman 'had it easy'. Before the next season started, the new champion was found to be suffering from tuberculosis, still in those days very often a fatal disease. Though, after missing one whole season, Gordon's recovery was rapid and complete, there were several other periods when falls, injuries and losing runs damaged his surprisingly fragile confidence. But truly brave men are not the ones who have no fear and Sir Gordon, highly intelligent and imaginative, was one of that much rarer breed, those who have doubts but overcome them.

He must also have overcome numerous temptations because his retirement came well before the modern era of huge prize money, multi-million dollar stud syndications and the gift of stallion shares to successful jockeys, which puts them among the world's best rewarded sportsmen. Sir Gordon Richards was certainly not a poor man when he retired, but his rewards did not begin to compare with those of his successors. In a sport which daily redistributes millions of pounds tax free, *any* first-flight jockey was – and still is – the object of many and various seductive approaches. But throughout his long career, and even in the gossip-ridden world of racing and betting, Sir Gordon's integrity was unquestioned. He was a rock in an often treacherous sea and his universally popular knighthood in 1953 was awarded at least as much on account of the example he set as the 4,870 winners he rode.

Although Sir Gordon became a successful trainer and later tireless and skilful manager of Lady Beaverbrook's good horses, it is – needless to say – as a jockey that he will be remembered. From the moment I started going racing until he retired, the one infallible recipe for making a dull day enjoyable was 'Watch Gordon Richards'. Trainers lucky enough to employ him have described the wonderful feeling of confidence that short, square figure inspired with its rolling sailor's walk. And though the price was often on the short side, young, hopeful punters felt the same.

There are no starting stalls in those days, but you knew that Gordon would get off precisely where he wanted. Then, though he preferred to be up near the leaders, any horse who needed relaxing could be 'put to sleep' just as effectively as Eddery lulls them nowadays. And then, best of all, you would see the shoulders start to hunch and the whip begin to wave and even if someone else was sitting motionless, you would know you still had hope. Because, with a longer rein and much longer stirrups and a much more upright back and an altogether different method from the modern masters, you *knew* the horse would run home straight and as fast as he was able. That was 'the most beautiful sight in the world' and, like many others, I shall always be grateful to Sir Gordon for creating it and proud that we were there to cheer him home.

———

9 NOVEMBER 1886

SUICIDE OF FRED ARCHER

When this startling announcement was displayed in Fleet Street yesterday afternoon it was at first received with incredulity, although it was known that the famous jockey was suffering from severe cold at his home at Newmarket. The information was soon verified, and when the details of his untimely decease by his own hand became known the shock was of an even more startling character, and widespread regret was manifested. The name of Fred Archer was so well known all over the world that his sudden demise was looked upon as a great calamity, and was the chief topic of conversation among all classes during the evening. On Thursday, Archer was in the saddle at Lewes, and while there he caught a cold, necessitating his return home that evening. The following day he became rapidly worse, although nothing serious was feared, until Sunday, when it was found that the patient was suffering from an attack of typhoid fever. Early yesterday morning a bulletin was published announcing that his condition was much more favourable, and hopes were entertained of his rapid recovery by his friends and relatives. About one o'clock Archer was attended by his sister, Mrs Coleman, and the nurse, when he desired the latter to retire. A short time later Mrs Coleman, who was at the window, hearing a movement, turned, and was horrified to see Archer staggering across the room with a revolver in his hand. With great presence of mind she at once attempted to disarm him, but before she could do anything Archer, while holding her tightly with one hand, deliberately placed the muzzle of the pistol in his mouth, fired, and immediately dropped dead. It was subsequently discovered that the bullet had severed his spinal column, and had passed out through the neck. The terrible news spread rapidly, and from all parts messages and inquiries poured in, the Prince of Wales being among the first to telegraph inquiries. Every other topic of conversation gave place to the decease of the great jockey, who was so much respected by all with whom he had dealings, and universally popular with all classes of sporting men.

Frederick Archer was the son of William Archer, a steeplechase rider, living at Cheltenham, and was born at Prestbury, near that town, on 11 January, 1857. From a very early age he was fond of riding, and so well did he figure in the saddle that when only 11 years of age he was apprenticed to Mr Matthew Dawson, of Newmarket. This was the first step to a career which has been of the most brilliant character, and which made the name of Archer famous all over the world, even among classes who know little of horse racing. Matthew Dawson took a great fancy to the boy, and gave him every opportunity for rapid advancement in his profession. His first winning mount was in a steeplechase at Bangor, where he rode a pony named Maid of the Mist, and at that time he only scaled four stone one pound. After going through the usual routine of a jockey's apprenticeship, he appeared in the saddle at Chesterfield Races in 1870, where he began his brilliant record by steering Athol Daisy to victory in a Nursery handicap. Before the end of that season young Archer had a record of two wins in his 15 mounts. In the following year he rode 40 times, being successful upon three occasions. The year 1872, however, saw him in the saddle upon 180 occasions, and his winning list numbered 27. H. Constable figured at the head of the list in 1873, while Archer was only two behind, having out of 422 mounts been first past the post 107 times.

Archer now became much sought after, his performance in the pigskin having brought him into general notice, and in 1874, with 147 victories, he headed the winning jockeys' record, while the following year he rode 172 winners of the 605 appearances in the saddle, among them being the One Thousand and Oaks on Lord Falmouth's Spinaway, while in the Chesterfield Stakes he steered that nobleman's Skylark to victory. In 1876 Archer failed to win any of the Classic events, but out of 662 mounts he scored 207 wins, including the City and Suburban on Thunder, and the Cesarewitch on Rosebery. The following year Archer was first past the post upon 218 occasions out of a total number of tries amounting to 602, among those victories being that for the Derby, while he was also victorious in the St Leger and City and Suburban, his Blue Riband success being on Silvio. Archer still further increased his winning list in 1878, when of the 619 times he sported silk he was first no fewer than 229 times, and whenever Archer rode he was sure of a big following. In the tenth year of his horsemanship Archer piloted 197 winners out of a total of 588 mounts, among them being the Oaks and One Thousand Guineas on Wheel of Fortune, the Two Thousand on Charibert, and the City and Suburban on the American horse Parole. It was in the following year that Muley Edris 'savaged' the popular jockey, which accident caused a temporary retirement from the saddle after the Goodwood meeting of that year, but he atoned for this in 1881 when he landed no less than 220 winners with 582 mounts, his chief win being on Bend Or, whom he got home for the Derby. Each succeeding year he has increased his winning list, and last season he reached his highest figure, having been successful upon 246 occasions out of 667 mounts. During his last five years Archer's principal performances have been winning the Leger on Dutch Owen in 1882, the Two Thousand Guineas on Galliard in 1883, the Derby and St Leger on Melton, the Oaks on Lonely, and Two Thousand Guineas on Paradox in 1885. The present year he won the Derby and Leger on Ormonde. The deceased was married to Miss Rose Nelly Dawson, the eldest of Mr John Dawson's daughters on 31 January 1883, but, after two years of married life, Mrs Archer died, her loss being keenly felt by her husband. Sunday was the anniversary of her death, and this fact may probably have had some bearing on the tragic event of yesterday.

A Newmarket correspondent, telegraphing last night, states: Between Saturday and Sunday Fred Archer became worse, and unmistakable symptoms of typhoid fever asserted themselves. This fever, acting on a spare and delicate frame, quickly raised the most serious apprehensions of his friends. Its effects on the deceased's mind, though not so outwardly observable, were, as the result showed, even more disastrous. This morning he was very ill. There seemed, however, nothing to be done but to wait the development of the disease. About 25 minutes after two o'clock this afternoon Archer's nurse left him alone with his sister, Mrs Coleman, in order that they might have some private talk. At a moment when Mrs Coleman was looking out at the window Archer suddenly got out of bed, and possessed himself of a revolver he had in the room. Mrs Coleman turned at the moment of his rising, and sprang towards him; but he was too quick, for, as she caught hold of him, he put the barrel of the revolver in his mouth and fired, he falling, bleeding and dying, in his sister's arms. Mrs Coleman was overpowered with the fearful sight, but she was able to get to the bell and ring for assistance. This was quickly at hand, but it was soon found to be unavailing. The doctor arrived very speedily and at once pronounced him dead. It is needless to say that the tragic end of a man so greatly beloved and so universally admired in the sporting world has elicited the deepest emotions of surprise and sorrow. In Newmarket every person is talking of his kindness of heart, and his incomparable achievements. As for the revolver, the unhappy proximity of which to his hand has caused so much grief, it appears that he had bought it in consequence of the exposed situation of the house, and some attentions it had previously received from burglars. Archer was a widower, his wife having died two years ago, and he leaves one child, a little girl. Since his illness commenced the telegraphic inquiries have been continuous. These have been followed tonight by innumerable messages of condolence with his brother, Mr Charles Archer, his sister, Mrs Coleman, her child, and other relatives.

On the 16th of last month Archer visited Ireland for the purpose of riding Cambustmore for Lord Londonderry in the Lieutenant's Plate at The Curragh. He attained the object of his visit as Cambustmore won the race easily on the following Thursday, and after a couple of other mounts on the same afternoon he returned home in order to ride St Mirin for the Cambridgeshire. In order to get down to the handicapped weight Archer underwent great privation, and for three consecutive days went without food, not a bit of any sort passing his lips, while on the other hand he dosed himself with trying medicine, and spent the best part of his time in the Turkish bath attached to his private residence at Falmouth House. By these means he was able to ride St Mirin at eight stone seven, or one pound overweight, in the Cambridgeshire, but the effort cost him his life, for it left him in such a weak state of health that, after riding at Brighton and on the first day of Lewes last week, he was compelled to relinquish his professional duties and seek rest. He was within two months of completing his 30th year. He stood five feet eight and a half inches in height, so that for a jockey he was tall, and his stature seemed the greater because of his slim figure. He worked tremendously hard to prevent his weight increasing to a degree that would have rendered it impossible for him to pursue his vocation. He had to undergo a regimen more severe than falls to the lot of most men, even in his own arduous profession. The perpetual strain of training had undoubtedly affected prejudicially a constitution none too robust to begin with. All this contributed to the catastrophe, the typhoid fever finding a ready victim when it flew to his head. This it did so suddenly that his friends can be excused for not being more on the alert. Dr Wright, his medical attendant, had only left him an hour before, and anticipated no such frenzy of the sick man. The consulting physician, Dr Latham, of Cambridge, was to have visited him again tomorrow. As might be expected, Mrs Coleman is tonight in an utterly prostrate condition, owing to the awful shock to her system. She should be the principal witness at the inquest tomorrow, but it is doubtful whether she will be able to undergo the ordeal involved in that inquiry.

24 MARCH 1945

STEVE DONOGHUE

Hotspur

Racing has lost its biggest personality by the sudden death of Steve Donoghue, who was 60, in London early yesterday morning. No jockey of this century rode so many famous horses. None was more admired by the experts for brilliant horsemanship or more beloved by the general public whose idol he was for 20 years. His fame and popularity were worldwide.

Donoghue rode six Derby winners beginning with Pommern (1915) and Gay Crusader (1917) in substitute races at Newmarket in the last War. Then came a wonderful Epsom hat-trick on Humorist (1921), Captain Cuttle (1922) and Papyrus (1923) followed by Manna in 1925.

But of all the horses he rode, Steve's favourite was old Brown Jack. They formed a wonderful partnership. Brown Jack won the Queen Alexandra Stakes at Ascot, the longest race run under Jockey Cup rules six times in succession. Steve rode him in 14 of his winning races which produced £23,500 in prize money for the owner Sir Harold Wernber. Describing the horses he had ridden Steve once said that Brown Jack was his favourite, Humorist the gamest, Gay Crusader the best, The Tetrarch the fastest and Tishy the slowest.

Donoghue was a fearless rider as well as a superb judge of pace. That is why the Epsom course was his happiest hunting ground. Horses with Steve up used to come bowling down the hill and round Tattenham Corner like a cricket ball. He won every race of importance in England and had ridden for nearly all the leading owners of the last quarter of a century. Steve took out a trainer's licence in 1938 and met with a fair measure of success.

---

19 OCTOBER 1995

NATIONAL HERO WHO DEFIED ALL THE ODDS

John Oaksey

Red Rum, who starred in five consecutive Grand Nationals, also played a unique part in preserving the great race and its Aintree home. His reign coincided with one of Aintree's most difficult periods and, but for him, it might easily now be a housing estate. A year before Red Rum's first Grand National in 1973, Mirabel Topham sold Aintree to Bill Davies, a self-made tycoon property developer. Three disastrously unprofitable years later, when Ladbrokes took over management of the course and race on a rental agreement, the future of both was in grave doubt.

In their energetic efforts to publicise and popularise the National meeting, Ladbrokes had one unbeatable trump card. 'Without Red Rum, Ginger McCain, all the help they gave us – and the luck of having them so close at Southport – our job would have been ten times as difficult,' said Mike Dillon of Ladbrokes. 'In fact, we might never have made it.' In Ladbrokes' first year, 1976, Red Rum, already a dual winner, ran second to Rag Trade. Twelve months later, he made sporting history by winning for a third time, and even in 1978 it was only on the eve of the race that the vets decided he was not fit to try again. 'Even then, Ginger let him lead the parade,' said Dillon. 'All those years, for most people, Red Rum was the Grand National . . .'

For many, despite his death yesterday at the age of 30, he still is – and his ascent to steeplechasing immortality will always remain one of racing's happiest, rags-to-riches, roller-coaster fairy-tales. Aesop and Dick Francis working in tandem at their most imaginative would have been hard-pressed to dream it up. The first time I saw Red Rum was on his first appearance at Aintree – in a five-furlong, two-year-old selling race, the day before Foinavon's sensational 1967 Grand National. They had no photo-finish in those days, and Red Rum, nearly a month short of his actual second birthday, was adjudged to have got up in the last stride for a dead-heat with Curlicue. This was a filly whose trainer, my late father-in-law Ginger Dennistoun, considered a certainty – and he encouraged all of us to back her.

This was the first of three occasions on which I have wished Red Rum on another planet. The other two were the day he caught an heroic Crisp in 1973, and the following year's Scottish Grand National, in which instead of having the decency to show signs of his successful Aintree exertions three weeks earlier, he made my mount, poor Proud Tarquin, look like a tortoise from the last. But long before he began making history himself, Red Rum had passed through the hands of several well-known racing personalities.

Tim Molony, whose five jockeys' championships and string of big-race triumphs never included a Grand National, bought him in Ireland for 400 guineas as a yearling. Molony's specific aim was to win that Aintree seller for Maurice Kingsley – on whose Sir Ken Molony won three Champion Hurdles. A year later, after another desperate Aintree finish (Red Rum's tenth and last Flat race in which, receiving the full Lester Piggott treatment, he was beaten a short head over a mile), Kingsley sold him to Mrs Lurlene Brotherton. Bobby Renton had won the 1950 Grand National for Mrs Brotherton with Freebooter and they had been searching in vain for a replacement ever since.

But, though Red Rum won three hurdle races and five steeplechases in the Brotherton colours, he was diagnosed, in the winter of 1971, as a victim of pedalosteitis — a usually crippling disease of the foot.

Some inspired veterinary treatment and the tender, loving patience of Red Rum's devoted stable-lass, Sandra Kendall, combined to achieve a miraculous cure. But the real miracle was still to come. For now, with younger, apparently sounder horses at her disposal, Mrs Brotherton insisted on sending Red Rum to the Doncaster Sales in August 1972. For poor Sandra and Anthony Gillam, the young man who had taken over the Renton stable when Tommy Stack decided to concentrate on riding, it was a heart-breaking decision. For the horse himself, with hindsight, it was a heaven-sent stroke of luck without which he would probably never have won a single National — because Donald McCain, the second-hand car dealer-turned trainer who paid 6,000 guineas to buy Red Rum for the Southport businessman Noel LeMare, did not have any fine grass gallops. His horses did all their serious work on Southport beach, paddling afterwards in the sea. It was the perfect training ground for any horse with inflamed feet — and almost certainly the only kind of launch-pad from which Red Rum could have rocketed to glory.

But do not put much else in this story down to luck. When a horse jumps round Aintree five years running without once looking in serious danger of a fall, you can bet your boots he has made a lot of his own luck. Brian Fletcher and Stack will both tell you how Red Rum used to see trouble before it even began to happen. 'He could sidestep with all four feet off the ground,' said Stack. 'As clever as he was brave, and that's saying something.'

Arkle and Desert Orchid, the only post-War steeplechasers to have achieved a comparable hold on public affection, both had a far easier, more carefully mapped-out climb to the top than Red Rum. Both, for instance, were trained throughout by one great expert and while Desert Orchid had three jockeys, Arkle, effectively, had only one.

Bred to be a precocious sprinter-miler, Red Rum was bought cheaply for just that purpose. Given a hard race before he was two, he had 109 more in the next nine seasons, and very few of them could be called 'easy'. He passed through the hands of five trainers, was ridden by 20 jockeys, and overcame one potentially fatal physical affliction. Yet, until his final illness, this marvellous survivor was still, essentially, a happy horse, in love with life. When you remember how it began, his whole career was a triumph over odds. Five times he played to a worldwide television audience of millions. No single horse, in fact, can have given pleasure and excitement to so many people. Let that be Red Rum's epitaph.

14 NOVEMBER 2006

HE NEVER GAVE UP, HE WAS THE FINEST HORSE I RODE IN MY CAREER

Richard Dunwoody

Dessie was, without doubt, the finest horse I rode in my career. What made him so special was not just natural ability but also his innate competitiveness; he never gave up, never knew when he was beaten and would keep on trying in races when other horses would quit and get swallowed up very quickly.

It was towards the latter stages of his career when I first rode Dessie, and he was still pretty exuberant to say the least. He was extremely free-running when Colin Brown rode him in his early days. It was this energy and power that made him distinctive, and he always liked to let his rider know who was boss. I once rode him, well after his retirement, in a parade at the Royal Welsh Show. Even with no race to win, he still ran away with me straight out of the show ring!

Although most famous for his great victories at Kempton, for me he put in his most memorable performance at Fairyhouse in the 1990 Irish Grand National. He lapped up the attention in the parade ring beforehand and come the race he was phenomenal, winning it while giving two stone and a half to most of the field.

It might be surprising that my most poignant memory of Desert Orchid was in a race when I was not even riding him. The 1989 Cheltenham Gold Cup was contested in the most horrendous conditions after heavy rain and snow. Despite the ground not being to his preference, nor the left-handed course, he gave Simon Sherwood an incredible ride, to win by a length and a half. I finished third on Charter Party and, on hearing the crowd erupt for Dessie, I realised that I was witnessing a rare moment in sporting history. It remains etched in my mind as a great memory of the horse and the sport.

Desert Orchid did more for National Hunt than any other horse in recent history since Arkle and Red Rum. The people loved him for many of the same reasons that I did as a jockey: the front-running style, gutsy perform-ances and never-say-die attitude to his racing. It was a great privilege to ride a true legend of the sport and he will be fondly missed and remembered.

10 FEBRUARY 1960

MISS DOROTHY PAGET DIES IN HER SLEEP

RACING LOSES ONE OF ITS WEALTHIEST OWNERS

Miss Dorothy Paget, who died in her sleep at her home at Chalfont St Giles, Buckinghamshire, yesterday, was one of the wealthiest and most enthusiastic owners in British horse racing. She was 54. The younger daughter of the late Lord Queenborough, the first baron, by his first marriage to Miss Pauline Whitney, she inherited a fortune from her grandfather, Mr William C. Whitney, a former United States Navy Secretary. Despite her great wealth, she lived quietly and was seldom seen by local people. She had suffered ill health for a number of years, but whenever possible she attended racecourses to watch her horses run.

HOTSPUR writes: The death of Miss Dorothy Paget, for a quarter of a century one of the leading owner breeders of the British Turf and famous as owner of Golden Miller, the most brilliant chaser of all time, is a severe blow to racing. At the time of her death Miss Paget had over 30 horses in training with Sir Gordon Richards for the Flat and ten jumpers with H.C.D. Nicholson at Cheltenham as well as nearly 100 horses including mares and young stock in Ireland.

Miss Paget was equally well known on the Flat and steeplechasing. But there was little doubt that over the years she was more successful as an owner of jumpers, though she won a War-time Derby with Straight Deal, which was bred at Elsenham, her stud in Essex. Miss Paget, who as a girl was extremely good on a horse, first came into racing under National Hunt Rules when she had a few humble horses in training with Alec Law, at Findon. She then sent her horses to be trained by Basil Briscoe at Newmarket.

She quickly became well known when Briscoe bought on her behalf Golden Miller who won five Cheltenham Gold Cups in succession for Miss Paget, and the 1934 Grand National in record time. Miss Paget gave 6,000 guineas for Golden Miller and in the same period 4,000 guineas for Insurance, with whom she won the Champion Hurdle at Cheltenham.

Golden Miller was her only winner of the Grand National, but she came very near to winning three others. Kilstar was third in the 1939 National to Workman, Legal Joy was second in 1952 to Teal and Mont Tremblant, the best chaser to carry her colours since the War, second under top weight to Early Mist in 1953. Nearly all Miss Paget's jumpers were home-bred, but Mont Tremblant was one of the exceptions. He was bought in France and won the

1952 Cheltenham Gold Cup as a six-year-old. Her third horse to win the Gold Cup was Roman Hackle in 1940.

On the Flat her outstanding horse was Straight Deal with whom she won the 1943 Derby. Straight Deal was trained at Epsom by Walter Nightingall and was ridden by the present Epsom trainer T.H. Carey. Previously she was a big buyer of yearlings, two or three of whom were notoriously unsuccessful. In 1936 she gave the then record price for a yearling of 15,000 guineas for Colonel Payne, a half-brother to the 1932 2,000 Guineas winner, Orwell. Colonel Payne was a moderate racehorse and was sold for 250 guineas. At the same time she gave 6,600 guineas for Tuppence who was equally mediocre, though he was all the rage for the 1933 Derby among women backers, starting at 10–1 and finishing nearer last than first.

In 1934, Miss Paget had started her own stud farm and once it was well established nearly all her horses on the Flat were home-bred. In previous days the best horse to carry her colours was Wyndham who as a Bossover colt was one of the best two-year-olds of his season, winning the New Stakes at Royal Ascot and other races. In post-War years her biggest winners were Aldborough, winner of the 1950 Doncaster Cup and the Queen Alexandra Stakes at Ascot, and Nucleus, winner of the 1955 Jockey Club Stakes and second to Meld in the St Leger. Probably Nucleus was the best horse she bred after the War.

Miss Paget, with her large figure and old-fashioned clothes, was known by sight by everybody who went racing, but she was shy and usually spoke only to her immediate entourage and her trainers. She undoubtedly enjoyed her racing thoroughly, loved to have a tilt at the Ring and trembled with excitement while watching her horses doing battle. It seems certain that her death will mean the biggest disposal sale of thoroughbred stock since the death of Mr J.A. Dewar.

OUR ESTATES CORRESPONDENT writes: Dorothy Paget has often been described as 'fabulous' and as an 'enigma'. The descriptions fitted her wealth and her life. She was the daughter of one of the wealthiest American families, the Whitneys, and of an English peer, Lord Queenborough, of ample means. Her American mother died in 1916 providing Miss Paget with some of the great financial resources which enabled her to keep her name in the forefront of British racing for so many years.

Her father died in 1949, leaving net estate of around £159,000. The residue, after £88,411 estate duty and minor legacies, went to the three daughters of his second marriage. He wrote that he had made no provision for his daughter, Dorothy Paget, because both she and her sister, Lady Baillie, who lives in Kent, had inherited liberal provision from their mother and American grandfather. This liberal provision, which it is said ran into several million pounds between the two girls, enabled Miss Paget to pursue her particular interests in life, first motor-racing in the early 1930s, and when this failed, the Turf.

She never lived ostentatiously. For about 20 years her home was the unhistoric creeper-clad mansion surrounded by 40 acres at Chalfont St Giles, known as Hermits Wood. Miss Paget lived a secluded life, unapproachable, with a well-paid staff of about 14 to run her establishment. In most things she was unorthodox. In an off moment she said she 'hated meeting people, but hated being alone'.

In 1949, she proposed selling her stud farm at Elsenham, near Bishop's Stortford, Essex, and moved all her breeding stock to the Ballymacoll Stud, near Dublin, which she owned at her death. The Essex land, still in her ownership, is used for farming. Though Miss Paget spent more money than anyone else chasing the Turf's major prizes, and had little else to interest her, she did not neglect charities. In the War she supplied funds to buy a number of ambulances. A more recent gift was the presentation of 2,000 cigarettes, one New Year, to the London Transport staff who served her Buckinghamshire home on behalf of her staff.

---

10 JUNE 1953

MR F. DARLING

GREATEST TRAINER OF HIS GENERATION

Hotspur

Three days after Pinza, whom he bred, had won the Derby, Fred Darling, the outstanding trainer of his generation, died at Beckhampton yesterday after a long illness. He was 69. Darling saddled three Derby winners before he was 40 and in all trained seven – Captain Cuttle in 1922, Manna (1925), Coronach (1926), Cameronian (1931), Bois Roussel (1938), his own Pont l'Eveque (1940) and Owen Tudor (1941). No other trainer in the 20th century has a comparable record.

It was not surprising that successes came to him early in life for his father, the late Sam Darling, was the creator of the great Beckhampton stable, which he handed on to his son and had himself sent out two Derby winners – Galtee More (1897) and Ard Patrick (1902). Fred started as a lightweight jockey, but soon grew too heavy for riding, and when he was only just turned 20 was appointed private trainer to the late Lady De Bathe (Mrs Langtry). One of his first feats was to win for her the Cesarewitch with Yentol in 1908.

He trained several winners for this patron, and when she reduced her stable he took a post in Germany as trainer to the brothers von Weinberg, for whom he won upwards of £50,000 in stakes in the course of two years. Then he returned to assist his father at Beckhampton and when Sam Darling gave up training to devote himself entirely to his 1,200-acre farm, he took over the control of the Beckhampton stable.

In the years immediately following the War, success followed success, and his establishment was easily the strongest in the country. The late Lord Woolavington was his chief patron, and then the late Lord Dewar joined the stable. The late Mr H.E. Morriss, owner of Manna, had horses bought for him by cable from Shanghai. During the First World War, Lord Woolavington, then Mr James Buchanan, had bought for 500 guineas a yearling by Marcovil, who was named Hurry On, was never beaten, and won a substitute St Leger. Great as he was as a race horse, he was greater as a sire, and at the time of his death, in 1936, his stock had won well over £300,000 in stake money.

It was with the stock of Hurry On that Fred Darling achieved some of his greatest successes. His first important winner was Captain Cuttle, who won the Derby and £15,037 in stakes. A few years later there came the slashing Coronach, who won the Derby, St Leger, Coronation Cup, and £48,224 in stakes. Manna was bought as a yearling at Doncaster for 6,000 guineas by Darling on behalf of Mr Morriss, and won the 2,000 Guineas and the Derby. Cameronian was bred by the late Lord Dewar and bequeathed to his nephew, Mr John A. Dewar, for whom he won the 2,000 Guineas and the Derby. Darling trained Four Course to win the 1,000 Guineas for Lord Ellesmere.

Darling was leading trainer for the first time in 1926, and for the last time when he retired owing to ill-health in 1947 – to be succeeded at Beckhampton by Noel Murless. In 1942, Darling saddled Big Game and Sun Chariot to win four of the five Classic races for King George VI. Sun Chariot won the 1,000 Guineas, the Oaks and the St Leger, and Fred considered her the best filly he trained.

No trainer turned out his horses better than Darling – the 'Beckhampton bloom' has for long been a byword in racing – and few trainers were better judges of a horse. His passing is a great loss to racing in this country.

---

10 JANUARY 1997

TOUGH MYSILV WAS MARE IN A MILLION

John Oaksey

As all animal lovers know, some of the saddest things in life are the dogs and horses you outlive. Several thousand people were painfully reminded of that tragic truth this week when their beloved Mysilv had to be put down. In fact, since the death in action of Dawn Run – whom Mysilv resembled in so many ways – no jumping race mare can have been so widely mourned or, come to that, have done much more for the winter game. Quite apart from courage, agility and 11 victories, Mysilv, who in her time had nearly 10,000 'owners', was the most successful so far of the welcome fashion for shared 'club' or 'syndicate' ownership.

David Minton, the bloodstock agent, had his eye on Mysilv in 1993. In her second season, trained by Chris Wall, she won a claimer and a handicap on the Flat. 'The form was quite respectable,' Minty says, 'but later when I bought her for 27,000 guineas at Newmarket, there were plenty who said I had paid far too much. I thought I might have, too…' But, not for the first time in Mysilv's career, the 'must-be-mad' school of thought were soon forced magnificently to eat their words. Trained by David Nicholson for the 130-strong Million In Mind syndicate, Mysilv, a smallish but compact and powerful chestnut, won her first six races over hurdles, including the Triumph Hurdle. Nicholson remembers: 'Her first morning here, she jumped 36 tree trunks, and from day one, she simply ate them. She just took to jumping as if she had been doing it for years – and she was even better on the racecourse.'

The Million In Mind rules dictate that all syndicate horses must be sold at the end of one season. So, to the dismay of at least one part-owner, the Triumph Hurdle winner was sent to Doncaster spring sales. And again, when Charles Egerton, acting on behalf of the Elite Racing Club, paid 155,000 guineas (a world-record price for a jumper) almost everyone said: 'He must be mad.' I have to admit that, despite showing a profit on the deal as an M-In-M shareholder, I was inclined to agree. Remarkably few Triumph winners have gone on to fame or fortune, and with that price tag round Mysilv's neck, Egerton faced what looked an uphill, 'hiding-to-nothing' task.

No wonder he and his staff are shattered by Monday's tragedy. Because Mysilv did both them and the Elite club proud – winning a Tote Gold Trophy, finishing an undisgraced fifth in Alderbrook's Champion Hurdle and, only two days after an even-closer sixth last year, fighting that memorable Stayers' Hurdle battle with Cyborgo. Mysilv's last four runs – two at Cheltenham, two in France – all ended in narrow, honourable defeat. But the French Champion Hurdle left her jarred and sore. So, with another Stayers' as her Cheltenham target, Egerton was in no hurry. Mysilv was only doing a steady canter when the fatal injury to her pelvis was sustained.

'What might have been?' pays no training bills but, as we mourn, it is hard not to reflect on the further and better services this courageous mare might still have done to racing. Both Adrian Maguire and Jamie Osborne, the two jockeys who knew Mysilv best, are convinced steeplechase fences would have been more a help than a hindrance. If Mysilv jumped fences as well as she did hurdles, the sky may have been the limit. And then, what about breeding? Suffering, as we are, a chronic shortage of good jumpers, the loss of a mare with Mysilv's potential is serious indeed. By the St Leger winner Bustino (maternal grandsire of Nashwan), she is a direct descendant in the female line of Aloe, one of the century's most productive foundation mares. Alcide, Parthia, Above Suspicion and the great American horse Round Table are just some of the winners from this famous line. If only Mysilv could have gone back to her birthplace Overbury Stud (just a few miles from the Nicholson stable), who knows what she might have produced?

---

6 APRIL 1932

PHAR LAP DEAD

'WONDERHORSE' WHO WAS COMING HERE
COST 100 GUINEAS; WON £66,450

Phar Lap, the 'wonder horse' of New Zealand and Australia, has died of colic at the E.D. Perry Stock Farm, in California. It was taken ill yesterday morning, says an Exchange message, and the illness developed so rapidly that the veterinary surgeons were helpless. The horse died at 2.20 p.m., but the news was kept secret for some time while efforts were made to communicate with the owner, Mr David Davis, who was flying to Los Angeles.

With the death of Phar Lap passes one of the greatest racehorses of all time. Bred in New Zealand from an English-bred sire, Night Raid, from a New Zealand mare, Eubreaty, Phar Lap was bought as a yearling by Mr Davis, at Wellington, for 100 guineas. He was afterwards sent to Australia, and won every honour on the Turf that country had to offer. Mr Davis intended to send the horse to England this year to run in some of our big handicaps, such as the Cesarewitch and Cambridgeshire. He has won over all distances from six furlongs to two miles.

Only last month Phar Lap carried off one of the richest prizes on the American Turf, the Agua Caliente Handicap, worth £10,000. His winnings in stake money amounted to £66,450, a total which has been surpassed by only one other, the American horse, Sun Beau, who won nearly £75,000.

Phar Lap's victory in the Agua Caliente Handicap may have led indirectly to his death. After the race he was being garlanded. He took fright at this, stamped on a concrete step and injured a foot. The injury, however, was stated to be not serious, and he afterwards wore a special shoe.

Phar Lap's name in Senegalese means 'wing of the sky' or 'lightning'. Phar Lap's owner issued a challenge in 1930 to race the gelding against any horse over any distance for any amount. On the eve of the Melbourne Cup, Australia's greatest Turf event, Phar Lap was shot at by hooligans, but celebrated the occasion by winning the cup and three other races during the meeting.

He was such a consistent winner that his entry for any race caused other owners to withdraw their horses. On the totalisator and with bookmakers in Australia, it was impossible to back the horse. A racing authority well known in England and Australia said last night: 'A horse capable of beating Phar Lap would be worth, I should think, quite £100,000.'

---

22 JULY 1976

MANDARIN 'BRAVEST OF THE BRAVE' DIES AT 25

Marlborough (John Oaksey)

If it is true that old soldiers never die, then one of the bravest there has been faded away at Lambourn yesterday when, in his 26th year, Madame Peggy Hennessy's Mandarin collapsed at Saxon House. It had been his home since he came from France as a three-year-old — 'one of the fattest,' his devoted trainer, Fulke Walwyn, says, 'that I have seen'. But it is not for his figure that Mandarin will be remembered.

More than anything else, it will always be for that hot summer day in 1962 when he and Fred Winter overcame the best chasers in France and the impossible handicap of a broken bit to win the four-mile Grand Steeplechase de Paris. I can see them now, crashing headlong through the Bullfinch, which, at Auteuil, is the second last, landing on the flat in front and struggling home, both desperately tired, for what was perhaps the most famous triumph in steeplechasing history. Without either brakes or steering after Mandarin's rubber snaffle broke at the fourth of 30 fences, Fred Winter had, of course, achieved a masterpiece of jockeyship. But, as he is the first to admit, it would have been impossible on any ordinary horse and, as Mandarin limped back, broken down on both forelegs, he richly deserved the title France gave Marshal Ney — the bravest of the brave.

Running 50 times in eight seasons, he won 19 races and nearly £50,000 — more, until Arkle, than any other European jumper. He had to his credit a Cheltenham Gold Cup, two Hennessy Gold Cups and two King George VI

Chases and his near misses in themselves made an heroic tale. They included another Grand Steeplechase of which he was only robbed by hesitation at an unfamiliar post-and-rails. Three times second in the Whitbread Gold Cup, he lost two of those by inches and, when third to Saffron Tartan at Cheltenham in 1961, two dreadful blunders had cost him far more than the four-and-a-half lengths by which, flying at the finish, he was beaten.

By that time, Mandarin had already been fired and cracked his fibula below the stifle, but neither injuries nor hard races nor bad luck could quench his will to win or, for that matter, his *joie de vivre*. When schooling his old friend and rival, Taxidermist (or, to be more exact, being schooled by him) I often saw Mandarin disappear over the Lambourn horizon stubbornly ignoring the strong arms of Gerry Madden, who rode him for so much of his career.

I also remember one terrifying night when Mandarin – long retired – was led into a farmers' dinner at Aylesbury. Startled by the noise and unfamiliar atmosphere he could easily have caused a bloodbath in that crowded room, but merely shot out through a side door, with his faithful attendant 'Mush' Foster trailing powerless behind him. 'Mush' will be one of many with memories and so will Fulke Walwyn, whose skill gave Mandarin so many chances. So will Madame Hennessy, Gerry Madden and Fred Winter and all the lucky men and women who shared those golden days at Saxon House. But for all of them there is no reason to feel sad. After delighting us for so long, Mandarin enjoyed a long and happy retirement, especially, perhaps, those days when he pranced like a two-year-old at Newbury before the Hennessy Gold Cup. Even heroes have to go some time, and he, who loved jumping, galloping and fighting, had plenty of all three. Fulke Walwyn yesterday called Mandarin: 'The gamest horse I trained.' I certainly never expect to see another like him.

---

1 JUNE 1970

ARKLE, MIGHTIEST OF CHASERS, IS DEAD

Hotspur

Arkle, almost certainly the greatest steeplechaser of all time, was put down in Ireland yesterday at the age of 13. He had been living in honoured retirement on his owner, Anne, Duchess of Westminster's estate at Maynooth, County Kildare, since the attempt to continue training him was finally abandoned in October 1968.

'Over the last few weeks Arkle had progressive arthritic lesions developing in both hind feet. As these became worse he was in a certain amount of pain,' said Anne, Duchess of Westminster, last night. 'All known drugs and anti-biotics were used. In spite of this no improvement was achieved. In the opinion of my veterinary advisors his condition was incurable and, rather than have him suffer, I had him put to sleep this afternoon.'

Three Cheltenham Gold Cup victories and at least one success in almost every other steeplechase of consequence except the Grand National, were among Arkle's 26 jumping wins worth a National Hunt record of £74,920 stake money. He also won on the Flat.

Arkle's brilliant pace, intelligence, superb jumping, courage under crushing handicap weights, and the fact that he never ran a bad race, nor fell, made this gentle-mannered champion the idol of racing men, and a household name.

Arkle was foaled on 19 April, 1957, at the Ballymacoll stud in County Meath and was bought as a three-year-old by Anne, Duchess of Westminster, for only 1,150 guineas at Goff's Dublin sales. He was trained throughout his career by Tom Dreaper and was generally ridden by Pat Taaffe.

Arkle broke a pedal bone in the hoof of his off-fore foot when running for the last time at Kempton Park in December 1966, yet he still struggled on to finish a close second. He was buried yesterday in the garden of his owner's estate.